palgrave advances in samuel beckett studies

Palgrave Advances

Titles include:

Phillip Mallett (*editor*)
THOMAS HARDY STUDIES

Lois Oppenheim (*editor*)
SAMUEL BECKETT STUDIES

Jean-Michel Rabaté (*editor*)
JAMES JOYCE STUDIES

Forthcoming:

Patrick Finney (*editor*)
INTERNATIONAL HISTORY

Robert Patten and John Bowen (*editors*)
CHARLES DICKENS STUDIES

Frederick S. Roden (*editor*)
OSCAR WILDE STUDIES

Anna Snaith (*editor*)
VIRGINIA WOOLF STUDIES

Nicholas Williams (*editor*)
WILLIAM BLAKE STUDIES

Jonathan Woolfson (*editor*)
RENAISSANCE HISTORIOGRAPHY

Palgrave Advances
Series Standing Order ISBN 1–4039–3512–2 (Hardback) 1–4039–3513–0 (Paperback)
(*outside North America only*)

You can receive future titles in this series as they are published by placing a standing order.
Please contact your bookseller or, in the case of difficulty, write to us at the address below
with your name and address, the title of the series and the ISBN quoted above.

Customer Services Department, Macmillan Distribution Ltd, Houndmills, Basingstoke,
Hampshire RG21 6XS, England

palgrave advances in samuel beckett studies

edited by
lois oppenheim
montclair state university

First published 2004 by
PALGRAVE MACMILLAN
Houndmills, Basingstoke, Hampshire RG21 6XS and
175 Fifth Avenue, New York, N.Y. 10010
Companies and representatives throughout the world

PALGRAVE MACMILLAN is the global academic imprint of the
Palgrave Macmillan division of St Martin's Press LLC and of
Palgrave Macmillan Ltd.
Macmillan® is a registered trademark in the United States,
United Kingdom and other countries. Palgrave is a registered
trademark in the European Union and other countries.

ISBN 1–4039–0352–2 hardback
ISBN 1–4039–0353–0 paperback

This book is printed on paper suitable for recycling and
made from fully managed and sustained forest sources.

A catalogue record for this book is available from the British Library.

Library of Congress Cataloging-in-Publication Data
Palgrave advances in Samuel Beckett studies / edited by Lois Oppenheim.
    p. cm.
Includes bibliographical references and index.
ISBN 1–4039–0352–2 — ISBN 1–4039–0353–0 (pbk.)
ˆ1. Beckett, Samuel, 1906—Criticism and interpretation. I. Oppenheim, Lois.

PR6003.E282Z7857 2004
848'.91409—dc22

                                                         2003066184

10 9 8 7 6 5 4 3 2 1
13 12 11 10 09 08 07 06 05 04

Printed and bound in Great Britain by
Antony Rowe Ltd, Chippenham, Wiltshire

contents

contents

notes on the contributors

H. Porter Abbott is Professor of English at the University of California, Santa Barbara. Among his many books are two on Samuel Beckett, *The Fiction of Samuel Beckett: Form and Effect* (1973) and *Beckett Writing Beckett: the Author in the Autograph* (1996). His most recent book is *The Cambridge Introduction to Narrative* (2002).

Linda Ben-Zvi is Professor Emerita in English and Theater from Colorado State University, and Senior Professor in the Department of Theater Studies, Tel Aviv University. A past president of the Samuel Beckett Society, she is currently Chair of the Beckett Working Group of the International Federation of Theater Research. She has published widely on Beckett and other modern and contemporary playwrights. Her books include *Samuel Beckett* (1986), *Women in Beckett* (1990), *Susan Glaspell* (1995), *Theatre in Israel* (1996), and *Writings from the Verge: the Life and Times of Susan Glaspell* (2004). She has also co-edited with J. Ellen Gainor the *Complete Plays of Susan Glaspell* (forthcoming 2005), and edited *The Road to the Temple* (2004) (Glaspell's biography of George Cram Cook), *A Casebook on Glaspell's Trifles* (forthcoming 2005), and *Drawing on Beckett: Portraits, Performance and Cultural Perspectives* (2003).

Peter Boxall is a lecturer in twentieth-century literature at the University of Sussex (England). He has published essays on Beckett in journals such as *The Yearbook of English Studies, Irish Studies Review, Samuel Beckett Today/Aujourd'hui* (9: 2000), and has published a reader's guide to *Waiting for Godot* and *Endgame*. He is currently writing a book entitled *Political Beckett*.

He is also completing a monograph on Don DeLillo for Routledge called *Don DeLillo: the Possibility of Fiction.*

Enoch Brater's publications on Beckett include *Beyond Minimalism: Beckett's Late Style in the Theater* (1987), *Why Beckett* (1989), *Beckett at 80/ Beckett in Context* (1986), and *The Drama in the Text: Beckett's Late Fiction* (1994). He is widely published in the field of modern and contemporary drama and is Professor of English and Theater at the University of Michigan.

Mary Bryden is Professor of European Literature at Cardiff University and president of the Samuel Beckett Society. Her books on Beckett include *Women in Samuel Beckett's Prose and Drama: Her Own Other* (1993), *Samuel Beckett and the Idea of God* (1998), and *Deleuze and Religion* (ed., 1998). She is currently completing a monograph on Deleuze and literature.

Elin Diamond is Professor of English at Rutgers University. She is the author of *Unmaking Mimesis: Essays on Feminism and Theater* (1997) and *Pinter's Comic Play* (1985), and editor of *Performance and Cultural Politics* (1996). Her essays on performance and feminist theory have appeared in *Theatre Journal, ELH, Discourse, TDR, Modern Drama, Kenyon Review, Cahiers Renaud-Barrault, Art and Cinema, Maska*, and in anthologies in the USA, Europe and India.

S. E. Gontarski is currently Sarah Herndon Professor of English at Florida State University where he edits the *Journal of Beckett Studies*. He has edited two volumes in *The Theatrical Notebooks of Samuel Beckett* series, *Volume II: Endgame* (1992) and *Volume IV: The Shorter Plays* (1999), and he has edited *Samuel Beckett: the Complete Short Prose, 1928–1989* (1995). His current book (with C. J. Ackerley) is *The Grove Companion to Samuel Beckett*, which will be published by Grove Press in 2004 both traditionally and electronically.

Leslie Hill is Professor of French Studies at the University of Warwick (England) and the author of *Beckett's Fiction: in Different Words* (1990), *Blanchot: Extreme Contemporary* (1997), and *Bataille, Klossowski, Blanchot: Writing at the Limit* (2001). He is currently working on a book on post-modernity, fragmentary writing, and affirmation in Blanchot, Beckett and some others.

Anna McMullan is Lecturer in the School of Drama, Trinity College, Dublin, and director of the M.Phil. in Irish Theatre and Film. She is the author of *Theatre on Film: the Later Drama of Samuel Beckett* (1993) and numerous articles on Beckett's drama and on contemporary Irish theater.

Angela Moorjani is Professor of French and Affiliate Professor of Women's Studies at the University of Maryland, BC (UMBC). The author of *Abysmal Games in the Novels of Samuel Beckett* (1982) and of books and essays on the psychopragmatics of art and literature, she recently co-edited volume 11 of *Samuel Beckett Today/Aujourd'hui* (2001).

Lois Oppenheim is Professor of French and Chair of the Department of French, German, and Russian at Montclair State University. A past president of the Samuel Beckett Society, she has published widely on philosophical and psychoanalytic aesthetics and in French studies. Her authored and edited books on Beckett include *The Painted Word: Samuel Beckett's Dialogue With Art* (2000), *Samuel Beckett and the Arts* (1999), *Directing Beckett* (1994 and 1997), and (co-edited with M. Buning) *Beckett On and On ...* (1996) and *Beckett in the 1990s* (1993). She is currently writing a book on neuro-psychoanalysis and the arts.

David Pattie is a Senior Lecturer in Performing Arts at Chester College of Higher Education (England). He is the author of *The Complete Guide to Samuel Beckett* (2000), and he has published articles on Beckett, contemporary theater and performance, and popular culture in performance.

Katharine Worth is Emeritus Professor of Drama and Theater Studies at the University of London, and Honorary Fellow of Royal Holloway University of London. Beckett gave her permission to produce *Eh Joe*, *Words and Music*, and *Cascando* and, in 1987, to adapt *Company* for stage performance. Her many books on theater include *The Irish Drama of Europe from Yeats to Beckett* (1986), studies of single playwrights – Wilde, Sheridan – and of single plays, such as *Waiting for Godot* and *Happy Days* in Macmillan's Text and Performance series. Her *Samuel Beckett Theatre: Life Journeys* was published in 1999 (paperback edition, 2001).

chronology

What follows are some principal dates in the life and career of Samuel Beckett. The dates and publishers are those of the first publication of a given text. This list is by no means meant to be comprehensive and the reader is referred to the extensive bibliography of Beckett's work (with translation and subsequent editions) contained in James Knowlson's *Damned to Fame: the Life of Samuel Beckett* (New York: Simon & Schuster, 1996), 747–50.

1906:   Samuel Barclay Beckett born in Dublin, 13 April
1923–1930: Undergraduate studies (in French and Italian) at Trinity College Dublin
1928–1930: Teaching post at the Ecole Normale Supérieure in Paris
1929:   Publishes first critical essay, 'Dante ... Bruno. Vico ..' Joyce', and first piece of fiction, 'Assumption' in *Transition* magazine
1930:   *Whoroscope* published in Paris (The Hours Press); returns to Dublin (to teach at TCD)
1931:   *Proust* published in London (Chatto & Windus)
1932:   Leaves TCD for Paris; writes *Dream of Fair to Middling Women* (published posthumously in 1992 in New York, London, and Paris [Arcade Publishing in association with Riverrun Press and Calder Publications])
1933:   Death of Bill Beckett (father) and Peggy Sinclair (cousin)
1933–1935: Lives in London
1934:   *More Pricks Than Kicks* published in London (Chatto & Windus)

1936: Travels to Germany
1937: Moves permanently to Paris
1938: *Murphy* published in London (Routledge & Sons)
1942–1945: War years in Roussillon; composes *Watt*
1945–1946: Visits family in Ireland; works for the Irish Red Cross
1946–1953: Writes the *Nouvelles*, ('First Love,' 'The Expelled,' 'The Calmative,' 'The End'); *Mercier and Camier*; The Trilogy (*Molloy, Malone Dies, The Unnamable*); *Texts for Nothing*; *Eleutheria* (published posthumously in 1995 in Paris [Les Editions de Minuit] and New York [Foxrock]); *Waiting for Godot*
1950: Death of May Beckett (mother)
1951: *Molloy* published in Paris (Les Editions de Minuit); *Malone meurt* (Malone Dies) published in Paris (Les Editions de Minuit)
1952: *En Attendant Godot* (Waiting for Godot) published in Paris (Les Editions de Minuit)
1953: First production of *Godot*, Paris (directed by Roger Blin at the Théâtre de Babylone); *L'Innommable* (The Unnamable) published in Paris (Les Editions de Minuit); *Watt* published in Paris (Olympia Press)
1954: Death of Frank (brother)
1955: *Nouvelles et textes pour rien* (Stories and Texts for Nothing) published in Paris (Les Editions de Minuit); *Godot* produced in London)
1957: *Fin de Partie* (Endgame) published in Paris (Les Editions de Minuit)
1958: *Endgame* and *Krapp's Last Tape* produced in London
1959: *Krapp's Last Tape* published in London (Faber & Faber)
1961: *Comment c'est* (How It Is) published in Paris (Les Editions de Minuit); *Happy Days* published in New York (Grove Press); marries Suzanne Descheveaux-Dumesnil
1962: *Happy Days* produced in London
1964: Shooting of *Film* (directed by Alan Schneider in New York); *Play* produced in London
1965: *Imagination morte imaginez* (Imagination Dead Imagine) published in Paris (Les Editions de Minuit)
1967: *Film* published in London (Faber & Faber); *Têtes-Mortes* published in Paris (Les Editions de Minuit); *No's Knife:*

	Collected Short Prose 1945–1966 published in London (Calder and Boyars)
1970:	*Mercier et Camier, Premier Amour* (First Love), and *Le Dépeupleur* published in Paris (Les Editions de Minuit)
1972:	*Not I* written and first produced, New York (directed by Alan Schneider)
1973:	*Not I* published in London (Faber & Faber)
1976:	*For to End Yet Again and Other Fizzles* and *Footfalls* published in London (John Calder and Faber & Faber respectively); *Fizzles* and *All Strange Away* published in New York (Grove Press and Gotham Book Mart respectively)
1977:	*... but the clouds ...*, *Ghost Trio*, and *Not I* collectively produced as *Shades* by the BBC in London; *Collected Poems in English and French* published in London (John Calder)
1979:	*Company*, published in London (John Calder)
1981:	*Mal vu mal dit* (Ill Seen Ill Said) published in Paris (Les editions de Minuit); *Rockaby* and *Ohio Impromptu* published in New York (Grove Press); *Quad* produced for German television
1982:	*Catastrophe* published in Paris (Editions de Minuit) and *Nacht und Träume* filmed for German television
1983:	*Worstward Ho* published in London (John Calder); *What Where* published in New York (Grove Press); and *Disjecta: Miscellaneous Writings and a Dramatic Fragment*, ed. Ruby Cohn, published in London and New York (John Calder and Grove Press)
1984:	*Collected Shorter Plays* published in London and New York (Faber & Faber and Grove Press); *Collected Poems 1930–1978* published in London (John Calder)
1988:	*Stirrings Still* published in New York and London (Blue Moon and John Calder); *Collected Shorter Prose 1945–1980*, published in London (John Calder)
1989:	*Comment dire* published in Paris (Les Editions de Minuit); *Nohow On* (*Company, Ill Seen Ill Said, Worstward Ho*) published in London (John Calder); Suzanne Beckett dies (17 July); death of Samuel Beckett (22 December)

1
introduction

lois oppenheim

'This is something I can study all my life, and never understand.'

Molloy[1]

Martin Esslin, author of an acclaimed classic on absurdist playwrighting, noted in his introduction to that 1961 volume that 'Godot' had infiltrated into the 'private language' of a local population that had viewed Beckett's play some four years prior. Entire phrases and even characters from the play bearing the name in its title were said to have become a 'permanent part' of the spectators' environment.[2] Esslin had no way of knowing just how far from the venue hosting that San Francisco Actors' Workshop production, the San Quentin Penitentiary(!), the infiltration would extend. Indeed, *Waiting for Godot* (first published in France in 1952) soon permeated the international theater community to revolutionize playwriting and establish its invisible protagonist as an icon of modernism in the art and philosophy of the Western world.

Samuel Beckett (1906–1989) was to become, arguably, the twentieth century's most important playwright. His work in the theater significantly impacted not only the art of dramatic writing, but of performance as well. So, too, his novels obliterated conventions of that genre and renewed our thinking on the meaning of narrative. Beckett wrote prose and poetry; he wrote for radio, television and film in addition to the stage. He wrote in English and French, publishing over 100 titles in all. Faced with a body of work so pivotal for the evolution of literature and performance, how have critics contextualized the writing? Has the writing itself continually compelled the critical contexts? Or have literary fads sometimes had the upper hand? What characterizes current critical debates and how might we assess the directions in which Beckett studies as a field is moving?

1

This volume addresses these questions and more; for not only is Beckett's work the subject of a formidable number of critical studies, but it inspires much thinking on the aims of criticism itself. In the 1960s, when Beckett studies came to the fore, Paris (where the writer was living) was still the center of post-war existential thought. The nature of Beckett's writing was such that critics fixed on the texts of the major existentialist philosophers were easily drawn to the profoundly reflective works of Beckett as well. Albeit in another mode of discourse, Beckett's novels and plays raised a lot of the same questions, harbored a lot of the same doubts, and contained a lot of references (some overt, many not) to the humanistic issues with which the French-speaking existentialist writers had long been concerned.

At the same time, though, Paris was home to the decade-old *nouveau roman*, a literary movement devoted to the reexamination of novel writing that, on several occasions, brought writers and their critics face to face.[3] Associated through the publisher, the late Jérôme Lindon of the Editions de Minuit, with a group whose preoccupation with the ways and means of the genre and with experimental investigations that in some ways resembled his own, Beckett's work fast became a focus of 'New Novel criticism' too.

Thanks to Barney Rosset, founder and former publisher of Grove Press, to Tom Bishop, Chair of the French Department at New York University, and to critics like Bruce Morrissette and Vivian Mercier, the *nouveau roman* quickly found a home away from home in the United States. Rosset published the New Novelists in English (in translations by Richard Howard, Barbara Wright, Maria Jolas, and others); Bishop brought them to lecture and teach in American universities, especially his own; and critical studies by American academics proliferated at an astonishing rate. Though, for his part, Beckett was loathe to come to the United States (and did so only once), as a literary persona (somewhat on the periphery of the movement), he was very much 'in the air.' Furthermore, with the rising notoriety of director Alan Schneider – who arrived on the New York scene with *Endgame* (in 1958), *Krapp's Last Tape* (in 1960), and *Happy Days* (in 1961) – and, also, with the proliferation of regional theaters outside New York where Schneider was a growing force, Beckett's theatrical presence in America, and its extension into the drama circle of the academy, were increasingly secured.

Coincidental with Beckett's pervasion of the philosophical, new novel, and academic arenas, criticism, in general, was growing ever more theoretical and interdisciplinary in its focus. Structural linguistics, anthropology, feminism, and psychoanalysis were permeating the literary domain in both Europe and the United States and, in the 1970s and 1980s, each had their Beckett. So varied were the commentaries, and so voluminous in number, that it seemed almost as if the critics were seeking revenge on the indeterminacy characteristic of the writing under review. It was not until the 1990s, when the debate over Beckett's place on the horizon of modernism (early, late, high, and post) intensified, that theory *qua* theory was relegated to the wings of Beckett criticism and biographical studies, on the one hand, and the exploration of affinities between Beckett's literary aesthetic and other forms of artistic expression, on the other, took center stage.

In a word, then, the field of Beckett studies (still finding new directions today) can be overwhelming. This volumes aims to assess its evolution and define the impact of the critical writings on our reading and viewing of Beckett's work. But how might essays devoted to so copious a secondary-source coverage be ordered to maximize the reader's grasp? Some have edited compilations of Beckett criticism arranging the contributions by chronology or genre; others have grouped essays according to critical approach. The objectives of this guide to Beckett criticism differ from previously published collections, however, in two significant ways: First, the over-riding effort is to demonstrate the usage of the various critical orientations while reflecting on them theoretically as well. And, second, not only does it seek to reveal both the evolution of Beckett criticism and the most recent developments in Beckett studies, but the chapters, to that extent possible, are interrelational; they play off the mutual consequences of the various critical approaches at hand.

Thus Porter Abbott's study of narrative theory and Beckett, his exploration of what he calls 'the art of gap management,' is followed by Enoch Brater's on intertexuality, a paper responsive to fundamental questions posed by Abbott about the degree to which preconception enslaves the reader's mind. 'Can you cognize a gap without filling it?,' Abbott asks. 'And what would you feel like if you could?' In uncovering 'shadows' of Yeats in Beckett, Brater seems to respond by having us read Beckett 'in terms of an assimilated literary past,' one set out, however, in a uniquely 'adventurous present.'

Similarly, Elin Diamond's chapter takes as its premise the interaction in the 1970s and 1980s of the texts of French feminist theory and Beckett's plays and prose. While she notes that there is no record of any personal interaction between Beckett and the feminist thinkers she discusses, she uncovers in three of his plays a feminized discourse, a 'parler-femme' (or 'woman-speak'), forging a fascinating intertextual connection to which Leslie Hill's poststructuralist reading of Beckett offers a provocative challenge. If Hill situates Beckett poststructurally, however, he also deflates the contextualization: No more than Blanchot, Foucault, Deleuze, Badiou, or Derrida can Beckett be said to *belong there*. In fact, Hill shows us Beckett's special sensitivity 'to what Deleuze calls "universal variation," described as a kind of ceaseless becoming, multiplying differences without identity, and showing at the core of all unity the intervention of perpetual foreignness or exteriority.' Anna McMullan, however, seems to reply to Hill by situating Beckett's work precisely within the historical contexts of Ireland of the 1920s and 1930s, of World War II France, and post-war Europe. 'Although Beckett does not represent these contexts mimetically,' she writes, 'his dislocations of personal and cultural memory constitute a critique of regimes which had the power to marginalize, exclude, or, in the case of Nazi Germany, exterminate those who did not conform to its definition of a national or ethnic subject.' So, too, Peter Boxall writes of communality: Juxtaposing homoeroticism as an important vehicle of connection, a 'new homosociality or community,' to a heteronormative reading of Beckett, he also puts deconstruction to the test.

Thus, to the volume's initial question of 'gap management,' as posed by Abbott, Brater, and Diamond seek phantom texts in the hollows of Beckett's own, while Hill delights in extending the recesses, the 'narrative blanks' (as Abbott calls them), and McMullan and Boxall explore vastly different referential contexts wherein they assume meaning.

Linda Ben-Zvi takes up both the intertexual thread and the motif of the body introduced by Boxall. Focussing her discussion of physical decrepitude in Beckett's works on the inscription of Cartesian and Johnsonian models, she reveals the body both as a 'seat of knowledge' and the site of its erased potency, another shaping of absence.

Mary Bryden and Angela Moorjani review two distinct traditions within which Beckett's critics have sought to 'manage' the gaps. With Bryden we have a comprehensive evaluation of Beckett criticism on the horizon of the religious or exegetical, whereas Moorjani gives us an exhaustive review of the psychoanalytic critical perspective. Each contributes an astute assessment of critics' efforts to determine how Beckett's texts communicate – not only in words, but in 'nonverbal and [other] contextual dimensions' (to cite Moorjani) – far more than what they say.

Though Beckett was deeply committed to the process of staging as 'creation,' his critics, Stan Gontarski tells us, have insufficiently tackled the vicissitudes of performance, feeling more comfortable within the confines of the published text. When they have veered toward questions of performance, they have tended to situate their commentaries within the frame of the fidelity of a given production to the work as it appears in print. Gontarski's justification of the need for a longer and stronger look at the nature of Beckett's theatrical art indicates an important direction for future studies.

The sources of attraction to Beckett's work – what in the past prompted the very great interest in the fiction and plays, but also ensures the continuity of this interest – are the subject of the essay by Katharine Worth. Noting that Beckett's entire stage oeuvre has recently been filmed, why, she asks, does the appeal continue to be so strong? The volume closes with a two-part study by David Pattie, a chronological overview of the entire critical corpus and a genre-specific guide for further reading.

A final word on the absence of a chapter devoted solely to Beckett and philosophy: The philosophical orientations to Beckett's work could not but appear in high relief everywhere throughout the volume. So endemic is philosophy to the critical corpus that its inevitable interweaving through the chapters was thought to yield a more substantive view of its significance. As critic Sidney Feshbach has stated, 'The multitude of philosophical approaches Beckett has attracted ranges from language analysis to phenomenology and even ethics. Properly so, for in addition to the ways of academic inquiry, his approach to writing has itself made varied use of philosophy.'

Feshbach has succinctly summarized Beckett's connection to philosophy as follows:

Clearly, Beckett read Schopenauer on pessimism and Bergson on memory, among many other philosophers. And his interest in René Descartes is incontestable. Carrying to Paris his college book on Descartes, Beckett found in that philosopher an image of the complete human who was divided into an isolated reasoning mind and a body-thing. (Was this division needed for dealing with his own painful medical and emotional problems?) In a France much influenced by Cartesianism, he approached that divided image of mind and body-thing using the literary, especially Irish, tradition of satire directed at the ironic self-tormentor. He repeated two images, a human calming and consoling himself in a rocking chair and a human struggling to travel on a bicycle, to satirize the desires of a mind locked into the mechanics of the body. Implicitly exploiting the Cartesian philosophy of duality, he ironically remembered, in the early poem 'Whoroscope,' that Descartes preferred to eat over-ripe eggs.

Beckett's wartime experiences and postwar encounters with Parisian existentialism and phenomenology influenced his great three novels, *Molloy*, *Malone Dies*, and *The Unnamable*. With these, the assumptions of Cartesianism seemed to linger, but the satire was diminished, farcical laughter changed into comic humor, and earlier verbal excesses were stripped to reveal the skeletal armatures of drama and prose and the anguish of a mind.

With his success as a novelist and playwright, Beckett moved from his early physical self-disgust, his desire for philosophical consolation and numbness in life, and his many reminders of illness to a somewhat more tranquil state in which he recalled momentary pleasures within elegiac memory.

If I quote Feshbach at length, it is because new directions for Beckett studies are suggested by the very evolution he describes. Some are evident already in this volume. Others will be so over time. For Beckett's literary philosophy and philosophical literariness are sine qua nonical to his work. Indeed, 'Beckett always read philosophy for its fictions of human existence and, never a philosopher, he always remained philosophical, telling great jokes in the graveyard.'[4]

notes

1. In *Three Novels* (New York: Grove-Black Cat, 1965), 169. Cited by Angela Moorjani and Carola Veit in the introduction to *Samuel Beckett: Endlessness in the Year 2000, Samuel Beckett Today/Aujourd'hui 11* (Amsterdam: Rodopi, 2001), 13.
2. Cited by Martin Esslin, *The Theatre of the Absurd* (New York: Doubleday: 1961), xvi–xvii.
3. I refer here to the several colloquiums in which the writers participated together with their critics. There was the famous 1971 conference at Cerisy-la-Salle, for instance, 'Nouveau Roman: hier, aujourdh'hui' and others at the same venue devoted to single writers associated with the *nouveau roman*. A retrospective held at New York University in 1982 was similarly unique in that a talk by each novelist was paired with one by a preeminent critic of his or her work (see my *Three Decades of the French New Novel*, Urbana: University of Illinois Press, 1986).
4. Sidney Feshbach, personal communication to L. O. dated 19 August 2002.

2
narrative

h. porter abbott

The twentieth century was the great age for critical commentary on
narrative jumps, ruptures, dehiscences, and sharp breaks of all kinds,
thanks in large part to the accumulated production of modernist and
postmodernist narratives that so often specialized in putting their broken
bodies on display. The commentary on Beckett's work is no exception.
What it has lacked is some perspective from within the subfield of narrative
gaps. My principal focus in this essay is Beckett's post-war (1944–52)
exploitation of a rare device, the egregious narrative gap, which is a kind
of narrative blank. If we look closely at a few examples of how Beckett
exploited this device, we can throw into relief a significant distinction
between Beckett's thematics of nothing – void, absence, emptiness,
naught – and the quite different experience of knowing nothing. This
focus can also bring out something of the great range of Beckett's art, both
within and beyond these experiments, and the extent to which it deploys
the ancient craft of fashioning gaps that are anything but egregious.

i. nothing

The theme of *nothing* shows up everywhere in Beckett, and much has been
written about it (see especially Hesla, Butler, Trezise, Uhlmann).[1] *'Nothing
is more real than nothing,'* Malone writes in perhaps the most famous of
Beckett's many oxymorons (Beckett 1965, 192). It is a line that quivers
with an energy of proximal self-contradiction: of 'more' and 'real' (how
can anything be more or less real – it's either real or it isn't, right?), of
'real' and 'nothing' (how can nothing be real?), and of the two kinds of
'nothing' that can freely trade places at the poles of the epigram (nothing
as 'not any thing' and nothing as the condition of 'nothingness').

7

Christopher Ricks, much of whose argument in *Beckett's Dying Words* takes aim at what he considers poststructuralist 'indeterminacy-mongering' (202), can speak for his reader's response to this line with modernist confidence: 'not only do you know what he means, you sense the chilly comfort of the thought' (203). The precise thought for Ricks is that of 'vacancy,' the absolute of nothing that comes with death. Ricks draws support from Malone's words in context: 'I know those little phrases that seem so innocuous and, once you let them in, pollute the whole of speech. *Nothing is more real than nothing.* They rise up out of the pit and know no rest until they drag you down into its dark.'

In an access of polemical zeal, Ricks narrows Beckett to fit his point, but the point he makes is nonetheless supremely important. The finality of death is one of Beckett's recurrent specialties: 'Grey light. Rain pelting. Umbrellas round a grave. Seen from above. Streaming black canopies. Black ditch beneath. Rain bubbling in the black mud' (Beckett 1984, 268). In the intervals between these tiny sentences, Beckett accumulates a grimly weighted precision. This is the end. It is a fact, indisputable. You will never, ever see her again. In this regard Ricks is dead right. There is much in Beckett that you can only appreciate by acknowledging the finality of death, to feel it without any cushion of indeterminacy. Death is one of the meanings of the phrase 'No's knife' and it cuts away at every living thing. In Beckett there is no end to the grieving.

There are two fine essays on nothing in Beckett that sit like bookends on both the subject and the criticism of the 1990s. At the near end (2001) is Eric Levy's 'The Beckettian Mimesis of Seeing Nothing,' which in different terms comes close to Ricks's position. Levy sees two kinds of nothing in Beckett: the 'wish for conscious oblivion' and the 'refusal to see anything in life but futility.' The one is positive – the long-sought peace of nothing – the other negative – the 'perturbation' at 'the spectacle of emptiness' (628). For Levy these come together in a sentence from *Texts for Nothing*: 'I'm up there and down here, *under my gaze*, foundered, *eyes closed*' (630, Levy's emphasis). Together they are a contradiction, since both cannot co-exist, yet together they correlate to the contradiction in the 'chilly comfort' that Ricks says we draw from the thought of such complete vacancy. The paradox of nothing so conceived is that it is at once awful and peaceful, a perception of futility and a blessed end, each sense of the term keeping the other alight. For it is the end that clinches the conviction of futility, and it is the conviction of futility that makes the end so attractive. Finally, it is worth noting that these two very different writers not only come to this shared perception, but can with confidence present it as Beckett's 'meaning,' distilled from his work. It is a truth about our condition on the planet that works as a core organizing principle of Beckett's writing.

At the far end of the last decade (1991) is a very different take on the subject by Steven Barker titled 'Recovering the *Néant*: Language and the Unconscious in Beckett.' Barker's essay is more elusive than Levy's, more a meditation or, as he calls it, a 'pensum' on the *Néant*, a word chosen for its alien feel and which, if I read Barker rightly, is in Beckett's texts at once the nothing, the unconscious, and language. Barker's focus is on nothing not as ending but as a source of continual beginnings. *Nothing* in his treatment is a plenitude and a denial of 'nihilism.' However much a pensum, Barker's language is every bit as assertive as that of Levy and Ricks: 'Beckett's words more and more energetically attempt to focus on this "moment of appearance," out of nothing, of words and their structural interactions. This (impossible) threshold of the *néant* is the emergent energy of the nameless and unnamable beginning, the origin of being and action, the desired *topos*, and the goal of Beckett's writing' (Barker, 129). And well it should be so assertive. Beckett's reflexive thematic treatment of the mystery of origination – the way new material keeps coming out of the dark (and the light) – is exceeded only by the originality of his writing itself, its ever-surprising swerves. In a somewhat similar argument, Shira Wolosky maintains that the whole 'negative way' of Beckett is a 'defiant creation from nothing,' an outpouring of 'reproductive and inventive energy,' which in turn tropes 'the generative power of what is as against the realm of what is not' (Wolosky 228).

Any full treatment of the theme of nothing in Beckett must credit both of these arguments – the Levy/Ricks argument and the Barker/Wolosky argument, nothing as ending and nothing as beginning. If they seem profoundly opposed, they are nonetheless, depending on where you look, undeniable readings of Beckett's work. But resting on top of this paradox is another: the venerable conundrum of Parmenides, cited by Barker (126), who echoes Beckett, who speaks through Sam, telling the story of Watt: 'the only way one can speak of nothing is to speak of it as though it were something' (Beckett 1976, 74). Words, as Beckett often laments, 'worsen blanks' (Beckett 1983, 39). Both of the above arguments appear to fill the nothing blank with something. And they do so with a rhetoric of conviction that is persuasive.

To speak of nothing as the place of generation (language, the unconscious) or, conversely, as a purity of emptiness (vacancy without end) is to put something there in the place of nothing and to that degree to anchor it. It also permits the comparative that Beckett subtly mocked when he allowed Malone to write: 'Nothing is more real than nothing.' Wordsworth, with grave sobriety, allowed the comparative in describing epic efforts to depict emptiness: 'Nor aught of blinder vacancy, scoop'd out / By help of dreams' (Wordsworth, ll. 25–6). Beckett's travesty of high romantic vacancy is the scooping motion of Gogo's and Didi's hands as they feel the emptiness of shoes and hats. As an idea, nothing is everywhere in Beckett, both represented and talked about. But there are also moments when he confounds the received discourse on nothing.

In one of the first critical responses to *Godot*, Alain Robbe-Grillet maintained that absolute vacancy was in fact what lay off-stage: 'everything that is *is here*, off-stage there is only nothingness, nonbeing' (Robbe-Grillet 123).

But if you look at the way Beckett manages the gap between Acts One and Two of *Godot*, it is hard to make this position fully accountable for Beckett's intentions. '*Next day. Same time. Same place*' are the stage directions, but also '*The tree has four or five leaves.*' Vladimir notices this from the start and won't let it drop: leaves 'in a single night.' 'It must be spring' says Estragon (Beckett 1956, 42), though in Act One, Pozzo had asserted it was autumn. The stage directions also tell us that the boots in the center of the stage as Act Two opens are Estragon's, boots whose tightness in Act One had caused Estragon much agony. Yet when he tries them on, they fit. In that same space between the acts, Lucky goes dumb and Pozzo goes blind. Moreover, Estragon, but not Vladimir, is beaten each night, though possibly by a different party each time, and possibly not at all, since he is a vivid dreamer. All this ground and more has been gone over many times in the last half century. My point is that Beckett takes pains here to prevent the viewer from filling this gap with any fixed ideas. It is an 'egregious gap' (about which more later). As such it allowed Beckett to perfect an art of ignorance, played out in performance as experience. There is no displacing this gap with an idea, however limited – even an idea of nothing. There is no resolving its uncertainties without disengaging from the work itself.[2]

ii. theory of gaps

Egregious gaps are not, and by a long shot, the only kind of narrative gap. Gaps in narrative, like the much more salient gaps in poetry, are any kind of opening in the text that requires filling in order for the text to do its work. As such, gaps are endemic in narrative and have been since people started telling stories. Narratologists have sometimes made much of these gaps. In *The Implied Reader*, Wolfgang Iser put the principle of the gap at the center of his theorizing. Gaps occur in all narratives, he argued, and it is only through them that 'the reader is enabled to bring both scenes and characters to life' (Iser 39). 'Indeed, it is only through the inevitable omissions that a story gains its dynamism. Thus whenever the flow is interrupted and we are led off in unexpected directions, the opportunity is given to us to bring into play our own faculty for establishing connections – for filling in the gaps left by the text itself' (280).[3]

Throughout his book, Iser had in mind the vital role of *significant* gaps, those 'points at which the reader can enter into the text, forming his own connections and conceptions and so creating the configurative meaning of what he is reading' (40). But actually gaps riddle narrative at all points, and we start filling them from the first words.

> When he saw us come in the door the bartender looked up and then reached over and put the glass covers on the two free-lunch bowls. (Hemingway 384)

Just to get past this first sentence of Hemingway's 'The Light of the World,' we have a bar to create, a bartender, the narrator, and his friend (or friends, we won't know for a few lines), and an action to interpret (the bartender covering the bowls), in terms of both the bartender's concerns and the implied appearance of the narrator and his friend. And though our sense of the characters and action deepens immensely as the story progresses, we are always imagining far more than comes from the page, drawing on what we know about bars, bartenders, drifters, and tough towns in hard times. We build characters, as we fill in scenes, imagine action, and apply significance and meaning. Narrative, like the universe, is comprised largely of dark matter. Just as the universe does not consist solely of the visible stars, narrative is not the marks on the page or even the images and sounds we see on the stage. We see points of light and then fill in the rest from the dark matter of our own imagining. This point becomes suddenly very clear when you read a novel like Nicholson Baker's *The Mezzanine*, in which the entire action consists of a one-storey ride up an escalator, with the narrator straining in an insouciant if doomed attempt to account for every particle of the action, mental and physical, during the course of this ride.

But in general, narrative is a blessed liberation from every little thing. We can be taken quickly to the important moments because we are presumed to be competent to fill in the gaps as needed. This view of the reader's contract with the writer is at the heart of Hemingway's theory that the art of fiction is an art of leaving things out. Those with the requisite experience supply what is missing from their own understanding. Hemingway's theoretical language was modernist and he was saying basically what Pound and Eliot said about poetry and what Eisenstein said about film: that reading is an art of filling in. The more informed the reader, the more fully are the gaps of art experienced. But whether we are as well equipped as Hemingway or Eliot demanded, narrative has always featured a stream of gaps. These come in all sizes, from the molecular (like those in the first sentence of Hemingway's story) to the very large. Some are gaps of discretion: Tolstoy drawing a veil when Vronsky and Anna first make love, Hardy spending a page not giving us any details of the rape of Tess. Though the action is veiled, we draw on our understanding of such events to fill in what happens. Other gaps are huge, covering years. In his *Confessions*, St Augustine marveled at the way in which memory chooses among millions of events those moments that are essential to the story of one's life. There is always much that a story does not need. We jump years in the lives of characters like Abel Magwitch, Michael Henchard, and Dick Diver, seeing them again, changed by the cumulative effect of untold events.

Finally, there are egregious gaps. These are gaps in the action that, however informed we may be as readers, still cry out for authorial assistance in filling them. In Robbe-Grillet's *La Jalousie*, is A . . . murdered? In Tim O'Brien's *In the Lake of the Woods* (1994), what happens to the protagonist's wife? In Christopher Nolan's film *Memento*, what is the full story of the protagonist's wife? Why doesn't she intervene? In *Vanity Fair*, does Becky Sharp kill Jos Sedley? Thackeray famously told inquirers that he himself didn't know the answer. In *Wuthering Heights*, does Heathcliff kill Hindley Earnshaw? Hindley was alive when Heathcliff sent Joseph for the doctor yet he was 'both dead, and cold and stark' (Brontë 185) when Joseph and the doctor got back. For good reason, the space in which Hindley dies has become a crux in the criticism of *Wuthering Heights*, and interpreters have filled it with several possibilities of which the main contenders are: murder, involuntary homicide, and death without further assistance. Egregious gaps have been handled in many different ways to serve different functions. Yet they share the capacity to call up immense interpretive energy. This in turn would appear to confirm the rule that we are so constructed that simply to know of a gap is to try to fill it.[4]

This view of how we relate to narrative gaps is strongly supported by work in cognitive science, social psychology, and the psychology of perception (Goffman, Mandler, Metzing, Rumelhart, Schank, Schank and Abelson, Thorndyke). In a continuing elaboration of Kant's original insight, such research has sought to articulate the extent to which we bring our knowledge to the world in the form of internalized frames, schemata, and scripts. Of the sensory input we obtain from the real world, we are at any one time consciously aware of very little. We see what we have a hand in shaping, drawing on an immense repertoire of generic structures that we carry within us. There are major differences between 'top down' cognitive scientists and 'bottom up' neurologists regarding the degree to which we are the prisoners of our preconceptions. But even the most sensory-biased neurologist will grant that to some degree we enter into the world we look at, adding our constructive input to scenes and sequences of action.[5] Perception, in the words of Roger Shepard, is an 'externally guided hallucination' (Shepard 436).[6] This is exactly what writers depend upon as they produce, from sentence to sentence and even from word to word, the fine stream of suspense and surprise that keeps readers reading. Since the work of David E. Rumelhart and P. W. Thorndyke in the late 1970s, a sector of the field of narratology has been devoted to the application of cognitive theory to the ways in which we, as it were, write what we read (see, for a few examples, Mandler, Spolsky, Stockwell, Schank, Storey).

In short, one finds repeatedly across the highly diversified spectrum of the theory of narrative gaps the point that we read by filling in, indeed that we are so constructed that we can't help it.[7] Is it possible, then, *not* to fill narrative gaps? Can you cognize a gap without filling it? And what would it feel like, if you could? For if there is nothing in your mind, where is the extra-mental receptor that lets you know it? It is just this impossible combination that Beckett's narrator prays for at the end of *Ill Seen Ill Said*: 'Grace to breathe that void. Know happiness' (Beckett 1981, 59). The answer to this prayer would appear to be No. But, as I suggested above in the case of *Godot*, there are other ways to know nothing, which I will get to in Section Four.

iii. beckett and the poetics of narrative

But first it is important to stress that, for all his complaints about how words 'worsen blanks,' Beckett was a robust collaborator with the regimes of narrative and cognition. Over six decades, with his well-chosen words, he invited his readers to fill narrative gaps. Guided by his cues, we make and remake his characters, giving them life – Murphy, Celia, Molloy, Malone, even the voice we listen to in *The Unnamable*. On stage, actors do much of this work for us, filling in from the marks they read in scripts. Krapp, Vladimir, Hamm, Winnie, Maddy, M(outh) come to life out of small marks interpreted by actors, with audiences extending the process, constructing on top of these constructions. And of course, we don't just help construct characters, but scenes, too, such as they are, and the action, such as it is. All this is true not only in the early work, but in the late work as well:

> Spreading rise and in midair palms uppermost come to rest. Behold our hollows. (Beckett 1981, 32)

Reading the gap between these two sentences, we connect them with implicit words – 'as if they [the palms] were to say' – and in doing so imagine how her hands look held out in midair. Other things, too: the ironic contrast between the epic grandeur of 'Behold' and the modesty of the subject, the sheer emptiness of these hands, the act of lifting up and displaying nothing. All of which is to say that Beckett wrote for human beings. Reading and watching his work, we do what humans do. We fill in the blanks, even if what we put in them is an idea of blankness ('our hollows'). He counted on us to do so.

The extreme of the verbal art of gaps is poetry, which is what Auden had in mind when he wrote somewhere that poetry is the only art you cannot half read. The quote above from *Ill Seen Ill Said* shows to what extent Beckett did in his later works what poets do, calling on readers to apply themselves at all points in an energetic, deeply felt and deeply thought transaction as they fill gaps everywhere.

> Riveted to some detail of the desert the eye fills with tears. Imagination at wit's end spreads its sad wings. Gone she hears one night the sea as if afar. Plucks up her long skirt to make better haste and discovers her boots and stockings to the calf. Tears. Last example the flagstone before her door that by dint by dint her little weight has grooved. Tears. (17–18)

Critical commentary on the strategic silences in Beckett's work has made this point. Herbert Blau has written of the 'Chekhovian silences' that complete *Godot*'s 'artful polyphony,' emphasizing that it is 'in silence, that the whole emotive tapestry of the theatrical event can be *heard*' (Blau 33). Enoch Brater has with loving attention tracked 'the supporting role of silence' in any number of passages in Beckett's later poetry and prose (Brater 142). Arguably, then, words 'worsen blanks' in the sense that they can dampen the resonances and emotional charge that fill the spaces between the words. It makes good sense of Beckett's reliance on the rhetorical figure of aposiopesis – 'an unexplained break into silence' – a 'central compositional resource,' to which Albert Cook attributed much of Beckett's emotional power (Cook, 586). Beckett's wonted austerity as an artist, in other words, has much to do with crafting spaces that are anything but empty.

> Can't go on . . . God is love . . . she'll be purged . . . back in the field
> . . . morning sun . . . April . . . sink face down in the grass . . . nothing
> but the larks . . . so on . . . grabbing at the straw . . . straining to hear
> . . . the odd word . . . (Beckett 1984, 221)

So much of the impact of *Not I*, a play which is a tissue of aposiopeses, lies in its ellipses. The remarkable gap between 'Can't go on' and 'God is love' contains not only the chemistry of transition from despair to hope but also, by its very abruptness, what must be a continuation of despair in the hope expressed. What follows emerges out of the faint idea that there is a God, that this God is in fact love, and that she will eventually 'be purged' if she can just start over again and get it right. At the same time, the ellipses express the strain of audition as Mouth listens for 'the odd word,' the anti-logos from a truly loving God that will undo this strange creation. The overriding point here is that much lies in these empty spaces, thanks to the craft that went into the spare words that frame them.

There are larger gaps in Beckett's work, gaps approaching the egregious, yet still recognizably within this ancient tradition of poets and story-tellers. Winnie's return in act two of *Happy Days*, buried up to her neck, is one of these. The narrative topos is the return after the passage of time, the same as Dickens used when he brought Abel Magwitch back into *Great Expectations*. The brilliance of Beckett's staging lies in the way it gives visual embodiment to Pozzo's words in *Godot*: 'They give birth astride of a grave.' Strange as this absurdly brilliant transition is, there is no narrative puzzlement in the gap out of which it comes. Life means getting buried, and the whole process seems to go like the wind: 'one day we were born, one day we shall die, the same day, the same second, is that not enough for you?' (Beckett 1956, 57).

Closer to the border of the truly egregious gap, yet still largely within this same topos of the return after long absence, is the transformation of Sapo into MacMann in *Malone Dies*.

> I have taken a long time to find him again, but I have found him. How did I know it was he, I don't know. And what can have changed him so? Life perhaps, the struggle to love, to eat, to escape the redressers of wrongs. (Beckett 1965, 226)

As with Winnie's return in Act Two, part of what is wonderful about this travesty of the topos is both the suddenness and the immensity of the transformation. As always in Beckett, travesty is lined with subtlety: 'And what could have changed him so? Life perhaps.' The transformation is so great that Malone acknowledges that this might not be Sapo, and indeed he renames him, but the eyes are the same, and the last we heard of Sapo was Mrs Lambert's message to her daughter 'that he was going away and would not come back' (217). Moreover, MacMann recapitulates the same condition of passivity and incomprehension that marked him as the boy Sapo. In this regard, the gap marks the persistence of bafflement over time and bodily decay – proof against all clichés about the wisdom that comes with age.

What is radical about this gap, pushing it right up to the border of the egregious, is that it is inflicted as much on the writer as on the reader. It involves a story of narrative production (a 'drama in the text,' to adapt Brater's title). After all, Malone is in charge; this is his fiction, undertaken in his determination to 'play.' That he should lose his own character and than find him again almost entirely transformed and then in the space of a few pages almost lose him again ('thank God, he's still there' [231]) seems counter-intuitive. Yet even this feature of the gap can be 'naturalized' – that is, filled from what readers know. On the one hand, it is a commonplace among writers that they discover as much as they make, their characters seeming to act independently of authorial control.[8] The classic instance is Tolstoy's account of writing ever faster to find out if Vronsky is actually going to attempt suicide (Gifford 48). Hapless Malone is no different from the rest and certainly shared this condition with Beckett, the self-described 'mole in a molehill' who, working in the dark, at once created and found Malone.[9]

On the other hand, the gap arrives much too fortuitously not to seem the product of calculation. After all, Malone needs to bring his character along swiftly if he is going to succeed in his plan: 'To show myself now, on the point of vanishing, at the same time as the stranger, and by the same grace, that would be no ordinary last straw. Than live, long enough to feel, behind my closed eyes, other eyes close. What an end' (195). The story of Sapo was going much too slowly; Malone needed somehow, and posthaste, to advance his character some sixty years. What could be more convenient than this narrative convention, allowing him at a stroke to remake Sapo more suitably in his own image and then to 'slip into him'? '[H]e is mine now, living flesh, and needless to say male, living with that evening life which is like a convalescence' (226). Malone tears this extrawide gap across his narrative and not a moment too soon, for within pages he feels the first warning shocks that his 'hour is at hand' (233). In this sense, Malone does exercise control over his material, making it do his bidding. Yet here is cause for genuine puzzlement, for Malone, in effect, gives life to what has life, creates the already created, writes what writes itself. This is the kind of mystery that sears the mind. The answer to it, if answer there be, lies somewhere in the gap between Sapo and MacMann.

iv. malone's egregious gap

Within this nine-page gap between the disappearance of Sapo and his reemergence as MacMann (217–26), tunneling into it as it were, is another gap when Malone loses his pencil. It lasts only two days rather than sixty years, though the comparison is somewhat fallacious since the two gaps belong to two different fictional universes. Narratologists distinguish between the world of the story and the world of the narrator telling the story – the diegesis and the scene of narration. The distinction is a little cumbersome, since in this case both are stories, one in the third person and one in the first. But that the former issues out of the latter might make one wonder: could this two-day gap be a wormhole from one universe to another, a kind of black hole, small but powerful enough to suck up sixty years from that other universe? Was Sapo lost in this two-day hole in the scene of narration?

Let's look into this truly egregious narrative gap:

I have spent two unforgettable days of which nothing will ever be known, it is too late now, or still too soon, I forget which, except that they brought me the solution and conclusion of the whole sorry business, I mean the business of Malone (since that is what I am called now) and of the other, for the rest is no business of mine. And it was, though more unutterable, like the crumbling away of two little heaps of finest sand, or dust, or ashes, of unequal size, but diminishing together as it were in ratio, if that means anything, and leaving behind them, each in its own stead, the blessedness of absence. (222)

This is a remarkable reversal of St Augustine's principle of self-recollection: That those few events that make up the history of one's true self can be culled from the myriad events that happen in one's life. In contrast, Malone writes that it is specifically the important action bearing on his self that is unrecoverable because 'unutterable,' the rest, as it turns out, being quite utterable, though 'no business of mine.' All there is of this unutterable business is the simile of two diminishing 'heaps of finest sand' that conclude in 'the blessedness of absence.' So we have here within a sixty-year gap another gap of two days that contains in its turn yet another gap – an absence that is beyond utterance. Could this be, at last, resting here in this gap now raised to the third power, the blank of blanks, the absolute of nothing? Has Malone been granted, even before his last breath, 'Grace to breath that void'?

Alas, words worsen blanks. Ever the narratorial recidivist, Malone the Anti-Augustine proceeds to fill the gap 'of which nothing will ever be known' with an account of all that unimportant activity which he has disclaimed as not his 'business' – his search for his pencil, the whitening of his floor, the loss and retrieval of his exercise-book. 'And all this time,' he notes, 'the sand kept trickling away and I saying to myself, It is gone forever, meaning of course the pencil' (223). Shades here of another narrative topos – the wayward soul, distracted by the things of this world ('it' meaning his pencil) when 'it' meaning the 'blessed' truth is so near at hand, there to be had but for the grasping. Then, veering back with an increase in the tremolo of religiosity, he turns again to his simile, now metaphor, for what may be (who knows?) a visitation of divine Truth:

And during all this time, so fertile in incidents and mishaps, in my head I suppose all was streaming and emptying away as through a sluice, to my great joy, until finally nothing remained, either of Malone or of the other. And what is more I was able to follow without difficulty the various phases of this deliverance and felt no surprise at its irregular course, now rapid, now slow, so crystal clear was my understanding of the reasons why this could not be otherwise. And I rejoiced, further-more, quite apart from the spectacle, at the thought that I now knew what I had to do, I whose every move has been a groping . . . (224)

But in Beckett no trope survives unmolested. The convention of confessional literature that he draws on and the metaphor he uses to feed it are from here on given several sharp twists from which neither survives:

And here again naturally I was utterly deceived, I mean in imagining I had grasped at last the true nature of [my[10]] absurd tribulations, but not so utterly as to feel the need to reproach myself with it now. For even as I said, How easy and beautiful it all is! In the same breath I said, All will grow dark again. And it is without excessive sorrow that I see us again as we are, namely to be removed grain by grain until the hand, wearied, begins to play, scooping us up and letting us trickle back into the same place, dreamily as the saying is. (224)

The contortion of both trope and topos continues into the next page until they are effectually dropped as 'all this ballsaching poppycock about life and death, if that is what it is all about, and I suppose it is, for nothing was ever about anything else to the best of my recollection. But what it is all about exactly I could no more say than take up my bed and walk. It's vague, life and death' (225). In effect, Beckett effaces the 'blessedness of absence' by laying waste the structures of belief and representation that gave it textual life, including any faint chance of miraculous intervention ('take up my bed and walk'). In terms of the art of gap management, this is a case of absence emptied – a narrative gap raised now to the fourth power. But note that in so augmenting the sense of an evacuated space Beckett has shifted his narrative emphasis from a postulated void in actuality ('blessedness of absence') to an actual void in knowledge, from *nothing there* to *nothing known*. In some schemes of thought, these two perspectives are the same thing, but as yet there is no compelling evidence that they are.

It may help at this point to put the way Beckett handles this egregious gap in *Malone Dies* beside the egregious gap in Brontë's canonical nineteenth-century novel, *Wuthering Heights*. I noted three different scripts that one could use to fill the gap in which Hindley dies – murder, involuntary homicide and neglect, depending on the degrees of passion, brutality, and cold calculation one attributes to the Heathcliff under construction. But it is possible to argue that there is no single Heathcliff occupying this critical gap, but a collection of Heathcliffs, all jostling together in the same space. And certainly elements in the interpretive theory of the last forty years – particularly the idea of a necessary and potentially endless chain of supplements in any and all acts of signification – would support the idea that Brontë's egregious gap is simply a continuation of what she does everywhere. Heathcliff is a moving target, an unfinished conversation of traits, in a process that continues through multiple readings.[11] It is also quite possible to make the case from cues elsewhere in the text that Brontë knew very well what she was doing when she both left this gap unfilled and gave cues that would arouse suspicion.[12] In this way, she was inviting us to feel what we are invited to feel at other moments in the novel: that Heathcliff will always be a stranger to us and that the springs of his character are beyond comprehension.

Brontë and Beckett make odd bedfellows, the differences between them being so immense, but in this regard (if you accept my reading of the egregious gap in *Wuthering Heights*) they share a similar object. The difference in Beckett is the degree to which he felt the urgency of making ignorance a felt condition of his readership and the corresponding degree to which he capitalized on the same device. He not only capitalized on it but, as I sought to show above, endeavored to make its potential for narrative discomfort unavoidable by nipping all in-filling schemata in the bud. His gaps are not empty, for given our nature there can be no imagined gaps without at the least some vaguely hypostatized place-markers. But what he *can* do is short-circuit the schematizing imagination.

If Beckett during his formative years as an artist assiduously honed an art of narrative's expressive gaps, an art that over the years right up to his final decade only grew in subtlety and evocative power, it would appear that in the 1940s, with the narrative interruptions of *Watt* and then the extraordinary gap between the two parts of *Molloy*, he began capitalizing in earnest on the heretofore rare device of the egregious gap. How he hit upon it, I am not sure, but it would appear to have spread rapidly in *Malone Dies*, and then, after the writing of *Godot*, spread like a virus to consume *The Unnamable* and *Texts for Nothing*. In this regard, the latter two texts are unprecedented events in the history of narrative, moments in which the architecture of narrative itself is pulled inside out, and what 'happens' (if the term can be used) takes place in a narrative void. The famous six words that begin *The Unnamable* – 'Where now? Who now? When now?' (Beckett 1965, 291) – initiate a stream of self-canceling attempts to fill a narrative gap that stretches out to the inconceivable 'door that opens on my story' (414). In many different ways and terms, the artful disintegration of narrative in these two works has been oft discussed. But putting Beckett's landmark literary experiments in the context of both the narrative and cognitive research on how we process gaps, several points stand out.

One is that the art of the egregious gap in Beckett's hands is a paradoxical art of emptying by energetic filling:

> [T]here's nothing here, nothing to see, nothing to see with, merciful coincidence, when you think what it would be, a world without spectator, and vice versa, brrr! No spectator then, and better still no spectacle, good riddance. If this noise would stop there'd be nothing more to say. I wonder what the chat is about at the moment. Worm presumably, Mahood being abandoned. And I await my turn. Yes indeed, I do not despair, all things considered, of drawing their attention to my case, some fine day. Not that it offers the least interest, hey, something wrong there, not that it is particularly interesting, I'll accept that, but it's my turn, I too have the right to be shown impossible. (Beckett 1965, 375)

Here in this immense 123-page narrative gap, Beckett hastens from one example to another of what Ricks identified as the 'Irish bull' – 'a form of linguistic suicide' that 'contradicts less itself than all we have learned to expect' (Ricks 153, 197).[13] From one to the next, Beckett expends unparalleled energy on the task of filling every page, even to the elimination of paragraph breaks, in order to empty all possible understanding. It is a project of enormous verbal business dedicated to the task of perfecting the purity of the gap in which it takes place. This point goes hand in glove with a second one, mentioned above: that this art of the egregious gap has less to do with signifying *nothing there* than *nothing known* – less to do with nothingness as an actual void, empirical or metaphysical, than with creating a felt conviction of the inability to know whether there is an actual void out there or something else, of whatever degree of strangeness.

But a third important point is that this bold experiment with the device of the egregious narrative gap, as anywhere else in Beckett's oeuvre, works in fine coordination with a powerful, pervasive, and quite traditional exploitation of the expressive gaps that have always given narrative its life. In the instance of this novel-length gap, what most significantly is built, calling on our willing assistance in every line, is, for want of a better term, a character. 'Character' actually is a good term, for this voicing entity comes through with all the sharp-edged clarity that is implied by the Greek root for 'character' (Χαρακτήρ) in the arts of engraving and minting. So even here, in this strange narrative pause, Beckett invites us to fill in, working with cues that allow us consistently to triangulate a consistent, agential narrative entity. We know this character by the wit of tautology ('If this noise would stop there'd be nothing more to say'), the logical sense that brooks no casual talk, no idiomatic excess ('Not that it offers the least interest, hey, something wrong there, not that it is particularly interesting, I'll accept that . . .'), the patrician formality ('Yes, indeed, I do not despair, all things considered'), and abrupt colloquialism ('good riddance,' 'this noise,' 'hey'). All these and much more sustain a voice that you would recognize anywhere and that directs attention to something that seems (important word) to lie behind the text, bringing it into being, and that can be nothing other than itself. This is a hard point to make, of course, since we all read differently, but I am pretty sure I have got it right, for without the company of this rare and wonderful character, I think there would be few readers who would last for long in the wilds of Beckett's mutant novel.

v. an atheology of gaps

In arguing that, with regard to the egregious gaps in the work of these eight years, interpretive priority should always go to the experience of ignorance, I am not calling for a reductive or impoverished criticism. Quite the reverse. Beckett's crafting of the texture and feel of ignorance is richly representational, not of the absence but of the feelings it engenders and the schemata that vie to fill it. After all, egregious gaps make the greatest appeal to the schematizing imagination, a gift in which Beckett's voices are as greatly endowed as they are in the honesty that fails to sustain it. In their struggles with ignorance, they open up to view what so often we allow ourselves to close.

How are the intervals filled between these apparitions? Do my keepers snatch a little rest and sleep before setting about me afresh, how would that be? That would be very natural, to enable them to get back their strength. Do they play cards, the odd rubber, bowls, to recruit their spirits, are they entitled to a little recreation? I would say no, if I had a say, no recreation, just a short break, with something cold, even though they should not feel inclined, in the interests of their health.

They like their work, I feel it in my bones! No, I mean filled for me, they don't come into this. (Beckett 1995, 122)

By its excess alone, the hypothesis of a crew of 'keepers' declares the utter impoverishment of information. Its elaborate futility is a project constructed out of bitterness and suppressed hilarity. But it says much about the deep structure of the speaker's imagination that the presumption, however factitious, should be totalitarian. He is a prisoner with keepers who 'set about' him. It is as if the feeling of helplessness cannot reflect on itself without the trope of some malignant other. Yet inside this imagined tyranny is the desire to tyrannize. He himself is a keeper *manqué* who, with subtle self-righteousness, would transfer control to himself: 'are they entitled to recreation? I would say no, if I had a say, no recreation, just a short break, with something cold.' All this meted out even against their inclinations 'in the interests of their health.' Which is to say that in the dark night of the soul, the scripts that are likely to rush in, invading the mystery, are often absurdly compounded of the power relations of self and other. Nothing so fully bears this out than the theological in-filling of the great religions of the Book, for which the universal gap is laced everywhere with hierarchy.

But Beckett's is a travesty quickly doomed: 'No, I mean how filled for me, they don't come into this.' The move inward in this last sentence, and its urgency, suggests a kind of Protestant extremity. Indeed, Declan Kiberd, thinking specifically of the trilogy, once called Beckett 'a supremely religious artist' (Kiberd 75). But there is considerable risk in using the term 'religious' since so much baggage comes with it. In the very process of giving insight, the term threatens what Beckett works so hard to sustain: that is, the effort to confound all pre-conceptions of how the question ('I mean how filled for me') might be answered. Mary Bryden has argued that 'Beckett's discourse of negativity, cancellation, and qualification' resonates with the mystical tradition of the '*via negativa*, or apophatic tradition' in which 'God is considered to be unknowable' (Bryden 181). Again, the parallel is striking, but the risks are the same, and Bryden works hard to steer clear of them. Paul Davies, in his second book on Beckett, went so far as to harmonize Beckett and Buddhism. Putting much pressure on a line in *That Time*,[14] he sees in Beckett an homage to the void. 'In the language of Buddhism, when one ceases to subscribe to the collective error of perspective known as self and world, the true nature of reality, the "clarity of emptiness", is what takes its place' (Davies 218). But in Beckett there is no certainty of this kind regarding the void. If

Beckett can be described as 'religious,' he is so in his characters' inability to let go of the question that Davies would have them abandon, that is: 'how filled for me?'

The passage cited above opens Text Six of the book that culminates Beckett's highly self-conscious deployment of the egregious narrative gap. *Texts for Nothing*, composed in 1951–2 on the heels of *The Unnamable*, incorporated into itself a series of wordless gaps (twelve of them) that operate as a repeated visual reflection of the wordfilled gaps they frame. Yet they are not just a 'reflection,' since, both wordless and wordfilled, they equally restate the title, *Texts for Nothing*. The whole thing is a 'farrago of silence and words, of silence that is not silence and barely murmured words' (125). There is to my knowledge no more fully sustained effort to maintain attention on the experience of unknowing in the face of apparent being. The 'keepers' quickly return as 'male nurses, white from head to foot,' then as 'ghouls, naked and soft as worm,' then as 'great clusters of bones, dangling and knocking with a clatter of castanets' (123). With each transformation, Beckett opens up different emotional and intellectual parameters of the encounter with the great unknown of self. As in *Malone Dies*, all this and more is projected into a gap within a gap, where ignorance is elaborated with exhaustive and exhausting beauty in a biding of time until the story can resume: 'a little story, with living creatures coming and going on a habitable earth crammed with the dead, a brief story, with night and day coming and going above, if they stretch that far, the words that remain, and I've high hopes, I give you my word' (126).

By looking at Beckett through the lens of narrative theory, one sees something of his extraordinary diversity. Before the 1950s were out, Beckett had written *Krapp's Last Tape*, in which an old man on perhaps his last day on earth listens to taped moments of his life. The darkness that is set off by the 'strong white light' in which he sits is the absolute vacancy of Ricks and Levy. Only by understanding it as such can the immense lyrical pathos of the play be released. Three years later, Beckett published the epic text, *Comment c'est* (*How It Is*), a work whose 825 white gaps are the generative void of Barker and Wolosky, the mud out of which creation comes, irresistibly (see also Abbott 95–108). Gaps abound in Beckett's many later works, some of them available to both readings, but free of the kind of retrospective worrying that Beckett expended on the egregious narrative gaps of his postwar art.

> Rediscovered miraculously after what absence in perfect voids . . . (Beckett 1995, 184)

> As hope expires of her ever appearing she reappears. (Beckett 1981, 24)

These are comparatively clean breaks, after which the narrator hastens on. Other gaps are everywhere in the later work, as are representations of nothing, as is the theme of our collective ignorance, the immediate and sustained experience of which was earlier so fully enabled by Beckett's exploitation of the egregious narrative gap. Beckett is an artist of such great range because he is so adept at controlling for different forms and different effects. As I argued at the outset, it is easy to overlook just how precisely he controls his art, inviting us to fill with comparable precision those gaps that are the life of any narrative. Included here are ideas of both the void and the mystery of origination that we know very well and that, properly invoked, give his work so much of its movement and depth. What I have focussed on, however, is a unique passage in the multi-faceted course of his career. His art here is every bit as razor-sharp as it is elsewhere, and much about the voice we hear in these egregious gaps is as precisely characterized as any voice in literature. But the larger referential object is to thwart the in-filling imagination. He does this by working with the way we apparently are designed to think, forestalling narrative and turning the mind back upon itself in what is its closest approach to the paradox of knowing what it feels like not to know.

notes

1. For a compact review of the principal work on nothing in Beckett see Levy (622, ftnt. 3). Three treatments of Beckett in which ideas of nothing play a central role and that Levy omits are Trezise, Wolosky and himself (Levy 1980). Wolosky's essay on *Texts for Nothing* includes a capsule overview of four different takes on nothing in Beckett criticism (225).
2. Robbe-Grillet's argument, literally applied, does work, I think, for Tom Stoppard's *Rosencrantz and Guildenstern Are Dead*, but it does so precisely because, unlike Beckett's characters, the characters in this play are overtly premised as fictional. They belong to *Hamlet* and, as such, their appearance outside that play references not so much the human condition as the ingenuity of the playwright. For this reason, at the beginning of Act Three,

the two characters emerge in wonderment from absolute non-being: 'GUIL: Are you there? ROS: Where? . . . ROS: We're on a boat' (Stoppard 97–8). The play owes much to *Godot* but, as Ruby Cohn has cogently argued, 'stylistically, rather than philosophically' (Cohn 114).

3. Compare Sternberg: 'The literary text may be seen as a dynamic system of gaps' (Sternberg 50). For two additional treatments of gaps see Spolsky and Rabinowitz.

4. Meir Sternberg made a closely related distinction between 'Permanent' and 'temporary' gaps (Sternberg 50–1, 238–41). My 'egregious gaps' are examples of Sternberg's 'permanent gaps,' yet they form a sub-class, the presence of which significantly frustrates interpretation. There are numerous permanent gaps (e.g., the unmentionable product that made Newsome's fortune in *The Ambassadors*) that do not clamor to be filled in the same way as, say, the question of whether or not there are ghosts in *The Turn of the Screw*.

5. That we are not the hopeless prisoners of our preconceptions is strongly indicated by our capacity to change our thinking despite the seduction of cultural frames and schemata. In a useful defense of the 'toolkit' as opposed to the 'latent-variable' view of cultural cognition, Paul DiMaggio divides the way we process information into two broad categories: 'Automatic cognition,' which is entirely a matter of the routine and uncritical application of schemata, and 'deliberative cognition,' in which attention, motivation, and the perception of 'schema failure' allow us to override our automatic responses (DiMaggio 268–72). The point remains, however, that in both modes of cognition we fill in. The very effort involved in deliberative cognition shows how important this object is.

6. More fully: 'I like to caricature perception as *externally guided hallucination*, and dreaming and hallucination as *internally simulated perception*' (Shepard 436).

7. Researchers at Duke University have recently located in a region of the prefrontal cortex what they believe to be the location of our automatic determination to find patterns in chaotic behaviors (Scott A. Huettel, *et al,* 'Prefrontal Cortex Activation is Evoked by the Violation of Local Stimulus Expectations,' <wysiwyg://39http://www.biac.duke.edu/research/talks/SFN_2001.asp>).

8. According to investigations by Marjorie Taylor and her colleagues at the University of Oregon into the phenomenon of children's autonomous imaginary friends, a condition found in eighteen percent of the population, successful published authors of fiction report a high incidence (forty per cent) of having had such imaginary companions in their own childhoods (Taylor *et al*, 'Fictional People with Minds of their Own: Characters Created by Adult Novelists and Imaginary Companions Created by Children,' unpublished study).

9. 'Je suis comme une taupe dans une taupinière' (Beckett, quoted in Juliet 19).

10. Correction based on the French original, *Malone meurt*, in which the possessive pronoun is included: 'mes absurdes tribulations' (Beckett 1951, 92).

11. The theory is both true and not true, depending on the reader one invokes. One of my students, a voracious reader and very bright, knew for a certainty

that Heathcliff did not murder Hindley. Throughout the gap in question, he sat there brooding, lost in his own thoughts, and for the moment at least, all passion spent. Clearly, my student was not that rare and informed reader, imagined by Paul de Man and Hillis Miller, who reads closely enough to know that reading is impossible. I don't think de Man and Miller made a fair move when they appropriated the meaning of the word 'reading' in this way, but the important issues in our context are how close, and according to what cues, and for what purpose or purposes, are we invited to approach maximal interpretive uncertainty?

12. Joseph: 'he warn't deead when Aw left, nowt uh t'soart!' (Brontë 185).
13. Ricks's chapter on 'The Irish Bull' (153–203) is a superb gathering of examples of this rhetorical figure, largely from Beckett's work.
14. 'gave up for good and let it in and nothing the worse a great shroud billowing in all over you on top of you and little or nothing the worse little or nothing' (Beckett 1984, 235).

works cited

Abbott, H. Porter. *Beckett Writing Beckett: the Author in the Autograph*. Ithaca: Cornell University Press, 1996.

Abelson, Robert. 'Psychological Status of the Script Concept.' *American Psychology*, 36 (1981): 715–29.

Baker, Nicholson. *The Mezzanine*. New York: Vintage, 1990.

Barker, Stephen. 'Recovering the *Néant*: Language and the Unconscious in Beckett.' In *The World of Samuel Beckett*, edited by Joseph H. Smith. Psychiatry and the Humanities, Volume 12, 125–56. Baltimore: Johns Hopkins University Press, 1991.

Beckett, Samuel. *Malone meurt*. Paris: Les Editions de Minuit, 1951.

——— *Waiting for Godot*. New York: Grove Press, 1956.

——— *Three Novels*. New York: Grove Press, 1965.

——— *Watt*. London: Calder, 1976.

——— *Ill Seen Ill Said*. New York: Grove Press, 1981.

——— *Worstward Ho*. New York: Grove Press, 1983.

——— *The Collected Shorter Plays of Samuel Beckett*. New York: Grove Press, 1984.

——— *The Complete Short Prose, 1929–1989*, edited by S. E Gontarski. New York: Grove Press, 1995.

Blau, Herbert. *Sails of the Herring Fleet: Essays on Beckett*. Ann Arbor: University of Michigan Press, 2000.

Brater, Enoch. *The Drama in the Text: Beckett's Late Fiction*. New York: Oxford University Press, 1994.

Brontë, Emily. *Wuthering Heights*. London: Penguin, 1995.

Bryden, Mary. *Samuel Beckett and the Idea of God*. London: Macmillan,1998.

Butler, Lance St John. *Samuel Beckett and the Meaning of Being: a Study in Ontological Parable*. London: Macmillan, 1984.

Cohn, Ruby. 'Tom Stoppard: Light Drama and Dirges in Marriage.' In *Contemporary English Drama*, edited by C. W. E. Bigsby, 109–120. New York: Holmes & Meier, 1981.

Cook, Albert. 'Minimalism, Silence, and the Representation of Passion and Power: Beckett in Context,' *Centennial Review*, 38:3 (1994): 579–88.

Davies, Paul. *Beckett and Eros: Death of Humanism*. London: Macmillan, 2000.

DiMaggio, Paul. 'Culture and Cognition.' *Annual Review of Sociology*, 23 (1997): 263–87.

Gifford, Henry (ed.). *Leo Tolstoy: a Critical Anthology*. Harmondsworth: Penguin, 1971.

Goffman, Erving. *Frame Analysis: an Essay on the Organization of Experience*. Boston: Northeastern University Press, 1986.

Hemingway, Ernest. *The Short Stories*. New York: Scribners, n.d.

Hesla, David. *The Shape of Chaos: an Interpretation of the Art of Samuel Beckett*. Minneapolis: University of Minneapolis Press, 1971.

Iser, Wolfgang. *The Implied Reader: Patterns of communication in Prose Fiction from Bunyan to Beckett*. Baltimore: Johns Hopkins University Press, 1974.

Juliet, Charles. *Rencontre avec Samuel Beckett*. Paris: Fata Morgana, 1986.

Kiberd, Declan. 'Beckett and the Life to Come.' In *Beckett in Dublin*, edited by S. E. Wilmer, 75–84. Dublin: Lilliput Press, 1992.

Levy, Eric P. *Beckett and the Voice of Species*. Dublin: Gill and Macmillan, 1980.

—— 'The Beckettian Mimesis of Seeing Nothing.' *University of Toronto Quarterly*, 70:2 (spring 2001): 620–32.

Mendler, Jean Matter. *Stories, Scripts, and Scenes: Aspects of Schema Theory*. Hillsdale, NJ: Lawrence Erlbaum Associates, 1984.

Metzing, Dieter (ed.). *Frame Conceptions and Text Understanding*. Berlin and New York: Walter de Gruyer, 1980.

Rabinowitz, Peter J. '"A Lot has been Built Up": Omission and Rhetorical Realism in Dostoevsky's *The Gambler*.' *Narrative*, 9:2 (May 2001): 203–9.

Ricks, Christopher. *Beckett's Dying Words*. Oxford: Oxford University Press, 1993.

Robbe-Grillet, Alain. 'Samuel Beckett, or Presence on the Stage.' In *For a New Novel: Essays on Fiction*, translated by Richard Howard, 111–25. New York: Grove, 1965.

Rumelhart, David E. 'Notes on a Schema for Stories' in D. G. Bobrow and A. Collins (eds), *Representation and Understanding*. New York: Academic Press, 1975, 211–36.

Schank, Roger C. *Tell Me a Story: Narrative and Intelligence*. Evanston: Northwestern University Press, 1990.

Schank, Roger C. and Abelson, Robert. *Scripts, Plans, and Goals*. New Jersey: Erlbaum, 1977.

Shepard, Roger. 'Ecological Constraints on Internal Representation: Resonant Kinematics of Perceiving, Imagining, Thinking, and Dreaming.' *Psychological Review*, 91:4 (October 1984): 417–47.

Spolsky, Ellen. *Gaps in Nature: Literary Interpretation and the Modular Mind*. Albany: State University of New York Press, 1993.

Sternberg, Meir. *Expositional Modes and Temporal Ordering in Fiction*. Baltimore: Johns Hopkins University Press, 1978.

Stockwell, Peter. 'Scripts and Schemas' in *Cognitive Poetics: an Introduction*. London: Routledge, 2002, 75–89.

Stoppard, Tom. *Rosencrantz and Guildenstern are Dead*. New York: Grove Press, 1967.

Storey, Robert. *Mimesis and the Human Animal: On the Biogenetic Foundations of Literary Representation*. Evanston: Northwestern University Press, 1996.

Thorndyke, P. W. 'Cognitive Structures in Comprehension and Memory of Narrative Discourse.' *Cognitive Psychology*, 9 (1977): 77–110.

Trezise, Thomas. *Into the Breach: Samuel Beckett and the Ends of Literature*. Princeton: Princeton University Press, 1990.

Turner, Mark. *Reading Minds: the Study of English in the Age of Cognitive Science*. Princeton: Princeton University Press, 1991.

Uhlmann, Anthony. *Beckett and Poststructuralism*. Cambridge: Cambridge University Press, 1999.

Wolosky, Shira. 'The Negative Way Negated: Samuel Beckett's *Texts for Nothing*.' *New Literary History*, 22 (1991): 213–30.

Wordsworth, William. 'Prospectus MS I.' In *Home at Grasmere*, edited by Beth Darlington, 255–63. Ithaca: Cornell University Press, 1977.

3
intertextuality

enoch brater

By the late 1950s, when Beckett was beginning to be taken seriously by literary critics on both sides of the Atlantic (and, indeed, by audiences all over the world), a pattern for talking about his work quickly developed. You could make sense of Beckett by placing him in the context of the European writers and philosophers who had come before him, and to which his fiction and drama so richly alluded. Hugh Kenner's intuitive early book on Beckett urged us to imagine what he called, impressionistically, the 'Cartesian centaur,' while Ruby Cohn's seminal study, *The Comic Gamut*, traced the evolution of comedic structures from Shakespeare to Bergson and beyond. Edith Kern found her way into Beckett through Kafka and existentialism; Rosette Lamont through the long history of the metaphysical farce; Katharine Worth through 'the Irish drama of Europe,' and Maurice Nadeau, Georges Bataille, and Leonard Pronko in their commentaries on the emerging *nouveau roman* and the always dynamic spirit of the French avant-garde. Martin Esslin's *The Theatre of the Absurd* inserted an enduring critical phrase into our dramatic vocabulary, one that relied on Sartre and Kierkegaard but also placed Beckett, however shakily, in a new tradition of post-war playwriting. More circumstantial studies of the relationship of Beckett's theater to Adamov and Ionesco, to Genet and Pinter and Arrabal,and later to its importance to Fornes and Sam Shepard and Heiner Muller, were not far away and were already predicted in Esslin's landmark book. Yasunari Takahashi reached beyond Europe and found stunning parallels between Beckett's theater and the Japanese traditions of the Noh.[1]

It is hardly surprising that Beckett became susceptible to so many rituals of comparison. His work, with its many invocations to Dante and so many parallels to the structure of memory he himself valorized in his early study of Proust, all but invited a series of academic discussions attuned to the multiple ways in which one literary text echoes, or is inseparably linked to, other texts. The Beckett 'text' came loaded with 'open or covert citations and allusions,' sometimes even the frank 'assimilation of the formal and substantive features of an earlier text' far beyond the chance participation in 'a common stock of literary and linguistic procedures and conventions.'[2] As early as the 1950s Roland Barthes attributed this phenomenon to language's 'secondary memory'; but in Julia Kristeva's radical formulation any text may, as a matter of course, be regarded as an 'intertext,' constituted by the intersection of all other texts, past and future.[3] Beckett would have loathed the term; he once warned his reader that 'literary criticism is not book-keeping' – of any sort.[4] Yet a term like 'intertextuality,' reformulated perhaps, can offer the student of his work a productive way of thinking about a given Beckett piece: the way it makes us read its presence in terms of an assimilated literary past, and most especially the odd way it makes us read that past in terms specifically set out in the adventurous present.

Beckett's connection with his two great Irish literary ancestors, for example, James Joyce and William Butler Yeats, has been the subject of considerable speculation, and continues to offer the student of intertextuality the prospect of much critical intrigue. In Joyce's case, of course, the relationship is well known and has been widely documented in both biographical and comparative terms.[5] And although it is true that Beckett was never Joyce's secretary, he did serve him from time to time in the capacity of amanuensis. Joyce, going blind, needed all the help he could get, especially in the Paris of the 1930s, the same years when his friendship blossomed with the young, impressionable, and particularly well-read Trinity College intellectual. 'Joyce had a profound effect on me,' Beckett once admitted. 'He made me realize artistic integrity.'[6] Beckett revered Joyce and always spoke of him in the present tense, even though he was to survive him by nearly half a century. Beckett's relationship with the poet he once called 'the Nobel Yeats,'[7] on the other hand, was far more vexed and ambivalent, and it will be far more difficult to track and trace. Yet it is precisely the complexities of this connection that reveal the dynamics of both Beckett's Yeats and Yeats's Beckett. As we shall see, in this instance the Beckett intertext moves, simultaneously and courageously, in both directions.

Early Beckett, as John Pilling (among others) has shown, is full of stubborn yet insistent Joycean locutions.[8] Works like the untidy *Dream of Fair to Middling Women* or even the retooled *More Pricks Than Kicks*, which in tone and mood, syntax and narration can never quite decide whether it sets out to mimic or parody *Dubliners*, may be remarkable for the light they shed on Beckett's breakthrough as an innovative writer of the *nouveau roman*, but they also display the perils of writing prose with James Joyce breathing down your back. In these early fictional enterprises Yeats is merely a point of reference – a literary allusion here and there, and not much more than that. Surely Dante can be more dependable, as is the occasional flourish from Baudelaire, St Augustine, Schopenhauer, Balzac, Mallarmé, Ruskin, Horace, Holderlin, Homer, Matthew Arnold, Lord Byron, Racine, Keats, Virgil, Ronsard, Dickens, Einstein, Freud, Nietzsche, Pushkin, Leopardi, Confucius, Plautus, and 'Bernard Pygmalion'[9] (my list is not complete). And at those rare moments when Yeats does distinguish himself within the rank and file of such a heady crowd, a poem like 'Sailing to Byzantium' can be subjected to some pretty hard knocks. As Beckett's Belacqua, Dante's stepchild, lies sprawled on the grass midway through *Dream of Fair to Middling Women*, for example, 'a group of aged compassionate contadine' can see that

> A fat June butterfly, dark brown to be sure with the yellow spots, the same that years later on a more suspicious occasion, it was inscribed above on the eternal toilet-roll, was to pern in a gyre about a mixed pipi champetre, settled now alongside his degradation.

Some few pages later, when the same Dantean prototype asks if a certain woman's dress is suggestively open or 'closed,' The Venerilla, as she is then called, is 'said to hold on while she called it to the eye of the mind.' Beckett's Malone can be similarly flippant and similarly Byzantine with his Yeatsian intertext: 'I am content, necessarily, but not to the point of clapping hands.'[10]

As a writer of poetry, which Beckett was trying to be at the same time that he was working on his short stories, Yeats's celebrated lyricism is similarly sidelined, if not discreetly avoided. Beckett's models here are typically classical and preferably medieval French, the more Provençal the better. And much later in his career, when Beckett turns his attention to writing for the stage, in order, as he said, 'to get away from the awful prose' that he was writing in the late 1940s,[11] Yeats seems to have been dropped altogether. Well, perhaps not quite. Estragon, who in Beckett's signature play, *Waiting for Godot*, claims to have been a poet ('Isn't that obvious?'), seems to have at least a nodding acquaintance with the Yeats canon, mediated in this case by the Gospel According to Saint Matthew:

ESTRAGON: You gave me a fright.
VLADIMIR: I thought it was he.
ESTRAGON: Who?
VLADIMIR: Godot.
ESTRAGON: Pah! The wind in the reeds.[12]

I have deliberately avoided reading too much Yeats into Beckett's first ventures into theater, though the temptation to do so should not go unremarked. Asked about the influence of Irish playwriting on his work, Beckett would admit to only Synge. He disliked Yeats in the theater, saying, for example, that compared to the Abbey productions of *The Resurrection* and *The King of the Great Clock Tower* he saw as a young man in Dublin, 'Balbus building his wall would be more dramatic.'[13] Nevertheless, the father–son endgame that plays itself out in *Purgatory* can emerge as a stunning parallel when featured on a double-bill with Beckett's second published play, just as the girl with green eyes celebrated and eulogized by the seedy old drunk in *Krapp's Last Tape* echoes the familiar trope of a love long lost that brings so much fire to the mature Yeats repertory, the poems Beckett grew to admire. Those 'unseeing eyes,' by way of *Othello*, are said to be 'like chrysolite' as Beckett's romanticization of memory, and of desire unfulfilled, begins to sound like this:

We drifted in among the flags and stuck. The way they went down, sighing, before the stem! (*Pause.*) I lay down across her with my face in her breasts and my hand on her. We lay there without moving. But under us all moved, and moved us, gently, up and down, and from side to side.

And later:

What remains of all that misery? A girl in a shabby green coat, on a railway-station platform? No?
Pause.[14]

The biographer James Knowlson also suggests that Hamm's intercalated lament in *Endgame* (the heavily rhetorical 'Can there be misery – [*he yawns*] – loftier than mine? No doubt. Formerly. But now?') ironizes the Sophocles Beckett knew from Yeats's versions of *Oedipus the King* and *Oedipus at Colonus*, both of which the playwright saw in his final two

years as an undergraduate at Trinity.[15] The intrepid Winnie, too, carries
with her handbag in *Happy Days* – the French translation is called, slyly
(pace Verlaine), *Oh les beaux jours* – some remarkable Yeatsian associations.
Move over, Molly Bloom. Part Cathleen-ni-Houlihan, part Crazy Jane,
this Mother Ireland, literally planted in a mound against a *trompe-l'oeil*
background, is the Mother Earth symbol to end all other mother earth
symbols, Celtic or otherwise.[16]

If in Beckett's four major plays the 'traces blurs signs'[17] of Yeats are
perhaps there, they are so largely by default, and mostly on the part of
the intertextual critic (in this case, the writer of this essay) who longs for
correspondences that may not necessarily stand up under further scrutiny
(Beckett's Murphy, too, it must be remembered, 'was one of the elect,
who require everything to remind them of something else').[18] Scenically,
however, we may be on much firmer and far more practical ground. In
Yeats's *At the Hawk's Well* we wait for a figure who never arrives. And
that 'empty' theater space so suggestive and elemental in *Purgatory*, so
revelatory and atmospheric in the Cuchulain cycle, is more than adequate
preparation for the minimalist *mise-en-scène* that brings with it the mark
of authenticity to the true Beckett style.

Oddly enough, that theatrical minimalism will reach for its most lyrical
expansiveness in Beckett's late, great works of the 1970s and 1980s, and
most surprisingly so in the pieces he designed for the mechanical media.[19]
It is here that the presence of Yeats, the poet rather than the playwright,
is at its most beguiling, its most haunting, and its most unequivocal.
Beckett's involvement with the mechanical media actually began as far
back as 1956, with the writing of the radio play *All That Fall* for the BBC.
A decade later, in part motivated by the poor distribution of his only
venture into cinematography, Alan Schneider's *Film*, he wrote his first
television play, *Eh Joe*, for his friend, the Irish actor Jack MacGowran. But
it was not until 1977 that the BBC broadcast two new television plays
that were to certify Beckett's mastery of the form.

Beckett originally intended . . . *but the clouds* . . . to be shown on a
double-bill with *Ghost Trio*, but when BBC television needed a third
piece to round out an evening's program, he tentatively agreed to an
adaptation of his 1972 stage play, *Not I*. On 17 April 1977, the three short
plays were broadcast together on a show called *Shades*, a title suggested
by the playwright himself. . . . *but the clouds* . . . displays its genealogy
proudly, taking its title, as well as the theme on which it works a stunning
variation, from the final stanza of Yeats's 'The Tower':

> Now shall I make my soul,
> Compelling it to study
> In a learned school
> Till the wreck of body,
> Slow decay of blood,
> Testy delirium
> Or dull decrepitude,
> Or what worse evil come –
> The death of friends, or death
> Of every brilliant eye
> That made a catch in the breath –
> Seem but the clouds of the sky
> When the horizon fades,
> Or a bird's sleepy cry
> Among the deepening shades.

Beckett owes a whole lot more than a line or two to Yeats. The television play, like the poem, features a 'troubled heart' in conflict with 'eyes' that in this case are quite literally 'impatient to be gone.' And the lines specifically not quoted from 'The Tower' can be the most cauterizing of all:

> Does the imagination dwell the most
> Upon a woman won or a woman lost?
> If on the lost, admit you turned aside
> From a great labyrinth out of pride,
> Cowardice, some silly over-subtle thought
> Or anything called conscience once;
> And that if memory recur, the sun's
> Under eclipse and the day blotted out.[20]

In . . . *but the clouds* . . . a male voice murmurs, 'Look at me' and 'Speak to me,' imploring the fleeting image of his beloved to restore memory back to life with 'those unseeing eyes I so begged when alive to look at me.' Beckett's variation on 'The Tower' is heart-rending; for whereas Yeats, 'lured by a softening eye, / Or by a touch or a sigh, / Into the labyrinth of another's being,' finds 'an answer in those eyes' to 'rise, / Dream and so create / Translunar Paradise,' at least in the inspiration they provide for his art, the solitary being who tramps in and out of Beckett's circle of hellish light is left only with a 'begging of the mind.' Beckett's wanderer

departs as he had previously arrived, with 'no sound,' no revelation, and
no Muse. What he finds in those cold eyes is emptiness. For Beckett's
bums there will be no soaring towers and no Byzantium, only a fading
horizon of memory, embers in 'the deepening shades.'

Donald McWhinnie directed Ronald Pickup and Billie Whitelaw in the
original English version of the play, the same team that worked on the
BBC *Ghost Trio*. Beckett was an active collaborator during the recording
sessions. While the companion piece was filmed in color but printed in
black and white, resulting in a tremendous variation in shades of gray,
the BBC . . . *but the clouds* . . . was designed for broadcast in the much
sharper contrast of two tones. The play features only two voices, the male
one who speaks and the female one who poignantly mouths Yeats's lines
in silence, proving once again that though (over)heard melodies may be
sweet, those unheard are sweeter. They are also, Keats notwithstanding,
far more dramatically effective; for this is, when all is *not* said and *not*
done, a visual display after all. The play should really be called:

'. . . . .'

And what might then be the unspoken 'intertext' for that?

In 1977, several months after the McWhinnie production was taped at
the BBC Shepherd's Bush studios in London, Beckett served as his own
director for a second 'go' at . . . *but the clouds* . . . , this one in German
for Suddeutscher Rundfunk. Entitled *Nur noch Gewölk*, this telecast uses
the final fourteen lines of 'The Tower' and makes another departure
from the BBC script in that Yeats's translated verse is not read against the
transparent face of a woman, but rather against the figure of the actor
bent over at his writing desk. The SDR version also has a male figure '*in
set*' who shuffles into and out of the camera light with a far more ironic
step. Yet despite the author's minor emendations to his original English-
language scenario, much of the poignancy of . . . *but the clouds* . . . was
lost in *Nur noch Gewölk*, relying as it did on a clumsy, though standard
translation of Yeats.

As . . . *but the clouds* . . . prominently displays, the Beckett intertext can
be subject to a variety of overlapping formulations. First and foremost,
of course, there is Beckett's rewriting of Yeats. But Beckett also rewrites
Beckett. And in this case there is a further complication: there are at least
three 'texts.' The original Beckett script in English, the McWhinnie BBC
production based on the same, and the German *Nur noch Gewölk*, directed
by the playwright himself, are in continual dialogue with themselves

and even more so with one another. In this Beckett × 3 any discussion of intertextuality will be heavily mediated by the impact of adaptation and interpretation through the sheer force of mechanical inscription. 'Text' in this case must embrace something more than 'script'; the so-called finished products 'canned' on electronic recording tape by the BBC and SDR confront us with new, competing and interlocking arrangements of Beckett's 'primary' and palpable manuscript.

Each text of . . . *but the clouds* . . . , nevertheless, aims to confront a television audience with the concision of an image, one which condenses even further the dimensions we remember from Yeats's initial poetic allure. Each involves only sixty camera shots, the shape of an hour or a minute, seeking to localize abstraction and present us with an authentic iconography, a complete language in pictures. In each case, too, it is difficult to determine if words (English? German?) are meant to imitate image, image words, or words (Beckett's? the speaker's?) words (Yeats's). Which – and what – is precisely 'there' before us to initiate, imitate or paraphrase which? Words, Yeats's as well as Beckett's, seem at first sight to be in charge of the dramatic action that takes place on the circular performance space. Yet, despite Yeats, 'words alone,' designed in this instance for recitation in a mechanical media like television, can no longer be relied on to foster anything even vaguely resembling some longed-for 'certain good.' They exist, instead, on a preprogrammed soundtrack, as ironically 'canned' in this medium as are the pictures themselves. Fated always to be delivered and rerun exactly the same way – they are, in fact, preselected 'takes' – these recorded words exist as once (and only once) spoken by 'Voice,' each text's elusive V. The trick here is twofold: in the process of witnessing the writing down of this story on tape, we are meant to 'see' the whole piece as part of an ever-evolving composition and, furthermore, that M = V.

In . . . *but the clouds* . . . an initially signaled 'he' tries to capture in words the picture he brings to mind, 'that MINE' lurking somewhere in the depths of his uneasy night-thoughts. The words this 'play' wants us to hear therefore serve a mediating function, halfway between the image M invents or remembers or desires and that quite different picture broadcast on the television screen. Beckett does not shy away from locating language at its source, in the writer's 'vision.' And as he does so, he relies on more than one Yeats text. Like the characters imagined in the play *The Words upon the Window-Pane*, the 'he' we meet in . . . *but the clouds* . . . sits, trance-like, at a séance, calling out to a face and a voice to appear: 'Look at me' and then, echoing Hamlet's appeal to a quite different ghost, 'Speak to me.' A scene from Yeats is all but impossible to dismiss:

DR TRENCH: I thought she was speaking.
MRS MALLET: I saw her lips move.[21]

Yet Beckett's face and Beckett's voice, unlike Yeats's, have been programmed to appear through the intercession of a quite different medium, the mechanical one of television. On this screen, word and image are made to participate in a dynamic relationship that is symbiotic and essentially poetic. Mutually supportive and telegenically sustainable, each has been recorded in advance to foster the re-envisioning of a Yeatsian illusion where we might have least expected to find it, in 'that MINE' of visual technology.

Beckett's embrace of technology in this play is nothing if not impressive. In the script he specifies only three camera shots, a near shot from behind for M, a close-up for the woman's face, and a long shot for the uninhabited set or the set with the single male figure. His stage directions make clear that each of the three shots is the '*same shot throughout.*' The use of this particular close-up, however, is something new for Beckett, especially as caught in the BBC production, where Billie Whitelaw's face appears as a transparency superimposed on the previously established video image. The requirements for such camera work present us with something a bit more complicated than three different images which move us progressively, as in an earlier television play like *Eh Joe*, inside a character's head. For in . . . *but the clouds . . .* the shots of M and the woman who shadows him (W) meet in an unpredictable collage, further eroding the barriers between one illusion and the next.

The reliance on close-ups, moreover, is as extraterritorial with time as it has been with televisual space. These exist, as Voice informs us, as 'three cases,' each one assigned its distinctive temporality. Sometimes they appear in the blink of an eye ('*2 seconds*'), sometimes as a lingering pose ('*5 seconds*'), sometimes long enough for the mouth to form in silence, after a moment, the words '. . . clouds . . . but the clouds . . . of the sky . . . but the clouds.' In this third case V murmurs, synchronous with W's lips, '. . .but the clouds' during the mouth's second movement on the screen. The reverse lip-synch allows us to hear, intertextually, Yeats in silence and Yeats in fact. After decoding this tripartite scheme for us, V has a surprise in store for us by saying, almost metatheatrically, 'Let us now run through it again.' We expect the camera to oblige, but it does so grudgingly and not nearly as scrupulously as we might have initially supposed. Before the inaudible mouthing of Yeats's lines from 'The Tower,' V quite unexpectedly makes an appeal directly to the longed-for apparition; the summons V intones, 'Look at me,' paraphrases Krapp's cry of 'Let me in.' After this interlude, V ups the ante by fine-tuning his supplication to 'Speak to me,' a bleak *cri de coeur* answered only by silence, then a quick dissolve to M. Pause. Soon the empty response to M's futile appeal is followed by mention of a previously undocumented 'fourth case,' or 'case nought,' which will be not only the most typical but also the most foreboding, the one in which the ghost-like W, like Godot, fails to keep her strange rendezvous with time.

Beckett's 'MINE' has all along been doubly ambiguous. In one sense it is a rich source of supply, but in another it is an exhausted pit from which all resources have been taken, as well as an encased weapon designed not to create, but to destroy. There is, then, a great deal in . . . *but the clouds* . . . that we do not see. We do not see the closet (east shadow) and we do not see the door (specified in the text as 'West, roads.'). Beckett makes darkness suggest other spaces, peripheries where other dramas may be enacted. Shadow space frames in a circle of light the drama we do see through that larger frame of the rectangular television box. Beckett graphically isolates his image here in a stark visual landscape that serves as a further emblem of the male figure's solitude. On the television screen shadow space is negative space, but Beckett uses it in . . . *but the clouds* . . . to confuse our sense of just what constitutes the positive and the negative. Removing his video image from its usual visual context, Beckett sets it free of any easy expository function in order to make us contemplate it in its seemingly pure state. Conceiving blacks and whites as forms of color, Beckett exhorts us to 'look' at the clarity of his figurative means. Affirming the primacy of representation in the 'face' of abstraction, . . . *but the clouds* . . . allows us to see even in things unseen how language controls vision:

When I thought of her it was always night.

The rest – and Beckett will show this to be the much greater part – is silence, where night and dreams take place.

It may seem strange that Beckett frames his final and most sustained encounter with Yeats in terms that are at once mechanical, mathematical and so geometrically precise. But in doing so, Beckett comes to terms not only with 'the Nobel Yeats,' but, as the artist grows old, with something in himself, an aspect of his writing that most Beckett critics have been reluctant to talk about. The late works for the stage and television, so concerned with the evocation of metaphors of night, rest and approaching death, reveal a surprising romanticism in which 'man,' as Yeats once said, 'is nothing until he is united to his image.'[22] Beckett's ambivalence in dealing with Yeats, which begins in parody and ends in eloquence, also reveals a Beckett who not only comes to terms with that romanticism, but who finally accepts and embraces it. Yet Beckett is no unqualified romantic; at best he will emerge before us in the guise of his fictionalized 'Mr Beckett,' who was of course only a 'dud mystic.'[23] That heavily intertextual machine that frames Yeats's lyrical voice in . . . *but the clouds* . . . is the only way Beckett can deal with this impulse, lest it overwhelm him completely. This is, after all, the same Beckett of last songs, of Schubert's lieder and of Beethoven's *Geister Trio*.

If W. B. Yeats never quite replaces the author of *Finnegans Wake* as the one true and always dependable ' – Hypocrite lecteur, – mon semblable, – mon frère!,'[24] it is nonetheless Yeats, rather than Joyce, who moves from background to foreground in Beckett's mature work. That old, rather dusty volume of forgotten lore that sits on a plain deal table in *Ohio Impromptu* contains many references indeed. While in some sense the text Reader intones is full of memories of Joyce – the walks Beckett took with him in Paris on the Isle of Swans, the fact that the Ohio is one more river of time mentioned in the *Wake* – somewhere, somehow Yeats lurks there, too:

> Seen the dear face and heard the unspoken word,
> Stay where we were so long alone together, my
> shade will comfort you.[25]

Reading Beckett, moreover, suggests that we may now want to read Yeats far less triumphantly. Yeats shadows Beckett, yet Beckett, too, inevitably shadows Yeats: this intertext is everywhere flexible and dynamic as it moves both ways. If Yeats emerges in the traditional modernist canon as the last great romantic, after Beckett he emerges as a decidedly desperate one. 'Dear shadows,' he wrote so hauntingly in his poem about Eva and Constance Gore-Booth, 'now you know it all.'[26] The grounding of such figurative means has shifted; we are all at once in the darkened world of . . . *but the clouds* . . . and *Footfalls*:

Will you never have done? . . . Will you never have done . . . revolving it all? . . . It? . . . It all? . . . In your poor mind? . . . It all . . . It all.[27]

Is Beckett Yeats? Probably not. But in those strange and luminous shadows cast by . . . *but the clouds* . . . has Yeats suddenly become – mirabile dictu – Beckett?

notes

1. For these early approaches to Beckett's work, see Ruby Cohn, *Samuel Beckett: the Comic Gamut* (New Brunswick: Rutgers University Press, 1962); Hugh Kenner, *Samuel Beckett: a Critical Study* (Berkeley: University of California Press, 1961); Edith Kern, *Existential Thought and Fictional Technique: Kierkegaard, Sartre, Beckett* (New Haven: Yale University Press, 1970); Rosette C. Lamont, 'The Metaphysical Farce: Beckett and Ionesco,' *French Review* (February 1959), 319–28; Katharine Worth, *The Irish Drama of Europe from Yeats to Beckett* (London: Athlone, 1978); Maurice Nadeau, 'Samuel Beckett, l'humour et le néant,' *La Littérature présente* (Paris, 1952), 274–79; Maurice Blanchot, 'Où Maintenant? Qui Maintenant?' Nouvelle Revue Française (October 1953), 676–86; Georges Bataille, 'Le Silence de Molloy,' *Critique* (15 May 1951), 387–96; Leonard Pronko, *Avant-Garde: the Experimental Theater in France* (Berkeley: University of California Press, 1962); Martin Esslin, *The Theatre of the Absurd*, revd. edn. (Garden City: Doubleday, 1969); and Yasunari Takahashi, 'Qu'est-ce qui arrive? – Beckett and Noh,' in Ruby Cohn (ed.), *Casebook on 'Waiting for Godot'* (New York: Grove, 1967). Beckett's relationship to contemporary playwriting has been widely studied; see, for example, Enoch Brater (ed.), *Beckett at 80/Beckett in Context* (New York: Oxford University Press, 1986), and Enoch Brater and Ruby Cohn (eds), *Around the Absurd: Essays on Modern and Postmodern Drama* (Ann Arbor: University of Michigan Press, 1990).
2. Abrams, 247.
3. See Roland Barthes, *Le Degré zéro de l'écriture* (Paris: Editions de Seuil, 1953); Julia Kristeva, *Desire in Language*, trans. Thomas Gora, Alice Jardine, and Leon S. Roudiez (New York: Columbia University Press, 1980); and M. H. Abrams, *A Glossary of Literary Terms*, 5th edn. (New York: Holt, Rinehart and Winston, 1988). For studies of Beckett's work in relation to Proust and Dante, see in particular Nicholas Zurbrugg, *Beckett and Proust* (Gerrards Cross, UK: Colin Smythe, 1988) and Daniela Caselli, 'Dante and Beckett: Authority Constructing Authority,' PhD diss., University of Reading, 1999.
4. Samuel Beckett, 'Dante . . . Bruno. Vico . . . Joyce,' in *Our Exagmination Round His Factification for Incamination of 'Work in Progress'* (New York: New Directions, 1972), 4.
5. For details of the Beckett–Joyce connection, see Richard Ellmann, *James Joyce* (New York: Oxford University Press, 1959) and James Knowlson, *Damned to Fame: the Life of Samuel Beckett* (New York: Simon & Schuster, 1996).
6. Quoted by Ruby Cohn, *Back to Beckett* (Princeton: Princeton University Press, 1973), 14.

7. Beckett used the phrase 'the Nobel Yeats' in his short story 'Walking Out'; see his *More Pricks That Kicks* (London: Calder & Boyars, 1970, 114). On Beckett's ambivalent attitude toward Yeats, see his 'Recent Irish Poetry' in *Disjecta: Miscellaneous Writings and a Dramatic Fragment*, ed. Ruby Cohn (London: John Calder, 1983), 70–6. For additional information about the Yeats–Beckett connection, see Gordon S. Armstrong, *Samuel Beckett, W. B. Yeats, and Jack Yeats: Images and Words* (Lewisburg: Bucknell University Press, 1990).

8. See John Pilling, *Beckett before Godot* (Cambridge: Cambridge University Press, 1997).

9. Samuel Beckett, *Dream of Fair to Middling Women*, ed. Eoin O'Brien and Edith Fournier (Dublin: Black Cat, 1992), 79.

10. Ibid., 129, 205. In *Malone Dies* (New York: Grove, 1956), Beckett's mid-trilogy protagonist has his own spirited but heavily qualified way with 'Sailing to Byzantium,' 2.

11. Quoted by Colin Duckworth (ed.), *En Attendant Godot, by Samuel Beckett* (London: Harrap, 1966), xiv.

12. Samuel Beckett, *Waiting for Godot* (New York: Grove, 1954), 13a. Yeats's 1899 collection of poems was entitled *The Wind Among the Reeds*.

13. See Knowlson, 181.

14. Samuel Beckett, *'Krapp's Last Tape' and Other Dramatic Pieces* (New York: Grove, 1960), 17, 27. For 'chrysolite,' see *Othello* V.ii.145.

15. Knowlson, 71.

16. See Enoch Brater *Why Beckett* (London: Thames & Hudson, 1989), 96–104 for additional configurations of Beckett's Earth Mother symbolism.

17. See 'Ping' in Samuel Beckett, *The Complete Short Prose, 1929–1989*, ed. S. E. Gontarski (New York: Grove, 1995), 193.

18. Samuel Beckett, *Murphy* (New York: Grove, 1957), 63.

19. For an extended discussion of Beckett's television plays, see Enoch Brater, *Beyond Minimalism: Beckett's Late Style in the Theater* (New York: Oxford University Press, 1987).

20. See *The Collected Poems of W. B. Yeats* (New York: Macmillan, 1966), 195, 197. All citations in my text from . . . *but the clouds* . . . are from *The Collected Shorter Plays of Samuel Beckett* (New York: Grove, 1984), 255–62.

21. See *The Collected Plays of W. B. Yeats* (New York: Macmillan, 1966), 385.

22. See Yeats's discussions on this point in *Explorations* (New York: Macmillan, 1962) and in 'Per Amica Silentia Lunae' in *Mythologies* (New York: Macmillan, 1959), 317–66.

23. *Dream of Fair to Middling Women*, 186.

24. Baudelaire, 'Au lecteur,' in *Poètes françaises du dix-neuvième siècle*, ed. Maurice Z. Shroder (Cambridge, MA: Harvard University Press, 1964), 92.

25. See *Ohio Impromptu* in *Collected Shorter Plays of Samuel Beckett*, 286.

26. 'In Memory of Eva Gore-Booth and Con Markiewicz' in *Collected Poems of W. B. Yeats*, 229.

27. See *Footfalls in Collected Shorter Plays of Samuel Beck*ett, p. 243. For additional discussions of Beckett's intertextuality, see *Samuel Beckett Today/Aujourd'hui*, 3 (1994).

works cited

Abrams, M. H. *A Glossary of Literary Terms*, 5th edn. New York: Holt, Rinehart and Winston, 1988.

Armstrong, Gordon S. *Samuel Beckett, W. B. Yeats and Jack Yeats: Images and Words*. Lewisburg: Bucknell University Press, 1990.

Barthes, Roland. *Le degré zéro de l'écriture*. Paris: Editions de Seuil, 1953.

Bataille, Georges. 'Le Silence de Molloy,' *Critique* (15 May 1951), 387–96.

Beckett, Samuel. *Waiting for Godot*. New York: Grove, 1954.

—— *Malone Dies*. New York: Grove, 1956.

—— *Murphy*. New York: Grove, 1957.

—— *'Krapp's Last Tape' and Other Dramatic Pieces*. New York: Grove, 1960.

—— *More Pricks Than Kicks*. London: Calder & Boyars, 1970.

—— 'Dante . . . Bruno. Vico . . . Joyce,' *Our Exagmination Round His Factification for Incamination of Work in Progress*. New York: New Directions, 1972.

—— 'Recent Irish Poetry,' *Disjecta: Miscellaneous Writings and a Dramatic Fragment*, ed. Ruby Cohn. London: Calder, 1983.

—— *The Collected Shorter Plays of Samuel Beckett*. New York: Grove, 1984.

—— *Dream of Fair to Middling Women*, ed. Eoin O'Brien and Edith Fournier. Dublin: Black Cat, 1992.

—— *The Complete Short Prose, 1929–1989*, ed. S. E. Gontarski. New York: Grove, 1995.

Blanchot, Maurice. 'Où Maintenant? Qui Maintenant?' *Nouvelle Revue Française* (October 1952), 676–86.

Brater, Enoch. *Beyond Minimalism: Beckett's Late Style in the Theater*. New York: Oxford University Press, 1987.

—— *Why Beckett*. London: Thames & Hudson, 1989.

Brater, Enoch (ed.). *Beckett at 80/Beckett in Context*. New York: Oxford University Press, 1986.

—— and Ruby Cohn (eds) *Around the Absurd: Essays on Modern and Postmdern Drama*. Ann Arbor: University of Michigan Press, 1990.

Caselli, Daniela. 'Dante and Beckett: Authority Constructing Authority.' PhD diss., University of Reading, 1999.

Cohn, Ruby. *Samuel Beckett: the Comic Gamut*. New Brunswick: Rutgers University Press, 1962.

—— *Back to Beckett*. Princeton: Princeton University Press, 1973.

Duckworth, Colin (ed.). *En Attendant Godot, by Samuel Beckett*. London: Harrap, 1966.

Ellmann, Richard. *James Joyce*. New York: Oxford University Press, 1959.

Esslin, Martin. *The Theatre of the Absurd*, revd. edn. Garden City, NY: Doubleday, 1969.

Kenner, Hugh. *Samuel Beckett: a Critical Study*. Berkeley: University of California Press, 1961.

Kern, Edith. *Existential Thought and Fictional Technique: Kierkegaard, Sartre, Beckett*. New Haven: Yale University Press, 1970.

Knowlson, James. *Damned to Fame: the Life of Samuel Beckett*. New York: Simon & Schuster, 1996.

Kristeva, Julia. *Desire in Language*, trans. Thomas Gora. Alice Jardine and Leon S. Roudiez. New York: Columbia University Press, 1980.

Lamont, Rosette C. 'The Metaphysical Farce: Beckett and Ionesco,' *French Review* (February 1959), 319–28.

Nadeau, Maurice. 'Samuel Beckett, l'humour et le néant,' *La Littérature présente* (Paris, 1952), 274–79.

Pilling, John. *Beckett before Godot*. Cambridge: Cambridge University Press, 1997.

Pronko, Leonard. *Avant-Garde: the Experimental Theater in France*. Berkeley: University of California Press, 1962.

Samuel Beckett Today/Aujourd'hui, 3 (1994). Special number on 'Intertexts in Beckett's Work/Intertextes de l'oeuvre de Beckett.'

Shroder, Maurice Z. (ed.). *Poètes françaises du dix-neuvième siècle*. Cambridge, MA: Harvard University Press, 1964.

Takahashi, Yasunari. 'Qu'est-ce qui arrive? – Beckett and Noh,' *Casebook on 'Waiting for Godot'*, ed. Ruby Cohn. New York: Grove, 1967.

Worth, Katharine. *The Irish Drama of Europe from Yeats to Beckett*. London: Athlone, 1978.

Yeats, W. B. *Mythologies*. New York: Macmillan, 1959.

—— *Explorations*. New York: Macmillan, 1962.

—— *The Complete Poems of W. B. Yeats*. New York: Macmillan, 1966.

—— *The Collected Plays of W. B. Yeats*. New York: Macmillan, 1966.

Zurbrugg, Nicholas. *Beckett and Proust*. Gerrards Cross: Colin Smythe, 1988.

4

feminist readings of beckett[1]

elin diamond

> There was father. That grey voice.
> There mother. That other.
> *A Piece of Monologue*

Who speaks? Who hears? In what language? These questions rise persistently from the oeuvre of Samuel Beckett, and have driven not only poststructuralist literary theory since the 1960s, but also, and perhaps more insistently, the theorizing of the major 'French feminists' of the early 1970s and 1980s: Luce Irigaray, Hélène Cixous, and Julia Kristeva.[2] To link Samuel Beckett with the latter writers may seem, at first blush, improbable. Beckett had no known allegiance to feminism *per se* and he consistently denied any political or social motives to his deracinated characters and bleak landscapes. Beckett's early critics helped to sustain his demurral, emphasizing the great author's solitary brilliance and the universal humanism of texts. Yet, if the dispossessed speakers of Beckett's fiction and plays seem to defy social even metaphoric labeling, they have, despite their fright wigs and greatcoats, gender. In fact, the displaced gender signifier – Krapp's banana and Winnie's pearls (from, respectively, *Krapp's Last Tape* and *Happy Days*) – is one of Beckett's more playful gestures. Further, the central tropes of French feminist theory, the hysteric, the maternal semiotic, and the performative *parler-femme* (speaking [as] woman) are contemporary with and, I will argue, at play in three brief, beautiful Beckett texts, *Not I* (1972), *Footfalls* (1976), and *Rockaby* (1982). This essay does not assume cross-influences among Cixous, Kristeva, Irigaray, and the ascetic Irishman who wrote in their midst. It does assume acknowledgment of Beckett's wide aesthetic and philosophical interests, among which, after two years of psychotherapy in the 1930s, were a keen interest in the relation of the unconscious to language, and in the psychosexual exertions and seductions of the maternal. Such issues, crucial to feminist theory, are not in a simplistic sense thematized in Beckett's work. Rather, in his *mises-en-scène* they are queried, ironized, and with painful visual images, explored. My argument, then, is that the polemical and performative gestures of feminist theory in its heyday of the 1970s and 1980s are critically and revealingly staged in Beckett's texts and, conversely, reading Beckett through the lens of feminist theory foregrounds significant features of his gender representations.

Perhaps a brief review of some major themes of poststructuralist thought will be helpful. In the 1960s and the following decades, poststructuralist theorists – semioticians, deconstructionists, linguists, psychoanalysts – sought to unravel the fundamentals of structuralist knowledge. Ferdinand de Saussure had demonstrated that linguistic signifiers produce meaning through phonemic difference – the difference between a present sound and absent ones – and not through a natural or transparent relation of signifier to signified, sign to referent. In *Of Grammatology* (1976, French edition 1967) and *Writing and Difference* (1978, French edition 1967), Jacques Derrida argued that meaning, arrived at through relations of differences, is meaning always deferred; there can be no structural center or 'transcendental signified' that could ground meaning or terminate this process of deferral. This notion in turn undermines the traditional authority of the speaker. Western thought, Derrida showed, is based on a 'metaphysics of presence'; it prefers speech over writing because it assumes that the presence of a speaker, an 'I,' will provide an origin to discourse as a guarantor to meaning. In *Problems in General Linguistics* (1971; French edition 1966), Emile Benveniste delinked this 'I' from the traditional fiction of selfhood. The referent for the 'I' is not the speaker uttering it but, rather, the act of discourse in which it is enunciated. Language, and only language, is the ground for the 'I,' but this ground is relational: The 'I' of enunciation only exists in relation to a 'you,' and both are positions, empty spaces, marked by pronominal shifters. 'I' is simply the one who 'utters the present instance of discourse containing the linguistic instance I' (Silverman 46). The notion of subjectivity preceded by and adrift in language is, of course, vintage Beckett. As the Unnamable puts it: 'I, say I. Unbelieving' (Beckett 1958, 291). The Unnamable's quarrel with any attempt to signify the subject might serve as an emblem of Parisian poststructuralism. Like the Derridean trace, Beckett's Unnamable eludes signifying form (except in the reader's desire) through a seemingly endless writing that tempts, but always forecloses, presence. In *The Unnamable* and the fiction that follows it, and in the stage plays under discussion here, Beckett goes out of his way to separate language from the intending consciousness of an 'I' that is assumed to govern the meaning of its utterance. As though acknowledging Beckett's precedence in poststructuralist theory, Michel Foucault began his seminal 'The Discourse on Language' by paraphrasing the last lines of *The Unnamable* – thus aligning himself with the linguistic homelessness of Beckett's characters and putting in crisis his own authority to speak.[3]

After 1968, amid contestation on many fronts, the feminist critique of gender in language emerged, forcing another crisis in the 'I.' Psychoanalyst Jacques Lacan, had, since 'The Agency of the Letter in the Unconscious' (1957), incorporated Saussurean insights into Freudian theory, rethinking the unconscious as a kind of writing system whose signifiers float free of the signified. The sexual determinations of identity in Freudian psychoanalysis became linguistic determinants in Lacan. Language, or the symbolic order, became the Order of the Father, and the phallus, the relational signifier by which all meaning is produced. The gendering process—the trajectory through the Oedipus in Freud – was resignified as the necessary acquisition of language. To take up one's place in language was to position oneself on one side or the other of the male/female divide, a process facilitated in male children for whom the unconscious terrors of castration are deflected by identification with the father's authority, his 'I.' The female child, lacking the organ to exchange for the phallic privilege of subjectivity, cannot assume that 'I' without an erasure of her unnamable – because unrepresentable – sexuality. In psychoanalytic terms, both genders enter the symbolic by extinguishing an intimate corporeal connection to, and splitting off from, the mother, their first 'other.' But the tiny girl, unable to identify with her father's sexual preeminence, experiences her body and sexuality as lack; in the symbolic order of the Father, she cannot symbolize her desire. There is no maternal order of language that allows her to say 'I' as a woman.

It is precisely at this psycho-linguistic impasse that feminist theory inserts itself. To speak, to enter linguistic and social normality, the female must choose between remaining outside the signifying system (a form of suicide) or using a language in which her position as object, not subject, is already given. Feminist theorists turn the supposed negative of the female – her inability to say 'I' except as a pseudo- or imitation man – into an explosive corpus of interpretations and formulations. That is, the early writings that became central to feminist theory absorbed and repositioned the themes of deconstruction and psychoanalysis, to make productive what language (and, by extension, gendered social and cultural relations) occludes. In *Revolution in Poetic Language* (1984, a shortened translation of her doctoral thesis *La Revolution du Langage Poétique*, 1974), Julia Kristeva distinguished the symbolic from a pre-Oedipal maternal 'semiotic,' linking the pulsional drives transmitted from the maternal body to the infant with the rhythms, repetitions, elisions, and wordplay of modernist poets since Mallarmé. In 'The Laugh of the Medusa' (1976, French version 1975), Hélène Cixous's coined *écriture féminine*, which famously celebrated the female body, not as disclosing or veiling its lack, but as the rich metaphoric ground of linguistic expression: 'And why don't you write? Write! Writing is for you. You are for you. Your body is yours, take it' (Cixous in Marks and de Courtivron, 146). In Cixous and Clement's *The Newly Born Woman* (1986, French edition 1975), hysteria, the condition, in psychoanalytic terms, of the refusal of correct gender positioning, is repositioned as resistance to the linguistic Law of the Father; the writers produce a sisterhood of 'luxuriant hysterics,' linking Freud's patients in *Studies on Hysteria* to a host of such mythological and literary viragos and madwomen as Medea, Clytemnestra, and Cleopatra.

Luce Irigaray's *Speculum of the Other Woman* (1985, French edition 1974) is an elaborate and dense uncovering of maternal repression in the master discourses of Plato and Freud. Philosophy and psychoanalysis are, Irigaray argues, based on the othering and silencing of the maternal; the woman/mother is reduced to a specular reflection of the masculine 'self-same.' Deconstructing Plato's famous Allegory of the Cave, Irigaray posits in effect two mimetic systems, one repressed by the other. Platonic mimesis assumes a model, an invisible Form or (for Aristotle) a universal, beyond or distinguishable from the shadow reflections on the cave walls. Ironizing and displacing classical mimesis is Irigarayan 'mimicry' in which the cave or womb is 'already a speculum ... [an] inner place of reflection,' and the shadows of Plato's cave proliferate into mere copies or 'fake offspring,' an incessant Medusan mimicry that troubles the rational I/eye (255). The philosopher wants to forget or prove illusory his maternal origins. Irigaray turns that wish into a playfully anarchic scenario: a hystera-theater that has lain in the 'womb' of Western thought and surfaces in the deformations of hysterics as well as modernist poets. Poststructuralists like Derrida say that representation is not a fall from presence, but is all we know of origins. Irigaray, enunciating a philosophy in the feminine register, trumps this position, placing the maternal (the womb/cave) at the origin of representation itself.[4] In *This Sex Which Is*

Not One (1985; French edition 1977), Irigaray offers a discursive fantasy for the impossibility of full female subjectivity: her *parler-femme* has been notoriously reduced to 'women's language' but it focuses on the more complex sense in French of *énonciation*, or the position of the speaker in discourse. Returning to Benveniste, we recall that the 'I' of language always implies an other, a 'you,' a positionality made vexing for women because of the relation of 'I' to a phallic system, woman as other to the masculine subject. As 'other' to the 'image of the one,' women are unable to achieve self-consciousness, linguistic mastery. Unlike Cixous's *écriture féminine*, which imagines a fluid maternal bodily writing, a writing of fluids, Irigaray's *parler-femme* (punning on *par les femmes*; or 'by women') seeks bigger game, a utopian 'place' in the symbolic wherein women speak to others and to each other as subjects.

In charting Samuel Beckett's gender representations, Mary Bryden gives ample evidence of the (hetero)sexual antagonism in Beckett's early work – his sardonic portraits of loathsome mothers, post-menopausal lovers, and ambivalent sons. She argues that in the later works such antagonisms morph into 'sexual mutuality or "indifference."'[5] At this point we might say that, as a modernist male writer, Samuel Beckett writes, inevitably, in the linguistic domain of the father, of that 'grey voice' (see epigraph above), but not by excluding the difficult effects of 'mother. That other.' His *parler-femme*, his version of 'speaking-as-woman,' works the territory of the repressed feminine, giving voice to the lacerating alienation of hysterical speech and to a maternal function that both encloses and pulses toward a kind of self-recognition.

not i

One starts speaking as if it were possible to stop at will.
The Unnamable

In the darkness, at a height of eight feet above stage level, Beckett's Mouth, as image of the female, rivals the fiercest creation of the surrealists. *'Fully, faintly lit,'* Mouth is the female body's metonymic reduction, both organ of speech and organ of sex/birth/reproduction.[6] The Unnamable describes a discourse from a 'liquified brain' (293); Mouth is a pulsing muscle that spews words like excrement, 'pouring it out' in a gasping, spittling, hysterical somatic mimicry of lexical and syntactic norms. Like the hysterics of Freud's *Studies on Hysteria*, Mouth suffers from 'reminiscences.' Her body, like theirs, 'is transformed into a theater for forgotten scenes ... bearing witness to a lost childhood that survives in suffering' (Cixous and Clement, 5):

> out ... into this world ... this world ... tiny little thing
> ... before its time ... in a godfor– ... what? ... girl? ... yes ...
> tiny little girl ... into this ... out into this ... before
> her time ... godforsaken hole called ... called ... no matter,
> parents unknown ... unheard of ... he having vanished ... thin
> air ... (*Not I*, 14)

Freud's case histories of hysterics were the basis of his 'new science' of psychoanalysis, and Cixous and Clement acknowledge the greatness of the listening doctor who, after the long sad history of medical resentment at resistent, incurable women, hears his own hysteria in his patients' somatic raving and verbal obsessions.[7] Mouth's raving is marked by a refusal of the pronominal that would inscribe her into normative discourse. The price for refusing that 'I' is a logorrhea marked by the classic symptoms of hysteria: withdrawal and silence ('practically speechless ... all her days,' 18); the analgesic attack ('whole body like gone,' 21); words that defy comprehension ('no idea what she's saying!,' 19), like the polysemia of Freud's Anna O. The 'I' that Mouth refuses to utter refers to a female speaker who is neither present nor absent but rather adrift in the elisions between four fragmented reminisces: lying face down in the grass; standing at the supermart; sitting on the bench noticing her own tears; and 'that time at court' (21). Like all Mouth's reminiscences, the latter is preceded by a reprise of the repressed first 'scene':

> tiny little thing ... before its time ... godforsaken
> hole ... no love ... spared that ... speechless all her days ... practically
> speechless ... how she survived!
> ... that time in court ... what had she to say for
> herself ... guilty or not guilty ... stand up woman ...
> speak up woman ... stood there staring into space ...
> mouth half open as usual ... (21)

Guilty or not guilty? Standing before the Law of the Logos, the female, by virtue of being born female, is already guilty, since, as the psychoanalytic story goes, she cannot assume subjectivity within the symbolic (she lacks a penis to be castrated) or outside of it. She has a guilty secret (her sexuality) that is both her disease and her resistance to cure. Hysteria, the body talking out of control, 'speaks' of this guilt and of this resistance: 'The hysteric is in ignorance, perhaps in innocence; but it is a matter of *refusal*, an escape, a *rejection* ...' (*Newly Born Woman*, 14). Mouth rejects the regulations of discursive logic, which order her to take up a subject position in a language that represses her secret. Empowering herself through the negative she is, at a minimum, 'not I.'

The hysteric, Margaret Whitford remarks, 'cannot assume her/his own discourse: everything is referred for validation to the "you"' (35). Beckett creates a poignant 'you' as stand-in for the audience. The story is often told that while vacationing in El Jadida, Morocco in 1972, Beckett observed a tall figure completely swathed in a djellaba, gender indiscernible, leaning against a wall, in an attitude, Beckett felt, of acute listening.[8] Raising and lowering arms in a *'gesture of helpless compassion'* (14), Beckett's figure seems silently to urge Mouth to staunch her verbal flow by symbolizing herself as 'I.' In a sense, Auditor acts the role of analyst, one who cannot modify the culture that makes his patient sick (*helpless* compassion), but attempts to, as Kristeva puts it, 'prevent [her] jouissance, [her] truth, and replace it with the plausibility of reasonable discourse' (Moi 236). The djellaba figure is not the only one to replace/ prevent Mouth's desire. Standing in for an overtaxed audience attempting to grasp the meaning of Mouth's truth, he also seems to be the relay for a much more powerful internal censor, a proscriptive voice that Mouth hears, reminding her of the buzzing and the flickering light, correcting her on empirical details (her age is seventy, not sixty, she was lying, not kneeling in the grass). Who is this Other that serves as the 'you' to Mouth? Mouth dutifully if frantically responds and corrects herself ('... sixty ... what? ... seventy? ... good God!,' 15), and even plaintively asks whether 'perhaps something she had to ... tell ... could that be it?' (21). However, intermingled with such questions are the signifiers of the raging and rejecting hysteric who refuses the healer's ministrations and his orders; who shrieks with laughter at the 'thought' of a 'merciful God'; and who, most of all, refuses ego-agency, or rather the fiction of ego-agency that would quell the violent symptom. Instead the 'mouth on fire' overcomes the repression barrier and does not cease: '*Voice continues behind curtain, unintelligible ...*' (23).

The hysteric's refusal to take up the position of a gendered 'I' appears subversive – a symptom that betrays and unravels the patriarchal symbolic. But to imply a marginal narrative of heroic proportions in *Not I*, or in feminist theorizing on hysteria, would be utterly simplistic. For one thing, as Clement puts it: 'The feminine role ... of the hysteric is ... antiestablishment and conservative at the same time. Antiestablishment because the symptoms – the attacks – revolt and shake up the public, the group, the men, the others to whom they are exhibited. ... The hysteric unties familiar bonds, introduces disorder into the well-regulated unfolding of everyday life. [But her role is] conservative ... because every hysteric ends up inuring others to her symptoms, and the family closes around her again, whether she is curable or incurable' (Cixous and Clement, 5). The compassionate gestures of Beckett's djellaba figure fade into immobility and the curtain will 'close around her again, whether she is curable or incurable.'

Mouth's signifiers 'speak,' throwing out flickering images of an anonymous life: a courtroom, a figure lying facedown in the grass or moving toward the sound of a bell. Yet the resonances of the play take us beyond Mouth. The elisions between word-images are the gaps or ruptures in the symbolic that are not indices of a fuller truth (if only we could get her to say 'I' and string a narrative together) but, rather, testify to the conundrum of enunciation itself: The I of discourse is *in* discourse; it is the fiction of humanist thinking that a 'not I,' an entity outside the language system, is speaking. *Not I* is a drama that gives the lie to that humanist fiction but that dramatizes the risk of not functioning as if the fiction were true. The drama of breaking off the maternal connection, of becoming socialized through language, is the drama of every human being, every 'tiny little thing,' and is best illustrated by those speakers for whom that accession to language can only be a struggle.[9] The female speaker, whose 'I' is never herself, enters speech as a 'no-body, dressed up wrapped in veils, carefully kept distant, pushed to the side of History and change, nullified, kept out of the way, on the edge of the stage ...' (Cixous and Clement, 69).

In the first French production of *Pas Moi* in 1975, Beckett allowed the Auditor to be dropped because of the company's technical problems, but in a new French production in 1978, that he himself directed, Beckett gave the imposing Auditor greater importance at the end: '[The Auditor] now covered his head with his hands "in a gesture of increased helplessness and despair, as if unable to bear any longer the torrent of sound"' (Brater 34). Also, in the French version, the Auditor 'adds a "gesture of blame" to his stance of helpless compassion' (34). This intensification of the Auditor's suffering, including the 'gesture of blame,' recalls the frustration of the Victorian doctors who began to blame the hysterics they could not cure. On a deeper level the Auditor's suffering speaks to the interdependence and fragility of the social-symbolic contract, and to the penalty suffered by those who fail to keep up their end of the 'I ... you' of normative speech. Perhaps, though, this increased role of the Auditor masks a repressed element in Beckett's original account: The djellaba-covered, seemingly genderless, figure leaning against a wall in El Jadida, a symbol to Beckett of acute listening, was, he later learned, a mother waiting for her child to leave school. Beckett's powerful use of the genderless djellaba figure is, of course, more important than what is revealed by this datum. Yet the datum is suggestive. As Bryden notes, most critics assume that the Auditor is male (119), which creates a familiar configuration of male healer, pathological female speaker. A female speaker and female listener are grist for another interpretative fantasy, where the suffering of Mouth's struggle is acknowledged by one who actually shares in it. This might lead us to wonder what might happen if the imaginary register, which Lacan designated for the infant–mother dyad, and Kristeva for the pulsional, maternal-semiotic ruptures of conventional language, were not devalued and repressed in the necessary accession to the symbolic. Psychoanalysis will not admit this possibility. 'The difficulty at the heart of being human,' Juliet Mitchell writes, is that subjectivity always entails a splitting off from the sources of nourishment, both real and fantasized: '[T]he subject is split and the object is lost' (Mitchell and Rose 25). As Beckett's characters have told us again and again, there is no help for the difficulty of being human.

Actresses who have opened themselves to the challenge of being Mouth testify to the mental and physical agony of producing her logorrheic utterance high above stage level, and in utter darkness.[10] For feminist theorists, *Not I* is a resonant and unforgettable image of precisely why *parler-femme* is impossible in our culture, yet why it persists as a critical performative, a proposition that has as yet no referent, but which, in its radicality, exposes the fissures and abrasions of the gender norms we take to be natural and eternal.

footfalls

> Forget me, Mother. Forget you in me, me in you. Let's just forget us. Life continues.
>   Luce Irigaray, 'And one doesn't stir without the other' (63)

The critique of patriarchal language and law through the figure of the hysteric is limited by the onus of her disease. Feminist theory has embraced a more significant human role – one impossible to marginalize, however silenced she has traditionally been. The mother, or more accurately the maternal function, because of her 'pre-Oedipal' role in nurturing, gendering, and socializing the infant, has become a metaphoric lever for dislodging patriarchal structures. In Kristeva's formulations of the 1970s, the pre-Oedipal or, to use her terms, the 'semiotic' (or 'chora') is central to her theory of artistic subversion. Kristeva locates the semiotic in the pre-verbal moment of mother–child bonding, when the child is most dependent on the maternal body, when instinctual drives are channeled and organized, when vocal/kinetic rhythms are unconsciously absorbed. The alliteration, repetition, melody, and harmony in modernist writing signifies not a referent but rather 'the influx of the semiotic' into the symbolic (Kristeva 1984, 62). The artist's incestuous appropriation of an 'archaic, instinctual, and maternal territory ...' (Kristeva 1980, 136) produces 'an irruption of the drives in the universal signifying order ...' (Kristeva 1984, 136). Importantly, Kristeva sees the semiotic as a 'dialectical' interference (Kristeva 1984, 24); the patriarchal symbolic is necessary to break the mother–child dyad, that space of nondifferentiation to release the child into separation and signification. Radically different is Hélène Cixous's concept of *l'écriture féminine*, a writing empowered by a 'woman-voice,' a 'maternal muse that the female writer ingests to create her own song for other women' (Stanton 167). This maternal voice is, like Kristeva's semiotic, the 'song before the law, before ... the symbolic' (167), but it brooks no interference from the symbolic, the Law of the Father. In this deep auditory intimacy, 'the voice is the uterus' which, merging with the breast, creates an absolute convergence: 'Voice. Inexhaustible milk. Is rediscovered. The lost mother. Eternity: voice mixed with milk' (167).[11]

> M: Mother. [Pause. No louder.] Mother.
> [Pause.]
> V: Yes, May.
> M: Were you asleep?
> V: Deep asleep. [Pause.] I heard you in my deep sleep. [Pause.] There is no sleep so deep I would not hear you there.
>
> (*Footfalls* 44)

Beckett's *Footfalls*, emerging from the darkness and a single chime, between May ('M') and her mother's voice ('V'), stages a crisis in feminist theories of the maternal: how celebrate the maternal origin, yet separate sufficiently from the mother to assume a subject position? While mother–daughter relations are privileged, and the collapse of boundaries between the two is applauded in *écriture féminine*, Irigaray's notion of *parler-femme* seeks to establish, through language, a space between subject positions for all women, including mothers and daughters. When Irigaray collapses 'woman' into 'mother' the gesture is polemical: In the symbolic order of language, all women are mothers in the sense of being positioned as objects or as the substratum, the 'ground' of discourse, never as subjects. The girl child has no means of symbolizing her own relationship to the mother, which leads, in Irigaray's discussion, to the 'nondifferentiation' of mother and daughter, the nonsymbolization of their relationship. And because, as Margaret Whitford writes, 'there is no genealogy on the side of women; the generational differences are blurred. [T]he man takes the woman as a substitute for his mother while *the woman simply takes the mother's place*. So that women in the symbolic are in a kind of continuous present ...' (Whitford 86, my italics).

Beckett's *Footfalls* poses the question of nondifferentiation between mother in stark yet mysterious terms. The obsessive May paces and 'wheels' nine steps to the right and left, in view of the audience, yet appears to be enveloped by her mother's voice. (In an early version of the play, V announced, 'My voice is in her mind,' recalling the censoring sounds to which Mouth must respond.) One can scarcely imagine metaphorical milk flowing between the ninety-year old 'V' and the spectral May with her 'disheveled' grey hair, her 'worn gray wrap ... trailing' (42) over unseen feet. Maternal rhythms have atrophied into a menopausal parody of the death drive, a linear repetitive dance by the daughter, whose steps the mother ghoulishly calls: 'But let us watch her move, in silence [M paces. Towards the end of second length.] Watch how feat she wheels [M turns, paces. Synchronous with steps third length.] Seven eight nine, wheel' (45). While V and May underscore their generational succession in the opening dialogue, and while May's story, following V's, is named a 'sequel,' Beckett, in his direction of *Footfalls*, explicitly insisted on echo, repetition and overlay between V and May's stories: 'One must sense the similarities of both narratives, [n]ot so much from the text as from the style, from the way the text is spoken ... "Not enough?" in the mother's story should sound exactly like the "Not there?" of Mrs. W in Amy's story' (Asmus 338; Gontarski 284). Beckett told the performer playing May in his German production, that her story should in effect sound like 'composing': 'It is not a story but an improvisation. You are looking for the words. You correct yourself constantly' (Asmus 340; Gontarski

285), yet the end of May's story is her beginning – the continuation of her pacing – and the reiteration of her mother's plaintive 'Will you never have done ... revolving it all?' (48).

Given Beckett's tight control over his texts, it is amazing that he uses the word 'improvisation' even as a directorial suggestion in the privacy of a rehearsal. For to improvise implies not merely access to the symbolic but an ability to play with and in language. May's stumbling, self-correcting discourse works athwart a powerful image-making in which she symbolizes herself ('A faint tangle of grey tatters,' 47) and sees herself ('Watch it pass ... watch her pass,' 47), and, in a sense, transcends herself, connecting her 'semblance' in fiction to that of the suffering god ('His poor arm,' 46). Pacing the 'arm' in the cruciform church ('up and down, up and down'), May, herself a ghostly semblance in the flickering candlelight, is there and not there, slipping across pronouns ('it ... her') breaking into a 'tangle' of alliteration and assonance: 'their light ... like moon through passing ... rack' (47). Another narrative frame retrieves or, rather, for the first time, produces a new object – an imaginary May called Amy and a mother called Mrs Winter, who has seen something 'strange' at church. Amy, May says, cannot confirm her mother's vision, because though her mother 'distinctly' heard her praying, Amy was 'not there.' Immediately, the created 'it,' the object/story, vanishes, swallowed back into the first dialogue by M's voice as she repeats her mother's lines: 'Will you never have done ... revolving it all?' (48).

If the referent for 'it' remains tantalizingly ambiguous, Beckett's meticulous choreography makes clear that the mental 'revolving' is physicalized in May's pacing. The first iteration of 'Will you never have done ... revolving it all?' ends just before May makes one of her turns (Asmus 338; Gontarski 283–4). These 'life-long stretches of walking,' Beckett told his German May, are 'the centre of the play; everything else is secondary' (Asmus 338; Gontarski 283). As such, May's pacing is linked to Beckett's perennial attraction/revulsion to the maternal, she who gives life and death simultaneously. Pozzo's line remains the most famous in this regard: 'One day we are born, one day we die, the same day, the same instant' (Beckett 1954, 57). In *Stories and Texts for Nothing,* as Mary Bryden writes, 'the birth/death dialectic is like an open lesion licked weariedly yet obsessively' by the mordant narrator (Bryden 165): 'the first step on the long travelable road: destination tomb, to be trod without a word, tramp ... tramp' (Beckett 1967, 118). Typically, the mother enters the image, as suffocating as the tomb: 'Yes, I'd have a mother, I'd have a tomb ... here are my tomb and mother, it's all here this evening, I'm dead and getting born, without having ended, helpless to begin, that's my life' (119). May's life, too, has never really begun. If we are to believe V's account, the disheveled middle-aged May began her pacing as a young child who demanded to hear, as though still inside the muffled space of the womb, the sound of footsteps, however 'faint they fall.' The repetitive pacing of nine steps (Beckett changed the number from seven to nine) marks not only the 'life-long stretches of walking' that is the compulsive insistent movement of life to death but the time of gestation. May marks the time of fetal development but parturition remains ambiguous. V herself refuses to utter the word 'born,' preferring 'began,' a deliberate echo, as Beckett tells it, of a lecture he heard in 1935 by C. G. Jung, at the Tavistock Clinic in London; Jung described a young girl whom he could not treat, and who died shortly after, because, according to Jung, she had never fully been born (Asmus 338; Gontarski 284). When the actress Billie Whitelaw, playing May, asked Beckett, 'Am I dead?,' he replied, 'Let's just say you're not really there' (Brater 60). Such is the insight of May's story, when her character Amy refuses to verify Mrs Winter's vision: 'I saw nothing, heard nothing of any kind. I was not there. Mrs. W: Not there? Amy: Not there' (48).

May's inability to be born, her inability to 'improvise' a story that separates herself from the engulfing suffocating womb/voice of her mother is a persistent thread in Beckett's texts and a brilliant theatrical metaphor of the paralysis of woman/mother's place in language. Three years after the first production of *Footfalls*, Irigaray published a 22-page monologue/essay, 'Et l'une ne bouge pas sans l'autre' (1979; 'And the One Doesn't Stir without the Other,' 1981), a plaintive yet defiant address from a tormented female 'I' to a maternal other:

> With your milk, Mother, I swallowed ice. And here I am
> now, my insides frozen. And I walk with even more difficulty
> than you do, and I move even less. (60)

In these opening lines of text, Irigaray's metaphor for maternal engulfment echoes May's fictional 'Mrs Winter' and the emotional temperature Beckett prescribed in his textual changes of *Footfalls*. The 'south' door in May's story became a 'north door' because it was 'colder.' 'You feel cold,' he told his actress, 'the whole time, in the way you hold your body too. Everything is frost and night' (Asmus 339; Gontarski 285). Irigaray's 'I' imagines her birth with a certain Beckettian detachment: 'A little light enters me. Something inside me begins to stir ... Waking me from a long sleep. From an ancient dream. A dream which must not have been my own, but in which I was a captive' (61). Captivity is soon imaged as the suffocation of nurturance and its attendant, agonizing collapse of boundaries between mother and daughter, I and you: 'You've prepared something to eat. You bring it to me. You feed me/yourself. But you feed me/yourself too much ... You put yourself in my mouth and I suffocate' (61). The theorist's 'I' pleads for a separation *and* intimacy: 'I would like both of us to be present. So that the one doesn't disappear in the other.' But, as with May's pacing, Irigaray's text, rather than advancing discursively, revolves it all and reprises her theme – again, in terms that appear haunted by *Footfalls*: 'And such an abyss now separates us that I never leave you whole, for I am always held back in your womb. Shrouded in shadow' (67; *Ensevelie dans l'ombre*, 21).

Perhaps we're closer to understanding the 'it ... all' of *Footfalls*. Amid ghostly semblances and flickering visions are veiled references to trauma or life-changing events ('Then one night'; 'Did you not observe anything ... strange?'). But more likely the 'it' is precisely (or imprecisely, given the dim stage lighting) what is before us: a verbal and visual image of mutual engulfment; an 'all' that brooks no individual destiny for either mother or daughter, since, as Irigaray puts it, 'one doesn't stir without the other.' Every woman is both mother and daughter (Irigaray: 'You look at yourself in the mirror. And already you see your own mother there. And soon your daughter,' 63) and Beckett encourages the slippage between the two. He designates 'V' as the voice of 'WOMAN,' leaving the traditional bio-social moniker to arrive with the play's first utterance: 'Mother.' When spoken by a female, this word designates both mother and daughter and, in this case, with Mother out of view, Beckett posits the suggestion that speaking to mother is a form of self-address. Unlike Mouth, both May and V say 'I'; they attempt, in dialogue, to verify each other's ages and separately to compose, symbolize, themselves and each other – an enactment of separation. Yet V, powerfully invisible, subsumes the otherness of May, despite the latter's attempt to invent herself as Amy. Jane Gallop links the paralysis perfomatively invoked in Irigaray's text to the anxiety of/between women concerning masculine privilege – who has access to phallic power? and will it threaten the integrity of she who does not? (Gallop 113–131). Perhaps this 'it' is another layer of May's 'it': The underside of the visual paralysis we see is the privilege to escape from the mother–daughter dyad, a choice *Footfalls* will not permit. Certainly Irigaray's engulfing mother belies Cixous's vision of the deep, productive (milk-giving) intimacy between the mother's voice and the listening daughter/writer.

Beckett's *Footfalls*, itself an unstable overdetermined 'it,' partakes of, and produces, both visions. V, the mother's voice, *both controls and is subsumed by* May's monologue. And the puzzle of the female self, different from, yet culturally, socially, linguistically collapsible into the maternal, remains. Beckett told the actress Billie Whitelaw to pronounce the word 'sequel' as though saying 'seek well,' thus having yet another good laugh at his interpreters. But perhaps he also shared with us the profounder puzzlement of the maternal. We may never have done 'revolving it all' – no doubt to our mental detriment – 'in our poor minds.'

rockaby

Because in order not to die, you must come and go, come and go ...

Samuel Beckett, *Malone Dies*

After the ghostly (non)presences of *Footfalls*, the emphatic materiality of W in *Rockaby* is an enormous relief. More or less. Certainly *Rockaby* inhabits the bleak verbal landscape now almost cozily familiar to Beckett readers. Short expressive lines, eschewing sentence structure, limn a solitary life, nearly but not quite extinguished. Familiar, too, is the technique of splitting and thus exploring the enunciative position: From a voice (claiming to be) separate from her utterance (*Not I*), to a recorded voice separate from (but inhabiting) an other (*Footfalls*), we have a woman, W, whose own voice, 'V,' emerges from a separate source; yet that voice replaces the pronominal 'I' with 'she,' and compared to V's recorded speech, the utterances of W are limited; she is spoken, rather than speaking. As with *Not I* and *Footfalls*, the fragments of utterances, whatever their source, while they describe experiences in a vague past, subtly and powerfully meld, over the course of the performance, with the image/sound we experience in the theater.[12] But Beckett gives *Rockaby*'s W a uniquely spectacular, grotesque femininity, exposing yet another layer of connection contemporaneous with feminist theory. Though alone and apparently dying, W's clothing activates and excites the eye; her 'black lacy high-necked evening gown' is covered in 'jet sequins' that 'glitter' as she rocks; an 'incongruous frivolous headdress set askew with extravagant trimmings catch[es] light when rocking.' In contrast, then, to her dirgelike discourse and 'expressionless white face,' W's sequin-covered dress and headdress are both light-catching, that is, light-reflecting, as is the rocker, which is 'polished to gleam when rocking' (22). Beckett's W is a spectacular, mirrorlike object whose words take us again into the labyrinth of the maternal, and a radical articulation of Beckett's *parler-femme.*

Mirrors are long associated with narcissistic women, objects of masculine disgust, and possibly envy. But the mirror is also crucial in Lacanian psychoanalysis as that which inaugurates the ego as other. In the story of the mirror stage, the infant, still wobbly on its feet, jubilantly identifies with an image of itself in the mirror, an image whose most impressive trait – bodily coherence – it does not share. Thus the ego, at this formative movement, is felt to reside not within the infant but in the mirror, as an image, an imaginary object. The infant's delighted self-recognition is in fact a self-alienating misrecognition, yet the lure of the image launches a lifelong, impossible journey to 'rejoin' this idealized version of the self (Lacan 2). Crucially, the mirror stage anticipates the alienation of language acquisition, in that the 'I' of language is situated *outside* the infant.

While both genders experience the mirror stage, while both enter language as speaking subjects, Lacan sees the mother as the support to the wobbly infant, separate from the reflection system that undergirds the ability of all subjects to say 'I.' For Irigaray, the setting aside of the mother is indicative of this setting aside of all women (including, eventually, the infant girl), for in the symbolic order the female is not positioned as subject. Women, then, are not in the mirror, but rather, as 'body/matter ... are the material of which the mirror is made' (Whitford 34).

With scores of mirrorlike sequins stitched into the material of her dress – a dress that calls attention to her femaleness – Beckett's W is the support of representation, but cannot represent herself as 'I.' Instead, as she rocks and is rocked, she conflates mother and child into one stage image. With 'famished eyes' the adult woman seeks to rejoin an imaginary version of herself ('another like herself/a little like'), and each time resumes her search – both rhythmic rocking and the recorded words – with the childlike demand: 'More.' In each section of text introduced by W's 'More,' the rocking rhythm is reinforced by the insistent repetition of key phrases: 'till in the end'; 'close of a long day'; 'to herself/whom else'; 'going to and fro'; 'all eyes/all sides'; 'high and low'; 'for another like herself/a little like'; and the line she uniquely speaks *with* V: 'time she stopped.' The latter contains the Beckett threnody of wishing for an end to life and to the words that prolong it. (The other meaning, that of stopping time, is merely laughable. The rocker rocks on, out of her control.) Each section introduces just enough substantive material to offer the audience the illusion of meaningful duration. From going 'to and fro' in the first section, V situates W 'at her window' still looking for another like herself, now nominated 'another living soul.' In the third section, V tells us that W's blinds are up, but all others down, recalling Krapp's memory of sitting outside looking up at his dying mother's window; the blind pulled down signalling her death (*Krapp's Last Tape*, 18–20). In the next and last section, not surprisingly perhaps, mother makes an 'appearance':

> so in the end
> close of a long day
> went down
> in the end went down
> down the steep stair
> let down the blind down
> right down
> into the old rocker
> where mother sat
> all the years in black
> best black

Here is the aforementioned melding point, where what has been described conjoins with what we see and hear. Past is present. And whereas the old woman before us seemed more mother than child, now the relation reverses and repeats: Mother is daughter, daughter mother. Is this the maternal genealogy, a place for the woman in discourse, that would signal a *parler-femme*? In the eight lines preceding the mention of 'mother,' 'down' is repeated six times. Penetrating the ear more deeply for being detached from the object/body before us, Beckett finds language for the unspoken, which is a hair's breadth away from the 'deepest' mental depths of the unthought. Effecting a change in our cultural modes of enunciation means drawing on, mobilizing, all psychic registers, including unconscious feelings and desires. W's rocking indeed mobilizes those feelings and what is revealed, in the smallest amount of linguistic space, is the articulation of a *range* of positions for a *parler-femme*. Twenty-three lines before her final silence, V stumbles on a new concept: 'time she went right down/was her own other/own other living soul.' Subjectivity, of course, means opening oneself to the other, the 'I ... you' of discourse. In her vision of *parler-femme*, Irigaray imagines women liberated from exclusively inhabiting the position of 'you,' the support and mirror of the masculine 'I.' She imagines women-as-subjects together, moving from 'you' to 'I' together. For this, women need a mirror too, 'a mirror that will send back to them an image that confirms them in their autonomous subjectivity' (Whitford 142). V supplies that reflection to W and, thus empowered, V finds, as the rocker slows, a language that dangerously and defiantly expands the representational frame of woman/ mother. Instead of 'yes,' W says 'no.' Instead of affirming/producing/ nurturing/supporting life, V says 'fuck life' (20). However, Beckett will not figure W's death as defiant release. The rocker that rocks her off is the 'mother rocker' with '*rounded inward curving arms to suggest embrace*' (22). With this reminder of the engulfing mother, of death as maternal suffocation of life, *Rockaby* leaves us with a bracing unsentimental vision of the possibilities *and* the limits of *parler-femme*. If the mother appears to control life (W is the rocker), she is also a female who, only feebly, emerges from her internal monologue to alter her representation (she is rocked). If maternal rhythms produce the 'semiotic' deformations in language we value in Beckett and others, Beckett reminds us that the rocker is 'controlled mechanically.' W's body, the woman's body, remains once again suspended between silent matter (nonsymbolization) and an ever-tenuous struggle to say 'I.'

Julia Kristeva praised the literary avant-garde 'for introducing ruptures, blank spaces, and holes into language [and thus calling] into question, the very posture of mastery' (Marks and de Courtivron 165). Doubtless she had Samuel Beckett in mind.[13] Beckett's own posture as venerated twentieth-century avant-garde author has been continually to link mastery to failure, speech to silence, syntax to gap. He has, in other words, 'feminized' his writing, permitted the other to invade his discourse and, in *Not I*, *Footfalls*, *Rockaby*, produced his own darkly resonant *parler-femme*. As the Parisian women of the 1970s and 1980s offered their version of the feminine body in discourse, the Irish writer who made Paris his home theatricalized their theory, ruptured and challenged *their* discursive mastery through powerfully denatured stage images.

notes

1. This article is an expanded version of 'Speaking Parisian: Beckett and French Feminism,' which first appeared in Linda Ben-Zvi (ed.), *Women in Beckett:*

Performance and Critical Perspectives (Urbana: University of Illinois, 1990), 208–16.

2. None of these three accepted the label of 'feminist.' For a good summary of the issues and the transatlantic misunderstandings, see Kelly Oliver, *Reading Kristeva: Unraveling the Double-bind* (Bloomington: Indiana University Press, 1993), 163–80.

3. Foucault unwittingly misattributes the source of these lines, claiming to cite 'the voice of Molloy' (215).

4. See my Introduction to *Unmaking Mimesis: Essays on Feminism and Theater* (Routledge, 1997), x–xii.

5. In her concluding chapter, Mary Bryden writes: 'The (male and female) beings who populate the work of this period are recognizably, persistently, searchingly human, but their quest is too elusive, too uncertain of outcome to permit them to glory in any fullness of gendered being. This factor alone ensures the absence not only of phallocentrism but also of its female (gynocentric) equivalent.' In Mary Bryden, *Women in Samuel Beckett's Prose and Drama* (New York: Barnes and Noble, 1993), 193. There are many wonderful insights in this book, but this one is misleading. Phallogocentrism (a tongue-in-cheek portmanteau coined by Derrida combining logocentrism with the 'phallus' of Lacanian psychoanalysis) is not a choice but rather the linguistic reality in which all human beings become subjects. There is no gynocentric alternative, except in the important theorizing of certain writers. Cixous's writing is a performance of *écriture féminine*, that is, a performance of a metaphor, and as such, slips the noose of authoritative label, including the 'gynocentric.' Furthermore, in the discourse of psychoanalysis, there is no 'fullness of gendered being' for either sex. Sexual identity rests on the unconscious experience of lack which is never overcome. This is why the 'split' subject yearns for imaginary completion in an other. And why perhaps Beckett's characters seek, as W puts it, for 'an other like herself,' (*Rockaby*).

6. The sense of Mouth as vagina is stunningly reinforced by Billie Whitelaw's televised performance (BBC, 1976) before a single camera (which eliminates the Auditor role). Spittle gathering at the corners of her mouth, lips quivering, teeth flashing, the viewer looks with horror and fascination at an orifice that, by implication, should not be seen. As Enoch Brater tells it, the shoot in color was so disturbing that it had to be 'neutralized by broadcast in black and white.' In Enoch Brater, *Beyond Minimalism: Beckett's Late Style in the Theater* (New York and Oxford: Oxford University Press, 1987), 35.

7. See 'Realism and Hysteria' in Diamond, *Unmaking Mimesis*, 3–39.

8. There are various accounts of this story which seem to emanate, more or less directly, from Beckett. One says the Auditor's attitude was one of 'intense listening' (Brater 24), another says 'intense waiting' (Bair 622). James Knowlson, combining the other known source of the play, Caravaggio's *Decollation of St John*, which Beckett saw in Malta in 1971, opines that the figure of 'intense listening' was probably a composite construction, conjoining Beckett's impression of the djellaba-clad figure and, as Knowlson describes it, the 'old woman standing to Salome's left' in the Caravaggio painting. 'She observes the decapitation with horror, covering her ears rather than her eyes'

(521–2). For my purposes, it is telling that the model for the listener in both sources is female.

9. In his 1933 essay 'Femininity,' Freud asks, 'how does [the little girl] pass from her masculine phase [desire for her mother] to the feminine one [identification with her mother] to which she is biologically destined?' He concludes that, 'the constitution will not adapt itself to its function without a struggle.' (Sigmund Freud, *The Standard Edition of the Complete Works of Sigmund Freud*, Vol. xxii, London: The Hogarth Press, 1953–74, 117, 119).

10. Jessica Tandy recalled that playing Mouth in 1972, eyes covered in black crepe, 'was a tremendous challenge.' 'There isn't another actor I can respond to – there isn't an audience I can see.' Billie Whitelaw performed Mouth at the Royal Court in 1973. 'What happened to me ... was a terribly inner scream, like falling backwards into hell.' After performing *Not I* for two seasons and taping it for television, she vowed: 'I will never do the play again. If I did, I think I would lose my sanity.' (All citations from Brater 30–1.)

    Wendy Salkind, who played Mouth in the Maryland Stage Company Production of *Not I* (November 1990), has these recollections: 'It began with black makeup painted around my mouth and on the tip of my nose, like a clown. Then the red mouth, wet. Then the hood with a strip of netting over the eyes. Finally the contraption. It was a helmet of metal bars that sat on my head and two long bars came down by my ears and extended way out below my chin. ... I was walked by hand down a dimly lit hallway to the scaffolding on stage. Always I felt I was walking to my execution. Because Xerxes [Mehta, the director] insisted on total darkness [backstage], I remember listening to the audience as the lights faded. I listened for them to become silent. ... Then I could feel my breathing quicken and it was as if I was about to lose my bowels, the words gushed up from deep down and, as I heard the curtain part, the light popped on, blinding me, so I shut my eyes and the words just poured out my mouth. It always began with a feeling of nausea until the word, "Out." That settled me. Somewhere, midway, I had the distinct sensation I was falling forward and that I would fly out into the audience, attached to my scaffolding. ... I couldn't wait to get to the screams' (letter to me, 2 December 2002).

11. Domna Stanton, quoting from Hélène Cixous's *Illa* (Paris: Editions des Femmes, 1980).

12. Ruby Cohn dubbed this effect 'theatereality' in *Just Play: Beckett's Theater* (Princeton, NJ: Princeton University Press, 1980), 28. For other fine writing about the plays under discussion here, see Steven Connor, *Samuel Beckett* (Oxford: Basil Blackwell, 1988) and the essays in Robin J. Davis and Lance St J. Butler, *'Make Sense Who May': Essays on Samuel Beckett's Later Works* (Totowa, NJ: Barnes and Noble Books, 1988).

13. Julia Kristeva's involvement in Beckett's writing goes back to 'The Father, Love, and Banishment' in *Desire in Language* (first published in *Samuel Beckett: Cahiers de l'Herne*, eds T. Bishop and R. Federman (Paris: Editions de L'Herne, 1976, xx, reprinted in *Polylogue*, 1977), which looks at the interplay of paternal meaning and maternal *jouissance* in Beckett's *First Love* and *Not I*. The latter play enters Kristeva's discussion of narcissism in 'Freud and Love: Treatment and Its Discontents' in *The Kristeva Reader*, ed. Toril Moi (New York:

Columbia University Press, 1986, 240–71) and in *Histoires d'Amour* (Paris: Denoel, 1983).

Hélène Cixous' interest in Beckett follows from a dissertation on Joyce (*L'Exil de James Joyce, ou l'art du remplacement*, 1972) and long interest in Jean Genet. Her appreciation of Beckett, 'Une passion: l'un peu moins que rien,' appeared in *Samuel Beckett: Cahiers de l'Herne*, 496–513. Other important texts on *écriture féminine* include *La Venue à l'écriture* (Paris: Editions des femmes, 1986) and 'Extreme Fidelity,' trans. A. Liddde and S. Sellers, in *Writing Differences: Readings from the Seminar of Hélène Cixous*, ed. S. Sellers (Milton Keynes: Open University Press, 1988, 9–36). See Mary Bryden's important readings of Cixous and Beckett in *Women in Samuel Beckett's Prose and Drama*.

Irigaray has never written on Beckett to my knowledge. In other works she has pursued the genre of, if I may coin a term, 'lyric theory': *Corps-à-corps avec la mère* (Ottowa: Editions de la pleine lune, 1981) and *Passions élémentaires* (Editions de Minuit, 1982). *Ethique de la différence sexuelle* (Editions de Minuit, 1984) continues the practice of reading with/against key philosophers (Plato, Aristotle, Descartes, Spinoza, Merleau-Ponty, and Levinas). *Je, tu, nous: Toward a Culture of Difference*, trans. Alison Martin (New York and London: Routledge, 1993) attempts to 'translate' theory into pragmatic questions and ordinary contexts.

works cited

Asmus, Walter. 'Rehearsal Notes for the German Premiere of Beckett's *That Time* and *Footfalls* at the Schiller-Theater Werkstatt, Berlin.' Trans. Helen Watanabe. *Journal of Beckett Studies, 2* (Summer 1977).

Bair, Deirdre. *Samuel Beckett: a Biography*. New York: Harcourt, Brace, Jovanovitch, 1978.

Beckett, Samuel. *Waiting for Godot*. New York: Grove Press, 1954.

—— *The Unnamable*. In *Three Novels: Molloy, Malone Dies, The Unnamable*. New York: Grove Press, 1958.

—— *Krapp's Last Tape*. New York: Grove Press, 1960.

—— *Happy Days*. New York: Grove Press, 1961.

—— *Stories and Texts for Nothing*. New York: Grove Press, 1967.

—— *Ends and Odds: Eight New Dramatic Pieces* [contains *Not I* and *Footfalls*]. New York: Grove Press, 1976.

—— *Rockaby and Other Short Pieces* [incl. *A Piece of Monologue*] New York: Grove Press, 1981.

Benveniste, Emile. *Problems in General Linguistics*. Trans. Mary Elizabeth Meek. Coral Gables: University of Miami Press, 1971.

Ben-Zvi, Linda (ed.). *Women in Beckett: Performance and Critical Perspectives*. Urbana: University of Illinois Press, 1990.

Brater, Enoch. *Beyond Minimalism: Beckett's Late Style in the Theater*. New York: Oxford University Press, 1987.

Bryden, Mary. *Women in Samuel Beckett's Prose and Drama*. New York: Barnes & Noble Books, 1993.

Cixous, Hélène. *Illa*. Paris: Editions des Femmes, 1980.

—— 'The Laugh of the Medusa.' Trans. K. Cohen and P. Cohen, rptd. E. Marks and I. de Courtivron. *New French Feminisms*. New York: Schocken Books, 1981.

—— and Clement, Catherine. *The Newly Born Woman*. Trans. Betsy Wing. Minneapolis: University of Minnesota Press, 1986.

—— *La Venue à l'écriture*. Paris: Editions des femmes, 1986.

—— 'Extreme Fidelity,' Trans. A. Liddle and S. Sellers, in *Writing Differences: Readings from the Seminar of Hélène Cixous*, ed. S. Sellers. Milton Keynes: Open University Press, 1988, 9–36.

—— 'Une Passion: l'un peu moins que rien.' *Samuel Beckett: Cahiers de l'Herne*, eds. T. Bishop and R. Federman. Paris: Editions de l'Herne, 1976, 496–13.

Cohn, Ruby. *Just Play: Beckett's Theater*. Princeton University Press, 1980.

Connor, Steven. *Samuel Beckett: Repetition, Theory and Text*. London: Basil Blackwell, 1988.

Davis, Robin J. and St. J. Butler, Lance. *'Make Sense Who May': Essays on Samuel Beckett's Later Works*. Totowa, NJ: Barnes and Noble Books, 1988.

Derrida, Jacques. *Of Grammatology*. Trans. Gayatri Chakravorty Spivak. Baltimore: Johns Hopkins University Press, 1976.

—— *Writing and Difference*. Trans. Alan Bass. Chicago: University of Chicago Press, 1978.

Diamond, Elin. *Unmaking Mimesis: Essays on Feminism and Theater*. New York and London: Routledge University Press, 1997.

Foucault, Michel. *The Archaeology of Knowledge* & *The Discourse on Language*. New York: Harper, 1972.

Freud, Sigmund. *Studies on Hysteria*. New York: Basic Books, 1955.

—— 'Femininity.' *The Standard Edition of the Complete Works of Sigmund Freud*, Vol. xxii. London: The Hogarth Press, 1953–74, 112–35.

Gallop, Jane. *The Daughter's Seduction: Feminism and Psychoanalysis*. Ithaca: Cornell University Press, 1982.

Gontarski, S. E. (ed.). *The Shorter Plays*, vol. IV of *The Theatrical Notebooks of Samuel Beckett*, general editor, James Knowlson. New York: Grove Press, 1999.

Irigaray, Luce. *Corps-à-corps avec la mère*. Ottowa: Editions de la pleine lune, 1981.

—— *Speculum of the Other Woman*. Trans. Gillian C. Gill. Ithaca: Cornell University Press, 1985.

—— *This Sex Which Is Not One*. Trans. Catherine Porter with Carolyn Burke. Ithaca: Cornell University Press, 1985.

—— *An Ethics of Sexual Difference*. Trans. Carolyn Burke and Gillian C. Gill. Ithaca: Cornell University Press, 1993.

—— *Je, tu, nous: Toward a Culture of Difference*. Trans. Alison Martin. New York and London: Routledge 1993.

—— 'And One Doesn't Stir without the Other.' *Signs*, 1981 7:1, 60–7.

Knowlson, James. *Damned to Fame: The Life of Samuel Beckett*. New York: Touchstone, 1996.

Kristeva, Julia. *Desire in Language: A Semiotic Approach to Literature and Art*. Trans. Leon S. Roudiez. (New York: Columbia University Press, 1980.

—— *Revolution in Poetic Language*. Trans. Margaret Waller. New York: Columbia University Press, 1984.

Lacan, Jacques. *Ecrits: A Selection.* Trans. Alan Sheridan. New York: W. W. Norton, 1977.

Mitchell, Juliet, and Rose, Jaqueline. *Feminine Sexuality: Jacques Lacan and the école freudienne.* Trans. Jacqueline Rose. New York: W. W. Norton, 1982.

Oliver, Kelly. *Reading Kristeva.* Bloomington: Indiana University Press, 1993.

de Saussure, Ferdinand. *Course in General Linguistics.* Trans. Wade Baskin. New York: McGraw-Hill, 1966.

Silverman, Kaja. *The Subject of Semiotics.* New York: Oxford University Press, 1983.

Whitford, Margaret. *Luce Irigaray: Philosophy in the Feminine.* London and New York: Routledge, 1991.

5
poststructuralist readings of beckett
leslie hill

i

'Whither literature?,' 'Où va la littérature?' It was with these deceptively simple words that, in July 1953, the French novelist, philosopher, and literary critic, Maurice Blanchot, returned to the radical rethinking of the question of literature that had concerned him for a decade or more. Blanchot's inquiry had many different aspects to it. It referred to literature's questioning relationship to the world at large. More important, it also had to do, in Blanchot's eyes, with literature's challenge to philosophy (and that pale shadow of philosophy, literary criticism), whose authority over literature, since Mallarmé, had become increasingly precarious. More significant still was the question that literature posed to itself as to its own origin, purpose, and destiny, for this was a question, Blanchot argued in *La Part du feu* (*The Work of Fire*) in 1949, that had become synonymous with literature itself. Ten years later, as Blanchot's thinking developed, it culminated in an influential and ground-breaking collection of essays entitled *Le Livre à venir* (*The Book to Come*).[1] The volume is an important one for many reasons, not least, as far as readers of Beckett are concerned, because it was one of the very first to identify the crucial importance of Beckett's trilogy for an understanding of modern (or postmodern) writing as such. Indeed, it was with a reprise of the famous opening words of *L'Innommable* (*The Unnamable*) – 'Where now? Who now?' – that in October 1953 Blanchot began to translate his own earlier question about the future of literature into contemporary terms.[2]

This was not Blanchot's first gesture in support of Beckett. Already two years earlier, together with Maurice Nadeau and Jean Blanzat, alongside his friend Georges Bataille, the author of a favourable early review of

Molloy that had notably drawn attention to the '*absence* of humanity' characterizing the author's writing, Blanchot had lobbied on Beckett's behalf to secure the 1951 Prix des Critiques for the novel.[3] Beckett failed to win the award, no doubt to his own secret relief, but it was clear that Blanchot's support for the novel was of some significance for Beckett. As Beckett's partner, Suzanne Dumesnil, put it at the time in a letter to Jérôme Lindon, 'whatever the final outcome, the main thing for Beckett will be to have had someone like Blanchot defending him.'[4] And some years later, when Gallimard suggested bringing out a critical introduction to Beckett in the *Pour une bibliothèque idéale* series, it was Blanchot's name that was immediately uppermost in Beckett's mind.

Le Livre à venir was remarkable not only for its prescient reception of Beckett, whom it boldly put alongside such other canonical (or soon-to-be-canonical) names as Mallarmé, Proust, Rimbaud, James, Artaud, Borges, Broch, Musil, Hesse, Bataille, and Duras. More generally, following Blanchot's *L'Espace littéraire* (*The Space of Literature*) of 1955, *Le Livre à venir* sought to draw the philosophical consequences of the claim, as Mallarmé put it, that something like literature exists.[5] Blanchot began by binding literature's question not to the past, i.e. tradition, order, certainty and truth, but to the future – the promise and challenge of what lies beyond the horizon of the familiar. Literature's future, in this sense, Blanchot argued, did not consist in a rendezvous with truth, grounded in humanism, religion, history, or philosophy. 'Literature,' instead, he wrote, in words that offer an unerring insight into the future course of Beckett's writing, 'is heading towards itself, towards its essence which is disappearance [*la disparition*].'[6]

What did Blanchot mean by this provocative formula? Blanchot's reading of Beckett, begun in 1953, continued in 1961 with a review of *Comment c'est* (*How It Is*), and concluded in 1980 with a brief obituary tribute, provides an answer.[7] Three main issues dominate Blanchot's reading of Beckett: the question of the end (and ends) of literature, of voice, and of value (or values). Not surprisingly, all three concerns were at the forefront of the earliest reception of Beckett's work, and have dominated the response of critics ever since. Blanchot's treatment of them shows, I think, the extent of his contribution to an understanding of Beckett's significance.

The initial context of Blanchot's thinking in the 1950s is provided by Hegel's celebrated remark, in the first of the *Lectures on Aesthetics* of 1820–21, that 'from the point of view of its highest determination, art is and remains for us a thing of the past [*ein Vergangenes*].'[8] Hegel explains that, as religion gives way to philosophy, art too in the modern age forfeits its higher or inner necessity, together with its 'authentic truth and vitality [*die echte Wahrheit und Lebendigkeit*].' Passing the mantle of truth to philosophy, art dies. In the process, it becomes an object of representation, of aesthetic, critical inquiry, and achieves recognition and autonomy. As it dies, then, art is also (re-)born – as itself. In one single movement, it receives from philosophy both a birth certificate and a death warrant.

The irony is that art is constituted as and in itself only by virtue of being separated from itself and from what it once was. Much about the fate of modern writing comes to be decided here, not only literature's preoccupation with the false, the fabricated or the fictitious, but also its strangely ambiguous relationship with literary criticism, consisting in equal measure (as Beckett's work eloquently shows) of provocation and defiance, reliance and resistance, dependence and insubordination. Blanchot's own response was complex and nuanced. His thinking begins with Hegel, but soon moves on, transforming Hegel's legacy to decisive effect by reinterpreting the event of art's fall from grace. For Blanchot, this fall from legitimacy is not a fall into errancy, if only because errancy – like that other night, *l'autre nuit*, of which Blanchot writes so powerfully in *L'Espace littéraire* – already inhabits philosophy as the open secret philosophy itself is forever unwilling to concede to its spectral offspring, literature. For Blanchot, art's fall – *felix culpa*! – is a happy event; for what it brings into the world is the possibility of art's radical self-questioning. Literature here no longer serves the cause of truth; it slides beyond philosophy's jurisdiction, which is not to say it does not have important things to say to philosophy. But as he works his way through and beyond the Hegelian dialectic, Blanchot rejects the claim or assumption that the history of modern art is a negative story of decline. For Blanchot, the reality is more nearly the reverse. For as art is abandoned by truth, so art comes to be characterized, with radical consequences, by nothing other than its essential inessentiality. Literature, reaching to the heart of human language as such, asserts itself here not as a monument vying with eternity, but that which is without beginning, or end, and tolerates neither justification nor purpose. And this is why, if it appears to itself at all, art does so as disappearance.

Art, then, is that which is essentially beyond, before, and outside itself. Literature knows that, like all things of language, it exists only within limits; but literature's limits, Blanchot argues, have become indeterminate, with the result that literature's relationship to itself and to the limits within which it exists has become limitless. Literature may search for itself, but it does so in vain. Though the quest is fruitless, however, there remains the unanswerable and limitless demand to go on. This, then, is what for Blanchot literature is, or rather *is* not. It is the reason why those famous opening sentences of *L'Innommable* have such poignancy for Blanchot. Read in this light they are not (at least not primarily) the words of a narrator, character, or persona consciously meditating on his or her identity, nor an author reviewing his present personal circumstances. In a more original sense, they are a series of unanswerable questions (not to be confused with self-reflexive ones) asked of literature by literature itself, and asked in respect of literature's own future, which is not a deferred present, but an undecidability that lies beyond the horizon of established meaning.

Literature is that which is perpetually in excess of itself. There is perhaps no clearer confirmation of Blanchot's argument than that provided by the writing of Beckett. For as Beckett's work proceeds, it is increasingly clear that literature itself – not to mention such generic labels as novel, play, or poem – has become a distant memory, like one of those old words Hamm once taught to Clov, redundant yet irreplaceable, infinitely contestable yet ever indispensable. The predicament is one all critics of Beckett's work face in their turn. For if names are no longer adequate, how to name what is at stake in Beckett's own writing? Is critical judgement still possible? If so, what criteria to adopt, what critical vocabulary to deploy? For his part, in responding to *L'Innommable* in 1953, Blanchot sought to address literature's excessive relationship to its own constitutive limits by deploying an ancient word, overlaid with more recent memories of Georges Bataille: the word experience. Experience here, however, did not refer back to an originating consciousness or subjectivity. From the outset, Blanchot refused what was shortly to become the most common critical reaction to *L'Innommable*, which was to see the novel as the expression of a tortured human self. *L'Innommable*, as Blanchot read it, did not rely on the inwardness of a deferred, but finally self-present consciousness; it was 'experience pursued under the threat of the impersonal, an approach to a neutral speaking that speaks to itself alone, traverses whoever is listening, is without intimacy, excludes all intimacy, and cannot be silenced because it is that which is unceasing, interminable.'[9]

'Who is speaking in the books of Samuel Beckett?,' asks Blanchot.[10] The question appears straightforward. But important issues are at stake, which have to do with the possibility or status of what Blanchot elsewhere calls the 'narrative voice,' or, more precisely, the 'narrat*ing* voice.'[11] Who or what – in ghostly, disembodied fashion – 'embodies' this voice? To what language does such a voice 'belong'? Is it the voice of an historical individual, whose relationship to any *one* language was famously problematic? Is it possible to equate it with an identifiable character, protagonist or textual persona? Or is the voice of *L'Innommable* simply the voice of literature? Such questions, Blanchot argues, both assume too much and claim too little. For literature's question begins here. To answer it, there are both too many words and yet too few. 'Tout langage,' says the narrator who calls himself Moran, 'est un écart de langage.' 'All language,' he replies to himself years later, in a language that both *is* and *is not* his own, as though to prove his own point, 'is an excess of language.'[12] The right words do not exist; there is only ever a long detour into errancy, as any bilingual writer, among others, is already more than aware. Works of fiction, Blanchot shows, never coincide with themselves. The possibility of the voice is always in excess of whatever actual form it might assume – and assumes under the guise of a pseudonym.

Strangely, if the narrating voice is able to inhabit the work, it is because that voice is also exterior to the work. The paradox is one Beckett himself explores with devastating consequences in *Le Dépeupleur* (*The Lost Ones*).[13] Fiction is traversed by an alterity for which it cannot account, and which it cannot incorporate except as an absent phantom, a ghost that undermines the closure of the work while being absolutely indispensable to the production of the work as such. As the narrator of *L'Innommable* has it, irreducibly, aporetically, self-defeatingly: 'Je le savais, nous serions cent qu'il nous faudrait être cent et un. Je nous manquerai toujours.' 'I knew it,' as his English-speaking counterpart has it, with less idiomatic ease, 'there might be a hundred of us and still we'd lack the hundred and first, we'll always be short of me.'[14] As Blanchot explains,

> The narrating voice that is inside only to the extent that it is outside, at a distance without distance, cannot embody itself: whether it takes on the voice of a judiciously chosen character, or even (this voice that ruins all mediation) creates the hybrid function of mediator, it is always different from whoever or whatever utters it: it is the indifferent-difference that disrupts the personal voice. Let us (for amusement) call it spectral, ghostlike.[15]

The literary work remains fatally split here between the completion to which it aspires and the incompletion that precedes and exceeds it, making ending possible but thereby also making ending impossible. The endpoint of *L'Innommable* may be a threshold, but that threshold is by necessity a new point of departure. Worklessness or unworking (what Blanchot calls *désœuvrement*) is a name for the demand of the work (*œuvre*); but it is also the reason why the work can never be completed, and the work's demand never fulfilled. But crucially, for Blanchot, worklessness is not a foundation or ground, and, unlike Hegelian negativity, cannot be subordinated to the logic of the work which it continually undermines. In this respect – and the convergence is anything but haphazard – its status is more like the famously corrosive 'Beethoven pause' ('devouring the tonal surface of Beethoven's Seventh Symphony with its great black pauses') described in Beckett's famous letter to Axel Kaun of July 1937.[16] Though it often intervenes in negative manner, qualifying words to disqualify them, the narrating voice cannot itself be silenced. Beckett's novel discovers this time and time again: to negate or interrupt the voice is to be returned, without end, to the evidence of its interminability. To write, then, is not to create a work, according to Blanchot; it is to be drawn irresistibly into a movement of spectral return, of repetition and difference, in which all distinctions are erased and reinscribed, multiplied and dispersed. As I have argued before, difference here is also indifference and indifference a name for endless fragmentation.[17] Writing is without beginning or ending, *archè* or *telos*. The demand that is worklessness and the work itself cannot be brought together in dialectical synthesis. To sacrifice oneself to the work is to fall victim to something that traverses the work, is outside the work, and is impatient of the work's very finality.

Who or what speaks, then, in Beckett? Some pages earlier in *Le Livre à venir*, Blanchot asks a similar question of Proust, and suggests the following answer:

> But who is speaking here? … We say Proust, but we sense that it is the wholly other writing, not simply somebody else, but the very demand of writing, a demand which uses Proust's name, but does not express Proust, which only expresses him by disappropriating him, by making him Other.[18]

These words help to identify the importance of Blanchot's understanding of Beckett. Blanchot is one of the earliest and most rigorous readers to refuse to address Beckett's writing within the terms of a dialectic of the work. Not for Blanchot the reductive belief, put forward by the Swedish Academy in 1969, and implicitly endorsed by many early critics, that Beckett's purpose was to provide humanity with solace in the face of the Nazi death camps. Nor the conviction that the aim of Beckett's writing, in the face of extreme human degradation, was to provide a cathartic dose of clarity and light. Nor the pious wish that the comings and goings of words can be stabilized and found to express the meaning of humankind's quest. Nor the assumption that Beckett's professions of ignorance were an expression of false modesty. For all these reasons and others too, Blanchot's Beckett is radically incompatible with the one described by the Nobel Prize Committee. Instead, Blanchot reads Beckett beyond negativism and beyond morality; and this, I want to argue, is why he remains acutely sensitive to the radical demand or exigency that writes itself in Beckett's texts as a form of resistance to incorporation, as a response to that which is anonymous, non-identical, and irreducibly other.

The fact is Beckett's writing from the trilogy onwards tends towards unreadability. In such circumstances, Blanchot maintains, it is the responsibility of the critic not to reduce writing to the values of the already known, but to affirm the text in its paradoxical refusal to allow reading to take place. This is the argument Blanchot adopts apropos of *Comment c'est*. In his review, Blanchot reiterates much of what he says elsewhere about the difficulty of maintaining a proper critical stance, based on traditional aesthetic values, in the face of works like these.[19] A book like *Comment c'est*, he says, disables criticism. 'There is a category of works,' Blanchot continues, 'that are more misunderstood by being praised than by being denigrated; to disparage them is to touch the power of refusal that has made them what they are and witness the distance that is their measure.'[20] In such cases, two responses are possible: the first is not to read at all, in the knowledge that such a stance is ultimately untenable, since in order *not* to read it is first of all necessary *to* read; the second is to affirm the text, whatever the cost.

But what might it mean to affirm *Comment c'est*? The question is one Blanchot asks not only of himself, but of all critics who aim to transform Beckett's writing into objects of cultural value, since to do so is not to affirm the text for what it is (or *is* not), but rather to fail to read it. Affirmation here, Blanchot argues, cannot mean asserting established values: aesthetic, ethical, moral, or political ones. That would be to impose upon literature a dogma expressive merely of criticism's will to mastery. 'The critic,' Blanchot reminds us, 'is a man of power.'[21] This is not to say critics should swoon in ecstasy at the self-sufficient perfection of the work. All 'literature' requires and obligates its readers. To affirm the writing of *Comment c'est*, Blanchot contends, can only mean affirming literature's absolute non-identity with itself; this implies, of course, a radical refusal of all established values in the name of that which is without name – what Beckett for his part calls 'the unnamable.'

To read in this way entails a fundamental transformation in critical discourse; this is why, in responding to *Comment c'est*, as in other texts of the late 1950s and 1960s, Blanchot allows his own text to fragment into a plurality of voices. The critic proposes no last word. In discussing *Comment c'est*, he ends rather with an unanswered question, belonging to both novel and readers: 'what is this voice?' In so doing, Blanchot responds, no doubt unwittingly, to a phrase of Beckett's that first appeared twenty-three years earlier. 'Art,' Beckett wrote, 'has always been this – pure interrogation, rhetorical question less the rhetoric.'[22] The observation announces Blanchot's own ending, which is also in the form of a rhetorical question: one which is unanswerable precisely because it already includes within itself not only its own tautological response ('this voice is this voice') but also the realization that no further development of that response is possible ('this voice *is* this voice'). Such unanswerability, which both requires an answer and yet forbids any answer that might efface the question, has another name in Blanchot, which it borrows from the philosophy of Emmanuel Levinas. The name is: responsibility – in the face of the Other.

Blanchot places us here before the same issueless predicament as Beckett's own writing. Blanchot does not attempt to explain it away by dialectical sleight-of-hand as a manifestation of pessimistic nostalgia; he does not seek to explicate Beckett's writing, but to expose his own language to its radical extremity. In grappling with Beckett's writing, Blanchot discreetly pushes the challenge of Beckett to its furthest point, where it can no longer be rescued by humanist dialectics. Blanchot reminds literary criticism of its responsibilities, and affirms his conviction that Beckett's writing is still to come, *à venir*, that it continues to speak to us, in a voice that is its own – that is, precisely *not* its own – from the imponderable distance of an incalculable future. As it does so, it calls upon us, its readers, to seek to give it a name, while also respecting in that writing what resists naming, because what it lays bare is the singular namelessness at the core of the name as such, of which namelessness is simultaneously the condition of both possibility *and* impossibility.

ii

Blanchot was not alone in greeting in Beckett's writing a philosophical as well as literary event. His awareness of the philosophical implications of the writer's work soon came to characterize a distinctive, enduring current in French critical responses to Beckett. Mediated in part by the response of Blanchot (and Bataille), the impact of Beckett's work spread far beyond the literary world. In 1983, for instance, Michel Foucault, looking back at his own mid-twenties, spoke for many when he identified the production of *En attendant Godot* at the Théâtre de Babylone in January 1953 as a key turning point in his own intellectual development. For it was the work of Beckett, he reports, that was instrumental in supplying him with the impetus to abandon the phenomenological existentialist model that had so dominated the French post-war intellectual scene.[23] And when Foucault took up his post at the Collège de France in 1970, it was under the tutelage of *L'Innommable*, the closing lines of which Foucault cited in the preamble to his inaugural lecture.[24]

There is further evidence, as we shall see, of an interest in Beckett's work on the part of other leading figures in recent French thought, notably the philosophers Gilles Deleuze, Alain Badiou, and Jacques Derrida. But it would be misleading to assume this receptivity to Beckett was shared by all. Other commentators were less impressed. Roland Barthes, for instance, arguably the most influential literary critic of the 1960s and 1970s, remained unenthusiastic, viewing Beckett almost exclusively as a member of an apolitical post-war theatrical avant-garde, whose subversive assault on convention, by the early 1960s, was largely exhausted.[25] In cognate, albeit more polemical vein, Philippe Sollers, the main protagonist in the influential *Tel Quel* group, as late as January 1968, could still be found professing his belief – citing Beckett as sole example – that 'a form may be apparently subversive and yet conceal a naturalistic mode of writing.'[26]

Other signs of resistance are apparent in the work of other members of the literary avant-garde. It was not until 1976 that *Tel Quel*'s most prominent literary theorist, Julia Kristeva, was moved to devote a paper to what she described, with obvious lack of relish, as Beckett's protestant aesthetic, which she constrasted with the incestuously transgressive writing of Joyce.[27] Mingling psychoanalysis with a largely Hegelian theory of cultural history, the argument was inevitably somewhat prescriptive, and Kristeva's main observation was that, for all its formal inventiveness, Beckett's work was ultimately locked into an obsessional labour of mourning for the dead father. Repressing the maternal body as an object of enjoyment, she argued, Beckett's writing was bereft of colour, and deployed only those many shades of grey that go by the name of asceticism, disenchantment, decay. Both the power and the limitations of Beckett's work, Kristeva concluded, belonged to the closed (and claustrophobic) world of Christianity in decline. This was faint praise with a vengeance. But by a curious twist it was Kristeva's own teleological prognosis that was to prove the more fragile; and by the mid-1990s the final disintegration of the avant-garde project she had defended in the early 1970s had prompted a return of sorts to Beckett, with Sollers – never slow to change his tune – now welcoming him, alongside Joyce, as one of the two 'greatest poets of the twentieth century.'[28]

Despite these dissenting voices, there is strong evidence of the strategic relevance of Beckett's work for philosophical engagement with literature in France for the whole second half of the last century. But in considering the influence of Beckett on the development of what has come to be known as French 'poststructuralism,' it is essential to enter two *caveats*. First, one should not minimize the considerable and at times irreconcilable differences that do exist, on the question of 'literature' (and much else besides), between the various thinkers – from Blanchot to Foucault, Kristeva, Deleuze, Badiou, and Derrida – who have happened to write about Beckett, albeit in some cases hardly at all, and who have often been erroneously presented as a homogeneous group. For if indeed – this is the second *caveat* – any contemporary French thinkers do share a minimal set of assumptions about 'literature,' it is to the extent that literature is precisely *not* reducible to a marginalium or subtext of philosophy. What is much rather at issue in the work of such philosophical writers in France as have been drawn to affirm Beckett's writing is a shared commitment, realized in a variety of different ways, to the need to respond to the singular event of 'literature' without subordinating that event to philosophy as such.

What, then, of the literary event signed 'Beckett'? How does recent French thought allow us to rethink Beckett's writing, not in its conformity with received literary or other models, but according to its essential and irreducible singularity?

A first sustained response to these questions came in 1992, some two-and-a-half years after Beckett's death, when the Editions de Minuit brought out a slim volume containing Beckett's four later plays for television.[29] Exceptionally, Beckett's own text, translated by Edith Fournier, was accompanied by a fifty-page essay by Gilles Deleuze, entitled 'L'Epuisé' ('The Exhausted').[30] Admittedly, this was not the first time Deleuze had written on Beckett. From 1970 onwards, he had made fleeting mention of Beckett in numerous books, essays, or interviews. Few of these references exceed two or three lines; the longest is a four-page analysis of Beckett's *Film*, first published in 1983 and recast three years later as 'The Greatest Irish Film Ever Made.'[31] In many ways, Deleuze's approach is hardly innovative. Like philosophical writers before him he approaches Beckett's text by extracting from it a scene, a phrase, or an affect, which is then used as a crux for Deleuze's own argument. The outcome, as far as readers of Beckett are concerned, often leaves something to be desired. Points are made in passing, yet rarely developed; and many of the same quotations are recycled time and again with little apparent concern for their specific context.

Nevertheless an original and provocative picture of Beckett does soon emerge. Three interrelated motifs predominate: First, there is the humorous or comic intensity of Beckett's prose, achieved 'by dint of dryness, sobriety, and willed impoverishment,'[32] far from any hint of reactive negativism or *ressentiment*. Second, we have the nomadic comings and goings of what *L'Anti-Œdipe* (*Anti-Oedipus*) calls 'the schizo's walkabout [*la promenade du schizo*],'[33] which is most often associated with *Watt*, Molloy's travels on his bicycle, or the scene at Saint John of God's at the end of *Malone Dies*, and which functions as an emblematic figure for the production of desire as a litany of what Deleuze calls inclusive or affirmative disjunctions – so many limitless series of differences no longer bounded by negativity, opposition, or contradiction. And, third, there is Beckett's so-called minority status as a bilingual writer (akin to that of the German-speaking Czech Franz Kafka), his moving back and forth between Anglo-Irish and non-native French, which makes him especially sensitive to what Deleuze calls 'universal variation,' described as a kind of ceaseless becoming, multiplying differences without identity, and showing at the core of all unity the intervention of perpetual foreignness or exteriority.

Deleuze might be thought here simply to be using Beckett's work as a convenient source of examples. The reality, however, is more complex. Literature for Deleuze (and Guattari) is not governed by signification; it has no representational function, nor can it be a simple vehicle for philosophical ideas. Instead, the artwork is portrayed as a monumental 'block of sensations, a compound of percepts and affects,'[34] no longer attributable to a subject of any sort, and therefore not bounded by the established horizons of lived experience. Its regimen is experimental or diagnostic. Moreover, philosophy and literature occupy clearly differentiated, though overlapping domains. While the former salvages the infinite by giving it (conceptual) consistency, according to Deleuze and Guattari, the latter invents finite entities whose role is to restore or reassert the infinite. In both cases creativity rules; what is paramount is not the horizon of the (merely) possible, but the unpredictability or indiscernability of the event – 'immaterial, incorporal, unliveable' – which exceeds actuality or teleology. Interminable and always in reserve, the event is irreducible to any state of things; it is what Deleuze and Guattari in *Qu'est-ce que la philosophie?* (*What Is Philosophy?*), citing Blanchot, describe as 'that which recommences without ever having started or come to an end.'[35]

The essay 'L'Epuisé' develops this argument, paying particular attention to the late television plays (*Ghost Trio*, *... but the clouds ...*, *Quad*, and *Nacht und Träume*). At first sight, Deleuze's title may be thought to imply a horizon of negativity, but this is far from the case. Exhaustion, Deleuze explains, is not a negative condition. It does not refer to an unavailable past or decaying present. What it does address, however, is Beckett's transformation of reality into an infinite number of inclusive disjunctions according to a criterion of exhaustivity. Beckettian *ars combinatoria* ('the art of combining,' as the narrator of *Enough* calls it) should not therefore be read as a husbanding of meagre resources, but as a positive principle of dispersion, a kind of radical cartography of the real. Reality is multiplied to excess, and Beckett's words end up (in *Watt* or *Molloy*) supplanting objective reality. Ever willing to conceptualize the multiple, Deleuze calls this layer of Beckett's writing: *Language I*. *Language II*, on the other hand, is what occurs when words, rather than the possible objects to which they refer, are taken to the limit, as in *L'Innommable*, turning into an endless string of possible voices, each with its own ramifying story (or stories), and all treated exhaustibly in their turn. But amidst this web of complexity, appearing everywhere but nowhere, in *Quad* or *Ghost Trio*, say, something unprecedented and unexpected irrupts, in the form of an in-betweenness – like, perhaps, the strangely indeterminable gender identity of the narrator of *Enough* – or as pure image or sound, dissipating itself and the space or time it occupies. Like a Beethoven pause. This, Deleuze tells us, is Beckett's *Language III*.

This schematic or diagrammatic presentation may seem dryly formalistic, though it does reflect an abiding belief on Deleuze's part that each singular case deserves and requires its concept, which it is philosophy's task to invent. It allows Deleuze to maintain an understanding of the dynamic unity of Beckett's writing, while also multiplying or dispersing that unity. The critical perspective Deleuze adopts is grounded in philosophical sobriety, but in its relationship to Beckett's work it is powerfully affirmative. As readers know, the late television plays are among some of the most challenging in Beckett's oeuvre. With their linguistic sparseness, their largely monochrome images, statuesque immobility, and lugubrious thematic material, they are most readily interpretable as so many last-ditch restatements of Beckettian pessimism. But this is precisely why, according to Deleuze, it is more urgent than ever to release Beckett's writing from the debilitating implications of the negative. Beckettian minimalism is not humanistic retreat, but nonhuman intensity. 'Creating,' Deleuze once told Raymond Bellour and François Ewald, 'is not communication, but resistance.' 'One writes in respect of a people of the future [*en fonction d'un peuple à venir*] and one that as yet is without language.'[36] The words are testimony to the philosopher's own project; but they also convey what indubitably was also at stake for Deleuze in Beckett: an ascetic, but uniquely inventive, vital, and vitalistic appeal to the future.

Deleuze was not alone in seeking to salvage Beckett's work from the ravages of the dialectic. A similar project, conducted in very different critical terms, had been begun in 1989 by Alain Badiou, himself an important novelist and playwright as well as a leading philosopher, whose first contribution to a reading of Beckett was entitled 'L'Écriture du générique: Samuel Beckett.' In 1995 Badiou's lecture was recast, in less explicitly philosophical terms, as a short book in the Hachette 'coup double' series, under the title *Beckett: l'increvable désir*.[37] Two years later, in that same series, Badiou published a study of Deleuze, in which he explained how between 1989 and 1995 the two men had been engaged in a complex debate on the question of how best to think multiplicity, or the multiple.[38] The exchange, however, was largely conducted in private, and came to an abrupt end with Deleuze's suicide in 1995 some six months after the appearance of Badiou's *Beckett*. The circumstances are worth recalling since what they suggest is the extent to which, during the early 1990s, Beckett's work served both Deleuze and Badiou as a kind of public proxy for explicating their respective – and distinctive – conceptions of the multiple and the event.

Badiou, for his part, begins his 1995 study by registering the impact of Beckett's work upon his own youthful understanding of the relationship between philosophy and literature, much influenced by Sartre. Reading Beckett, for many of Badiou's generation, put paid to any belief in the transparent transitivity of language. But in his response to Beckett, Badiou did not just leave Sartre behind. He also jettisoned both received versions of Beckett then current, not only the grim existential absurdist, but the derisive Stoic comedian too. So far, so good. However on Badiou's part this was merely one step in a more ambitious project consisting in the endeavour to think beyond or outside the so-called linguistic turn in modern philosophy (without which the entirety of modern literary theory is quite simply inconceivable).

Even so, what Badiou proposes to put in the place of the critical stereotypes he rightly denounces is surprising: 'Beckett's lesson,' he writes, 'is a lesson in measure, exactitude, and courage.'[39] Dispatching, then, in one fell swoop the romanticism, tragic pathos, and nihilism that for most literary critics are inseparable from Beckett's work, Badiou affirms a rather different, almost neo-classical Beckett, animated by a methodical, ascetic, subtractive reappraisal of the great themes of human existence (beauty, movement, love, the relation with others). The main inspiration for this, suggests Badiou, thereby declaring his own philosophical allegiances, lies in a kind of latter-day Platonism. 'If Plato the philosopher, in *The Sophist*, determines the general conditions of all thought,' Badiou explains, 'Beckett the writer, by the ascetic movement of his prose, aims to present in fiction the intemporal determinants of humanity.'[40]

Beckett's work is seen by Badiou as following an essentially philosophical itinerary. Its starting point, during the period up to 1960, reflected in the questions: *where?* and *who?*, is the long-standing ontological inquiry: 'what is the meaning of what is?'; while after that date, Badiou contends, in the wake of *Comment c'est*, the focus of the work shifts to concentrate on the relation with the Other and the key issue of the event, which Badiou formulates as follows: 'how to name what comes [*ce qui arrive*]?'[41] And what comes in Beckett, says Badiou, necessarily to one in the dark, comes as a supernumerary, incalculable, indiscernable, undecidable event – irreducible to all established protocols of being, nameable only as something ill seen ill said, of which all that can be said is what is missaid. And so on. Missaying, however, is not a failure of language, nor is it the language of failure; it is what occurs as sole possibility when a name meets an event. That encounter, Badiou suggests, is not grounded in its intensity, as it was for Deleuze, as one indication among many of the univocity of being. The discontinuity to which it bears witness points rather to what, using an old-fashioned word, Badiou describes as truth – and which endows Beckett's writing, according to Badiou, with extraordinary courage, courage that comes from a desire, and capacity, to affirm what Badiou calls 'the pure multiple [*le multiple pur*],' the (mathematical) empty set that is the only proper name of being itself.[42]

To seasoned readers of Beckett Badiou's argument may seem oddly literal-minded or one-sided. But this would be to miss the extent to which a stubborn and deeply original rethinking of the relationship between philosophy and literature is at work in Badiou's analysis. A later essay, devoted to Edith Fournier's 1992 French translation of *Worstward Ho*, makes this more readily apparent.[43] Admittedly, of all the readings of Beckett considered so far, Badiou's is the most purely philosophical; this is reflected for instance in the suggestion that *Worstward Ho*, say, be read as a 'short philosophical treatise.' Beckett's text, Badiou writes, consists of a 'stenography of the question of being.'[44] Importantly, however, this is not to reduce literature to the status of an example or an illustration, to being merely a convenient means of expression for properly philosophical ideas. Badiou's project has a very different purpose, which is to envision a new dispensation in the long history of dealings between literature and philosophy, one in which the relationship between art and truth is immanent and singular. As Badiou explains in *Petit Manuel d'inesthétique*, this is to make two crucial points: first, that 'art is rigorously coextensive with the many truths it provides'; and, second, that 'these truths are nowhere given except in art.' 'Art,' Badiou adds, 'is a way of thinking [*une pensée*] whose works are the real (not its effect). And this way of thinking, or the truths it sets in motion, are irreducible to all other (scientific, political or love-related) truths. Which also means that art, as a singular way of thinking, is irreducible to philosophy.'[45] Art then thinks, and thinks for itself, in its own manner. Here lies the force of Badiou's demonstration; his reading of Beckett is significant therefore not only for its cogent dismantling of a swathe of pseudophilosophical assumptions that have become inseparable from Beckett's work, but also because it points in the direction of a sustained rearticulation of the relationship of Beckett's writing with thought itself.

The power and influence of the institutions of literary criticism are formidable. Few can have guessed in the early 1950s that, within a generation, criticism of the work of Samuel Beckett would have turned into an industry. More is known today about the textual history, intellectual circumstances, biographical background, internal structure, or performance history of Beckett's work – and much else besides – than can ever have been dreamed possible at one stage. But the more that is known about Beckett leaves the enigma of his writing intact. The paradox is one that has strongly affected the relationship between Beckett and philosophy. For at the heart of Beckett studies there remains an unrelenting demand for philosophical explanation which by its nature is impossible to satisfy. Thus it is, for instance, that some have wondered why Jacques Derrida – surely of all the philosophical writers to address the question of literature in recent decades the most influential – seems to have avoided writing about Beckett. What is at stake in this missed encounter between Beckett and deconstruction? The question was put to Derrida himself in an interview in April 1989 by Derek Attridge. Derrida made the following guarded, but unambiguous reply: '[Beckett] is an author,' he said, 'to whom I feel very close, or to whom I would like to feel myself very close; but also too close. Precisely because of this proximity, it is too hard for me, too easy and too hard.' And Derrida went on to explain that – 'for the moment' – he had given up the idea of writing 'in the direction of Beckett.'[46]

What is to be made of this oblique engagement, this proximity that is a distance, this distance that is a proximity? On one level, Derrida's evasiveness is – knowingly – disingenuous. To decline to read Beckett is itself already a reading, and it is not hard to imagine Derrida, at some future date, beginning to write on Beckett by exploring the relationship between proximity and distance he evokes in the interview. Beyond this horizon of expectation, however, Derrida's intervention – this reading without reading of Beckett – embodies an incisive performative dimension. Derrida is well aware that Beckett's works are the object of one of the most thorough efforts at critical institutionalization of modern times, one that, like the Joyce industry, albeit for different reasons, is premised on the very impossibility of its fulfilling the task it has set itself.[47] That paradox is one all critics of Beckett, past, present, and future, have to confront. And this is Derrida's point. He replies to Attridge by asking a series of unanswerable questions of his own. 'How could I write, sign, countersign texts,' he says, 'which "respond" to Beckett performatively? How could I avoid the platitude of a supposed academic metalanguage?'[48] Derrida's resistance to the demand to write on Beckett speaks volumes. For by discreetly side-stepping the invitation, and thus the requirement that he name the unnamable, what Derrida does is to hold open a promise – one that he (or others) may or may *not* ever honour (since that is a necessary condition of promising anything) – which is that at some future time (one can never know!) words might (or might *not*) be available to say, or missay, something more – something other – in response to the infinite demand of Beckett's writing.

The indication is a precious one. The phrase: 'poststructuralist' Beckett is a misnomer and a nonsense for many reasons, not least because few, if any, of the authors discussed in this chapter might with remotest plausibility be described as 'poststructuralist.' But if the term preserves some strategic force, it may be because it obliges us, as Blanchot, Foucault,

Deleuze, Badiou, and Derrida in their different ways have already done, to imagine a Beckett breaking with the present, and belonging – *not* belonging – to the future. To a future that, necessarily, is beyond the horizon of the possible; and because, in the absence of the possible, it is still necessary to go on. 'On. Say on. Be said on. Somehow on. Till nohow on. Said nohow on.'

notes

1. See Maurice Blanchot, *Le Livre à venir* (Paris: Gallimard, 1959). The essays on which the book is based first appeared between 1953 and 1958; see my *Blanchot: Extreme Contemporary* (London: Routledge, 1997).
2. See Maurice Blanchot, *Le Livre à venir*, 256–64. The essay was first published in *La Nouvelle Nouvelle Revue française*, 10, October 1953, 678–86; an English translation by Richard Howard appears in *Samuel Beckett*, edited by Jennifer Birkett and Kate Ince (London: Longman, 2000), 93–8.
3. Bataille's review 'Le Silence de Molloy' first appeared in *Critique*, 48, May 1951, 387–96. A translation by Jean M. Sommermeyer is given in *Samuel Beckett*, 85–92.
4. The letter, dated 25 May 1951, is cited by Anne Simonin, *Les Editions de Minuit, 1942–1955: Le devoir d'insoumission* (Paris: IMEC Editions, 1994), 378. By then, Blanchot would have been known to Beckett as the author of such shorter fiction as *L'Arrêt de mort* (1948) or the second version of *Thomas l'Obscur* (1950) or the essay collections *Faux Pas* (1943) and *La Part du feu* (1949). In Jérôme Lindon of the Editions de Minuit the two men shared a publisher. Blanchot's responsiveness to Beckett was not self-evident. Beckett was barely known in 1951 and, as a native Irishman writing in French, was viewed with some puzzlement in Paris literary circles. According to Simonin, *Molloy* in its first year sold 694 copies, while *Malone meurt*, two years later, managed only 241. Sales of *L'Innommable* reached 476.
5. See Maurice Blanchot, *L'Espace littéraire* (Paris: Gallimard, 1955), 35; *The Space of Literature*, translated by Ann Smock (Lincoln and London: University of Nebraska Press, 1982), 42–3.
6. Maurice Blanchot, *Le Livre à venir*, 237; 'The Disappearance of Literature,' translated by Ian Maclachlan, *The Blanchot Reader*, edited by Michael Holland (Oxford: Blackwell, 1995), 136; translation modified.
7. On *Comment c'est*, see Maurice Blanchot, 'Notre épopée,' *La Nouvelle Revue française*, 100, April 1961, 690–8, republished as 'Les Paroles doivent cheminer longtemps,' *L'Entretien infini* (Paris: Gallimard, 1969), 478–86; translated by Susan Hanson as 'Words Must Travel Far,' *The Infinite Conversation* (Minneapolis: University of Minnesota Press, 1993), 326–31. For Blanchot's obituary, see 'Oh tout finir,' *Critique*, 519–20, August–September 1990, 635–7; 'Oh All To End,' translated by Leslie Hill, *The Blanchot Reader*, 298–300. Surprisingly, there has been little sustained analysis of Blanchot's reading of Beckett, which is often misrepresented. Bruno Clément, in an otherwise sympathetic account,

charges Blanchot (whom he misquotes) with neutralizing *L'Innommable*, claiming that he 'abolishes the necessary distance between critic and writer, between the speaking voice and the commenting ear.' ('Les Premiers Lecteurs de Samuel Beckett,' *Critique*, 467, April 1986, 287–307 [p. 304].) But this is to misunderstand the extent of Blanchot's break with the traditional discourse of aesthetics and to elevate Beckett's work to the status of a totalizing myth that always already includes its own reading. More spectacular still in its misunderstanding is the attack on Blanchot's interpretation of Beckett by Pascale Casanova in *Beckett l'abstracteur* (Paris: Seuil, 1997), in which the critic contrives to take Blanchot to task for espousing a (largely Heideggerian) view that is precisely the opposite of that found in *Le Livre à venir*!

8. G. W. F. Hegel, *Werke*, edited by Eva Moldenhauer and Karl Markus Michel, 20 vols (Frankfurt: Suhrkamp, 1970), XIII, 25. See *Blanchot: Extreme Contemporary*, 103–14.

9. Blanchot, *Le Livre à venir*, 259; *Samuel Beckett*, 96–7; translation modified. For a critique of the reliance of Beckett criticism on existential humanism, see Thomas Trezise, *Into the Breach: Samuel Beckett and the Ends of Literature* (Princeton: Princeton University Press, 1990).

10. Blanchot, *Le Livre à venir*, 256; *Samuel Beckett*, 94; translation modified.

11. See 'La Voix narrative (le «il,» le neutre),' *L'Entretien infini*, 556–67; *The Infinite Conversation*, 379–87. Blanchot's use of the term should be distinguished from that current in narratology, where it refers to the type of narration or narrator used in a given narrative: extradiegetic or intradiegetic, heterodiegetic or homodiegetic. Blanchot's usage is at once simpler and more complex than this; it refers to what might be called more properly, in English, the 'narrating voice,' i.e. the voice in so far as it gives rise to the possibility of narration as such, prior to the typological categories elaborated by narratology.

12. Samuel Beckett, *Molloy* (Paris: Minuit, 1951), 179; *Molloy, Malone Dies, The Unnamable* (London: Calder and Boyars, 1959), 116.

13. See my *Beckett's Fiction: In Different Words* (Cambridge: Cambridge University Press, 1990), 155.

14. Samuel Beckett, *L'Innommable* (Paris: Minuit, 1953), 106; *Molloy, Malone Dies, The Unnamable*, 342.

15. Maurice Blanchot, *L'Entretien infini*, 565–6; *The Infinite Conversation*, 386; translation modified.

16. See Samuel Beckett, *Disjecta*, edited by Ruby Cohn (London: John Calder, 1983), 53.

17. For an attempt to trace the consequences of this movement, see my *Beckett's Fiction: In Different Words*.

18. Maurice Blanchot, *Le Livre à venir*, 254; 'The Pursuit of the Zero Point,' translated by Ian Maclachlan, *The Blanchot Reader*, 149; translation modified.

19. See Maurice Blanchot, *Lautréamont et Sade* (Paris: Minuit, (1949) revised 1963), 9–14; 'The Task of Criticism Today,' translated by Leslie Hill, *The Oxford Literary Review*, 22, 2000, 19–24.

20. Maurice Blanchot, *L'Entretien infini*, 481; *The Infinite Conversation*, 328.

21. Maurice Blanchot, *L'Entretien infini*, 479; *The Infinite Conversation*, 327.

22. Samuel Beckett, 'Denis Devlin,' *transition*, April–May 1938, 289–94 (p. 289).

23. See Michel Foucault, 'Archéologie d'une passion,' interview by C. Ruas (15 September 1983), in *Dits et écrits 1954–1988*, 4 vols (Paris: Gallimard, 1994), IV, 598. Foucault notes: 'I belong to a generation of people who, as students, were trapped within a horizon marked by Marxism, phenomenology, existentialism, and so on. All extremely interesting, stimulating things, but which after a while become rather stifling and make you want to look elsewhere. I was the same as every other philosophy student at the time. For me, the break came with Beckett's *Waiting for Godot*. When I saw it, it took my breath away.' The early influence of Blanchot was also crucial, as Foucault acknowledges; see *Dits et écrits 1954–1988*, I, 593.

24. See Michel Foucault, *L'Ordre du discours* (Paris: Gallimard, 1971), 8.

25. See Roland Barthes, 'Le Théâtre français d'avant-garde' (1961), *Œuvres complètes*, edited by Eric Marty, 3 vols (Paris: Seuil, 1993), I, 915–21. Surprisingly, in the whole of Barthes there are less than a dozen mentions of Beckett, almost all referring to *En attendant Godot* and dating back to the period before 1965.

26. Philippe Sollers, 'Le Réflexe de réduction,' *Théorie d'ensemble* (Paris: Seuil, 1968), 396. On the *Tel Quel* group, see Patrick ffrench, *The Time of Theory* (Oxford: Oxford University Press, 1995).

27. See Julia Kristeva, 'Le Père, l'amour, l'exil,' *Polylogue* (Paris: Seuil, 1977), 137–47; 'The Father, Love, and Banishment,' *Samuel Beckett*, 248–58.

28. Philippe Sollers, *La Guerre du goût* (Paris: Gallimard-folio, 1996), 499.

29. See Samuel Beckett, *Quad et autres pièces pour la télévision* (Paris: Minuit, 1992).

30. See Gilles Deleuze, 'The Exhausted,' *Essays Critical and Clinical*, translated by Daniel W. Smith, Michael A. Greco, and Anthony Uhlmann (London: Verso, 1998), 152–74

31. See Gilles Deleuze, *L'Image-mouvement* (Paris: Minuit, 1983), 97–100, *Cinema I: The Movement-Image*, translated by Hugh Tomlinson and Barbara Habberjam (London: Athlone, 1986), 66–8; and *Critique et clinique* (Paris: Minuit, 1993), 36–9, *Essays Critical and Clinical*, 23–6. For two recent attempts to mobilize Deleuze for a reading of Beckett, see Anthony Uhlmann, *Beckett and Poststructuralism* (Cambridge: Cambridge University Press, 1999); and Timothy S. Murphy, 'Only Intensities Subsist: Samuel Beckett's *Nohow On*,' *Deleuze and Literature*, edited by Ian Buchanan and John Marks (Edinburgh: Edinburgh University Press, 2000), 229–50.

32. Gilles Deleuze and Félix Guattari, *Kafka : pour une littérature mineure* (Paris: Minuit, 1975), 35; *Kafka: Towards a Minor Literature*, translated by Dana Polan (Minneapolis, University of Minnesota Press, 1986), 19.

33. See Deleuze and Guattari, *L'Anti-Œdipe* (Paris: Minuit, 1972), 7–8, *Anti-Oedipus: Capitalism and Schizophrenia*, translated by Robert Hurley, Mark Seem, and Helen R. Lane (London: Athlone, 1983), 1–2; translation modified.

34. Gilles Deleuze and Félix Guattari, *Qu'est-ce que la philosophie?* (Paris: Minuit, 1991), 154; *What Is Philosophy?*, translated by Graham Burchell and Hugh Tomlinson (London: Verso, 1994), 164.

35. Deleuze and Guattari, *Qu'est-ce que la philosophie?*, 148; *What Is Philosophy?*, 157.

36. Deleuze, *Pourparlers* (Paris: Minuit, 1990), 196; *Negotiations*, translated by Martin Joughin (New York: Columbia University Press, 1995), 143; translation modified.
37. See Alain Badiou, *Conditions* (Paris: Seuil, 1992), 329–66; and *Beckett: l'increvable désir* (Paris: Hachette, 1995). An English translation of Badiou's work on Beckett is forthcoming from Clinamen Press, 2003.
38. See Alain Badiou, *Deleuze: 'la clameur de l'être'* (Paris: Hachette, 1997).
39. Badiou, *Beckett: l'increvable désir*, 9.
40. Badiou, *Beckett: l'increvable désir*, 24. Elsewhere, in *Manifeste pour la philosophie* (Paris: Seuil, 1989), 85, Badiou describes himself as a 'Platonist of the multiple [*platonicien du multiple*].'
41. Badiou, *Beckett: l'increvable désir*, 39.
42. Badiou, *Beckett: l'increvable désir*, 79.
43. Alain Badiou, *Petit Manuel d'inesthétique* (Paris: Seuil, 1998), 137–87.
44. Badiou, *Petit Manuel d'inesthétique*, 139.
45. Badiou, *Petit Manuel d'inesthétique*, 21.
46. Jacques Derrida, *Acts of Literature*, 60, 62.
47. On the relationship between Joyce's text and the critical industry it has rendered both necessary yet impossible, see Jacques Derrida, *Ulysse gramophone* (Paris: Galilée, 1987); *Acts of Literature*, 256–309.
48. Derrida, *Acts of Literature*, 60.

works cited

Badiou, Alain. *Manifeste pour la philosophie*. Paris: Seuil, 1989.
—— *Conditions*. Paris: Seuil, 1992.
—— *Beckett: l'increvable désir*. Paris: Hachette, 1995.
—— *Deleuze: 'la clameur de l'être.'* Paris: Hachette, 1997.
—— *Petit Manuel d'inesthétique*. Paris: Seuil, 1998.
Barthes, Roland. *Œuvres complètes*. ed. Eric Marty, 3 vols, Paris: Seuil, 1993.
Beckett, Samuel. 'Denis Devlin.' *transition* (April–May 1938): 289–94.
—— *Molloy*. Paris: Minuit, 1951.
—— *L'Innommable*. Paris: Minuit, 1953.
—— *Molloy, Malone Dies, The Unnamable*. London: Calder & Boyars, 1959.
—— *Disjecta*, ed. Ruby Cohn. London: John Calder, 1983.
—— *Quad et autres pièces pour la télévision*. Paris: Minuit, 1992.
Blanchot, Maurice. *Le Livre à venir*. Paris: Gallimard, 1959.
—— *Lautréamont et Sade*. Paris: Minuit, 2nd edn 1963.
—— 'Oh tout finir.' *Critique*, 519–20 (August–September 1990): 635–7.
—— *L'Espace littéraire*. Paris: Gallimard, 1955; *The Space of Literature*, trans. Ann Smock. Lincoln and London: University of Nebraska Press, 1982.
—— *L'Entretien infini*. Paris: Gallimard, 1969; *The Infinite Conversation*, trans. Susan Hanson. Minneapolis: University of Minnesota Press, 1993.
Birkett, Jennifer and Ince, Kate. (eds). *Samuel Beckett*. London: Longman, 2000.
Buchanan, Ian and Marks, John (eds). *Deleuze and Literature*. Edinburgh: Edinburgh University Press, 2000.
Casanova, Pascale. *Beckett l'abstracteur*. Paris: Seuil, 1997.

Clément, Bruno. 'Les Premiers Lecteurs de Samuel Beckett.' *Critique*, 467. (April 1986): 287–307.

Deleuze, Gilles. (with Félix Guattari), *L'Anti-Œdipe*. Paris: Minuit, 1972; *Anti-Oedipus: Capitalism and Schizophrenia*. Trans. Robert Hurley, Mark Seem, and Helen R. Lane, London: Athlone, 1983.

—— *L'Image-mouvement*. Paris: Minuit, 1983; *Cinema I: The Movement-Image*. trans. Hugh Tomlinson and Barbara Habberjam, London: Athlone, 1986.

—— *Kafka: pour une littérature mineure*. Paris: Minuit, 1975; *Kafka: Towards a Minor Literature*. Trans. Dana Polan, Minneapolis, University of Minnesota Press, 1986.

—— *Qu'est-ce que la philosophie?* Paris: Minuit, 1991; *What Is Philosophy?* Trans Graham Burchell and Hugh Tomlinson, London: Verso, 1994.

—— *Pourparlers*. Paris: Minuit, 1990; *Negotiations*. Trans. Martin Joughin, New York: Columbia University Press, 1995.

—— *Critique et clinique*. Paris: Minuit, 1993; *Essays Critical and Clinical*. Trans. Daniel W. Smith, Michael A. Greco, and Anthony Uhlmann, London: Verso, 1998.

Derrida, Jacques. *Ulysse gramophone*. Paris: Galilée, 1987.

—— *Acts of Literature*. ed. Derek Attridge, London: Routledge, 1992.

Foucault, Michel. *L'Ordre du discours*. Paris: Gallimard, 1971.

—— *Dits et écrits 1954–1988*. 4 vols, Paris: Gallimard, 1994.

ffrench, Patrick. *The Time of Theory*. Oxford: Oxford University Press, 1995.

Hegel, G. W. F. *Werke*. ed. Eva Moldenhauer and Karl Markus Michel, 20 vols, Frankfurt: Suhrkamp, 1970.

Hill, Leslie *Beckett's Fiction: In Different Words*. Cambridge: Cambridge University Press, 1990.

—— *Blanchot: Extreme Contemporary*. London: Routledge, 1997.

Holland, Michael (ed.). *The Blanchot Reader*. Oxford: Blackwell, 1995.

Kristeva, Julia. *Polylogue*. Paris: Seuil, 1977.

Simonin, Anne. *Les Editions de Minuit, 1942–1955: Le devoir d'insoumission*. Paris: IMEC Editions, 1994.

Sollers, Philippe, 'Le Réflexe de réduction,' *Théorie d'ensemble*. Paris: Seuil, 1968.

—— *La Guerre du goût*. Paris: Gallimard-folio, 1996.

Trezise, Thomas. *Into the Breach: Samuel Beckett and the Ends of Literature*. Princeton: Princeton University Press, 1990.

Uhlmann, Anthony. *Beckett and Poststructuralism*. Cambridge: Cambridge University Press, 1999.

6
irish/postcolonial beckett

anna mcmullan

His being was in the marge,
he had chosen the marginal part[1]
Dream of Fair to Middling Women

> when you started not knowing who you were from Adam trying
> how that would work for a change not knowing who you were
> from Adam no notion who it was saying what you were saying
> whose skull you were clapped up in whose moan had you the way
> you were was that the time or was that another time there alone
> with the portraits of the dead black with dirt and antiquity and the
> dates on the frames in case you might get the century wrong
>
> *That Time*

In 1906, Samuel Beckett was born on the outskirts of Dublin into an upper middle class Protestant family, part of the settler population of an island that was invaded by the Vikings and the Anglo-Normans and was planted by the English and Scottish in the Elizabethan and Tudor ages. Ireland, at the beginning of the twentieth century, had been annexed to Britain by the Act of Union in 1800, but, following the Anglo-Irish Treaty of 1921, twenty-six of the thirty-two counties of Ireland formed the independent Free State of Ireland, the Saorstat, when Beckett was fifteen.[2] The other six, which included the strongly Protestant counties of Antrim and Down, and therefore had a Protestant majority, were carved out of the formerly nine-county northern province of Ulster, renamed Northern Ireland, and remained under the political jurisdiction of Britain. While many members of the Protestant minority in the Free State retained economic privileges (though there was also a Protestant working class), they were politically marginalized in the new state which was dominated by a hegemonic, conservative nationalism allied with and legitimated by the Catholic Hierarchy. As a young adult, Beckett was ill at ease in this climate, and having experienced the cosmopolitanism of Paris through an exchange between the Ecole Normale Supérieure and Trinity College, Dublin (his Alma Mater) in 1928–30, he moved there in 1937. This chapter investigates Beckett's dislocation of the boundaries of nation and identity through these particular national and international contexts and through the lens of postcolonial theory, but argues that it is in the contradictions and interstices within and between Irish Studies and Postcolonial Studies[3] that a dialogue with Beckett's work can be developed.

J. C. C. Mays argues that between 1890 and 1930, in the prevailing climate of nationalism and subsequent consolidation of the state, an 'Irish' writer was supposed to write about traditional Irish subjects (Mays 1992). However, Beckett chose, like his mentor, James Joyce, an iconoclastic, international, and hybrid aesthetic, even when evoking Ireland. Beckett vehemently refused the parameters of Irish cultural nationalism as he encountered it in the first decades of the Irish Free State. On 31 January 1938 he wrote to his friend Thomas MacGreevy (who strongly identified himself as 'Irish' and became the Director of the National Gallery of Ireland in 1950): 'I can't think of Ireland the way you do.' In the same letter, he refers to his 'chronic inability to understand as member of any proposition a phrase like "the Irish people"' (TCD MS 10402).

Beckett's relation to 'Ireland' and 'Irishness' was therefore complex: While throughout his life he continued to draw on memories, landscapes, and cultural references (such as Yeats, Synge, or Berkeley) from his childhood or early adulthood, the unstable and multiple modes of identification embodied in his work were incompatible with existing categories of 'Irish writing.' Indeed, for several decades, Beckett's work was largely ignored by the dominant Irish cultural institutions, though he had a number of individual admirers and supporters in Ireland.[4] Mays argues that in the 1960s there was little interest in or knowledge of Beckett's work in Ireland in academic or literary circles. While Vivian Mercer and Mays published studies in the 1960s and Deirdre Bair published her unauthorized biography in 1978, it was not until the 1980s that two journals, the *Irish University Review* (1984) followed by Trinity College's *Hermathena* (1986) published special editions on Beckett's work, and that Beckett's 'Irishness' began to be a significant issue in Beckett criticism.

Since the 1980s, Beckett's oeuvre has been placed in the contexts of Irish landscape (O'Brien), drama (Roche), poetry (Coughlan), and culture (Kearney), particularly in the Anglo-Irish or Protestant tradition (Kenner, Kiberd, Mays, McCormack, Mooney). Indeed, the reclaiming of Irish references and contexts in Beckett's work also invites a redefinition of the historical and geographical boundaries of 'Irish' culture.[5] Mays emphasizes that, though Beckett does not fit easily into the Celtic Twilight movement that was dominant in the Ireland he chose to leave, he can be placed within older, pre-Revival genealogies of Irish writing, from Swift or Congreve to Burke. Beckett's work therefore challenges both the historical and the cultural boundaries of what was being constructed as a national 'tradition' of Irish writing. In more recent years, as the Irish Republic interrogates and challenges its own foundational myths of identity and nation, and yet, in some respects, reveals itself as resistant to otherness and difference, Beckett's voice, which is that of a dissenter, has acquired greater resonance in Ireland than ever before. The Beckett Festival of the author's nineteen stage plays (excluding *Eleutheria* whose performing rights remain unavailable), mounted by Dublin's Gate Theatre in 1991 and remounted at New York's Lincoln Center in 1996 and the Barbican Centre in London in 1999, marked an important moment in Beckett's Irish 'rehabilitation.' As Irish culture opens up to an increasingly diverse range of identities and genres, Beckett remains a pioneer, exploring and contesting the construction of identity and its others, in individual or national terms.

The first major study of Beckett's work within an Irish postcolonial framework, David Lloyd's chapter on 'Writing in the Shit: Beckett, Nationalism and the Colonial Subject' in his book, *Anomalous States: Irish Writing in the Postcolonial Moment*, places it in the context of a critique of hegemonic nationalism's drive to integrate 'a highly differentiated population into the modern nation state, a project which has always sought to transcend antagonisms, contradictions and social differences for the sake of a unified conception of political subjectivity. [O]ne principle and consistent dynamic of identity formation has been the negation of recalcitrant or inassimilable elements in Irish society' (Lloyd 1993, 5). Lloyd therefore aims to 'situate the significance of [Beckett's] writing in relation to Ireland's postcolonial moment and to read his anti-nationalism as a critical political intervention'(4). He suggests that Beckett's *First Love* 'approaches the threshold of another possible language within which a postcolonial subjectivity might begin to find articulation' and that 'it is in whatever lies in the gapped, disjointed songs of

Anna/Lulu, in the unrepresentable in the narratives of identity which Beckett's work excoriates, that the project of decolonization finds its unpredictable resources. In the meantime, Beckett's own oeuvre [...] stands as the most exhausting dismantling we have of the logic of identity that at every level structures and maintains the postcolonial moment' (56).

This chapter takes Lloyd's arguments as its point of departure, and links these to some of Homi Bhabha's theoretical concepts in *The Location of Culture*. These two writers are not 'representative' of a homogenous set of discourses named 'postcolonial theory' which is rather heterogeneous and vigorously contested, but their work, like the work of Edward Said, whose *Orientalism* is a foundational work of contemporary Postcolonial Studies, investigates the impact of representation in the construction of cultural or political identities and their 'others.' *Anomalous States* focuses on the forging of national identities in the postcolonial state, and stresses 'the hegemonic role of culture in the formation of citizen subjects' (Lloyd 1993, 7). Both Lloyd and Bhabha, in their individual ways, are interested in counter-hegemonic aesthetic strategies geared towards uncovering and presenting the 'inassimilable' (Lloyd) or 'incommensurable' (Bhabha) narratives and histories that disrupt the homogenizing force of state legitimated national culture. However, Ireland's 'postcolonial' status is itself contested, and Beckett's work can be seen to reflect the ambivalences and contradictions not only within the category of 'Irish,' but within the category 'postcolonial' in so far as it can be applied to Ireland.

Joe Cleary has argued that 'The emergence of colonial and postcolonial studies within the Irish academy as a distinct mode of critical analysis can be dated to the start of the 1980's' (Cleary 2002, 101). While postcolonialism analyzes the discourses and material practices which legitimated and sustained the colonial projects of imperial nations such as England or France and the struggle for liberation on the part of decolonizing peoples, it also analyzes the legacies of colonialism (and late capitalist neo-colonialism) in postcolonial nation states. The analysis and critique of nationalism as the main strategy of decolonization is a major area of debate within postcolonial studies, with recent studies insisting on the need to distinguish between particular forms of nationalism at particular historical moments, while suggesting that the historical development of global capitalism has favored the modern state and its 'grid of determinate, national identities' (Chatterjee 1997, 238). From this perspective, Beckett's experience of the newly instituted Irish Free State, and his experience of pre- and post-World War II Europe can be seen as formative contexts for his rejection of unitary and exclusive structures of identity.

There has been much debate as to whether the relation between England and Ireland was a colonial one. In his immensely influential study, *Inventing Ireland*, Declan Kiberd emphasizes that Ireland was sometimes subject to colonial policies, and sometimes seen as an extremity of the imperial center's domestic realm (Kiberd 1994). In his essay 'Postcolonialism: the Case of Ireland,' Terry Eagleton evokes the ambivalence of the historical relationship between Ireland and Britain: 'Ireland before its partial independence was that impossibly oxymoronic animal, a metropolitan colony, at once part of the imperial nation and peripheral to it. What other British colony had MPs at Westminster? As such, divided between colonial and metropolitan, august kingdom and primitive periphery, the juridical fiction of union and the political reality of subjugation, it figured as a kind of political monstrosity' (Eagleton 1998,127). The current status of Northern Ireland as part of the British Isles further complicates any description of Ireland as resolutely 'postcolonial.' While connections can be made with other colonized nations and, indeed, Stephen Howe cites historical research that colonial 'managers' used Ireland as a testing ground for English imperial ventures elsewhere (Howe 2000), Ireland's particular history makes it an anomalous case, but one which troubles the borderlines between imperial history and its margins.

Beckett was not ignorant of the complexities of Irish history. The 'Notebooks'[6] Beckett kept during his student years and a decade or so beyond, and held in the Library of Trinity College, Dublin, include notes from a chronological study of Irish history, from Celtic pre-history to the Anglo-Irish wars of 1919–21. One phrase in these largely routine history notes is given a paragraph unto itself, and refers to the Protestant settlers in Ireland as the 'Middle Nation – Irish to the English and English to the Irish' (TCD MS 10971/2/10). This recalls Joe Cleary's definition of Ireland as 'a settlement rather than an administrative colony,' and of the Protestant settlers as 'an independent third factor that intervened between the imperial mother-country and the colonized native peoples' (Cleary 2002, 115). Dublin's Protestant elite often referred to their location as 'West Britain,' a name that both elided the boundaries between Ireland and Britain, and obliterated native Celtic culture or pre-history, the narrativizing of which became central to the nationalist imagination of an independent Irish state. Beckett located himself in neither of these camps. His move to Paris (and later the French language) offered a release from the dominant national polarities of British/Irish.

In her essay on Beckett's poetry in the context of Irish Modernism, Patricia Coughlan stresses Beckett's experience of difference at a number of levels, relating to State, social milieu, and family:

> [B]y background a Protestant in a state increasingly and aggressively Catholic in ideology, by conviction an atheist in a family devoutly low church and Evangelical, member of the suburban middle class in a cultural milieu officially devoted to enthusiastic imaginative celebration of the rural peasantry, bohemian and cosmopolitan by taste and inclination and, in a household governed by respectability and propriety, valuing the life of the intellect and the arts above bourgeois professional status or security. 'They want me to wear a bowler hat', he complained to MacGreevy upon one of his returns from Paris; and, more plaintively: 'I don't want to be a professor.' (Coughlan 1995, 182)

From an economically and educationally privileged but politically and culturally marginalized social milieu, Beckett might be compared to Pierre Bourdieu's subaltern elite, well equipped with the privileges of educational and cultural capital so as to critique the social and cultural orthodoxies from which they feel alienated (Bourdieu 1984, 176).

Beckett's alienation seems to have been both against the 'proper' bourgeois expectations and values of his respectable family, and the narrow cultural and ethnic boundaries of the Catholic Free State, and indeed perhaps Northern Ireland. The Constitution of 1937 (coincidentally, the year Beckett settled in Paris) institutionalized many of the doctrines of the Catholic Hierarchy, while the province of Northern Ireland was created as a Protestant State for a Protestant people. As well as being educated in Enniskillen's Portora in Northern Ireland, Beckett taught briefly at one of the educational bastions of middle-class Protestant Northern Ireland, Campbell College in Belfast, both of which were concerned with shaping a future Protestant elite, a role that Beckett vehemently rejected.

Neither did he embrace the celebration of the Celtic past in the writers of the 'Celtic Twilight' led by W. B. Yeats, and referred to by Beckett in his review of 'Recent Irish Poetry' as 'our leading twilighters' (Cohn 1983, 71). In the same essay, initially published in 1934, Beckett specifically rejects the twilighters' reification of cultural memory into artifacts venerated by the 'antiquarians,' with their 'segment after segment of cut and dried sanctity and loveliness' (Cohn 1983, 71).

The postcolonial critic Homi Bhabha describes such an 'antiquarian' approach to national history as 'pedagogic' and contrasts it with the incoherence of the moment of 'the performative' before it has been shaped into history: 'The scraps, patches and rags of daily life must be repeatedly turned into the signs of a coherent national culture, while the very act of the narrative performance interpellates a growing circle of national subjects. In the production of the nation as narration there is a split between the continuist, accumulative temporality of the pedagogical, and the repetitious, recursive strategy of the performative' (Bhabha 1994,145–6).

A major and contentious issue in postcolonial historiography is the questioning, not only of Western imperial history, but the counter construction of national histories and national subjects in the service of the postcolonial state. In other words, the mechanisms whereby individuals come to identify with a national history and a nation state tend to replicate or mirror the mechanisms of the colonial regime, 'because both, albeit competing visions and discourses were being produced within the framework of identity thinking, which held as self evident the origin of meaning in a unitary self' (Coughlan 1995, 179). David Lloyd emphasizes 'the conjunction between identity formation and the emergence of the state' (Lloyd 1993, 4). The concept of 'authentic' origins, history, and language are all crucial elements of national identity formation.

Within both an individual and a national framework, managing memory is the key to constructing history and identity. The narratives of personal or cultural history shape the past according to the exigencies of the present. In Beckett's work, the personal and cultural past continually returns, but as dislocated fragments, which fail to be assimilated into an 'authentic' identity, history, or language. The transmutation of pedagogic history in Beckett's oeuvre into the 'scraps, patches and rags' of memory involves a radical interrogation of the basic mechanisms whereby identity and authority are constituted, which has implications for the critique of European imperial identity and for the construction of postcolonial identities.

Edward Said's investigation of Western imperial 'Orientalist' discourse exposes the assumption of a 'sovereign Western consciousness' (Said 1979, 8) which casts the 'Orient' as its object of knowledge and scrutiny. Beckett's oeuvre can be seen as a sustained critique or parody of that sovereign consciousness which seeks to see, know, and record its objects. From his earliest writings, both fictional and critical, Beckett was concerned with the breakdown of the relation between self and world, or subject and its representable object: the 'visible,' 'knowable' world.

Postcolonial theory analyzes the imperial control over naming and definition which situated the imperial center as the seeing and knowing agent, and the colonized peoples and culture as the object which is seen, known, and acted upon. How, then, does a postcolonial nation go about reconstituting a non-oppressed and non-oppressive sense of identity? This is one of the major sources of contention in postcolonial studies. Does not the undermining of the mechanisms of authority and power debilitate the agency of the colonized people/nation? On the other hand, Lloyd and Bhabha insist that if the new nation is not to replicate exclusive boundaries of who or what can be represented, thereby creating its own marginalized internal others, the very field of representation and the limits of legitimate identities need to be reimagined, beyond 'the perspective of a state formation for which neither political subjectivity nor agency are conceivable outside the framework of representative narratives' (Lloyd 1993, 10). This is where Beckett's aesthetics of radical dislocation intersect with the cultural politics of the postcolonial.

Yet Beckett also troubles postcolonial theory as a writer identified with European metropolitan culture and with the presentation of a dislocated individual consciousness amidst the ruins of history rather than on communal interaction and the construction of alternative histories. However, while primitivism and Orientalism were recurrent tropes within European metropolitan culture of the late nineteenth and early twentieth centuries, the European avant-garde itself assimilated writers and artists from a range of cultures and there were more politicized interventions into the areas of anti-imperialism and racial oppression. Beckett in fact made a major contribution to one of the more radical of these, *A Negro Anthology*, compiled by Nancy Cunard, for which he translated several articles. W. C. McCormack reminds us that 'Nobody contributed more to it than Beckett who translated nineteen pieces in all, a body of prose work amounting to well over one hundred thousand words' (McCormack 1994, 386). Tim Brennan has described the anthology as a 'groundbreaking compilation' and 'an unprecedented documentary record of African influence in society and the arts as well as an anticolonial compendium' (Brennan 2002, 196). Yet, even though Beckett may personally have lent his support or actively intervened in particular political or historical struggles, his writing insists on an aesthetics of disintegration and non-mimeticism.

Beckett's review of the Irish dramatist Sean O'Casey's collection of diverse writings, *Windfalls*, in *The Bookman* of 1936, interestingly focuses not at all on the urban, Irish location or issues of class and nation, but notes that O'Casey 'discerns the principle of disintegration in even the most complacent solidities, and activates it to their explosion' (Cohn 1983, 82). He suggests that O'Casey's *Juno and the Paycock* 'communicates most fully this dramatic dehiscence, mind and world come asunder in irreparable dissociation.' There is even a prefiguring of *Eleutheria* when Beckett cites O'Casey's one act 'knockabout,' *The End of the Beginning*, 'where the entire set comes to pieces and the chief character, in a final spasm of dislocation, leaves the scene by the chimney'[7] (Cohn 1983, 83).

David Lloyd suggests in relation to the Irish poet W. B. Yeats that the foregrounding of 'moments of disintegration' can 'open the space for another history' (Lloyd 1993, 5). Such dehiscence can therefore be viewed as an interruption of the mechanisms by which the subject is constructed into a 'proper' shape, history, or body, and an articulation of the quest for alternative modes of identity and authority, emerging from within the ruins, debris, and margins of 'Western' aesthetics.

In this sense, Beckett's work may be seen as a response to the historical contexts of Ireland of the 1920s and 1930s and, as Antony Uhlmann argues in *Beckett and Poststructuralism*, to the France of World War II and post-World War II Europe, that of Pétain and de Gaulle, mediated through the metropolitan avant-garde of Paris in the interwar years. Although Beckett does not represent these contexts mimetically, his dislocations of personal and cultural memory constitute a critique of regimes that had the power to marginalize, exclude or, in the case of Nazi Germany, exterminate those who did not conform to its definition of a national or ethnic subject. I would argue, therefore, that Beckett's rejection of the national boundaries of identity and history was informed not by a refusal of the struggle for national independence or liberty, which in Ireland had already happened by the time Beckett reached adulthood (he did not of course hesitate to join a collective struggle during the Resistance), but within the context of a hegemonic social structure (both that of the family, and that of the established state) and the symbolic systems which legitimized and sustained that structure. Beckett's strategies of assault included the parody of those systems, as in *Watt*'s relentless lists, categories, and genealogies, as well as the embrace of liminal and 'incommensurable' structures and identities. Moreover, the particularization of cultural references in Beckett's work (including the identification of Irish references in the works mentioned above) reveals the recurrent strategy of cultural hybridization as he juxtaposes diverse and even conflicting cultural contexts.

Antony Uhlmann (Uhlmann 149–50) draws attention to the slippage and ambiguities in Beckett's use of pronouns to indicate Irish or French nationality in his 1946 talk on his experience of the Irish hospital at Saint-Lô written for Irish National Radio (RTE), though never broadcast:

> When I reflect now on the recurrent problems of what, with all proper modesty, might be called the heroic period, on one in particular so arduous and elusive that it literally ceases to be formulable, I suspect that our pains were those inherent in the simple and necessary and yet so unattainable proposition that their way of being we, was not our way and that our way of being they, was not their way.

Beckett appears to identify with the Irish 'we' and yet this identification slips across the borders of nation, and at the end of the piece the Irish have become 'they,' as Beckett considers

> the possibility that some of those who were in Saint-Lô will come home realizing that they got at least as good as they gave, that they got indeed what they could hardly give, a vision and a sense of a time-honoured conception of humanity in ruins, and perhaps even an inkling of the terms in which our condition is to be thought again. These will have been in France. ('Capital of the Ruins,' Beckett 1986, 337)

The provisionality of these pronouns and tenses, and the sense of occupying simultaneously positions that appear to be exclusive according to the classificatory systems of nation, space, and time, will recur in Beckett's writing.

In his early work, Beckett achieved a sense of national dislocation through the superimposition of Irish, European, and, indeed, Eastern geographical and cultural references. His first novel (unpublished until 1993) *Dream of Fair to Middling Women* which, as Beckett's biographers have demonstrated, draws on much autobiographical material, hinges on a double geography of Germany and Ireland, with some scenes in Paris, but even the Irish scenes and stories are given an Italianate slant through the naming of the central character as Belacqua and other Dantean references (not to mention the tissue of quotations direct and indirect to Western and Eastern philosophical and literary works). At one point, the author, a Mr Beckett, directly mentions meeting his creature,

Belacqua, in a timeframe later than the main narrative. Belacqua offers the author a portrait of himself:

'John' he said, 'of the Crossroads, Mr Beckett. A border man.'[8] (Beckett 1993,186)

Since he has just been referring to the poems of St John of the Cross, Belacqua's liminality is as much ontological as national. Belacqua also crosses class boundaries: He frequents both popular Dublin drinking dens and the social milieux of the upper classes and intelligentsia; yet the narrative is very aware of class divisions, and the position of Belacqua within the hierarchies of postcolonial Dublin, even though his appearance and behaviour often belie that position. In the second scene of the novel, after Belacqua has failed to find any coins with which to passify the wharfinger upon whose pier he has trespassed, he reasserts his status as 'an obvious gentleman' by his courteous 'good evening' as he takes his leave, which only mollifies a little his identity as vagrant trespasser in the wharfinger's eyes (8). *More Pricks Than Kicks*, which incorporates some of the material of the unpublished *Dream*, including the central character, Belacqua, refers to the 'weary proletarians at rest on arse or elbow' ('Ding Dong,' Beckett 1970, 45) and the 'incontinent bosthoons of his own class' ('Dante and the Lobster,' Beckett 1970, 15). Belacqua is in no sense a man of the people, but a man apart. In Beckett's later work, all specificities of class, nation, or geography will give way to abstracted and formalized spaces of representation which can accommodate strange reciprocities, metamorphoses, and inversions of identities and corporealities. But the tension here between Belacqua's liminal sense of identity and the particularities of his cultural, social, and national milieu leads to a dynamic of cultural dislocation that can be traced also in the early drama.

Beckett's early attempts at drama betray a certain struggle with the temporal and spatial conventions of stage setting. The fragment *Human Wishes* which entailed reams of historical research, is set in a room in the household of the eighteenth-century encyclopedist, Dr Johnson. However, while supported by copious historical research, and dated very precisely as the evening of 14 April 1781 (125 years before Beckett's birth date), it focuses, not on the Doctor himself, but on the morbid wranglings of his raggle taggle household (a kind of anti-family). Death dominates the conversation, as the characters debate whether two particular figures from Anglo-Irish theatrical history, Henry Kelly and Oliver Goldsmith, are or are not dead. The historical registering of death notices is contrasted with Marcel Proust's 'intermittences du Coeur' through Mrs Williams's distinction between her mental registering of the death of her father and its belated coming to the notice of her heart the following Christmas (Cohn 1983, 164). Lionel Kelly's article on *Human Wishes* in *The Ideal Core of the Onion* points to Beckett's further destabilizing of the locational and historical parameters of that aborted play, through his alleged attempts to transpose the accents of Dr Johnson's hybrid eighteenth century household into an Irish register. (Presumably, at one point he envisaged an Irish production.) (Pilling and Bryden, 1992, 25.) Beckett's notes suggest a shift of focus from the 'social comedy' of Johnson's household and milieu to a fascination with the interior struggles of Johnson who was terrified of going mad, but he abandoned the play, and, a decade later, he worked through a similar tension in *Eleutheria*.

Eleutheria (from the Greek word for freedom) stages Beckett's discarding of the convention of showing an individual in relation to their environment, in terms of geography, family, community, or nation. Victor Krap rejects his bourgeois family and the family home, which finally disappears from the stage to make way for Victor's bare, anonymous room. Peter Boxall has written of the crossed cultural references in the play, which presents specific autobiographical details rooted (as we now know from biographical research) in Dublin, but in the French language and in a Parisian setting: 'The reality effect that sustains the Krap's salon is prone to collapse both towards Victor's geography of pure negativity, and towards an Irish/Beckettian geography.' The space/time of Victor's consciousness is contrasted with 'the other characters' attempt to protect the referents that hold their space in place from slippage into the negativity of Victor's liberty' (Boxall 1998, 250). Victor's freedom is defined not as a collective political ideology, though he professes solidarity with other marginalized beings, but as an individual attempt to withdraw from being as much as possible.[9] Victor is upbraided for having no 'proper' shape or boundaries:

> GLAZIER: Define yourself, that's it. It's time you defined yourself. You sit there like a kind of ... how can I put it? Like a kind of oozing pus. Like a kind of sanies, that's it. Get a bit of body, for God's sake. (*Eleutheria*, 82)

Victor is also particularly aware that his power to disturb lies in the fact that he cannot be simply dismissed as 'other' in the eyes of his bourgeois family and milieu – one of those suffering creatures who are of such a different class or category that their fate is a matter of indifference: 'Saints, madmen, martyrs, victims of torture – they don't bother you in the least, they are in the natural order of things' (Beckett 1996, 145). But he is both an insider and an outsider. This might be applied also to Beckett's own relationship to the categories of 'colonial/postcolonial.' Inhabiting these borderlands, Beckett, like his creature Watt, seems to have opted for the role of 'witness': 'A needy witness, an imperfect witness. The better to witness, the worse to witness' (Beckett 1963, 203). He makes no attempt to reconcile or assimilate the material he witnesses into a world or a self that, like the imperial globe, can be seen and 'understood' at a glance: 'the whole thing there, all there, staring you in the face. You'll see it. Get off me' (*Play*, Beckett 1986, 317). The rags, scraps, and patches of experience fail to cohere despite the mechanisms of pedagogical or imperial interrogation.

To investigate Beckett's work within a postcolonial framework is to emphasize the modes of perception and knowledge which underpinned imperial colonialism and its impact on the parameters and definitions used to construct 'reality' and 'normality,' and their 'others': the deviant and the abject. Postcolonial discourses such as Bhabha's or Lloyd's therefore intersect with deconstructionist theories which have been applied to Beckett's work for some time, but they tend to focus on the political and cultural contexts and implications of the aesthetic. In other words, they refer the aesthetics of indeterminacy back to historically-specific, determining political and cultural institutions, against which the indeterminacies of the work labor, without necessarily seeing those contexts reflected mimetically in the aesthetic product.

Indeed, a postcolonial approach questions the separation between the frameworks of European and colonial histories, emphasizing that the empire's colonial histories are central and internal to its own history. Anne McClintock suggests that, in the Victorian era, the categories of race, class, and gender were produced in and through each other as a way not only of maintaining British colonial supremacy, but of supporting the 'self-definition of the middle classes' and 'the policing of the "dangerous classes": the working class, the Irish, Jews, prostitutes, feminists, gays and lesbians, criminals, the militant crowd and so on' (McClintock 1995, 5). The relation between 'English' and 'Irish' (featured in Victorian cartoons as negroid or simianized) or 'Anglo-Irish' (featured as a graceful young 'Hibernia,' of the same class and race as the English, but feminized, deferring to and dependent upon the stern Britannia or paternalistic

John Bull) was clearly also mediated through these categories. Imperial systems of knowledge, identity, perception, and classification are therefore central to Western domestic, intellectual, and social histories as well as to its colonial histories. Stephen Howe argues that if 'Ireland's story was indeed a colonial one, it was as part of a picture in which, literally, all European history is colonial history' (Howe 2000, 16). It is perhaps the increasing erasure of geographical or national references in Beckett's work that enables it to be interpreted as a critique of the imperial sovereign subject and as an articulation of colonized subjectivities. Specificity is provided by the particular cultural and political context of the work's reading, production, or appropriation.

In the 2002 Annual Beckett Lecture at Trinity College, Dublin, on 'Beckett's "Ghost Notes",' Joseph Roach placed *Waiting for Godot* within both a genealogy and a geography of performance which spanned the historical oceanic trajectories of exchange between European, African, and American continents. He linked it with the practice of leaving silent notes or 'Ghost Notes' in the musical fabric of New Orleans Jazz funereals and with Susan Lori Parks's *The America Play* (1994) and *The Oriki of a Grasshopper*, written in the 1980s by Nigerian postcolonial playwright, Femi Osofisan. In Osofisan's play, the spaces of 'metaphysical' crisis in *Waiting for Godot*, which is being rehearsed in a university drama department, allow other layers of more local, immediate, and socio-political crises to be substituted (from waiting for an actor to appear, with the knowledge that he may have been incarcerated, to waiting for social/political/economic revolution in Nigeria). Roach argued that it is Beckett's insistence on the 'violence of the unutterable,' the silence after catastrophe which defies representation that enables *Waiting for Godot* to figure as a palimpsest for other global and local struggles and catastrophes. It may indeed be partly Beckett's refusal to appeal to a specific or national interpretative community that enables his work to be reproduced and appropriated in diverse contexts, and particularly those that have known violent political oppression and conflict.

By *Waiting for Godot*, Beckett had cleared the stage of any specific spatio-temporal coordinates, though the names of the characters, Estragon (French), Vladimir (Russian), Pozzo (Italian), and Lucky (Anglo-American), as has been frequently noted, evoke hybrid cultural contexts. *Waiting for Godot* features five characters who share the here and now of the stage present, and the enunciative moment of dialogue or monologue, but their worlds do not coincide – their individual discourses indicate that they inhabit radically heterogeneous temporalities and spatialities. Estragon is beaten at night, but Vladimir isn't (paralleling the boy and his brother). Vladimir remembers other times and spaces, but Estragon doesn't. The Boy moves between Godot's quasi mythical space-time and that of the stage. Pozzo refers to his manor and his possessions, reproducing through his relationship with Lucky the discourse of imperial/capitalist exploitation: 'I am bringing him to the fair, where I hope to get a good price for him' (Beckett 1986, 32). Lucky's speech is an atrophied parody of academic discourse whose disintegration represents and mimes the collapse of a logocentric concept of a 'merciful God' and of the intellectual and corporeal disciplines of the academy and sport, revealing in the splinters of his speech a vision of famine/catastrophe: 'the skull to shrink and waste [...] I resume alas alas abandoned unfinished the skull the skull in Connemara [...]' (Beckett 1986, 43). As Joseph Roach noted, each of the characters has a distinct relationship to food and hunger:

VLADIMIR: Does he give you enough to eat? (*The* BOY *hesitates*.) Does he feed you well?
BOY: Fairly well, sir.

(Beckett 1986, 50)

In *Godot* and *Endgame*, Beckett presents both the material subjection of Lucky, Clov, Nagg, and Nell, through corporeal discipline, and the ambivalence of the authority of the master/oppressor, in ways which recall Bhabha's insistence on the insecurity of colonial rule. While Said's *Orientalism* was crucial in identifying the West's strategies of 'Othering,' critics pointed out that he posits for diverse European imperial projects an apparently secure and unified identity – 'the West,' and tends to present the Orient as the passive victim of the West's identificatory power. Bhabha's controversial intervention,[10] was to insist that, at the level of discourse and rhetoric, the supposedly stable and superior identity of the colonizer is anxious and ambivalent and needs to be continually reasserted. Pozzo and Hamm are dependent on those they subject to produce and perform their identity, while they anxiously maintain positions of linguistic and corporeal dominance.

Bhabha has used the term 'mimicry' to underline the contradictions of colonial authority:

For the epic intention of the civilizing mission, 'human and not wholly human' in the famous words of Lord Rosebery, 'writ by the finger of the divine' often produces a text rich in the traditions of *trompe-l'oeil*, irony, mimicry and repetition. In this comic turn from the high ideals of the colonial imagination to its low mimetic literary effects mimicry emerges as one of the most elusive and effective strategies of colonial power and knowledge. (Bhabha 1994, 85)

In fact, in Beckett's world, authority is almost always a masquerade. Pozzo comes across as a rather pathetic and parodic substitution for the absent Godot. He is also the mimic man of his 'slave,' Lucky, who taught him his rhetoric. Vladimir and Estragon mimic the roles of Pozzo and Lucky at the beginning of Act Two. Lucky, in turn, has internalized his subjection and mimics his master when he places the whip back in the hands of Pozzo in Act Two. Clov in *Endgame* recalls Caliban in Shakespeare's *The Tempest* (a text that has often been read in a colonial/postcolonial context) as Hamm rules him and has imposed his language and customs on him:

> CLOV: I use the words you taught me. If they don't mean anything anymore, teach me others. Or let me be silent.
>
> (Beckett 1986, 113)

Yet Hamm is the ultimate player-king, whose authority must be continually mimed through well-rehearsed and self-consciously theatrical routines. In recognizable colonial/postcolonial terms, Hamm's authority is shored by his narration of origins – his story. But as Paul Lawley has argued, *Endgame* is full of inauthentic origins, adoptions, betrayals, and substitutions (Lawley 1997, 22). Therefore, while Beckett stages authority as invested in the power to name and know who, what, and where, and in the corporeal subjection of others, that authority is framed as masquerade and mimicry. Most of the authoritarian figures in Beckett's drama, while appropriating the labor of others, are themselves required to perform. As Lloyd argued of *First Love*, Beckett presents identity not as pedagogical, but as performative and interactive: '[O]ne labours to produce oneself for others' (Lloyd 1993, 50).

In the late work, images of the past are torn from any sequential narrative, and, as in *That Time, Not I, Company*, or *How It Is*, are continually reproduced in the present moment of narrative or performative utterance. While the images appear to be static, like the pictures in the gallery that Voice C in *That Time* contemplates ('the dates on the frames in case you might get the century wrong'), they are constructed through the temporality of performance. Even if scraps of the past keep returning, they are also being continually revised in and for the moment of utterance, in the demand to account for oneself or the hope of being witnessed.

Hence Beckett's increasing focus on the mechanisms of consciousness and identity formation in relation to the other/Other. I'm using the 'other' here in three ways: Firstly, as that which is abjected or disidentified with in order for the bounded identity of the self/nation to be defined. In *The Making of Political Identities*, Ernesto Laclau, drawing on Lacanian psychoanalysis, emphasizes that political or national borders are founded in order to offer an imaginary coherence and identity which will mask the lack or loss at the heart of our fantasies of identity. In the constitution of such an identity, he maintains, the positing of an 'other' is crucial: '[A]ll identity is constituted through an externalization of the other via the drawing of political frontiers' (Laclau 1998, 121). Mary Bryden has pointed out the ways in which Beckett's early work posited women as material and often suffocating 'others' (Bryden 1993), but in Beckett's later work the positing of such frontiers is disturbed, so that the masks of self and other keep slipping, revealing precisely 'the lack or loss at the heart of our fantasies of identity,' but also providing a space for the articulation, however traumatic, of fragmented incommensurable identities. Secondly, the Other refers to the Symbolic Other, the dominant cultural and linguistic laws of representation (aesthetic, social, or political) which shape 'legitimate' individuals. Beckett often figures the demand of the Other as interrogation, from *Eleutheria* to *What Where*. The demand to account for herself fuels the desperate confessions of Mouth in *Not I*, and the heads in *Play* reenact their petrified narrative in scraps and fragments to try to pacify the Light. Thirdly, the (at least partially or virtually) embodied other refers to the potential relations of interactivity between subject and other.

Several commentators, including Declan Kiberd and Hugh Kenner, have seen in Beckett's late work the mechanics of the isolated Protestant conscience. Sinead Mooney argues that in Beckett's work, 'Bereft of the occasion to "confess" to another, an instance of utterance which it would be presumptuous to dub a self confesses under the goad of a relentless imperative in classic Protestant fashion, but can never be sure of being shriven, and is thus doomed to seemingly endless repetitions of the same non-narrative in ever-decreasing hope of some eventual expiation. [...] This is the DNA pattern, so to speak, of Beckett's imagination – a fiat with regard to which disobedience is unthinkable – rather than any fundamentally self-delighting inventiveness' (Mooney 2000, 230). She stresses Beckett's refusal of tradition and any 'induction into a community of forcibly shared meanings' and refers to the 'immaculate solipsism' of his aesthetics (Mooney 235). Yet this seems to reduce the complex and plural positions of self and other/Other that I have suggested above.

Beckett's work certainly bears witness to the calamitous cruelty that human beings and nations inflict on each other, by corporeal, psychological, linguistic, or technological means. It bears witness as well to the sense of alienation and subjection inflicted on the human subject through the laws of identity and language inherited not only from the forms of Judeo-Christian religion, but also the epistemic and material conditions of post-Cartesian capitalist modernity. Yet I would argue against the 'immaculate solipsism' of Beckett's work. Beckett's texts are interwoven with rags and patches of hybrid cultural references that certainly do not interpellate any homogeneous 'community' of interpretation or recognition, but incorporate (for example) Classical, European, Celtic, Protestant, Catholic, Jewish, and Buddhist elements. *Ill Seen Ill Said* is an extraordinary combination of Celtic and Christian, including Marion imagery. Moreover, the inability of Beckett's so-called 'characters' to keep silent is not only in passive obedience to the omniscient Other. It is also an insistence, as Lloyd notes, on the production of self for the other in the hope and desire of being witnessed. In a chapter on Beckett's paradoxes in *Crazy Jane and the Bishop*, Terry Eagleton notes that 'Lamenting by means of sounds, or better still words, is a vast liberation, because it means that the sufferer is beginning to produce something' ('Beckett's Paradoxes,' Eagleton 1998, 302).

Indeed, several of Beckett's late plays transform the lack of definition of self, into a fluidity of borders between self and other. In *Ohio Impromptu*, the other/Other is not punishing or coercive but sends a mediator, a translator, an other self to comfort the Listener. The stage image is of two figures 'as alike in appearance as possible' seated at a table, one the Reader, one the Listener. The Reader reads to the Listener from the book on stage what appears to be the Listener's own story, of the loss of a loved one, followed by the apparition of a man who resembles the Reader we see on stage. (Nothing of course is certain):

> One night as he sat trembling head in hands from head to foot a man appeared to him and said, I have been sent by – and here he named the dear name – to comfort you. Then drawing a worn volume from the pocket of his long black coat he sat and read till dawn. Then disappeared without a word. [...] So from time to time unheralded he

would appear to read the sad tale through again and the long night
away. Then disappear without a word.
[*Pause.*]
With never a word exchanged they grew to be as one. (Beckett 1986,
447)

While this seems to be the incorporation of the different in order to
reproduce the same, the text and the stage image do not coalesce but
contradict each other at the end. In the text we are told that the figures
remain: 'Buried in who knows what profounds of mind' (Beckett 1986,
448). On stage, however, they raise their heads to meet each other's
eyes in mindful contemplation. Rather than the self incorporating or
subjecting the other, the performance works against the construction
of the boundaries of self and other, and prevents the audience from
categorizing the figures before us. They remain profoundly uncanny,
both familiar and unfamiliar. The production of self for the other and
via the other creates a liminal being who is neither self nor other (and
is both self and other).

If placing Beckett's oeuvre within the frames of Irish and Postcolonial
studies troubles their boundaries, to place him outside those frames
would equally be a kind of blinkering. This is why I have argued that
Beckett's work performs a dislocation of the frames of nation, identity,
or theory. These days, when we are very legitimately concerned with
agency and empowerment, Beckett's theater questions the establishment
of our emergent identities and how they negotiate the relationship with
the other. In Beckett's work, the dehiscence of the spatial and temporal
coordinates of self, family, or nation, might allow the space, body, or
voice of the other to emerge in a different relation to the self. Indeed, it
might provide 'an inkling of the terms in which our condition is to be
thought again' ('Capital of the Ruins,' 1986, 337).

Acknowledgement: permission to quote from a letter of Beckett's to MacGreevy
(TCD MS 10402), and from Beckett's 'Notebooks' (TCD MS 10971/2/10) has been
given by the Board of Trinity College Dublin.

notes

1. The description is of Belacqua.
2. Ireland did not become a Republic until 1949.

3. The title 'Irish Studies' and 'Postcolonial Studies' have emerged in response to the increasing legitimation within academia of theoretical disciplines such as Cultural Studies, Gender Studies, etc. Indeed the term 'Irish Studies' as opposed to the Study of Irish Literature(s) reflects the impact that these theoretical disciplines have had in widening and theorizing the field.

4. *Waiting for Godot* was produced at Alec Reid and Carolyn Swift's Pike Theatre in Dublin very shortly after its London premiere in 1955. Anthony Roche in his book, *Contemporary Irish Drama from Beckett to McGuinness*, points out that 'what followed was a year long run. *Godot* in Ireland was to prove a popular rather than an avant-garde success' (p. 4). Trinity College, his Alma Mater, awarded him an honorary doctorate that he accepted in person in 1959.

5. See Kearney 1985.

6. Currently being edited by Everett Frost and Jane Maxwell.

7. The review ends with a reference to the 'doomed furniture' which, in *Eleutheria*, will end up apparently in the orchestra pit.

8. Samuel Beckett, *Dream of Fair to Middling Women* (London & New York: Calder and Riverrun, 1996 (1993)) 186. The reference is Belacqua's self-description as recorded by 'the author'.

9. Beckett used the Greek word previously in *Murphy*, in an ironic reference to some turf that, 'truly Irish in its eleutheromania [...] would not burn behind bars.' Samuel Beckett, *Murphy* (London: John Calder, 1963) 130.

10. See, for example, McClintock's critique of Bhabha's concept of colonial ambivalence (McClintock 1995, 62–5).

works cited

Beckett, Samuel. *Murphy*. London: John Calder, 1963.

—— *Watt*. London: John Calder, 1963.

—— *More Pricks Than Kicks*. London: John Calder, 1970.

—— *The Complete Dramatic Works*. London: Faber & Faber, 1986.

—— 'Capital of the Ruins.' *The Beckett Country*. Eoin O'Brien. (ed.), Dublin & London: The Black Cat Press in assocation with Faber & Faber, 1986, 333–7.

—— *Dream of Fair to Middling Women*. London: Calder, 1993.

—— *Eleutheria*. London: Faber & Faber, 1996.

Bhabha, Homi. *The Location of Culture*. London: Routledge, 1994.

Bourdieu, Pierre. *Distinction*. London: Routledge 1984.

Boxall, Peter. 'Freedom and Cultural Location in *Eleutheria*.' *Samuel Beckett Today/ Aujourdhui*, 7 (1998): 245–59.

Bryden, Mary. *Women in Samuel Beckett's Prose and Drama: Her Own Other*. London: Macmillan – now Palgrave Macmillan, 1993.

Chatterjee, Partha. *The Nation and its Fragments: Colonial and Postcolonial Histories*. Princeton: Princeton University Press, 1993.

Cleary, Joe. 'Misplaced Ideas: Locating and Dislocating Ireland in Colonial and Postcolonial Studies.' *Marxism, Modernity and Postcolonial Studies*. Ed. Crystal Bartolovich and Neil Lazarus. Cambridge: Cambridge University Press, 2002. 101–24.

Cohn, Ruby (ed.). *Disjecta: Miscellaneous Writings and a Dramatic Fragment by Samuel Beckett*. London: John Calder, 1983.

Connor, Steven (ed.). *Waiting for Godot and Endgame*. London: MacMillan – now Palgrave Macmillan, 1997.

Coughlan, Patricia. "The Poetry is Another Pair of Sleeves': Beckett, Ireland and Modernist Lyric Poetry.' *Modernism and Ireland: the Poetry of the 1930s*. Ed. Patricia Coughlan and Alex Davis. Cork: Cork University Press, 1995, 173–208.

Eagleton, Terry. 'Postcolonialism: the Case of Ireland.' *MultiCultural States*. Ed. David Bennett. London: Routledge, 1998, 125–34.

—— *Crazy Jane and the Bishop and Other Essays in Irish Culture*. Cork: Cork University Press in association with Field Day, 1998.

Kelly, Lionel. 'Beckett's Human Wishes.' *The Ideal Core of the Onion: Reading Beckett Archives*. Ed. John Pilling and Mary Bryden. Beckett International Foundation, 1992, 21–44.

Kenner, Hugh. *A Reader's Guide to Samuel Beckett*. New York: Farra, Strauss & Giroux, 1973.

Kiberd, Declan. *Inventing Ireland*. London: Jonathan Cape, 1995.

Kearney, Richard (ed.). *The Irish Mind: Exploring Intellectual Traditions*. Dublin: Wolfhound Press, 1985.

—— *Transitions*. Manchester: Manchester University Press, 1988.

Laclau, Ernesto. *The Making of Political Identities*. Edinburgh & Australia: Edinburgh University Press, 1998.

Lawley, Paul. 'Adoption in Endgame.' *Waiting for Godot and Endgame*. Ed. Steven Connor. London: MacMillan – now Palgrave Macmillan, 1997. 119–27.

Lloyd, David. *Anomalous States: Irish Writing in the Postcolonial Moment*. Dublin: Lilliput Press, 1993.

—— *Ireland After History*. Cork: Cork University Press in association with Field Day, 1999.

McClintock, Anne. *Imperial Leather: Race, Gender and Sexuality in the Colonial Contest*. New York & London: Routledge, 1995.

McCormack, W. J. *From Burke to Beckett: Ascendency Tradition and Betrayal in Literary History*. Cork: Cork University Press, 1994.

Mays, J. C. C. 'Irish Beckett: a Borderline Instance.' *Beckett in Dublin*. Ed. Steve Wilmer. Dublin: Lilliput Press, 1992, 133–46.

Mooney, Sinead. '"Integrity in a Surplice": Samuel Beckett's (Post) Protestant Poetics.' *Samuel Beckett Today / Aujourd'hui*. 9 (2000): 223–37.

O'Brien, Eoin (ed.). *The Beckett Country*. Dublin & London: The Black Cat Press in assocation with Faber & Faber, 1986.

Pilling, John, and Bryden, Mary. (eds) *The Ideal Core of the Onion: Reading Beckett Archives*. Beckett International Foundation, 1992.

Said, Edward. *Orientalism*. New York: Vintage, 1979.

Roche, Anthony. *Contemporary Irish Drama from Beckett to McGuinness*. Dublin: Gill & MacMillan, 1994.

Uhlmann, Anthony. *Beckett and Poststructuralism*. Cambridge: Cambridge University Press, 1999.

7
beckett and homoeroticism

peter boxall

'Alone together so much shared'
Ohio Impromptu

Samuel Beckett's most famous play, *Waiting for Godot,* has an all-male
cast, and centers around two protagonists who appear to have shared
each others' lives for decades. They bicker, they embrace each other, they
depend upon each other. It has been suggested by many that they might
be thought of as a married couple. But critics have generally been slow
to reflect upon the possibility that there might be an erotic dimension
to their quasi-marital relationship, even despite Vladimir's claim, in
the opening moments of the play, that he has a tendency to 'go all
queer.'[1] In what could be thought of as an extraordinary demonstration
of mass denial, Beckett studies has worked under the assumption that
Vladimir and Estragon are just good friends. Like Holmes and Watson,
they may have breakfast together, but in the critical imagination they
have remained resolutely straight. Masculinity in the play has most
often been read as a metonym for the human condition, and as a result
any homoerotic drives that may emerge from the play's depiction of a
loving male partnership are effaced by an insistence upon compulsory
heterosexuality. The relationship between man and man is allowed to
stand in for a relationship between man and woman, and any transgressive,
subversive, or dissident erotics in the play are accordingly subsumed
under the figure of a normative humanity. Vivian Mercier's 1977 work
Beckett/Beckett is an example of such a general refusal of homoeroticism
in Beckett's writing. He suggests that Beckett's universalism both belies
and rests upon a number of structuring oppositions – between Ireland
and the world, gentleman and tramp, artist and philosopher, even woman

110

and man.[2] But the opposition (if it is one) between gay and straight gets not so much as a mention. Heterosexuality is a condition that does not admit of contradiction.

As Beckett studies has evolved, along with wider trends in literary criticism, critics have become less insistent upon the capacity for Beckett's work to incorporate difference into an overarching universalism, and more inclined to view his writing as engaging in various forms of identity politics. The consensus which dictated that masculinity in Beckett's drama should be read merely as shorthand for our general condition has been challenged by those critics who prefer to think of him as offering a critique of the cultural and textual mechanics by which gender is produced, along with other markers of identity such as race and (less often) class. The sudden proliferation and diversification of approaches to Beckett's writing in the late 1980s led to a reassessment of his relationship particularly with women and with Irish politics, and the work that this reassessment continues to produce has been amongst the more influential that has appeared in the last decade.[3] Despite this increasing flexibility in approaches to 'Beckettian man,' however, he remains more or less as straight as ever.

AnJanette Brush's contribution to the 2001 volume entitled *Beckett and the Political* offers an analysis of gender performativity in Beckett's prose, which illustrates the tenacity of Beckettian heterosexuality in the critical imagination. In her essay, entitled 'The Same Old Hag: Gender and (In)Difference in Samuel Beckett's Trilogy,' Brush suggests that a 'liberatory politics' might be found in the trilogy by tracing the ways in which the narrators and characters move 'out of and away from the confining logic' of the 'metanarratives' that produce gendered subjectivity.[4] The tendency of Beckett's characters, particularly in the trilogy, to disintegrate, and for the boundaries of their being to become blurred and porous, could be regarded as opening onto a radical, 'postmodern' contestation of subject positioning:

> As contemporary theoretical sensitivities call for the multiplication of sites of subjectivity, for the creation of varying and contestatory rather than normative identifications, Samuel Beckett's collapsing figures might be considered exemplary of just such a process.[5]

Her conclusion, however, contrary to a recent current in Beckett criticism which has been rather enthusiastic about the liberatory possibilities of his representation of feminine subjectivity, is that his writing is, in fact, held in place by gendered markers which resist such multiplication, slippage, or collapse. It may be that female identity in Beckett is in such flux that all his women can be regarded as 'the same old hag,' and it may be that the borders of Beckett's male characters are so weak as to produce moments of gender uncertainty even amongst the most hoarily masculine of his creations – Molloy prancing about in a lavender nightie during his stay at Lousse's house might be an example. But for Brush, what prevents Beckett's writing from producing a radical critique of gender performativity is its heterosexuality. Where critics such as Mary Bryden and Linda Ben-Zvi have been able to produce feminist readings of Beckett without seriously challenging assumptions about his representation of heterosexuality, Brush finds it difficult to separate his treatment of gender from his treatment of sexuality.[6] However hard one looks for it, she argues, and however uncertain other forms of identification become, it remains difficult to find a developed homoerotic in Beckett's writing. The free play of subject positions is closed down, and gendered identity is fixed in a normative position, by the heterosexual economy which persists in his writing. So, for Brush,

> One would certainly be hard-pressed to find evidence of a coherent character 'Molloy', but whether or not that which Adrienne Rich was first to term 'compulsory heterosexuality' is also missing is questionable. It is clear that Beckett has shaped a tremendously fragmented figure in Molloy – one split between mind and body, ambivalence and action. It is not quite as clear, however, whether his radical indifference to his sexual partners somehow signifies more than the fact that they are all nevertheless women, that these are in fact heterosexual encounters, encounters between a man whose voice is shifting and a woman whose name he shifts himself.[7]

Through her laudable refusal to join a trend which has given Beckett's gender and sexual politics the benefit of the doubt, then, Brush finds that Beckett's writing is shaped by a heterosexual male gaze that can't be argued away, that fixes gender in place, objectifies women, and that makes their bodies matter.

That Brush, along with the vast majority of other commentators, should find it so difficult to detect or articulate a Beckettian homoerotics is both mystifying and understandable. It is mystifying because of the sheer preponderance and centrality of homoerotic moments in Beckett's writing. I would argue, in fact, that it is difficult to think of many Beckett texts which are not driven, to some extent, by a homoerotic impulse. *The Calmative*, for example, turns around a highly sexualized encounter between the narrator and a dubious character with shining teeth, who offers the calmative of the title in return for a kiss. The mixture of the violent and the erotic in this encounter is both disturbing and comic:

> All of a sudden his hand came down on the back of my neck, his sinewy fingers closed and with a jerk and a twist he had me up against him. But instead of dispatching me he began to murmur words so sweet that I went limp and my head fell forward on his lap. Between the caressing voice and the fingers rowelling my neck the contrast was striking [...] And if you gave me a kiss, he said finally. I knew there were kisses in the air [...] Come, he said. I wiped my mouth in its tod of hair and advanced it towards his. [...] He took off his hat, a bowler, and tapped the middle of his forehead. There, he said, and there only. He had a noble brow, white and high. He leaned forward, closing his eyes. Quick, he said. I pursed my lips as my mother had taught me and brought them down where he had said.

This passage is a key moment in the story, a moment at which the erotic and spatial dynamics of the novella meet in a critical, epiphanal juncture. *The Calmative*, along with all of the four novellas, is concerned with finding one's place in a part-Dublinesque, part-Parisian landscape of memory. This landscape, in its extreme instability, is composed as much of an obscured semi-autobiographical geography as it is of a kind of network of sexual and aesthetic drives. It is studded with evocative symbols that place the land within a highly charged Beckettian psycho-sexual economy. The close of each of the novellas has the narrator trying to find his way around this sexual/geographical territory, attempting to navigate his way by reference to the stars, whose constellations his father had taught him (rather badly) to interpret.[8] The narrator's struggle to locate himself is a struggle to accommodate and negotiate the conflicting drives that produce the story, and that hold the landscape in its fragile and evocative shape. He is adrift in a country whose shifting contours are determined by a nostalgia for homeland, combined with a hateful rejection of homeland, combined with a longing for and fear of the protective spirit of the father, combined with a desire and disgust for the body of the mother. The above passage in *The Calmative* is one in which these desires and dreads come together, negotiated by and refracted through the desire and dread that the narrator feels for the gentle, violent stranger. The encounter between the narrator and the stranger is, in part, what the narrator had 'come out for.'[9] He is expelled from the peace and silence of an unwritten home, into an alienated and terrifying landscape composed of all the homes that have been written for him, and he subjects himself to the agony of this expulsion in order to put himself at the mercy of another. It is through the erotics of this encounter with the other that the narrator seeks to find a new home, to find a new relationality in which the conflicting needs and pathologies which produce the story might be worked through, and might open onto a new form of community or placedness. That this new community should be glimpsed through a *homo*erotics and, what is more, a homoerotics born from and wreathed about with violence and loathing, is not incidental. The narrator's desire is not indifferent to the stranger's gender, and the stranger's masculinity cannot be feminized. Rather, it is the homoerotics of this encounter that opens onto the possibility of a new kind of homeland for the narrator. The calmative that the stranger offers in return for the kiss, contained in a glittering phial which reappears time and again in Beckett's writing,[10] offers entry to the impossible territory of fulfilled desire, in which the narrator is finally 'sated with dark and calm.'[11] The homoerotic encounter offers a fleeting glimpse of a sexual relationality that can accommodate the various antagonisms which determine the narrator's social being.

Homoerotic desire is accorded this centrality, in various ways, throughout Beckett's oeuvre. *Watt*, for example, turns around the extraordinary relationship between Watt and Sam, where the novel's dictation, its very possibility, arises from the erotic encounter between the fences of their respective 'pavilions.'[12] Similarly, *How It Is* is entirely dominated by the slithery s/m erotics of Pim and his band of victims and tormentors who crawl through the mud prodding each other's anuses with can-openers. And *Ohio Impromptu* offers a compelling model of the homoerotics of reading and textual production. The centrality and preponderance of these moments might, as I have suggested, make the general refusal of a homoerotic Beckett seem rather mystifying. But it is also the very centrality of these encounters as I have described them, in all their force and violence and strangeness, that has made such a refusal understandable. Homoeroticism in Beckett isn't confined to a few transgressive encounters in an otherwise normative environment. Rather, it is everywhere in his writing. The eroticism produced by central male relationships bleeds out to color the entirety of his oeuvre, and it does so in such a way as to defy, or at least impede the attempt to understand it as a drive, an impulse, or a tendency. All of the ingredients that go to make up the characteristic Beckettian scenario – hatred of the body and of its functions, a gluttonous revelling in the body, resistance to forms of community, longing for community, longing for an impossible companionship, the persistence of companionship under straitened conditions, love for and hatred of the father and the mother, a generalized violent misanthropy and misogyny, a gently poignant nostalgia – are bound up with this central homoerotic. But because these things are routed so directly through an underlying gay economy, they can easily appear not to be homoerotic at all. Homoeroticism is such an important connecting and networking element in the Beckettian psychosexual complex, that it can become invisible, and can shade over into those features that have become standard attributes of a straight Beckett. Homoeroticism in *Godot*, for example, can be thought of as simply a form of brotherly companionship, and much of the love between men in Beckett can be thought of as evoking the love between father and son. The pleasure taken in the penis, and in erections and ejaculations, throughout Beckett's writing, might be thought of as evidence not of a homoerotic element in his writing, but of his misogynistic refusal of women, or his masturbatory refusal of the Other. And the grotesquely sexual figure of the mother looms so large that much of the dissident sexual energy that Beckett's oeuvre produces and contains can be thought of as stemming from an underlying failure to contain and navigate sexual drives which are nevertheless heterosexual.

Indeed, the terms in which AnJanette Brush rejects the possibility of a queer economy in the trilogy illustrate with some clarity both the prevalence of homoerotic moments in the novels, and the tendency for such moments to be re-read and re-routed into a heterosexual interpretive framework. So she quotes the passage in *Malone Dies* where Malone becomes embroiled in a lurid fantasy about his penis: 'I mean the tube itself, and in particular the nozzle, from which when I was yet a virgin clouts and gouts of sperm came streaming and splashing up into my face.'[13] But in doing so she demonstrates how this surplus homoerotic investment in the aesthetics and pornographics of ejaculation can be effaced by a reading strategy which approaches masturbatory fantasies in Beckett solely through his negotiation of the relations between men and women. Brush suggests, in reference to Malone's masturbatory habits, that 'some parts of the body become conceivable locations of pleasure precisely because they correspond to a normative ideal of a gender-specific body.'[14] For Brush it is Malone's straightness that leads him to privilege the phallus as a biological site of pleasure, and the joy taken in the ejaculating penis is located, by default, in a heterosexual matrix. Similarly, Brush plays down the uncertainty surrounding Molloy's sexuality, insisting that his potential homosexuality is really just another form of heterosexuality. Molloy's recounting of his one experience of 'true love,' however you look at it, does betray a confusion or a vacillation about his sexual preference. His narration of his brush with erotic delight demonstrates such confusion at the outset:

> Was such an encounter possible, I mean between me and a woman? Now men, I have rubbed up against a few men in my time, but women? Oh well, I may as well confess it now, yes, I once rubbed up against one. I don't mean my mother, I did more than rub up against her. And if you don't mind we'll leave my mother out of this.[15]

This opening to Molloy's relation might suggest that he defaults to a gay rather than a straight sexuality, finding it more natural, as he does, to 'rub up' against men rather than women. The decision nevertheless to tell the story in terms of a straight encounter seems to be mediated, to some extent, by the figure of the mother, who looms here, both inviting sexual attention to her own physicality and, perhaps, directing Molloy's sexual energies towards an appropriate sexual object. As the story opens, then, we have uncertainty both about Molloy's object choice, and about the status of the mother either as an object herself of transgressive (and fiercely repressed) sexual desire, or as a lawmaker who enforces Molloy's heterosexuality. As the story continues, these uncertainties and transgressions only deepen. When Molloy comes to describe the act itself, he evinces surprise at the nature of Ruth's or Edith's (he forgets the name) anatomy. She had, he says, a 'hole between her legs, oh not the bunghole I had always imagined, but a slit, and in this I put, or rather she put, my so-called virile member.'[16] The suggestion is, then, that Molloy had 'always imagined' anal rather than vaginal sex, but the hand of Ruth or Edith seems to be directing him towards good, reproductive heterosexual practice. As the story continues further, however, Molloy allows himself to imagine that the encounter might have been anal after all:

> Perhaps after all she put me in her rectum. A matter of complete indifference to me, I needn't tell you. But is it true love, in the rectum? That's what bothers me sometimes. Have I ever known true love, after all?[17]

The extent to which we accept Molloy's claim that the difference between anus and vagina is a matter of complete indifference is perhaps key here. But however you read this disclaimer, and the attendant anxieties about whether love in the rectum can be considered 'true,' it is unmistakably the case that the story is progressing away from normativity towards transgression, beneath the simultaneously admonitory and concupiscent gaze of the mother which Molloy is so anxious to evade. It comes as no surprise, then, that as we reach the climax of the narration, the original uncertainty about the gender of Molloy's belle/beau should return:

> She [...] was an eminently flat woman and she moved with short stiff steps, leaning on an ebony stick. Perhaps she too was a man, yet another of them. But in that case surely our testicles would have collided, while we writhed. Perhaps she held hers tight in her hand, on purpose to avoid it.[18]

This story, then, is composed of a number of erotic elements, which jostle against each other in a way that is both comic and dangerous. The tension, itself erotic, between a transgressive heterosexuality and a (perhaps fantasized) homosexuality is played out in the shadow of the sexualized figure of the oedipal mother. All in all, this constitutes quite a heady sexual brew. But Brush's approach to this passage is guided by a tendency to close down, and to normalize the multiple sexual transgressions that are at work here. For Brush, Ruth or Edith's masculinity is easily accommodated within an overarching femininity. The extra set of testicles that intrude into Molloy's writhings lose their power to sexualize and genderize Molloy's loved one, because the testicles are said by the narrator to be 'hers.' The structural tension that is set up by the phrase 'her testicles' is resolved by Brush in favor of the 'her.' Brush insists that the 'multiple confusions/blurrings' that are on display in the passage 'take place only within the figure of *her*.'[19] This leads Brush to suggest that the femininity of Edith or Ruth, and the heteronormativity that such femininity would guarantee, is privileged over, and works to erase, all of the other sexual and erotic possibilities that are contained in the passage. The heterosexual framework within which Beckett has almost always been read, and which determines so many of the political and critical formulae within which he has been understood, leads to a willed repression of such homoerotic possibilities.

A queer reading of Beckett's writing, in opposition to this kind of heteronormative reading, might open up some of those possibilities which have until now been closed to us. It might work to shift the centre of gravity of his reception, so that the network of homoerotic signification that lies at the heart of his writing is allowed to come into view. And this work of rebalancing may in turn open the way to a new homosociality or community in Beckett's writing, a new way, as Beckett puts it in 'The Capital of the Ruins,' of 'being we.'[20] The question that Molloy asks himself in the above passage – is it 'true love, in the rectum' – is one that even the supremely indifferent Molloy admits 'bothers [him] sometimes.' But the heterosexual model that relies upon Beckettian indifference to sexuality (an indifference which produces normative sexuality by default) has not allowed us to attempt a response. Can the love that is posited, for example, in *First Love*, a love which it would be more conventional to regard as either the narrator's misogynistic love for Lulu/Anna, or his patriarchal love for the 'great disembodied wisdom' of the father, be found, instead, in the rectum?[21] Is there a way of discovering a new relationality in Beckett's writing, a new mode of connectedness and desirousness, that would open onto a form of community or spatial politics that has not so far been imagined? And could the rectum, as a site of transgressive sexuality and a site of homoerotic desire, be the portal to such a new relationality? Has Beckett studies been blind to the dangers, pointed out as it happens by Molloy himself, of 'underestimating' the arse-hole? Molloy's brief paean to the anus might point to some of the possibilities and difficulties of such an inquiry:

> Perhaps it is less to be thought of as the eyesore here called by its name than as the symbol of those passed over in silence, a distinction due perhaps to its centrality and its air of being a link between me and the other excrement. We underestimate this little hole, it seems to me, we call it the arse-hole and affect to despise it. But is it not rather the true portal of our being and the celebrated mouth no more than the kitchen-door. Nothing goes in, or so little, that is not rejected on the spot, or very nearly. Almost everything revolts it that comes from without and what comes from within doesn't seem to receive a very warm welcome either.[22]

The rectum emerges, in this comic ode, as a site of silence and anticommunality as much as, if not more than, a site of eroticism or new relationality. It is a symbol 'of those passed over in silence,' and what seems most to endear it to Molloy is its function as a bar to connectedness, rather than as anything that opens up new channels of communication.

It is preferred to the mouth partly because, unlike the mouth, it doesn't speak, and it is congratulated most warmly for its capacity to reject and to revolt (although it remains unclear what 'little' goes into it that it might *not* reject). But despite this emphasis on its excretionary muteness, it is nevertheless heralded as a portal and as a link between one's being and the rest of the world. In fact, it is directly through such muteness that the anus acquires its function as portal. This combination of inarticulate resistance to communality with the production of a new channel of communication, however playfully intended here, is suggestive for an understanding of the ways in which a new queer territory might be envisaged in Beckett's writing. Leo Bersani has suggested that 'the most politically disruptive aspect' of what he describes as the 'homoness' in gay desire is 'a redefinition of sociality so radical that it may appear to require a provisional withdrawal from relationality itself.'[23] His analysis of homoness turns around the possibility that it points towards an 'anticommunal mode of connectedness,' a mode of connectedness which remains scarcely articulable because its contours do not match the 'already constituted communities' within which we currently live.[24] A reading of Beckett that is able to approach the homoerotic connectedness that is implied in the 'link' that the rectum establishes between 'me and the other excrement' might discover a new way of understanding the politics of Beckett's violent antisociality, as well as of his movement towards silence. It might provide a map of a psychosexual and political geography, in which silence and aggressive anti-communitarianism open onto the space of a community whose political and erotic contours are unimaginable from the perspective of a compulsory heterosexuality.

In his essay 'Sociality and Sexuality,' Bersani briefly sketches the possibility that Beckett's writing could suggest the outlines of a 'new relational mode.'[25] For Bersani, a theoretical model which would be able to account for the relational possibilities figured in homoerotic desire would have to look elsewhere than the existing model offered by psychoanalysis. This is because psychoanalytic formulations of sexuality turn around absence or lack as the propelling motor of desire. Bersani suggests that 'psychoanalysis has conceptualised desire as the mistaken reaction to a loss; it has been unable to think desire as the confirmation of a community of being.'[26] The understanding of desire that emerges from psychoanalysis is one which necessarily grounds desire in alienation, loss and self-immolation; but homoerotic desire points towards a form of relationality that might be grounded not in lack, but in self extension. It suggests the 'possibility of love, or desire, as including within itself its object.'[27] As he argues in *Homos*, it may be that 'desire for the same can free us from an oppressive psychology of desire as lack (a psychology that grounds sociality in trauma and castration).'[28] A theory of homoness, Bersani speculates, could lead towards a notion of difference 'not as a trauma to be overcome (a view that, among other things, nourishes antagonistic relations between the sexes), but rather as a nonthreatening supplement to sameness.'[29] This sketch of homoerotic desire as that which embraces rather than rejects the Other, and which as a result opens up loving rather than antagonistic relations (opposite as well as same sex), seems rather far removed from the relations imagined in Beckett's sometimes viciously misanthropic writing. But Bersani implies that it is Beckett's anti-communitarian impulses that help to excavate the ground of such a relationality. All art, for Bersani, 'celebrates an originating extensibility of all objects and creatures into space.'[30] Art is the 'principle site/sight (both place and view) of being as emergence into connectedness.'[31] It is in the art work that the fact of our existence in relation to one another, and in relation to our surroundings, is both acknowledged and celebrated. If this is accepted, then, it is in those artworks which strip relationality back to its barest forms (Beckett, Rothko, Resnais) that this fundamental, emergent connectedness can best be approached.[32] It is Beckett's refusal to accept existing forms of community, despite all of the comically bitter residues that such a refusal leaves, that allows him to 'go back,' to approach an original emergence into community:

> The Beckettian narrator goes back to a place where he never was as the only way to account for his being anywhere, for it was from 'there' that he was summoned into relations, called up from the immobility of perfect self-adequation to be displaced within a language that, before meaning anything, operates as a directional motor, an agent of spatial dispersion.[33]

So, in this model, the language of Beckett's texts both offers a route back to a perfect self-adequation, and propels the self away from such a condition of sameness with its environment. Language itself, as a mode of expression which opens up a reflective distance between the self and the world, necessarily drives the narrator away from his utopian haven of self-adequation. Indeed, the ways in which language drives a wedge between the self and its perfect home have been agonizingly depicted in the plight of Beckett's non-character Worm.[34] But Bersani suggests that

Beckett's use of language enables him to live through the dispersing and alienating effects of language, whilst simultaneously finding in language a way to return to a self-adequacy that is immune to the distancing effects of desire or of speech. And for Bersani, this route back to an unbroken connectedness between self and not-self is found through the mechanics of homoerotic desire.

This reading of art, and Beckett's art in particular, as offering entry to a kind of homo-community, a space that is undivided by the action of language or loss, may seem a little starry eyed and, indeed, Bersani has elsewhere been more skeptical about the capacity for Beckett's writing to open onto a prelinguistic space of self-adequation.[35] But the model which reads Beckett's language as both a vehicle for loss of self and a route back towards homoerotic connectedness suggests some powerful ways of thinking about the relation between homoeroticism and community in his oeuvre. The passage from *The Calmative* quoted above can be seen to conform to this model of reading. If Beckett's language is a motor of spatial dispersion, then the space into which the narrator is being ejected is the *unheimlich* landscape of the novellas, alienated, surreal, sliced up as in a nightmarish montage. But the direction of the novella is also towards what the Beckett narrator has described as his 'true home.'[36] As the story balances between these two spatial matrices, it is the kiss of the cruising stranger that acts as the alternator, switching us from language as dispersion, to language as the path towards a kind of homo-coital calm, in which erotic love for the stranger and spiritual love for the father are allowed to meet in a communal space which is not riven by oedipal injunctions or disfigured by lack. And the spatial erotics that are worked through in the novellas are only the blueprint of a territory that Beckett builds upon, elaborates, and hones, throughout the rest of his writing career. Through the middle and late prose, and throughout the drama, a homoerotic register is at work, the elaboration of which might enable us to recalibrate the relative values of silence and community, and to approach, in a new critical spirit, the bi-directional movement in Beckett both away from and towards connectedness.

It is perhaps in the novels of the trilogy that the spatial-erotic politics that can be glimpsed in outline in the novellas is most fully and most painstakingly worked through. The novels are choreographed, both individually and as a series, in accordance with an economy of repetition, a persistent re-emergence of the same. This economy is in turn organized around the possibility of glimpsing, through the hostile, barren landscapes that proliferate in the novels, an original Beckett country which the narrator has never left. This repetitive structure is present, as Steven Connor has persuasively demonstrated,[37] at almost every point in the trilogy, so it is possible to draw examples at random from the text.

An instance which, as it happens, draws upon the stellar motif already established in the novellas, occurs at the beginning of *Molloy*. The narrator, describing the barren ground across which the lonely wayfarers A and C wander, slips into a gently lyrical mode, evoking the 'wild straining' of his soul both towards the strangers, and towards the landscape itself, which he invests with a Friedrich-esque beauty. As part of his panoramic description of the view towards which his spirit leaps out, 'as if on elastic,' the narrator turns first to the land which comes into view in a 'sharpening line of crests,' and then to the evening sky where, 'without seeing them I felt the first stars tremble.'[38] This sense of straining towards a beauty or a possibility that is intuited, but which lies hidden behind a barrier or a veil, is a recurrent motif in Beckett's writing.[39] Indeed, the simultaneously melancholy and fervent desire that the narrator feels for A and C itself evokes the sense of a frustrated grasping after a trembling, fragile possibility that remains unrealized. But as the lyrical passage continues, things take a slightly stranger turn. The narrator says that he feels this same spiritual pull 'towards my hand also, which my knee felt tremble and of which my eyes saw the wrist only, the heavily veined back, the pallid row of knuckles.'[40] This shifting of the narrator's desirous gaze, from the strangers and the landscape to his own hand, immediately throws into confusion the romantic mode in which the passage has up to now been working. We are no longer dealing here with a self-identical subject who looks longingly upon a landscape which remains separate from him. Rather, the body in which the narrative voice is lodged becomes, itself, part of the scenery to which the narrator feels drawn, and from which he feels himself divorced. And the key moment in this rearrangement in perspective comes with the repetition of the word 'trembling.' The stars tremble, hidden but divined behind the 'taut skin'[41] of the sky; the narrator's hand trembles, lying on his lap. The trembling of the hand is registered, like that of the stars, through a kind of highly tuned narrative sensibility, rather than through any sense that the hand belongs to the narrator, that the trembling is his own trembling. His eyes, the narrator says, could not see his hand. It was his knee that felt the hand tremble, that empathized with the hand's 'nervous act of life.'[42] But in the newly arranged relationality between narrator, landscape, and body, it is difficult to imagine how far the narrator's knee, which registers the trembling hand, can be regarded as *his* knee. Nor, for that matter, is it clear how far the narrator's eyes, which could have viewed the hand directly and obviated the need for any intuitive grasping after the hand's trembling essence, can be thought of as *his* eyes. And as the repetition of the act of trembling causes relations to become displaced, another economy of repetition between narrator and landscape comes into view. The hand itself bleeds over to become part of the landscape in which Molloy finds himself marooned. The heavily veined back becomes suggestive of the land scored by roads along which the strangers walk, clothed in the beauty of their strangeness and their difference from Molloy; and the pallid row of knuckles becomes the 'line of crests' receding into the distance, over which the road takes the strangers, the rises and falls of which hide them from each other's view. Through this rather delicate set of adjustments to perspective and positionality, a hole opens up in the land and in the text, through which the narrative voice itself threatens to leak. Hands, eyes, and knees join with strangers, land and sky, and the voice itself, coming from nowhere, slips beyond the horizons of the scene. The network of relations between men dispersed in space, towards which the narrator strains with a wild desire, moves beyond the grasp of the narrative through the action and recounting of the desire itself.

This bleeding together of the material of the text, to produce an unbroken continuity between landscape, character, and narrator as character, occurs both locally, and across body of the text and of the oeuvre. Indeed, this opening scene of *Molloy*, in which Molloy cowers in the shadow of a rock, lusting after A and C, repeats and reverberates through *Molloy*, and through the rest of the trilogy. An example of such a reemergence of the A and C scenario occurs in the passage already quoted, in which Molloy describes his affair with Ruth or Edith. Towards the end of the A and C passage, Molloy comments that 'I must have been on the top, or on the slopes, of some considerable eminence, for otherwise how could I have seen, so far away, so near at hand, so far beneath, so many things, fixed and moving.'[43] This necessity for Molloy to have been elevated in order to witness the strangers' activities bothers him, however, because he has cast the landscape, up to this point, as a flat, empty desert space. He asks himself, with the ingenuous anxiety that things should hang together so characteristic of Beckett's narrators, what an 'eminence' was doing 'in this land with hardly a ripple.'[44] In some ways, this attention to the physical mechanics of observation inaugurates a new geographical diversity in the novel. Molloy admits that he must have been high up to see the landscape clearly, and this admission brings an end to the skeletal scene of A and C's journeying across empty space and opens the account of Molloy's own journeying through a more richly realized, Dublinesque city space. But Molloy's concession to narrative credibility, along with the growth of a diverse and coherent storyscape that such a concession enables, is partly undermined by its morphed reappearance later in the novel. As Molloy is recounting his brush with Ruth or Edith, forty pages later, he describes her as an 'eminently flat woman.'[45] This point in the Ruth or Edith episode is an important one because, as I have already suggested, it marks the beginning of her gender transformation, and hastens the movement of the passage towards its underlying and forbidden homoeroticism. But the capacity of the phrase 'eminently flat' to describe Ruth or Edith's anatomy, and in turn to suggest her masculinity, is compromised by the ghostly reappearance of the A and C landscape effected by the trace repetition of eminence and flatness. The comic contradiction between flatness and eminence which plays briefly in the description draws more emphasis from this overlaying: Ruth or Edith's body is laid over the land with scarcely a ripple across which A and C walk; the eminence which constitutes both Molloy's vantage point and Ruth or Edith's breasts is eroded by the partial breakdown in mimesis consequent on this repetition; and the erotics at work in the wild straining after both Ruth or Edith and A or C are cancelled out by the flattening of the textual surface, the collapse of detail and difference into a murky and barren sameness. As the details of the text blur together, as the diverse scenery of the novel collapses into what Estragon describes as the undifferentiated 'muckheap' of the 'Cackon country,'[46] then the tendency is for the narrator to lose any purchase in the landscape, to fall away and out of the scene. If the rectum, in Molloy's figuration, offers a way of mediating and corresponding between 'me and the other excrement,' then the collapse of distinctions which the persistent reemergence the of the same brings about can work to eradicate the possibility of such correspondence. 'Me' becomes both indistinguishable from the cacky muckheap, and too distant or removed from it to achieve any kind access to it.

This structural repetition, and the structural collapse that it brings about, occurs, in much more obvious ways, throughout the trilogy. The objects, such as the sawing horse and the lacquer tray, that crop up in Molloy's, Moran's, and possibly Malone's narratives, the reemergence of Molloy as Moll, the repetition of the letter M as surname initial throughout, the snowballing repetition of Beckett's own litany of characters as the trilogy progresses, are just some of the better recognized of these. If, to return to Bersani's snapshot description of the oeuvre quoted above, Beckett's narratives are composed both of a 'going back' to an original point, and a dispersal in an alienated landscape, then this structural collapse might suggest that such a bi-directional movement springs from and results in a loss of connectedness. The narrator who is ejected from the landscape of sameness returns to silence and absence, whilst the landscape that he cannot inhabit or penetrate falls into barrenness and meaninglessness. This, indeed, has been the assumption that has laid at the foundation of Beckett's reception. But it may be that a reading of Beckett's work that is alive to its homoerotic mechanics might find that there is a different form of connectedness at work, a form of relationality that survives the cleaving between narrator and text that has always returned the narrative voice to antisociality and silence. The homoerotic straining towards connectedness that imbues the A and C scenario, and in manifold ways permeates the entire oeuvre, might be salvaged from the normative reading practice that has not allowed it as a possibility, by a reading that is itself guided by a homoerotic spirit. The sameness that threatens the diversity and mimetic security of Beckett's landscapes, and that threatens to eject the narrative voice from relationality to a silent exile that remains beyond the boundaries of the text, might reveal a new kind of erotics when viewed under a queer optic. The tendency for difference to collapse into sameness may point towards a form of narrative desire that can 'include within itself its object,' rather than towards a desire that is structured around loss, or lack.

Malone Dies, as the middle installment of the trilogy, exhibits with great clarity both the tendency for the narrator to slide beyond the boundaries of the text, and the opposite tendency for the text to absorb the voice into its repetitive matrix. The trilogy as a whole moves towards an increasingly bald depiction of a scenario in which an unnamable narrative voice shelters behind the masks of its creatures, in order to make itself heard whilst remaining silent. As the novels progress, this unnamable voice, 'howling behind my dissertation,'[47] becomes increasingly intrusive, and increasingly destructive of the fictional geographies it partly inhabits. So in *Molloy* we are presented with landscapes and narrators who hang together with a certain resilience. Beneath the surface of the Turdy and Bally landscapes, and the Molloy and Moran narratives, it is possible to intuit the restless trembling of the unnamed narrator, waiting for his time to come, but the fictional world of the novel nevertheless remains able to withstand the corrosive effects of his underlying influence. But by the time we have reached *The Unnamable*, any mimetic coherence that the earlier novels might have had has eroded away. Molloy, Moran, Malone, Murphy, Mercier, Watt, all these characters are cast as merely 'vice-existers' for the unnamable narrative voice, the narrator who lives in an original silence and nothingness, and who cannot be revealed.[48] All of the landscapes, the characters, the houses, buildings, seascapes, and skyscapes, are deemed, by the time of *The Unnamable*, to be fashioned from the same muck, repuked puke puked from the mouthless mouth of the absent narrator.[49] The novel oscillates agonizingly, perpetually on the brink of an impossible revelation, living in the impossible moment of the separation between the narrator and the voices that allow him to speak. It is in *Malone Dies* that the transition between these two states is articulated with the utmost poetic delicacy. Malone holds together as voice and body and presence in a way that the surreally displaced, partial figure of the Unnamable simply doesn't. But the unnamed narrative voice stirs behind the surface of Malone's narrative with a force and a persistence that is not found in *Molloy*. *Malone Dies*, seen in a certain light, is the story of a kind of gradual poetic occupation. What is perhaps most surprising about this military incursion into the Malone province, however, is that it generates both a fierce antagonism, and an extraordinarily poignant love. Malone fights against his occupying force, defending as he has to the boundaries of his own being. But he also finds, in the narrative force that is invading him, another way of becoming himself. In a passage that is reminiscent of the love between Vladimir and Estragon, Malone suggests that the tender love that he feels for his invader might lead him towards his true home; that his intention in becoming himself is really to become this other who inhabits him, and who comes to him from Bersani's 'place where he never was':

> What I sought, when I struggled out of my hole, then aloft through the stinging air towards an inaccessible boon, was the rapture of vertigo, the letting go, the fall, the gulf, the relapse to darkness, to nothingness, to earnestness, to home, to him waiting for me always, who needed me and whom I needed, who took me in his arms and told me to stay with him always, who gave me his place and watched over me, who suffered every time I left him, whom I have often made suffer and seldom contented, whom I have never seen.[50]

In this passage, the voice which speaks from nowhere and nothingness, and which lives in the poetic emptiness of a complete and original self-adequation, is offering an embrace to Malone, an embrace which suggests an intimate and tender connection between Malone's spatially dispersed being, and a form of unseen being which has not yet been 'summoned into relations.' And perhaps unsurprisingly, where we find such a powerful homosocial love, we also find a simultaneously violent and tender homoeroticism. As Malone attempts to describe his sense of occupation, his sense that he is a mannekin in a long series of mannekins who are controlled by a superior narrating being, the eroticism of this relation is palpable:

> I must say that to me at least and for as long as I can remember the sensation is familiar of a blind and tired hand delving feebly in my particles and letting them trickle between its fingers. And sometimes, when all is quiet, I feel it plunged in me up to the elbow, but gentle, as though sleeping. But soon it stirs, wakes, fondles, clutches, ransacks, ravages, avenging its failure to scatter me with one sweep.[51]

If Malone is a puppet here, then the unnamed narrator is the fisting hand of the puppeteer, plunged invasively, erotically, and lovingly in Malone's body. If Molloy conceives of the rectum as a link between the self and the world, then here the rectum is the site of poetic occupation. The hand both fondles and ravages, it reassures and destroys. There is a pleasure and a masochistic delight in the hand's plunge; Malone accepts with a kind of joy both its destructiveness, its intention to annihilate him, and its capacity to confirm his being, its capacity to animate him. As with Donne's Divine Meditation 'Batter my heart, three-personed God,' this is a homoerotic rape fantasy, a call to be occupied, to be broken, blown, burned, and made anew.[52] It is a call to be usurped, in order to be transformed into that which you already are, to be filled with your own spirit.

A reading which can gain access to this homoerotic link between the narrator who is 'plunged beyond recall'[53] into the spatially dispersed world of the novels, and the narrator who remains harboured in the darkness and nothingness of a true home, could transform the ways in Beckett's treatment of relationality and community have been understood. The repetitive networks which have led to the collapse of relations in Beckett, and which have taken the narrator back to silence, solipsism, and solitude, can be rearranged, through this reading, to open on to the site of a new community. The reemergence of the same, the reiteration of objects, of landscapes and seascapes, the over-investment in particular moments and places and features, is recalibrated by the terms of this homoerotic attachment. Those Beckettian features that pepper the landscape of *The Calmative*, and that reemerge time and time again throughout the trilogy and after, are welcomed into a new, unalienated geography, through this homoerotic. A landscape can be glimpsed, through the simultaneously violent and loving relation between Malone and the narrative spirit that inhabits him, that is composed both of otherness and of sameness, that is both alien to the narrator, and fundamentally a part of him, a landscape in which solitude and togetherness might be shared.

As the conditional mood of much of this essay might suggest, however, such a reading is still some way beyond our grasp. The community that a queer reading of Beckett might glimpse trembles still, like Molloy's stars, beyond the horizon of possibility. In fact, it is to Beckett's own writing that we might turn for a dramatization of the conditions of possibility that determine such a reading. As the Reader and Listener of *Ohio Impromptu* sit facing each other, in the gloaming both of their relationship and of Beckett's writing career, the play performs at once the possibility and the continuing impossibility of a reading that opens onto an undivided, homoerotic community. The Reader in *Ohio Impromptu* brings book and text to the Listener, who has been cast out 'to where nothing ever shared,' to a Parisian-Beckettian geography of exile.[54] The book, as well as providing the script of the play itself, contains the 'unspoken words' of the Listener's loved one, of a narrator figure who lives still in that haven of self-adequation where he and the Listener were so long 'alone together,' and between whom so much was shared.[55] The Listener, marooned on the left bank of the Seine, overlooking the 'extremity of the Isle of Swans,'[56] lives a life divorced from the dear name, and the dear face, of the loved one. But the act of reading, the performance of the text and of the play that has been smuggled over the boundary by the Reader, allows, briefly, for the unspoken words to be heard again, the dear face to be once more seen. The play itself, contained in the unspoken words that emanate from the Listener's true home, opens up a passage to this undivided country. As the Isle of Swans divides the Seine, so exile divides Listener from his unnamed partner; but the words read by Reader offer an image of confluence. At the 'tip' of the islet, the Reader tells the Listener, the Listener 'would always pause to dwell on the receding stream. How in joyous eddies its two arms conflowed and flowed united on.'[57]

The performance of the play itself, in its ephemeral brevity, offers a fleeting possibility of this liquid confluence, this joyously erotic commingling. But, powerful as this collapse of difference into sameness is, the focus of the play is on the recedence of this possibility. The knocking of the Listener's hand on the table, a bathetic wooden contact which itself contrasts so starkly with the streamy interweaving of the Seine, is the only control Listener has over Reader. The knocking causes the Reader to slow down, to recap, to go over. As the play comes to a close, though, as the source of the unspoken words dries up, this knocking becomes a vain and painful entreaty, a poignant and impotent protest against the material and textual conditions which have stranded the Listener by his islet, and seated him, like so many of Beckett's writing figures, at a deal table. For Reader, Listener, and audience alike, the space of an abandoned homoerotic confluence remains as a trembling possibility that is circumscribed by the prevailing, heteronormative modes of reading, of writing, and of production.

notes

1. Samuel Beckett, *Waiting for Godot*, in Samuel Beckett, *Complete Dramatic Works* (London: Faber and Faber, 1986), 11.
2. See Vivian Mercier, *Beckett/Beckett* (Oxford: Oxford University Press, 1977).
3. See, for example, David Lloyd, 'Writing in the Shit: Beckett, Nationalism and the Colonial Subject,' in David Lloyd, *Anomalous States* (Dublin: The Lilliput Press, 1993), 41–58; Declan Kiberd, 'Religious Writing: Beckett and Others,' and 'Beckett's Texts of Laughter and Forgetting,' in Declan Kiberd, *Inventing Ireland: the Literature of the Modern Nation* (London: Vintage, 1996), 454–67, 530–50, and Mary Bryden, *Women in Samuel Beckett's Prose and Drama* (London: Macmillan – now Palgrave Macmillan, 1993).
4. AnJanette Brush, 'The Same Old Hag: Gender and (In)Difference in Samuel Beckett's Trilogy,' in Henry Sussman and Christopher Devenney (eds), *Engagement and Indifference: Beckett and the Political* (New York: State University of New York Press, 2001), 127.
5. Brush, 'The Same Old Hag,' 127–8.
6. See the collection edited by Linda Ben-Zvi, *Women in Beckett: Performance and Critical Perspectives* (Urbana: University of Illinois Press, 1992), and Bryden, *Women in Samuel Beckett's Prose and Drama*.
7. Brush, 'The Same Old Hag,' 134–5.
8. See Samuel Beckett, *First Love*, 30, Samuel Beckett, *The Expelled*, 47, and Samuel Beckett, *The End*, 93, in Samuel Beckett, *The Expelled and Other Novellas* (1977; Harmondsworth: Penguin, 1980). For a reading of the Dublin and Parisian elements in the *Novellas*, as part of a geography of memory, see Peter Boxall, ' "The Existence I Ascribe": Memory, Invention and Autobiography in Beckett's Fiction,' *The Yearbook of English Studies* (2000).
9. Beckett, *The Calmative*, 67.
10. See, for example, Beckett, *The End*, 82, where the narrator finds 'a phial in my pocket.'
11. Beckett, *The Calmative*, 67.

12. See Samuel Beckett, *Watt* (1953; London: Calder, 1976), 160–1.
13. Samuel Beckett, *Malone Dies*, in Samuel Beckett, *Molloy, Malone Dies, The Unnamable* (1955; 1956; 1959; London: Calder, 1994), 235.
14. Brush, 'The Same Old Hag,' 134.
15. Samuel Beckett, *Molloy*, in Beckett, *Molloy, Malone Dies, The Unnamable*, 56.
16. Beckett, *Molloy*, 56.
17. Beckett, *Molloy*, 57.
18. Beckett, *Molloy*, 57.
19. Brush, 'The Same Old Hag,' 133.
20. Samuel Beckett, 'The Capital of the Ruins,' in Samuel Beckett, *The Complete Short Prose, 1929–1889* (New York: Grove Press, 1995), 277. For an excellent unpacking of the cultural and communitarian implications of the phrase 'way of being we,' see Daniel Katz, *Saying I No More: Subjectivity and Consciousness in the Prose of Samuel Beckett* (Illinois: Northwestern University Press, 1999), 46–8.
21. Beckett, *First Love*, 13.
22. Beckett, *Molloy*, 79–80.
23. Leo Bersani, *Homos* (Cambridge: Harvard University Press, 1995), 7.
24. Bersani, *Homos*, 10.
25. See Leo Bersani, 'Sociality and Sexuality,' in *Critical Inquiry* (Summer 2000), 641, where Bersani draws on Foucault's use of the expression 'new relational modes.'
26. Bersani, 'Sociality and Sexuality,' 644.
27. Bersani, 'Sociality and Sexuality,' 651.
28. Bersani, *Homos*, 7.
29. Bersani, *Homos*, 7.
30. Bersani, 'Sociality and Sexuality,' 643.
31. Bersani, 'Sociality and Sexuality,' 643.
32. See Leo Bersani and Ulysse Dutoit, *Arts of Impoverishment: Beckett, Rothko, Resnais* (Cambridge: Harvard University Press, 1993).
33. Bersani, 'Sociality and Sexuality,' 643.
34. See Samuel Beckett, *The Unnamable*, in Beckett, *Molloy, Malone Dies, The Unnamable*, 351, where the narrator struggles to invoke Worm, without going through the alienating process of naming him as such. As soon as Worm is named, the narrator accedes, 'Then it's the end. Worm no longer is. We know it, but we don't say it, we say it's the awakening, the beginning of Worm, for now we must speak, and speak of Worm. It's no longer he, but let us proceed as if it were still he.'
35. See Bersani and Dutoit, *Arts of Impoverishment*, 51, where the authors suggest that '*Molloy* and *The Unnamable*, for all their magnificent originality and complexity, are perhaps somewhat naïve in their assumptions about the sympathy that literature can provide to a straightforward defense of prelinguistic essential being.'
36. See, for example, Samuel Beckett, *How It Is* (1964; London: Calder, 1996), 111.
37. See Steven Connor, *Samuel Beckett: Repetition, Theory and Text* (Oxford: Blackwell, 1988), particularly chapter 4, 64–87.
38. Beckett, *Molloy*, 11.

39. See Samuel Beckett, *Dream of Fair to Middling Women* (London: Calder, 1993), where the image of a rat scuffling on the other side of a wall is evoked repeatedly, to symbolize an ungraspable possibility. See, particularly, 16–17, where the fidgeting rat is used to demonstrate one of the more pompous theories of aesthetic production: 'The mind suddenly entombed, then active in anger and a rhapsody of energy, in a scurrying and plunging towards exitus, such is the ultimate mood and factor of the creative integrity, its proton, incommunicable; but there, insistent, invisible rat, fidgeting behind the astral incoherence of the art surface.'
40. Beckett, *Molloy*, 11.
41. See Beckett, *Dream*, 27.
42. Samuel Beckett, 'Dante and the Lobster,' in Samuel Beckett, *More Pricks than Kicks* (1934; London: Picador, 1974), 18.
43. Beckett, *Molloy*, 14.
44. Beckett, *Molloy*, 14.
45. Beckett, *Molloy*, 57.
46. Beckett, *Godot*, 56. Molloy himself builds on the muckheap analogy, opining that 'if all muck is the same muck that doesn't matter, it's good to have a change of muck, to move from one heap to another a little further on, from time to time,' Beckett, *Molloy*, 41.
47. Beckett, *The Unnamable*, 317.
48. Lists of Beckett characters, cast as puppets, mannekins, or vice-existers recur throughout *The Unnamable*. At one point, the unnamable narrator says 'I believe they are all here, at least from Murphy on.' Beckett, *The Unnamable*, 295.
49. See Beckett, *Watt*, 43.
50. Beckett, *Malone Dies*, 195.
51. Beckett, *Malone Dies*, 225.
52. See John Donne, *Divine Mediations*, 'Meditation 14,' in A. J. Smith, (ed.), *John Donne: the Complete English Poems* (Harmondsworth: Penguin, 1971), 314: 'Batter my heart, three-personed God; for you/ as yet but knock, breathe, shine, and seek to mend;/ That I may rise, and stand, o'erthrow me, and bend/ Your force, to break, blow, burn and make me new.'
53. Samuel Beckett, *Molloy*, 111.
54. Samuel Beckett, *Ohio Impromptu*, in Beckett, *Complete Dramatic Works*, 445.
55. Beckett, *Ohio Impromptu*, 446.
56. Beckett, *Ohio Impromptu*, 445. The Listener is exiled on an extremity, and he also finds himself in a personal, emotional extremity (446). This is a recurrent blurring in Beckett between landscape and state of mind. Victor Krap, for example, has a bedsit in the 'Impasse de L'Enfant Jésus,' and the play turns around the impasse in which Victor finds himself stuck. See Samuel Beckett, *Eleutheria* (London: Faber and Faber, 1996), trans. Barbara Wright, 8.
57. Beckett, *Ohio Impromptu*, 446.

works cited

Beckett, Samuel. *More Pricks than Kicks*. 1934; London: Picador, 1974.
—— *Watt*. 1953; London: Calder, 1976.

—— *Molloy, Malone Dies, The Unnamable*. 1955; 1956; 1959; London: Calder, 1994.

—— *How It Is*. 1964; London: Calder, 1996.

—— *The Expelled and Other Novellas*. 1977; Harmondsworth: Penguin, 1980.

—— *Complete Dramatic Works*. London: Faber and Faber, 1986.

—— *Dream of Fair to Middling Women*. London: Calder, 1993.

—— *The Complete Short Prose, 1929–1889*. New York: Grove Press, 1995.

—— *Eleutheria*, trans. Barbara Wright. London: Faber and Faber, 1996.

Ben-Zvi, Linda. *Women in Beckett: Performance and Critical Perspectives*. Urbana: University of Illinois Press, 1992.

Bersani, Leo. *Homos*. Cambridge: Harvard University Press, 1995.

—— 'Sociality and Sexuality,' *Critical Inquiry*, Summer 2000.

Bersani, Leo, and Dutoit, Ulysse. *Arts of Impoverishment: Beckett, Rothko, Resnais*. Cambridge: Harvard University Press, 1993.

Boxall, Peter. '"The Existence I Ascribe": Memory, Invention and Autobiography in Beckett's Fiction,' *The Yearbook of English Studies* (2000).

Brush, AnJanette. 'The Same Old Hag: Gender and (In)Difference in Samuel Beckett's Trilogy,' in Henry Sussman and Christopher Devenney (eds) *Engagement and Indifference: Beckett and the Political*. New York: State University of New York Press, 2001.

Bryden, Mary. *Women in Samuel Beckett's Prose and Drama*. London: Macmillan – now Palgrave Macmillan, 1993.

Connor, Steven. *Samuel Beckett: Repetition, Theory and Text*. Oxford: Blackwell, 1988.

Donne, John, ed. A. J. Smith. *John Donne: the Complete English Poems*. Harmondsworth: Penguin, 1971.

Katz, Daniel. *Saying I No More: Subjectivity and Consciousness in the Prose of Samuel Beckett*. Illinois: Northwestern University Press, 1999.

Kiberd, Declan. *Inventing Ireland: the Literature of the Modern Nation*. London: Vintage, 1996.

Lloyd, David. *Anomalous States*. Dublin: The Lilliput Press, 1993.

Mercier, Vivian. *Beckett/Beckett*. Oxford: Oxford University Press, 1977.

8

biographical, textual, and historical origins

linda ben-zvi

'Body Worlds' is the title of one of the most shocking, controversial, and successful exhibits to be mounted in Europe in recent history, drawing over eight million people during its tour through Austria and Germany before moving on to England (Rapp 2002).[1] What has attracted the notoriety and the crowds are the 'objects' on display: twenty-five preserved human male and female corpses in various poses, and 150 body parts – torsos, heads, and limbs – all treated with a newly-developed process which replaces bodily fluids with a variety of hardening plastic substances that allows for a variety of body positioning. In the case of the most shocking display, entitled 'Suit of Skin,' a flayed male, his bones and blood vessels delineated in white and red plastic, stands upright looking at his raised left hand which holds the actual skin that covered his body. There is a slight smile on the man's face. Answering charges that such an exhibition is a desecration of the dead and a ghoulish, cynical attempt to provide a sated, contemporary society with yet another grotesque thrill, the inventor of the process and organizer of the exhibit, a professor at the Institute for Plastination at Heidelberg University, argues that his work is, in fact, a continuation of the long tradition of 'anatomical theatre' practiced for centuries by surgeons to gain further knowledge of the human body.

'Body Worlds' could serve as a powerful contemporary coda to Francis Barker's study *The Tremulous Private Body: Essays on Subjection*, which traces the ways in which conceptions of the body shifted in the seventeenth century, the body losing its place as a privileged site of subjectivity, becoming progressively more disguised, veiled, hidden, and subdued. Only when neutralized and no longer threatening was it reinscribed, in the name of science and progress, as an object of inquiry, a *thing* to be studied, dissected, manipulated, and displayed, like the man holding his 'body suit.' Barker's own example of 'anatomical theatre' is the 'Anatomy Lesson of Dr. Nicolaas Tulp,' preserved in Rembrandt's famous painting (Barker 1984, 73–112). In the canvas, as Barker points out, none of the seven black-clad men who have come to observe the dissection of the executed criminal, Aris Kint, look at the corpse. Instead, most concentrate their gazes on a point at the lower right-hand corner of the painting, presumably focusing on a text describing the dissection that the surgeon, Dr Tulp, is beginning to perform. The body is present – in fact it occupies the center of the composition practically touching the assembled observers – but it is no longer a fleshly body but rather an object, 'the anatomy of a conception'(96), explained and delineated on the pages of Tulp's medical manual, according to accepted categories, rather than apprehended where it lies before the assembled group. For Barker the painting is a clear example of the way in which the body in the seventeenth century underwent a disappearing act, Hamlet's call for this 'too too sullied flesh' to 'melt/Thaw, and resolve itself into a dew' [I.ii.129–30] ... taken at his word'(12).

This dismissal and reinscription of the body follows the model of Descartes, who writes in the *Meditations*:

> I have a body to which I am very closely united, nevertheless, because, on the one hand, I have a clear and distinct idea of myself in so far as I am only a thinking and unextended thing, and because, on the other hand I have a distinct idea of the body in so far as it is only an extended thing but which does not think, it is certain that I, that is to say my mind, by which I am what I am, is entirely and truly distinct from my body, and may exist without it. (Descartes 1968, 156)

However, just as in 'The Anatomy Lesson' (which Barker claims Descartes may have attended while in Amsterdam), the body is not totally banished in Cartesian analysis; it can be reinstated as an object of study, a means by which knowledge of the body's workings can be gained, in an attempt to alleviate disease. This reinscribed body, like those on display in the 'Body Worlds' exhibit – also claimed as examples of medical progress – is one without flesh, a constructed body, no longer threatening. This new body, the positive, healthy body, is one that can be reintroduced as an element in the construction of a theory of self, as long as its corporeality and pain have been carefully stripped and drained.

i

There are no such pretty, healthy bodies in Beckett. Anyone reading his texts or seeing performances of his plays is immediately struck by his infirm, decrepit figures, who are, as Beckett described them, 'falling to bits' (Shenker 1979, 148). There is no attempt to beautify or idealize the body in Beckett, no airbrushing of flaws; on the contrary, his women and men are presented in all their fleshly imperfections. Few are young, most are incapacitated, and almost all are depicted in the process of physical decay, graphically played out and accelerated in the stories and theater works in which they appear, this decay a central theme Beckett returns to again and again. On most are the marks of some physical sort of physical ailment or illness. Watt suffers from poor healing skin; Camier has a cyst, Mercier a fistula; Belacqua, Molloy, Moran and assorted unnamed protagonists suffer from cramps, arthritis, corns, and lameness of legs and feet. Walking, a passion they share, is, therefore, particularly arduous. In order to move at all, characters usually resort to complex series of motions to propel them forward, including splayed feet and a bent or contorting trunk to bear the shocks of stiff limbs, or crutches and wheelchairs to see them on their way. In the later fiction, bodies in closed spaces proliferate: still cramped, crabbed with age, not even sure of their physical contours or conditions. In the plays, through the agency of the body of the live actor, the spectacle of decrepitude and contortion is visually repeated, the characters' infirmities, as actor Pierre Chabert puts it, becoming that 'lack' or limitation 'which gives the body its existence, its dramatic force and its reality as a working material for the stage,' since 'one's body exists all the more strongly when it begins to suffer'(Chabert 1982, 24). And there is plenty of suffering in the plays. Vladimir endures prostate problems, Estragon a weak left lung and sore, smelly feet, Pozzo goes blind, Lucky mute, Hamm is blind and confined to a wheelchair (his infirmities divided between A and B in *Rough for Theatre I*), Clov barely able to walk, and the 'wearish' Krapp is nearsighted, chronically constipated and hard of hearing. Even the most basic human functions – breathing, urinating, and defecating – are sources of great pain. Dan Rooney's question in *All That Fall*, 'Did you ever know me to be well?' (Beckett 1984, 31), could be asked by most who inhabit the Beckett canon.

Progressively, in both fiction and dramas, bodies in decay give way to bodies barely visible or gradually disappearing. Winnie is a torso that becomes merely a talking head in the course of *Happy Days*; M, the solitary walker in *Footfalls*, literally walks herself to oblivion on the stage, a shade to join the shade of her specter mother alive only in her head, or she in her absent mother's words. While most are, as Maddy Rooney observes, 'not half alive nor anything approaching it'(Beckett 1984, 16), some are no longer even that: Malone dead by the end of the novel that bears his name, the Unnamable a voice beyond the grave in the book that follows, the three talking heads in *Play* interned in burial urns, Mouth, just lips, tongue, and teeth 'whole body like gone' in *Not I* (Beckett 1984, 220). Yet, even when it is barely possible for the speakers to discern their own forms, the very absence bespeaks a body that was and still is struggling to be seen and experienced. Mouth may be a tiny orifice on the stage, but her words continually return, like a litany, to body parts, their positioning, and their functioning. The same pull between corporeal presence and absence can be found in the late fiction as well as in the late plays. The speaker in *Company* may begin as a voice in the dark, but he is fully aware that he is on his back, feeling 'the pressure on his hind parts'(Beckett 1980a, 7), and he ends his chronicle of memory in the same way, in the dark, still in his body, a body even more invasive and demarcated than it was at the beginning of the text. The narrated 'she' in *Ill Seen Ill Said*, 'This old so dying woman' (Beckett 1981, 20), continues to leave 'a tenacious trace' (59), even when, presumably, there is 'Not another crumb of carrion left' (59). And in *Worstward Ho*, Beckett's last extended fiction, the struggle of the 'nohow on' is still to 'Say a body'(Beckett 1983, 7). The threnody echoed twice in *Waiting for Godot* seems applicable to them all, seen or unseen, shade or ghost: 'Astride of a grave and a difficult birth. Down in the hole, lingeringly, the grave-digger puts on the forceps. We have time to grow old. The air is full of our cries' (Beckett 1956, 58). The air is also full of pants, wheezes, coughs, hiccups, farts and screams, as well as those smells 'the living emit [from] their feet, teeth, armpits, arses, sticky foreskins and frustrated ovules' (Beckett 1974, 1) used by Beckett as if to ensure that the physical is not erased in the drive toward the metaphysical. Even beyond the grave, presumably beyond corporeality, M in *Play* can still hiccup, indicating either that Beckett's people never entirely give up the ghost or that what passes for life is in fact in question.

It is difficult to think of another modern writer who has so consistently, thoroughly, and relentlessly focused on questions of the body. Repeatedly in his early works, his characters talk about the dream of ridding themselves of their corporeal states, of becoming pure mind. Murphy goes as far as to bind his naked body to a rocking chair, attempting to rock himself into a state in which he would be 'free in the mind' (Beckett 1957, 2); Belacqua attempts to enter a similar gray umbra by pressing his body down on his mattress. Neither succeeds. Beckett characters may dream of somatic-free lives, but such a state eludes them. The central given in Beckett's works can be said to be the very recalcitrance of the body against dismissal and its gross insubordination in refusing to assume its place in the Cartesian hierarchy where mind holds ultimately sway.

Beckett's particular bodywork is central to his writing; it is also highly complex. On the one hand, Beckett seems to accept, as Steven Connor says, 'the impossibility of disembodied thought' refusing 'the refusal of the body' (Connor 1992, 101). His problem is how to invoke this body without resorting to the very methods of objectification that deny its presence; how to represent what is constantly in the process of decomposition; and how to convey pain, something that is ultimately unrepresentable. As Elaine Scarry has argued, the 'it' of pain is 'so incontestably and unnegotiably present' for the sufferer while 'so elusive that "hearing about pain" may exist as the primary model of what it is "to have doubt,"' (Scarry 1985, 4).[2]

To further complicate the matter, Beckett, early in his career, recognized the very instability and limitations of language that in his fiction would be an essential means of conveying subjectivity or the body. In his first published work, the 1929 essay 'Dante... Bruno. Vico.. Joyce', a defense of James Joyce's 'Work in Progress' (*Finnegans Wake*), he applauds Joyce's ability to bypass 'abstraction' and 'metaphysical generalization'(Beckett 1972, 16) in order to 'snare the sense'(14) through creating words, themselves embodying life and able to present 'a statement of the particular'(16–17). By 1937, however, Beckett had become more concerned with 'that terrible materiality of the word surface' (Beckett 1983b, 172), and more determined to find an alternative solution to the one Joyce embraced. In a letter to a German acquaintance, Axel Kaun, Beckett calls for a 'literature of the unword' (Beckett 1983b, 173), that is, a way of writing that would free literature from the ultimate sway of language. Rather than Joyce's 'apotheosis of the word'(172), Beckett suggests the possibility of 'somehow finding a method by which we can represent this mocking attitude towards the word, through words' (172), using 'some form of Nominalist irony' (173). The notion of using words to indict words was an idea Beckett came across in 1929 when, at Joyce's behest, he read the *Beiträge zu einer Kritik der Sprache (Contributions Towards a Critique of Language)* by Austrian skeptical nominalist Fritz Mauthner.[3] Mauthner, in his three-volume critique, argues that all knowledge comes through the body, but the body itself is a poor conductor of experience, given its physical limitations. In addition, what little it does know it cannot say because of the vagaries of language, the only vehicle through which a sense of self and of the world can be ascertained or shared.[4] The solution Mauthner describes is to find a means whereby language will call attention to its own paucity. In 'Three Dialogues With George Duthuit,' in 1949, in which Beckett describes the situation of the artist who acknowledges that 'there is nothing to express, nothing with which to express, nothing from which to express, no power to express, no desire to express, together with the obligation to express'(Beckett 1965), he seems to have Mauthner in mind, practicing what Mauthner preached.[5] Beckett's problem was how to somehow use language without being caught in the net of signification it imposed. At the same time, how to make this writing live without doing what Joyce did, and without imposing extraneous forms and conditions that denied the very impotence that he recognized as inevitable. As John Pilling notes, no wonder at the end of 'Three Dialogues' Beckett says 'ironically, but wearily "Yes, yes, I am mistaken, I am mistaken"' (Pilling 1997, 228). He knew the difficulty of the road he had followed and what lay ahead.

Beckett's skepticism outstrips Descartes and goes as far as to put into doubt not only language but also the very possibility of knowing the self. Unlike Descartes's claim, quoted above, in Beckett's works there would be no 'clear and distinct idea of myself,' nor 'a distinct idea of the body,' *I* and *myself* vie for attention, locked in combat over the possession of the first person singular and the body that experiences but can not coalesce or say them. Beckett's great discovery was not to resolve the dilemma of subjectivity but present the struggle both in his fiction and, then, through the agency of the actor, on the stage. Just as he explodes traditional notions of narrative in his fiction – 'the Balzac thing' Beckett's first fictive narrator calls it in *Dream of Fair to Middling Women* – and Aristotelian principles in his drama – 'the Ibsen thing' Beckett indicated to an interviewer – he explodes notions of the body as a coherent, unified entity, capable of being captured, subdued and objectified. Instead, he offers up a fleshly, decaying body, whose very contours are constantly shifting and indeterminate, on page and stage, not the positive, healthy body Descartes reinscribes as an object of inquiry, but, rather, a body marked by its own impotence.[6] The positive, healthy body in Beckett's works becomes coterminous with the lucid narrative and ineluctable dramatic plot, something to be unveiled as fraudulent and disposed of as a given in fiction and drama. In its place Beckett introduces a body that can be brought to life, if at all, through its infirmities.[7] It is this decaying body that becomes one of the central marks of what is meant by the term 'Beckettian.' As Connor notes, 'It is especially in Beckett's attention to the defective or otherwise deviant body that his work runs parallel to some of the most important and influential rethinkings of the relation between rationality and physicality in our culture' (Connor 1992, 101–02).

That Beckett found a way of both presenting the body as seat of knowledge and then erasing its potency and even, at times, its corporeality is striking. What is even more striking is that he began turning out his 'gallery of moribunds' (Beckett 1955, 137) when he himself was just thirty. One of the questions that is often asked but not often explored is how such a young man had such an affinity with illness and decrepitude, and how he came to settle on this technique as one means of both invoking and problematizing bodies in his work. A starting point, of course, is in Beckett's own biography. In fact, although photographs of him indicate a tall, lean athletic figure, James Knowlson, in *Damned to Fame*, lists under the heading 'Beckett's illnesses' 109 entries on the 704 pages of the biography, organized under eight specific medical problems including poor eyesight, lung problems, panic attacks and racing heart, and a general category of 'other illnesses.' These do not include Beckett's near-fatal stabbing on a Paris street in 1938, the wound just missing the heart and lung. To create people dealing with illnesses, Beckett did not have to use great leaps of imagination.

In addition to his own medical problems, Beckett could also draw from those he observed in his family. When, for example, Lady Beatrice Glenavy, a Beckett family friend, first saw *Endgame,* she immediately associated the crippled Hamm with Beckett's Aunt Cissie (Beckett) Sinclair (Knowlson 1996, 264–65, 407), whose Parkinson's disease and severe arthritis so greatly incapacitated her that Beckett wheeled her to the hospital to visit her husband, Morris 'Boss' Sinclair, himself dying of tuberculosis, just as their daughter, Peggy had four years earlier. Later in his life, on trips back to Dublin, Beckett would witness his mother's gradual deterioration, also from Parkinson's disease, and the dementia it precipitated (Knowlson 1996, 382–3). Then there were those physical sufferers he encountered in Dublin, London, and, later, in France: old men for whom he had a particular fondness, 'gerontophilia,' he called it (Smith 2002, 90); the patients he visited in Bethlem Royal Hospital in 1936; those whose extreme suffering he witnessed in France under the Nazi regime, and later in the hospital at St-Lô. He could also have found models for his physically infirm in the literature and art to which he was partial: in Dante and Shakespeare, in the paintings of the Bruegels and Bosch (Knowlson 1996, 58, 609).[8] From all of these sources, Beckett had ample validation for Hamm's cry in *Endgame,*

'Use your head, can't you, use your head, you're on earth, there's no cure for that!' (Beckett 1958, 53).

Examples of Beckett's use of decrepitude can be found in his writing as early as *More Pricks Than Kicks* – the blind paralytic 'all tucked up' in 'Ding Dong' and 'A Wet Night' (Beckett 1972, 39, 47), Belacqua's 'grotesque exterior' in 'Ding Dong' (Beckett 1972, 41), with his 'spavined gait,' and feet 'in ruins'(15). In *Pricks*, *A Dream of Fair to Middling Women*, and *Murphy*, however, these references to the body are still filtered through a perceiving mind that comments on infirmity rather than living it, as Beckett illustrates in chapter 6 of *Murphy*. The early fictions, in general, John Pilling argues, still hold to formal markers of the genre. 'As long as Beckett hoped to "snare the sense" [...] the snare of arbitrary form claimed him as its victim' (Pilling 1997, 230). So, to an extent, did the language of Joyce. Beckett, when describing the Smeraldina-Rima, in *Dream* could still write: 'Poppata, big breech, Botticelli thighs, knock-knees, ankles all fat nodules, wobbly, mammose, slobbery-blubbery, bubbub-bubbub, a real button-bursting Weib, ripe' (Beckett 1992, 15). By 1937, however, as Beckett indicated to Kaun, he was already looking for a different way of writing. What is significant is that at exactly the time when he wrote the Kaun letter, July 1937, Beckett was in the throes of a project that he may have imagined could lead him to this new type of writing less confined by formal means or, at least, a form that might move him out of the Joycean sway. The theme was to be impotence in the face of desire, the subject was to be Dr Samuel Johnson.

ii

Johnson holds a special place in Beckett studies. Of all those writers, philosophers, and intellectuals to whom Beckett was drawn and from whom he gained inspiration, Samuel Johnson proved in many ways one of the most compelling and the most intractable. While Beckett was able to distill elements of his study of Descartes in the 1930 poem 'Whoroscope' (Beckett 1984*b*, 1–6), and the next year turn his intensive reading of Proust into a seventy-one page essay (Beckett 1931), as revelatory of Beckett as it is of Proust, his extensive work on the life and times of Dr Samuel Johnson, the eighteenth-century classicist, lexicographer, critic, poet, and renowned figure in Augustan literary circles, resulted in no completed work. It produced over 200 pages of detailed notes and one eleven and a-half page typed scene of an aborted play Beckett entitled *Human Wishes* (derived from Johnson's famous poem 'The Vanity of

Human Wishes').[9] Beckett later admitted to the critic Ruby Cohn that he could not remember what it was that first drew him to Johnson (Cohn 1980, 145), why he decided to write about him, or why he chose drama as his form, since he had never before attempted to write a play.[10] What he was certain of was that he was motivated by the theme he clearly wished to pursue: Johnson in love.

Beckett was already interested in Johnson's writing in the early 1930s. His *Whoroscope* notebook, that covers the years 1932–38, includes some notes on Johnson's *Rasselas*, a nihilistic fable that he continued to admire – 'a grand book' Beckett would call it many years later (Knowlson 1996, 536) – not surprisingly given its theme that 'life is everywhere a state in which much is to be endured and little to be enjoyed' (Johnson 1969, 1031). He also copied down materials from Johnson's *The Lives of the English Poets* and from James Boswell on Johnson,[11] and in 1935 Beckett paid a visit to Lichfield, Johnson's birthplace.[12] At the end of September 1936, before setting out on an extended trip to Germany in order to visit museums and view the new art being done there, he began thinking of writing about Johnson, and turned his attention to finding materials for what he soon was calling his 'Johnson fantasy' (Smith 2002, 110–31). During the six months that he traveled, he did not actually work on the topic (Knowlson 1966, 270), but he had not left Johnson behind. In a 13 December letter to his friend Mary Manning, he wrote, 'There are 50 plays in [Johnson's] life' (Pilling 1997, 163). The one he fixed on was based on his hypothesis that Johnson had been in love with Mrs Hester Thrale. Thrale had served as his closest confidant and support over the fifteen-year period during which she and her husband had taken the widowed, lonely man into their family, providing him with the comforts of wealth and the companionship of caring friends that the brooding Johnson, for all his wit and conviviality, seemed desperately to need.[13] When Henry Thrale died on 4 April 1781, Hester was forty-one, a mother of thirteen children, four living, a still attractive woman, who had been a partner in an arranged marriage to a husband ten years older, and who, now free of 'Thrale's bridle … off her neck,' as Johnson described her situation (Boswell 1934, 277), could plot a new life for herself. This she did. She soon declared her love for her children's Italian music teacher, Gabriel Piozzi, married him in 1784, and moved to Italy.

Johnson at the time of Thrale's death was seventy-two, a sick man who grew progressively more enfeebled in his last years. All his life he had been plagued with illness. 'Born nearly dead,' he wrote in his *Annals* (Wiltshire 1991, 13), a phrase Beckett copied in his notebook. He suffered

from scrofula, a form of tuberculosis, which left its mark on his features
and may have given rise to many of those compulsive ticks, gesticulations,
and odd bodily habits for which Johnson was infamous, particularly his
way of walking: with legs stretched as far as they could go, heels pressed
down, body hurtling forward as if from some internal volition (Bate 1977,
357), another description that Beckett wrote down. In addition, Johnson
was plagued throughout his life by deafness, poor eyesight, depression,
fears of insanity, and preoccupations with death and mortality, symptoms
alleviated, Mrs Thrale notes, only by constant companionship late into
the night (which she provided) and by arithmetic, something Beckett's
sufferers would also find soothing. Counting, Johnson explained, was
'a way of steadying his mind generally, or steadying his resolve' (Bate
1977, 72) by 'breaking things down into smaller, more manageable units'
(Bate 1977, 106). In his youth, Johnson had sought to overcome his
infirmities by vigorous physical activity, swimming in rough seas and
undertaking extensive walking programs, but by 1781, the year that
Beckett fixed on to begin his research, Johnson's body overtook his
resolve. He became increasing afflicted by dropsy, circulatory problems,
bronchitis, emphysema, congestive heart failure, and sarcocele of the
testicle, illnesses too debilitating to slough off even with his prodigious
will. It is this Johnson, the towering intellect now in decay, who seems
to have captured Beckett's imagination, or rather the thought that such
a physical wreck could wish to be the next husband of Hester Thrale.
'What interested me especially was the breakdown of Johnson as soon as
[Mr] Thrale disappeared,' Beckett wrote to Manning, 'the platonic gigolo
or house friend, with not a testicle, auricle or ventricle to stand on when
the bluff is called' (Knowlson 1996, 269).

During Beckett's extensive travels in Germany, he kept a diary which
Knowlson details in his biography. There is no mention of Johnson; it is
taken up almost entirely with two subjects: Beckett's impressions of the art,
people, and places he was seeing; and his own physical ailments, which
uncannily resembled several from which Johnson suffered, particularly
a cyst on the scrotum that made walking excruciating, and bouts of
extreme lethargy, thrown into sharp relief by the 'industriousness' of
those around him.[14] However, on 25 April 1937, only three weeks after
his return to Dublin, Beckett could report to his friend Tom MacGreevy
that he was 'working ... on the Johnson thing to find my position ... more
strikingly confirmed than I had dared hope' (Bair 1978, 253–4). Beckett's
supposition was that Johnson was impotent, a theory he admitted for

which 'there is no text' (Smith 113), and when finally free to woo Thrale, he could not do so.[15]

For the next six months, except for an extended period in May while he was recovering from the death of Boss Sinclair, Beckett seems to have spent much of his time in the National Library in Dublin voraciously reading all available books and related material on the life of Johnson, Hester Thrale, and the wide circle of people who interacted with them. His primary sources were Birkbeck Hill's 1887 edition of Boswell's *Life of Johnson*,[16] C. E. Vulliamy's *Mrs. Thrale of Streatham*, published in 1936, as well as Mrs Piozzi's *Anecdotes*, entries from the *Dictionary of National Biography*, and related letters and secondary material, particularly John Hawkins's *Life of Samuel Johnson* (Cohn 1980). Relying on these and numerous other primary and secondary sources, Beckett filled three notebooks on his reading. Ruby Cohn (1980) provides the most detailed descriptions of these notebooks and analyses of their contents. They indicate that while Beckett may have left academe several years before, he was still very much a scholar, taking copious notes about every possible detail related to his subject, going so far as to copy down the dates of birth of each of Thrale's thirteen children. He also attempts early in his research to provide some structure for the facts he is amassing. On the inside cover of notebook one, Beckett jots down a chronology of events concerning his main characters during the target dates of 1781 to 1784 (Henry Thrale's death and Johnson's), and inside the back cover he lists several alternative dramatic arrangements, organized into three acts, all taking place during 1784 or, alternatively, four acts or scenes covering the entire four-year period. On a facing page, usually reserved for his comments or for materials he found particularly significant, Beckett writes a third alternative: 'or Bolt Court.'

Beginning as early as notebook two, it becomes apparent that Beckett was becoming drawn more to Johnson's body and its physical decay than to love and marriage. In this notebook he writes down all of Johnson's sicknesses of those last years, even copying his autopsy or 'neuopsy,' translating its medical terms from Latin. He also copies quotations and comments about Johnson's fear of death and annihilation and preoccupations with the infirmity of his body. At one point, when Johnson describes his friend Sir John Flower, an asthma specialist who 'panted on to 90 as was supposed,' he underlines the phrase in blue pencil, his way of indicating something that might be useful for his project, and repeats the phrase twice, once on verso, noting 'spoken towards end of last act, when, with J panting in silence after "sent to hell, Sir, etc.," curtain falls' (Cohn 1980, 158).[17]

Beckett's third notebook has material on Thrale, and several of the people Johnson had given home and shelter in his private residence, Bolt Court: blind Mrs Anna Williams, a friend of Johnson's late wife, now his taciturn, official hostess; Mrs Elizabeth Desmoulins, another of Tetty Johnson's companions, inherited by Johnson; Dr Robert Levett, a lay doctor, serving those who could not afford trained help; Francis Barber, a black Jamaican-born young man, who came and went in the household; and Johnson's cat Hodge. Beckett also tries once more to synthesize his material into a four-act, four-year structure. At this point, Beckett moved to loose leaf paper, filling thirty-seven more pages with material on each of the 'Bolt Court inhabitants,' including a Miss Poll Carmichael, who seems to have been a prostitute whom Johnson found lying in the street one night and brought home to nurse and to 'put her into a virtuous way of living' (Bate 1977, 502). N. F. Löwe, in a comprehensive study of the notebooks and their sources, concludes that Beckett turned in the direction of the Bolt Court 'seraglio,' as Johnson called them, because he was aware that his earlier research had reached an impasse, and he could not proceed with his original theme of love and marriage. His decision to shift emphasis, Löwe persuasively argues, is indicated by the fact that Beckett chose a different edition of Boswell, L. F. Powell's revised edition of Hill, since it contained more notes on the group, and Beckett supplemented this with Leslie Stephen's chatty biography of the writer in the English Men of Letters series that has an entire chapter on Johnson's last years.

In a scurrilous wedding hymn Boswell circulated about the possibility of Johnson marrying Thrale, he writes, '"Desmullins [sic] may now go her ways," cries the ecstatic Johnson, "And poor blind Williams sing alone ... I with my arms encircle heaven"' (Bate 1977, 554). When it became clear that heaven in the person of Mrs Thrale and her home had eluded him, Johnson was forced to rely for succor and companionship on those he had assembled at Bolt Court, at best poor substitutes. Among Johnson's friends it was well known that they were 'anything but a happy family' (Stephen 1878, 147). Johnson in a letter to Mrs Thrale, which Beckett copied, admits the same: 'Williams hates everybody; Levett hates Desmoulins, and does not love Williams; Desmoulins hates them both; Poll loves none of them' (Ben-Zvi 1986, 53). It was clearly a disgruntled group; it was also elderly. In 1781 Mrs Williams was seventy-five, Dr Levett seventy-six, Mrs Desmoulins sixty-five, and the cat Hodge, indeterminably aged.

During the time period Beckett investigated, both Levett and Williams died, and Desmoulins departed the residence. At his death, Johnson was nearly alone.

iii

Beckett's work on his Johnson project was one of the most protracted in his career. He began in 1936; worked on it for six months in 1937, until he left permanently for Paris; still had it in mind, he informed Tom MacGreevy, in August 1938 (Löwe 1999, 193); and finally on 21 May 1940 reported to George Reavey: 'I wrote half of a first act of Johnson' (Cohn 2001, 107). However, despite the time he spent and the extensive research he gathered, the Great Cham fails to materialize in *Human Wishes*. He is only referred to obliquely twice, as 'he' and as 'the doctor' who 'is late'; the man himself does not appear. Waiting for his return, on 4 April 1781, the day of Henry Thrale's death, are Williams, Desmoulins, Carmichael, and Hodge respectively meditating, knitting, reading, and sleeping (if possible). Engaging more in mutual monologues than dialogue, the three women touch on a variety of subjects, including their dislike for each other, an extended inquiry on who in the household could be considered merry (the conclusion 'nobody'), and a list of those who have 'departed,' whose 'debt to nature is discharged,' or, as Mrs Williams finally shouts, are 'Dead. D-E-A-D.' The theme of death is extended and reinforced by a quotation from the book Poll is reading, Jeremy Taylor's *The Rule and Exercises of Holy Dying*.[18] However, more than death, it is 'the peevishness of decay' (Beckett 1980b, 296) that pervades the scene, illustrated by the petty bickering and punctuated by the repeated silences that threaten to stop what little action there is. Blind Mrs Williams, an early avatar of Hamm, aggressively seeks to control the action; Mrs Desmoulins, an unwilling Clov, continually comes and goes (as she did in the Bolt Court household); and Levett performs the first of Beckett's silent pantomimes, entering midway through the scene 'slightly, respectably, even reluctantly drunk' (one of Beckett's best stage directions), and emits a powerful hiccup that almost knocks him off his feet. His otherwise silent appearance and disappearance precipitate a metatheatrical exchange, Mrs Williams commenting, 'Words fail us' (Beckett 1980b, 300) and Mrs Desmoulins replying, 'Now this is where a writer for the stage would have us speak no doubt' (300).

There are several theories about why Beckett finally abandoned his Johnson project. Deirdre Bair reports that Beckett told her the problems of putting the eighteenth-century phrasing into 'the Irish accent' for a production scheduled for Ireland proved too daunting (Bair 1978, 255–6), while Cohn and Löwe question this reason, arguing that much of the phraseology of the play already comes from primary sources and is consistent with modern usage and understanding. Knowlson cites a growing identification between Beckett and his subject as the reason for his long struggle with the work (Knowlson 1996, 250). Cohn suggests that finally Beckett 'could not resolve the conflict between the realistic biographical drama he had painstakingly prepared himself to write and the verbal ballet he actually found himself writing' (Cohn 2001, 106). Frederick Smith, in a detailed discussion of the Johnson play, also argues that during the course of Beckett's research, he became progressively more fixated on Johnson the man, shifting his emphasis from the comic possibilities in the marriage theme to the tragic situation of Johnson's physical deterioration and decline (Smith 2002, 116–17).[19]

Even while he was still struggling with the Johnson material, and as yet, as he put it, unable to 'degrade it to paper' (Löwe 1999, 193), Beckett sensed its importance to his writing in general: 'I have not written a word of the Johnson blasphemy,' he informed Manning. 'I trust that acts of intellection are going on about it somewhere. Which will enable me eventually to see how it coincides with the Pricks, Bones and Murphy, fundamentally and fundamentally with all I shall ever write or want to write' (Knowlson 1996, 271). *Human Wishes* does offer indications of what Beckett would later do in *Godot* and beyond: the use of circuitous conversations, overlapping ideas, long silences, habitual activities, name calling, and sudden arrivals and departures to fill time while waiting for someone who never arrives. But that is far from fulfilling its intended promise, as Beckett imagined it.

However, in another way, it can be argued that Beckett was prescient about his Johnson project and the ways it could serve to throw light both on what had preceded it and on what was to come. What Beckett had gathered was a welter of facts about Samuel Johnson, yet try as he might, he was not able to impose form upon this voluminous material. No formal pattern seemed adequate to embody the man or his life. At this point in his writing career, Beckett had little sense of the principles of drama; that certainly was an impediment in his work, but only part of the problem. Looming larger was the recalcitrance of the subject itself, particularly Johnson's own preoccupation and overwhelming concern with his body and its decline. As Löwe points out (1999), Johnson, when writing his poem 'The Vanity of Human Wishes,' based on Juvenal's Tenth

Satire, omitted the body in his translation of Juvenal's famous '*mens sana in corpore sano.*' The sound body could not be his. The Johnson body was a body in pain, a sick, decaying body; and it was this body that finally pushed all else aside in the life of the man and in the notebooks of Beckett, who sought to use him as material for a play. Samuel Johnson, one of the great intellects of the eighteenth century, the man who single-handedly – despite what he argued was his innate lethargy – set himself to writing a dictionary and the *Lives of the English Poets*, heir to the seventeenth-century philosophers Descartes and Locke, had tried, like them, to subdue body to mind, but finally could not escape his own corporeality and decaying flesh. Beckett must have recognized the direction his research was taking. His recourse to the Bolt Court surrogates may point to a last ditch attempt to deal, at least indirectly, with the subject of bodily deterioration which was submerging his project and which, in 1940, he was not able to address directly in his play.

The scholarly approach he used had also failed him; his reading and note taking had not led to Johnson. The impotence had been his. This awareness that 'scholarly thoroughness is not guarantee of truth' (Smith 2002, 117) became a central theme in Beckett's next novel *Watt*, written during the war years. Sam, the narrator in the novel, describes his own inability to fit all the details concerning Watt into any coherent form 'though I was most careful to note down all at the time, in my little notebook' (Beckett 1976, 124), a possible reference to the Johnson project, Smith conjectures. Certainly, Beckett's parody of the scholarly method – the eleven pages on the Lynch family, the elaborate system describing the disposal of Mr Knott's food, the repeated question marks that punctuate the text – points to the bankruptcy of rational enquiry, as Beckett had experienced it during his work on Johnson. Yet, Watt, too, is still glimpsed from the outside, just as Murphy and Belacqua had been, described but not experienced in the flesh. The Johnson fiasco had still not altered Beckett's form, although it probably influenced this novel.

Only in 1946, after the war, did a different kind of Beckett fiction appear and a different kind of fictive presence emerge. Beginning with *Molloy*, Beckett turns to French and adopts the first person pronoun for his speakers. Central to the 'revelation' that precipitated this novel, and the outpouring that followed, was Beckett's awareness, as he told Knowlson, that 'my own way was in impoverishment, in lack of knowledge, in subtracting rather than adding' (Knowlson 1966, 352). Instead of focusing on the world of ideas, apprehensible through logic and rational means, Beckett now focused on what could not be known, and on what could only be vaguely sensed and felt. He began to write using the experiences of the body, from the inside out. 'Impotence' and 'ignorance' – the words Beckett employed to explain this new authorial position – (Shenker 1979, 148) replaced logic and rationality. And they were manifested in the decrepit, infirm bodies that began proliferating in his fiction and in his plays.

Beckett's focus on the body from *Molloy* on can be traced to many causes, his experiences in the war probably contributing most directly to his awareness that logic as well as words are, as Arsene recognizes in *Watt*, finally 'doomed to fail, doomed, doomed to fail' (Beckett 1976, 62). However, his work on Johnson may have provided him with the physical correlative for the impotence he now embraced. By presenting the infirm body, he could overthrow the Cartesian legacy, making this body the seat of knowledge, little enough but all he could.

In taking this position, Beckett was, in fact, a precursor of recent eighteenth-century scholarship[20] that claims that Johnson, along with Swift, Defoe, and Fielding, began to rethink Cartesian theories of mind and body in their own lives and their writings, no longer submerging corporeality or veiling it, as the seventeenth-century thinkers had attempted to do. They became increasingly obsessed with the body, particularly the body in decay. As Carol Flynn puts it: 'After Hobbes, after Locke, and in spite of Descartes, the body, at least in eighteenth-century England would not go away easily. It became instead matter difficult, perhaps impossible, to idealize – matter in the way' (Flynn 1990, 1). It was this 'matter in the way,' present in the public and private writing of Samuel Johnson that seems to have thwarted Beckett in *Human Wishes*. In Beckett's later work, however, the very recalcitrance of the body becomes one of the dominant themes that drives his work: how to say the body, and how the body says itself to itself. In this sense, Beckett was correct: His work on Johnson did have implications for what preceded it and what was to come.[21]

However, Beckett did not simply reverse the Cartesian equation, substituting body for mind, and reinscribing a clearly delineated, positive somatic entity at the center of his work, a unified subject that replaces a failed intellect. His decrepits are, as Leslie Hill warns, not be taken as 'simply illustrative of ontological decay' (Hill 1990, 117). On the contrary. Beckett, after 1946, began an interrogation of what it means to have a body, how that body is constructed, how it struggles to emerge, and how it is thwarted by its own corporeal limitations, and those imposed on it by social, cultural, and political forces and institutions that seek to control and define it. Many of the central issues raised over the past twenty years by feminist, Foucauldian, and poststructuralist studies can be found embedded in Beckett's fiction and dramas. Recent Beckett scholarship has illustrated this point by employing a variety of contemporary critical theories from these areas to discuss Beckett's works, particularly related to his depiction of the body. Mary Bryden (1993) and Elin Diamond (1990), for example, have discussed the ways in which Beckett illustrates gender issues; Steven Connor (1988, 1992), Leslie Hill (1990), and Anthony Uhlmann (1999) have shown how themes in Beckett's fiction antedate and illustrate issues central to poststructural theory, and Anna McMullan and Stan Gontarski, among many others, have focused on the body in Beckett's theatre in relation to recent theories of performativity. Most of these studies have pointed to the complex ways in which body and text interrelate in Beckett's works. Most have also concluded that what Beckett offers is 'a new idea of the body' (Hill 1990, 117), although they have not always agreed on what that is. For Hill the body becomes 'less image than gestural rhythm, more flickering energy than calm appendage, not a support for apperception but more a flesh in process of disintegration' (Hill 1990, 117). McMullan and Gontarski describe the emerging body on the stage and the interplay between presence and absence in the theatre work, particularly in the late plays, and the ways in which Beckett provides the audience with the same 'ill seen' sense of corporeality and presence that the stage characters themselves experience. Through performative means, Beckett 'simultaneously effaces and reinscribes the body in the body' of the drama, Gontarski concludes (Gontarski 2001, 176).

As a recent book declares in its preface, 'There's no escaping the body' (Kelly and von Müke 1994, 1). Certainly not in life and certainly not in the outpouring of critical studies undertaken in the past twenty years and growing in number over the last five. Beckett knew this over fifty years ago. His canon, therefore, is a rich source of illustrations for ever-expanding critical discussions of the body, and new readings of Beckett will surely emerge using these approaches. However, the 'anatomy lesson' of Dr Johnson should be kept in mind. The body demands that it be seen; it denies that it can be reduced to or contained in any medical or intellectual schema or theory. It challenges the observer to see *it* and not some text about it. So does the body of Beckett's work. It illustrates 'the irreducibility of the body, and reminds us that it remains an agent of disclosure' (Chabert 1982, 27).

notes

1. As of October 2002, an additional 500,000 had viewed the ongoing exhibit in London, and close to a million had attended the overlapping Seoul exhibit.

For more information about the exhibit, also called Köreperwelten, visit their website, www.koerperwelten.com.

2. Scarry's theories, presented in *The Body in Pain*, prove useful in discussing Beckett's work. Her central argument, that the experience of pain cannot finally be communicated by the one who experiences it to the one who does not, is illustrated in the 'It hurts' exchange between Didi and Gogo in *Waiting for Godot*. Scarry's description of the nature of torture also parallels what Beckett stages in *What Where*: 'Torture [...] consists of a primary physical act, the infliction of pain, and a primary verbal act, the interrogation. The verbal act, in turn, consists of two parts, "the question" and "the answer," each with conventional connotations that wholly falsify it' (35). She writes, 'the "it" in "Get it out of him" refers not just to a piece of information but to the capacity for speech itself' (49). In her book, Scarry uses the case of Winnie in *Happy Days* to make her point about ageing and the possibilities of 'self-extension' (33). She also discusses Beckett's writing in her book *Resisting Representation* (1994).

3. In a letter to me (2 September 1979), Beckett indicated that 'I skimmed through Mauthner for Joyce in 1929 or 30.' However, based on the *Whoroscope* Notebook, James Knowlson suggests that Beckett 'may have been mistaken' and, in fact, read Mauthner later, or that he may have been returning to the subject at a later date (Knowlson 1996, 760).

4. For a discussion of Mauthner's connections to Beckett, see Ben-Zvi (1980, 1984). For other discussions of Mauthner and Beckett, see Knowlson (1996), and Pilling (1997). Everett Frost is now working on the newly-available Beckett notebooks at Trinity College Dublin, which Knowlson used in his biography, but which only now have become available to scholars. They contain additional Beckett notes on Mauthner.

5. Beckett's own repetitions of 'nothing' and 'to express' might be seen as his playing the Mauthner game: using language to both critique itself and to communicate.

6. Although I use the word 'marked' here, it is possible, in performance, to imagine Beckett's decrepits, as somehow refusing 'marking,' by their very indeterminacy as performed by actors whose bodies become the 'raw material' (Chabert 1982, 23) for such indeterminacy. In this sense, the work of Peggy Phelan, in *Unmarked* (1993), offers interesting possibilities for a reading of Beckett's late theatre.

7. For a discussion on how this might work in performance, see Chabert (1982, 24).

8. For a comprehensive discussion of the importance of Beckett's perception of art in relation to his work, see Oppenheim (2000).

9. *Human Wishes* has been published twice, in Cohn (1980 and 1983). In the latter, however, the date given for the scene is incorrectly written as 14 April. It should read 4 April. In addition to Cohn (1980), for other discussions of the play and the Johnson notebooks, see Cohn (2001), Smith (2002), Knowlson (1996), and Ben-Zvi (1986).

10. Knowlson indicates that the 1931 play *Le Kid*, a parody of Pierre Corneille's *Le Cid* sometimes attributed to Beckett, was the work of Beckett's university

friend Georges Pelorson, Beckett supplying only the title (Knowlson 1996, 123–5). See, also, Bair (1978, 126–8).

11. Knowlson mentions an additional 'private notebook' (755) dating from 1936 in which Beckett translated Johnson's famous 'Letter to Lord Chesterfield' into German, perhaps in preparation for his forthcoming trip to Germany. Beckett, having just completed *Murphy* with no outside assistance, must have enjoyed Johnson's spurning of Chesterfield's praise for his dictionary, since the Lord had refused his earlier entreaties for help.

12. Beckett often visited the homes of writers he admired. On his first trip to France, in the summer of 1926, he included in his itinerary visits to the homes of Ronsard, Rabelais, Descartes, and Balzac (Knowlson 1996, 64).

13. For a discussion of Johnson's dependence on friends and associates, see Reichard (1980).

14. One of the interesting questions that arises about Beckett's travels throughout Germany at this time was his reactions to the growing influence of Nazism. Knowlson's summary of the diary Beckett kept has relatively few references to the tightening Nazi stranglehold of the country, save its effects on the art community. However, one comment is telling. Beckett, bemoaning his own lethargy – a problem for Johnson as well – writes, 'I am always depressed and left with [a] sense of worthlessness at the beautifully applied energy of these people, the exactness of documentation, completeness of equipment ... and authenticity of vocation' (Knowlson 1996, 252).

15. There was, however, some text for the possibility of a match between these two so mismatched people. Boswell, Johnson's faithful chronicler and hero worshipper, in fact wrote an anonymous 'epithalamium'/('in appalling taste' Johnson's biographer W. Jackson Bate calls it [1977, 554], in which an ardent Johnson expresses his joy that, 'I myself am Thrale's entire, the pun on *entire* pointing to a stud not a gelding, as another Johnson biographer, John Wain, points out (Wain 1974, 355).

16. Beckett would later misplace Boswell's *Life of Johnson*, and repurchase it in 1961, while in Folkestone, England, waiting to establish residency in order to marry. It was still in his personal library, Knowlson indicates, when he died (Knowlson 1996, 482).

17. N. F. Löwe provides the complete sentence 'Sent to hell, sir, and punished everylastingly' (Lowe 1999, 197).

18. It should amuse Beckett students to know that Taylor's collected writings appear under the title 'The Whole Works.'

19. In addition to discussing Johnson's influence on Beckett, Smith's important study focuses on other eighteenth-century writers, including Swift, Sterne, Fielding, and Pope, whose works and whose lives were possible sources for Beckett. Smith also discusses major literary and philosophical trends during the period.

20. See, for example, Flynn (1990), Kelly and von Müke (1994), and Wiltshire, whose book *Samuel Johnson in the Medical World* details prevailing attitudes of the period concerning the body and Johnson's contributions to the discourse.

21. In 'Cascando,' a poem that probably dates from the same period in which he was struggling with Johnson, Beckett writes, 'is it not better abort than be barren'

(Beckett 1984b, 29). He may have had *Human Wishes* in mind. In relation to the writing which followed, the answer is yes. For a discussion concerning the dating of 'Cascando,' see Cohn (2001, 271–4).

works cited

Bair, Deirdre. *Samuel Beckett: a Biography*. New York: Harcourt Brace, 1978.

Barker, Francis. *The Tremulous Private Body*. London: Methuen, 1984.

Bate, W. Jackson. *Samuel Johnson*. New York: Harcourt Brace, 1977.

Beckett, Samuel. *Proust*. New York: Grove Press, 1931.

—— *Waiting for Godot*. New York: Grove Press, 1956.

—— *Murphy*. New York: Grove Press, 1957.

—— *Endgame*. New York: Grove Press, 1958.

—— 'Three Dialogues.' In *Samuel Beckett: a Collection of Critical Essays*. Ed. Martin Esslin, 16–22. Englewood Cliffs, NJ: Prentice-Hall, 1965.

—— 'Dante ... Bruno. Vico ... Joyce.' In *Our Exagmination Round his Factification for Incamination of Work in Progress*. 1–22. London: Faber & Faber, 1972.

—— *More Pricks than Kicks*. New York: Grove Press, 1972.

—— *First Love and Other Shorts*. New York: Grove Press, 1974.

—— *Watt*. London: John Calder, 1976.

—— *Three Novels: Molloy/Malone Dies/The Unnamable*. New York: Grove Press, 1977.

—— *Company*. New York: Grove Press, 1980a.

—— 'Human Wishes.' In *Just Play*. Ed. Ruby Cohn, 295–305, 1980b.

—— *Ill Seen Ill Said*. New York: Grove Press, 1981.

—— *Worstward Ho*. London: John Calder, 1983*a*.

—— 'Letter to Axel Kaun.' In *Disjecta*. Ed. Ruby Cohn, 70–173, 1983b.

—— *The Collected Shorter Plays*. New York: Grove Weidenfeld, 1984a.

—— *Collected Poems 1930–1978*. London: John Calder, 1984b.

—— *Dream of Fair to Middling Women*. Ed. Eoin O'Brien and Edith Fournier. Foreword Eoin O'Brien. New York: Arcade, 1992.

Ben-Zvi, Linda. 'Samuel Beckett, Fritz Mauthner, and the Limits of Language.' *PMLA*, 95.2 (March 1980): 183–200.

—— 'Fritz Mauthner for *Company*.' *Journal of Beckett Studies*, 9 (1984): 65–88.

—— *Samuel Beckett*. Boston: Twayne Publishers, 1986.

—— (ed.). *Women in Beckett*. Champaign: University of Illinois Press, 1990.

Boswell, James. *Boswell's Life of Johnson*, Vol. IV (1780–84). Ed. G. B. Hill, Revd. L. F. Powell. London: Oxford University Press, 1934.

Bryden, Mary. *Women in Samuel Beckett's Prose and Drama*. Lanham, MD: Barnes and Nobel, 1993.

Chabert, Pierre. 'The Body in Beckett's Theatre.' *Journal of Beckett Studies* (Autumn 1982): 23–28.

Cohn, Ruby. *Just Play*. Princeton: Princeton University Press, 1980.

—— (ed.). *Disjecta*. London: John Calder, 1983.

—— *A Beckett Canon*. Ann Arbor: University of Michigan Press, 2001.

Connor, Steven. *Samuel Beckett: Repetition, Theory, and Text*. Oxford: Blackwell, 1988.

—— 'Over Samuel Beckett's Dead Body.' In *Beckett in Dublin*. Ed. S. E. Wilmer, 100–08. Dublin: Lilliput Press, 1992.

Descartes, René. *Discourse on Method, and Meditations*. Ed. F. E. Sutcliffe. Harmondsworth, Middlesex: Penguin Books, 1968.

Flynn, Carol Houlihan. *The Body in Swift and Defoe*. Cambridge: Cambridge University Press, 1990.

Gontarski, S. E. 'The Body in the Body of Beckett's Theatre.' *Samuel Beckett Today/ Aujourd'hui* 11. Ed. Angela Moorjani and Carola Veit (2001): 169–77.

Hill, Leslie. *Beckett's Fiction: In Different Words*. Cambridge: Cambridge University Press, 1990.

Johnson, Samuel. *Rasselas*. In *Eighteenth-Century English Literature*. Ed. Geoffrey Tillotson *et al*. New York: Harcourt, Brace, 1969.

Kelly, Veronica and von Müke, Dorothea. *Body and Text in the Eighteenth Century*. Stanford: Stanford University Press, 1994

Knowlson, James. *Damned to Fame: the Life of Samuel Beckett*. London: Bloomsbury, 1996.

Löwe, N. F. 'Sam's Love for Sam: Samuel Beckett, Dr. Johnson and "Human Wishes."' *Samuel Beckett Today/Aujourd'hui* 8 (1999): 189–203.

McMullan, Anna. *Theatre on Trial: Samuel Beckett's Later Drama*. London: Routledge, 1993.

—— 'Versions of Embodiment/Visions of the Body in Beckett's ... *but the cloud...*' *Samuel Beckett Today/Aujourd'hui* 6 (1997): 353–64.

Oppenheim, Lois. *The Painted Word: Samuel Beckett's Dialogue with Art*. Ann Arbor: University of Michigan Press, 2000.

Phelan, Peggy. *Unmarked: the Politics of Performance*. London: Routledge, 1993.

Pilling, John. *Beckett Before Godot*. Cambridge: Cambridge University Press, 1997.

Rapp, David. 'Anatomy of an Exhibition.' *Ha'aretz*, 2 August 2002.

Reichard, Hugo. 'Boswell's Johnson, the Hero Made by a Committee.' *PMLA*, 95.2 (March 1980): 225–33.

Scarry, Elaine. *The Body in Pain*. New York: Oxford University Press, 1985.

—— *Resisting Representation*. New York: Oxford University Press, 1994.

Shenker, Israel. 'An Interview with Samuel Beckett.' In *Samuel Beckett: the Critical Heritage*. Ed. Lawrence Graver and Raymond Federman, 146–9. London: Routledge, 1979.

Smith, Frederick. *Beckett's Eighteenth Century*. New York: Palgrave – now Palgrave Macmillan, 2002.

Stephen, Leslie. *Samuel Johnson*. New York: Harper and Brothers, 1878.

Taylor, Jeremy. *The Rules and Exercises of Holy Living and of Holy Dying*. Revd. and corrd. edition. Charles Page Eden. Hildesheim: Georg Olms Verlag, 1969.

Uhlmann, Anthony. *Beckett and Poststructuralism*. Cambridge: Cambridge University Press, 1999.

Wain, John. *Samuel Johnson*. New York: Viking Press, 1974.

Wiltshire, John. *Samuel Johnson in the Medical World*. Cambridge: Cambridge University Press, 1991.

9
beckett and religion
mary bryden

Since the earliest days of Beckett criticism, commentators have recurrently sought to identify religious, spiritual, and mystical underpinnings within Beckett's writing. This is from one point of view surprising. Beckett's work can hardly be said to dramatize a journey to faith, an experience of the divine. At the extempore prayer meeting held by Hamm, Clov, and Nagg in *Endgame*, the participants fail to apprehend the presence of God, and quickly abandon their attitudes of prayer. Hamm's disgusted observation about the *deus absconditus* is: 'The bastard! He doesn't exist!' (Beckett 1964, 38). Indeed, a few years before *Endgame*'s first appearance, Harold Pinter was already communicating in a letter his admiration of what might be termed Beckett's resourcelessness: 'The more he grinds my nose in the shit the more I am grateful to him. [...] He's not flogging me a remedy or a path or a revelation or a basinful of breadcrumbs' (Graver and Federman 1979, 12).

If, then, there is no 'path,' no 'remedy,' no 'revelation,' why does a persistent strain of Beckett commentary assign spiritual values to his work? What turns a groan into a *miserere*, or a sigh of relief into a *deo gratias*? Why introduce a putative addressee into a landscape of abjection in which groans and sighs may simply be the exhalations of material beings? This essay will explore that paradox in relation to a range of orientations within Beckett criticism over the past forty years. It will conclude by considering both the strengths and the limitations of bringing Beckett's work into dialogue with religious or exegetical traditions.

beckett's religious background

Beckett's early upbringing was marked by an observance of religious practice within his own household, upheld notably by a mother who reinforced it with her own values of piety and discipline. The environment for this religious observance was that of a well-to-do Protestant minority in Dublin. Recent scholarship has brought to prominence what had been an under-exploited dimension of Beckett studies – his Irishness – and this has contributed to understandings of Beckett's religious awareness as it developed within a very specific historical and cultural context.

Living in the affluent suburb of Foxrock, the Becketts' neighbours were, as Vivian Mercier points out, predominantly Protestant: 'The males and some of the females of the typical Protestant family took the train every weekday to office, school or university in Dublin. In all these places they were likely to be associating almost exclusively with fellow Protestants – as Beckett did at Earlsfort House School and later at Trinity College. Irish Catholics, rich or poor, played walk-on parts in their lives' (Mercier 1977, 28). (The same was true of Portora Royal School, attended by Beckett after Earlsfort.) This is not to say that Beckett did not eventually develop close friends amongst Catholics. Tom MacGreevy is an outstanding example of an *âme frère* who was also a committed Catholic. Nevertheless, it is significant to note that when, in his early writing, Beckett directs a wry, Joycean-style satire towards elements of Catholic organization and ritual, he does so from the perspective of an observer rather than from the insider perspective acquired by Joyce.

In his influential *A Reader's Guide to Samuel Beckett* (1973), Hugh Kenner does in fact situate Beckett firmly within a specifically Protestant tradition: 'Beckett's work draws on two spiritual traditions by which history has shaped the specifically Protestant character: the personal testimony, and the issueless confrontation with conscience' (Kenner 1973, 134). Hence, without attributing to Beckett a denominational adherence, Kenner argues that, in contrast with the 'rigorous externality' associated with a Catholic sacramental theology, still 'persisting beyond Joyce's loss of belief,' Beckett's endlessly self-questioning protagonists share in 'a habit of mind that since the seventeenth century has received a specific religious shaping,' that shaping being Protestant (Kenner 1973, 134).

Although the distinction, as posed, is not entirely clear, it seems that, by the term 'issueless confrontation with conscience,' Kenner means that the self-implicated penitent, having confessed, does not receive absolution or assurance of forgiveness from an external mediator, as in the Catholic tradition. Taken to an extreme, this is the stereotypical view of Catholicism – that wrongdoing is easily remedied by confession to a priest. Yet the very requirement of confession (with its precondition of repentance and resolution of amendment) may itself induce excessive feelings of guilt (as Joyce's *A Portrait of the Artist as a Young Man* memorably illustrates). Moreover, though sacraments are indeed dispensed through visible, material means, these can only be the external signs of an inner, spiritual event. Nevertheless, Kenner does issue the caveat that 'these are by no means exclusively Protestant categories' (Kenner 1973, 134), and his emphasis upon early debates about justification by faith (rather than by external works) is indeed valid within the Protestant tradition.

Anthony Cronin renders the Protestantism in which Beckett was raised as 'mainly a system of punishments and rewards, with the Bible as the principal source of authority' (Cronin 1996, 19). As touched upon in later discussions in this essay, Beckett's exposure to, and knowledge of, the Bible was profound. Cronin points out that, despite Beckett's professed evasion, in later life, of doctrinal outreach, 'he always possessed a Bible, at the end more than one edition, and Bible concordances were always among the reference books on his shelves. He certainly knew the book backwards and as a boy he won a prize for knowing it in the diocesan synod examination' (Cronin 1996, 21). Such knowledge is not easily rendered null and void. As James Knowlson points out, 'the roots of Beckett's religious upbringing were very tenacious,' the play *All That Fall* being an example of a work which is 'grounded in a Protestant outlook and terminology that recalls Charles Wesley's use of the word "home" and "haven" in his hymns' (Knowlson 1996, 429–30).

For Vivian Mercier, aligning his own Huguenot ancestry with that of Beckett, the particular consciousness in which Beckett participated was that of what he calls 'Southern Irish Protestants,' a minority intelligentsia 'that draws its ideas and general culture from outside its native country' and which, far from opting for unqualified settlement, faces a quadripartite pathway: 'expatriation, impatriation, and return to the mother country. A fourth choice was simply to stay put' (Mercier 1977, 27). While Synge chose impatriation (i.e., a willed adhesion to Ireland, and, more particularly, to the Aran Islands), Beckett chose expatriation from the mother country and the mother tongue.

Ciaran Ross, in an article entitled 'Homewards to the Centre of Nowhere: Difference and (Irish) Identity at Play in Samuel Beckett's Theatre,' acknowledges that 'it is perhaps only the young Protestant in Beckett who could have described, as Beckett did, Belacqua Shuah, the hero of Beckett's *More Pricks Than Kicks* (1934) as a "low-down Low Church Protestant of Huguenot stock"' (Ross 1993, 100). However, Ross challenges Mercier's analysis by stating that 'Beckett's Irish Protestant identity was [...] much more disturbing than Mercier is willing to admit'

(Ross 1993, 101). For Ross, Beckett's self-transfer to France and to French was not so much an escape from a problematical cultural heritage as a positive search for a 'transitional' or 'potential' space (Ross 1993, 102). In a close reading of *Waiting for Godot*, Ross counters any 'pre-established objective relations between Beckett and society' (Ross 1993, 109), and argues that 'in inviting us to un-do and re-do our experience of theatre in general, and in particular Irish Protestant theatre, Beckett radically deprives us of having to choose between theatre and social reality' (Ross 1993, 115).

In fact, Mercier eventually slips out of the armour assaulted by Ross, by claiming that 'Beckett's universality, in the last analysis, does not depend on impatriation or expatriation, on Irishness, Frenchness or cosmopolitanism: it depends on the paradox of a unique self' (Mercier 1977, 45). Having posited a very specific cultural consciousness, Mercier 'in the last analysis' jettisons it in favour of 'universality.' The apparent volte-face may appear to be an attempt at 'having it both ways.' More significantly, however, it illustrates the difficulty of making statements about Beckett which retain their applicability throughout the wide generic and chronological spread of his writing career (or even, indeed, throughout the text of a single work). Declan Kiberd illustrates this tellingly by stating that Belacqua Shuah, in *More Pricks Than Kicks*, 'fondly imagines himself to be an indolent bohemian, but at heart he is a puritan, seeking to replace the smooth Catholic rituals of the aesthetic adventure with a more literal-minded low-church honesty. He is, in fact, an anti-bohemian, and so the narrative deliberately trips over itself, with jagged phraseology, intrusive footnotes, and authorial interruptions' (Kiberd 1992, 78).

Beckett's own self-positioning *vis-à-vis* religion at this period is similarly ambiguous. In answer to a defence counsel question in 1937 (during a libel action undertaken by his uncle) as to whether he was a Christian, Jew, or atheist, Beckett replied: 'None of the three' (Knowlson 1996, 279). In contrast to his mother's apparently unwavering Christian faith, and his father's apparently docile tolerance of denominational membership, the status of Beckett's own religious attitudes remained mobile and provisional. Like many an atheist, he remained fluent in God-talk; like some theists, he remained fluent in the discourse of scepticism. At the age of fifty-five, Beckett could simultaneously own (in an interview with Tom Driver) to a quickening of faith at an important *rite de passage* and a subsequent disaffection with the notion that religion might aid or anaesthetize at the climax of human misery: 'I have no religious feeling.

Once I had a religious emotion. It was at my first Communion. No more. [...] The family was Protestant, but for me it was only irksome and I let it go. My brother and mother got no value from their religion when they died. At the moment of crisis it had no more depth than an old-school tie. Irish Catholicism is not attractive, but it is deeper' (Driver 1961, 217).

Is Beckett here equating 'depth' with 'emotion'? Is 'emotion' desirable? If Catholicism is 'not attractive,' does its 'depth' constitute 'value'? A first Communion service is a special circumstance. It is perhaps true of all the major religions of the world that what might pass for a 'religious emotion' is more readily elicited by a sense of liturgical occasion, in the presence of family and friends, and attended by a beauty of language and music to which Beckett undoubtedly remained susceptible throughout his life. But how does 'religious emotion' relate to religious conviction? And, if 'religious emotion' cannot be experienced at the moment of death, is such emotion meaningless? Beckett's diagnosis, as always, remains elusive. What is certain is that Beckett wished to inoculate his artistic production against the encroachment of religious formalism. When interrogated, in the 1937 legal case referred to earlier, about an arguably blasphemous reference to Christ in *More Pricks Than Kicks*, Beckett 'replied that the character who spoke these words and the priest were both fictitious and that, as a writer, he could put words into their mouths that he did not agree with' (Knowlson 1996, 279).

the voicing of pain

Beckett's early credo, voiced in the pressurized capsule of the courtroom, concerning the inherent independence and anarchy of fictional creation, is an important one. It is clear that the question of Beckett's status as believer, non-believer, partial believer, or suspender of belief, and in what, cannot satisfactorily be resolved. Nor is it necessarily desirable that it should be resolved. Nevertheless, it is also inconceivable that a writer can somehow deliver text from a zone which is culture-free, devoid of the anxiety of influence, neutralized from hard-won insights and convictions. When Tom Driver asked Beckett whether his plays dealt with concerns which might also be deemed religious, Beckett replied, citing his experience of travelling in a London cab: 'Yes, for they deal with distress. [...] On the glass partition between me and the driver were three signs: one asked for help for the blind, another help for orphans, and the third for relief for the war refugees. One does not have to look for distress. It is screaming at you even in the taxis of London' (Driver 1961, 221).

How many of us read such notices? How many of us, even if we read them, allow them to impinge more than momentarily upon our daily lives? Although Beckett's writing contains protagonists who sometimes display a cavalier callousness to suffering in others, it also contains movements of compassion and solicitude (one might cite the portrait of Celia at the close of *Murphy*, the ministering hands of *Nacht und Träume*, or the opening of *Footfalls*). Insofar as it is preoccupied with the pained riddle of suffering afflicting the innocent, Beckett's work may be said to be exploring territory which is also the grazing-ground of theologians. At the 1982 Drawbridge Memorial Lecture, the Reverend Richard Harries, then Dean of King's College London, began his lecture with the words: 'Samuel Beckett is of particular importance to Christians. This is not just because of his genius as a writer, though this in itself is enough to win our attention. It is because his central themes are those with which religion has traditionally been concerned and because his treatment of them raises a question-mark against every other version, particularly the Christian one' (Harries 1982, 2). Citing words traditionally recited at the graveside – 'Man that is born of woman has but a short time to live, and is full of misery'[1] – Harries remarks: 'This view of life underlies every line Beckett writes' (Harries 1982, 2).

Jean Onimus, author of arguably the most important French book (in Desclée De Brouwer's 'Ecrivains devant Dieu' series) on religious approaches to Beckett, underlines this perception in equally stark terms: '[Beckett] ne cesse de répéter sous toutes les formes possibles et jusque dans ses jongleries de cirque la formule des Chartreux: Frère il faut mourir' (Beckett never stops repeating in every possible context, and even in his clowning about, the Carthusian motto: Brother, you must die) (Onimus 1968, 124–5).

Of course, these unsettling meditations do not remain the preserve of Christians: thinking people of all faiths and of none contemplate them at one time or another. Nevertheless, at a formative stage of his development, an array of attempts to answer them impinged upon Beckett from the specific perspective of Christianity, and couched in the texts of Christianity. Laura Barge underlines this perspective with a litany of questions which preoccupy Beckett's protagonists: 'Who am I? How and why have I come to be here? Who or what is responsible for my existence? What am I supposed to be doing, and how free am I to do it? [...] Why is my life such a miserable affair?' (Barge 1990, 34). Yet these questions hang in the air, unanswered. Moreover, as Barge notes, the 'existential needs' of Beckett's people 'remain urgent and unmet' (Barge 1990, 43).

For Vladimir in *Waiting for Godot*, one of these urgent existential needs concerns the authenticity or otherwise of Gospel accounts of the Crucifixion – in particular, of the differentiated salvation prospects of the two thieves crucified with Christ. Why does only one Gospel (that of Luke) mention the incident of Christ assuring the more benevolent thief of salvation? And 'why believe him rather than the others?' (Beckett 1965, 13). More importantly, goes the subtext, 'what implications does this have for us? Will one, both, or neither of us be saved?' Yet Estragon, implicated as he is (at least, in Vladimir's mind) in the conundrum's applicability, has only a foggy idea of what salvation might constitute: 'Saved from what?' (Beckett 1965, 12).

The short-circuiting which occurs here – a key religious concept, that of 'salvation', is deployed but then disrupted by poor reception – has many parallels, both in this play and in other areas of Beckett's writing. These interrupted processes mean that any attempt to translate Beckett's work into a sustained engagement with 'religion' will inevitably encounter difficulty. For Günther Anders, *Waiting for Godot* 'is certainly not a religious play; at most it deals with religion. "At most": for what he presents is ultimately only a faith that believes in itself. And that is no faith' (Anders 1965, 145).

Yet, *in extremis*, perhaps 'a faith that believes in itself' may be the only attainable one. In his early years, Beckett exhibited a remarkable fascination with the sickliness and decline of Samuel Johnson. In one of his notebooks on Johnson (Reading University Library MS 3461/2), compiled before his attempt at the (subsequently abandoned) play *Human Wishes*, he copied out a detailed extract from Johnson's autopsy, an account which elicits no small measure of wonder at Johnson's powers of endurance when alive.[2] In an exemplary study on Beckett and the eighteenth century, Frederick Smith comments that 'the figure of the declining Johnson became for [Beckett] a sort of metaphor of Western man, academic and witty, alone, afraid of dying and yet intrigued by his own physical deterioration' (Smith 2002, 111). Though immune from the religious presuppositions which animate Johnson's *Prayers and Meditations* – (a text he carefully read) – Beckett admired in Johnson the dogged struggle to write from within a failing and paining body and a melancholic, fearful mind.

This linkage between the experience of apparently gratuitous pain and the commitment to an activity which does not exclude it but which bypasses it – writing – is an important one. What many commentators have noted in Beckett (both in his own writing career and in his beset fictional creatures) is precisely the quality which he admired in Johnson: persistence in finding and retaining a voice. The writer Hélène Cixous remarks of Beckett in an early essay: 'pour cette résistance comment ne pas aimer Beckett, pour cette lutte, [...] cette *passion* qui le fait parler jusqu'à plus – souffle' (For this resistance, how can we not love Beckett, for this struggle, [...] this *passion* which makes him speak until no more – breath) (Cixous 1976, 398).

Within the French context, Jean Onimus inserts this characteristic into a mode of being which has encountered 'religious' questions but which refuses to domesticate them: 'Un homme? Ce déchet dans une poubelle, cette chenille dans la boue, ce tas de hardes dans un fossé! Non, plus un homme: une chose. Mais cette chose parle! Ce qu'elle dit n'a pas de sens: un mélange délirant de rires et de rages. Mais elle parle. Quand tout est perdu, il reste la Parole' (A human being? That refuse in a trashcan, that caterpillar in the mud, that pile of rags in a ditch! No, no longer a man: a thing. But this thing speaks! What it says has no meaning: a delirious mixture of laughter and rage. But it speaks. When all is lost, the Word remains) (Onimus 1968, 13–14). For Onimus, Beckett does not simply repudiate Christianity. Rather, he outdistances it by casting a clear and stark light upon those areas which a comfortable version of Christianity would prefer not to acknowledge: 'Il déconcerte les chrétiens pour qui la créature humaine est à l'image de Dieu et qui refusent de se reconnaître dans des larves souillées de boue, des clochards séniles, des hébétés cruels' (He disconcerts those Christians for whom the human creature is in the image of God, and who refuse to recognize themselves in worms soiled with mud, senile tramps, cruel and stupefied people) (Onimus 1968, 15).

These potentially disconcerted Christians may include those who see church membership as a convenient form of social inclusion, those who wish to perpetuate the reassurance provided by a set of rules, or those who wish to participate in the triumphalism of a single world-view. There are also, however, those who see in it a forum for questioning, a radical opportunity to work for justice and peace, one means amongst others of palliating human misery. This same dichotomy is apparent in prevalent images of Christ. The Christ who is evoked in various textual contexts throughout Beckett's writing is not the triumphalist version: Christ

Pantocrator, the majestic Second Person of the Trinity, the one throned in glory whose gaze penetrates the beholder in so many Byzantine Greek and Sicilian churches and, in a more recent example, in the great Graham Sutherland tapestry of Coventry Cathedral. Neither is it the glowing, lantern-carrying 'Light of the World' as portrayed by Holman Hunt and contemplated without trauma by the Victorian public. Rather, it is the 'man of suffering,' the bloody, suffering, enfleshed Christ, rendered object, victim, by the human imposition of crucifixion.

Thomas Carlyle was one of the few critics of Hunt's famous painting. During a visit to Hunt's studio, he dismissed the carefully planted symbolism of the painting, and proceeded to argue that Christ should be envisaged 'toiling along in the hot sun, at times in the cold wind, going long stages, tired, hungry often and footsore, drinking at the spring, eating by the way [...]. I see Him dispirited, dejected, and at times broken down in hope' (Hunt 1913, 263). This is precisely the Christ with whom Estragon, in *Waiting for Godot*, can empathize. For him, Christ is not the landowner, well-heeled and well-shod, but the peasant. When Vladimir reproaches him for contemplating walking barefoot, he replies: 'Christ did. [...] All my life I've compared myself to him' (Beckett 1965, 52). Perhaps Estragon has at one time benefited from the comparison; now, however, it is the dispossessed, barefoot Christ with whom he can identify. Beckett's description of the eponymous Watt also exemplifies this latter tendency: 'His face was bloody, his hand also, and thorns were in his scalp. (His resemblance, at that moment, to the Christ believed by Bosch, then hanging in Trafalgar Square, was so striking, that I remarked it)' (Beckett 1976, 157). This is the Christ – 'no longer a man, a thing' – which underlies Onimus's observation of the Beckett creature *par excellence* and which, in its voicing in Psalm 22, has also been conventionally seen as a foreshadowing of the Christ-predicament: 'But I am a worm, and no man; a reproach of men, and despised of the people' (Psalm 22: 6).

It is this objectification, this 'thingness' of Christ which Beckett responds to in the clown-Christs of Rouault's paintings.[3] As Alfred Simon remarks: 'Chez Rouault, la condition humaine trouve une symbolisation exhaustive dans une trinité formée par le Christ (aux outrages), le Roi (déchu), et le Clown (lugubre). Chacune de ces trois figures médiatise les deux autres. Chacune est à la fois christique, clownesque et royale. Il en va ainsi chez Beckett' (In Rouault, the human condition finds an exhaustive symbolization in a trinity composed of Christ (mocked), the King (demeaned), and the Clown (lugubrious). Each of these figures promotes the other two. Each is christlike, clownish and kingly. This is how it is with Beckett) (Simon 1983, 112). Hence, Hamm in *Endgame* is, at one and the same time, a dying king, a sinister clown, and a Christ (complete with veronica cloth).

The Christ figure of Beckett's fiction is, therefore, not a God/Man, a privileged being, a personifier and dispenser of salvation, but simply a recognizable paradigm of extreme forms of human suffering. In Ludovic Janvier's terms, 'Jésus représente la douleur humaine exemplaire, sa Passion est l'acte de souffrance par excellence. [...] Surtout [la figure de Jésus] apparaît vidée de toute signification théologique' (Jesus represents the exemplar of human anguish, his Passion is the act of suffering *par excellence*. [...] Above all [the figure of Jesus] appears emptied of all theological significance) (Janvier 1969, 118–19).

Moreover, this figure of Christ the predecessor and predeceaser is the one who dies not in calm rectitude, but with a screeched question that goes unanswered: 'My God, my God, why hast thou forsaken me?' (Matthew 27: 46). His cry is echoed in various forms in Beckett's work, in screams (*Not I*) or in wails for help, as with Estragon in the second act of *Waiting for Godot*, when the waiting becomes unbearable: 'God have pity on me! [...] On me! On me! Pity! On me!' (Beckett 1965, 77). In thus crying out, Estragon haplessly echoes the opening words of Psalm 51, the *miserere*: 'Have mercy upon me, O God.'[4] The psalmist's self-conviction – 'For I acknowledge my transgressions: and my sin is ever before me' (v.3) – even finds experimental echoes in the play when Vladimir ponders: 'Suppose we repented?' (Beckett 1965, 11). Yet, whereas the psalmist 'owns' his guilt, seeing it as inborn – 'in sin did my mother conceive me' (v.5) – the two men are at a loss as to what they could efficaciously repent of, other than 'our being born,' an idea which results in a 'hearty laugh' from Vladimir (Beckett 1965, 11). (The same sense of being punished for an unfathomable offence is voiced in other Beckett texts, notably *The Unnamable*). Nevertheless, just as Psalm 51 consists wholly of aspiration, of verbs of request, attaining in its course no assurance of external succour, *Waiting for Godot* remains similarly bounded by unfulfilled expectation.

The examples given above draw attention to an ambiguity in Beckett's writing concerning the status of Biblical texts. For Gérard Durozoi, the matter is more straightforward. In his wide-ranging book *Beckett* (in Bordas's 'Présence Littéraire' series), he asserts that Beckett's use of the scriptures is straightforwardly satirical and dismissive: 'C'est en se rappelant l'attitude de constante dérision que Beckett maintient par rapport à la culture occidentale qu'il convient d'aborder la question de Dieu, qui ne mérite certainement pas qu'on lui accorde un examen aussi développé que le font certains critiques' (We should be mindful of the attitude of constant derision which Beckett maintains in respect of Western culture when we approach the question of God, which certainly does not deserve the weight of attention which certain critics have devoted to it) (Durozoi 1972, 200). In an accompanying footnote, Durozoi makes clear that the 'certain critic' he has in mind is Jean Onimus, whose work is referred to above. Sweeping together a range of texts, including Dante, Proust, Shakespeare, and the Bible, Durozoi declares Beckett's use of them to be 'systématiquement parodique,' and wholly the fruit of Beckett's ironic humour, 'qui consiste à rapprocher du noble (culturel) et du trivial (le texte actuel), non pour faire ressortir leur similitude, mais pour insister sur leur différence' (which consists in bringing together the noble (cultural) and the trivial (the current text), not to highlight their similarity, but to insist upon their difference) (Durozoi 1972, 196–7).

Certainly this description is applicable on many occasions in Beckett's writing, both published and unpublished. His 'Whoroscope' notebook from the 1930s, for instance, contains many examples of quipping quotations or manipulated aphorisms (for example, 'Christ had his ups and downs').[5] There is a plethora of examples, especially in Beckett's early writing, of biblical texts being customized or perverted, often to humorous effect.[6] In the early novel *Murphy*, for example, Wylie speaks of Murphy as 'the creepy thing that creepeth of the Law' (Beckett 1973, 121), thus adverting to but subverting the verse from the Book of Leviticus which includes among the taxonomy of unclean foods 'every creeping thing that creepeth upon the earth' (Leviticus 11: 41).

Nevertheless, to classify as uniformly parodic every occurrence of a Biblical resonance in Beckett's writing would be to resolve prematurely a turbulence which is undoubtedly present. Beckett once famously stated, with regard to his own accessing of Biblical and spiritual material, that 'Christianity is a mythology with which I am perfectly familiar, so naturally I use it' (Duckworth 1972, 18). By using the term 'mythology' (i.e., a body of stories), Beckett acknowledges the unwieldy anatomy of the phenomenon he is describing. Just as the Bible is a collection of diverse literatures from a multiplicity of epochs and cultures, Beckett's use of it is similarly diverse. In an article entitled 'A Stuttering *Logos*: Biblical Paradigms in Beckett's Trilogy,' Jan Hokenson tries to convey the complexity of these patternings: 'The three novels each reverberate with echoes from each other and from the gospels, *Job*, the prophets, the *Divine Comedy*; the result is a dense, involuted, and fragmentary series of Christian allusions which interweave throughout the trilogy, as variations on several themes in addition to the Biblical *Logos*' (Hokenson 1971, 294).

There are undoubtedly occasions when, recognizing the stubborn weightiness of these texts within his own memory, Beckett is content to assert his control over them, to jump upon them, using them as a springboard towards lighter, more elastic, or more comic configurations. On other occasions, however, he embeds the texts in ways which allow them to acquire or retain resonance or poignancy. For Lance St John Butler, 'there simply is too much *sympathy* scattered through Beckett, too many allusions to Christ that are not blasphemies [...] for this to be the whole story' (Butler 1992, 181). One such case would be the desperate *miserere* from Estragon referred to earlier, a Job-like cry from the belly which would provoke laughter only from the sadist. In *Endgame*, as Ruby Cohn has convincingly shown, the web of scriptural allusions serve as a grim reminder that '*Endgame* is unmistakably a play about an end of a world' (Cohn 1969, 44). These allusions do not wrench the text into predetermined patterns. As Kristin Morrison remarks with reference to *Endgame*: 'The allusion itself does not change or add anything to the sense of misery and hopelessness that the play has previously established; it simply intensifies what is already there' (Morrison 1983, 95).

As his work progresses, Beckett often uses Biblical texts in half-hidden guises, so that recognition of the prompt-text is merely optional. As Morrison concludes, Biblical allusions are 'present often only as subtle verbal echoes, whispered reinforcements of moods, themes, ironies already established' (Morrison 1983, 97). Many of these texts (increasingly taken from the Old Testament) embrace the theme of the brevity of life and the transience of the material world. Hence, in *How It Is*, the phrase 'I remembered my days an handbreadth' (Beckett 1964, 88) recalls Psalm 39: 5: 'Behold, thou has made my days as an handbreadth.'

The sheer obduracy of both overt and subtextual Biblical or devotional allusion in Beckett's oeuvre cannot be overlooked or dismissed. Considering his work for the theater alone, Louis Barjon observes that 'la première chose qui saute aux yeux, lorsqu'on interroge le théâtre de Beckett, c'est le caractère presque obsessionnel que revêt l'idée de Dieu' (the first thing to leap to the eye when one scrutinizes Beckett's drama is the way in which the idea of God takes on an almost obsessional nature) (Barjon 1965, 651). Though always careful not to deduce belief from such a wealth of reference, Barjon concludes that, while Beckett's work admits of no 'réalité divine,' it nevertheless returns, repeatedly and significantly, to the 'mystère inconnaissable, "l'Innommable"' (unknowable mystery, the Unnamable) (Barjon 1965, 660).

mysticism

The reference to mystery and to unknowing leads to an element of Beckett's religious consciousness which cannot be overlooked. Of course, the term 'mysticism' is a gathering-point for a vast collection of traditions and practices, and there is no space here lengthily to examine them. As Hélène Baldwin is careful to state in her study, *Samuel Beckett's Real Silence*: 'To say what mysticism is without being misunderstood is extremely difficult. In his famous *Studies of English Mystics*, Dean Inge offered twenty-six definitions of mysticism' (Baldwin 1981, 16). Today, after several further decades of experimentation, of inter-faith dialogue, and of New Age mysticism, these definitions have no doubt multiplied further.

My own book, *Samuel Beckett and the Idea of God*, covers material relating to Beckett's extensive reading of, and quotation from, a range of spiritual writers. These include John of the Cross, Teresa of Avila, Thomas à Kempis, Augustine of Hippo, Jeremy Taylor, and Julian of Norwich, to name only the most well known. He was well versed in apophatic spirituality, as represented by writers such as Meister Eckhart and Pseudo-Dionysius. There is also a particularly privileged value accorded in Beckett's writing to qualities seen as preconditions to the mystical experience, such as stillness and solitude.[7]

The pursuit of mystical spaces in Beckett's work has led to a wealth of investigations. In an early article entitled 'God and Samuel Beckett,' Richard Coe follows Murphy as he girds himself up for an experience akin to the self-emptying of the mystic: 'Murphy's supreme virtue is his silence. Relying as he does largely on his visual symbols and his senses, he jettisons bit by bit the whole apparatus of intellect and thus manages to escape entanglement in the net of words' (Coe 1965, 76). In connection with this dismantling of logical argumentation, it is notable that, in what was Beckett's own copy (now preserved in Reading University Library) of the first volume of Maeterlinck's theatrical work, one passage has been carefully underlined in pencil by its owner, as follows: 'La vérité suprême du néant, de la mort et de l'inutilité de notre existence, où nous aboutissons dès que nous poussons notre enquête à son dernier terme, n'est, après tout, que le point extrême de nos connaissances actuelles. Nous ne voyons rien par delà, parce que là s'arrête notre intelligence. Elle paraît certaine, mais en définitive rien en elle n'est certain que notre

<u>ignorance</u>' (The supreme truth of nothingness, death, and the uselessness of our existence, where we end up as soon as we pursue our enquiries to their final end, <u>is only</u>, after all, <u>the far point of our present knowledge</u>. We see nothing beyond, because that is where <u>our intelligence comes to an end</u>. It seems certain, but in the last analysis nothing in it is certain except our ignorance).[8]

The selectivity of these underlinings is eloquent. The mystic must indeed be prepared to relinquish the 'apparatus of intellect' in order to move to a space of receptivity, ungoverned by order and logic. It is this attitude of committed receptivity, only distinguished from quietism or passivity by its quality of intentness, which Beckett singles out in response to a question from Charles Juliet: 'J'évoque les mystiques, mentionne Saint Jean de la Croix, Maître Eckhart, Ruysbroeck ... , lui demande s'il lui arrive de les relire, s'il aime ce qui émane de leurs écrits. – Oui ... j'aime ... j'aime leur ... leur illogisme ... leur illogisme brûlant ... cette flamme ... cette flamme ... qui consume cette saloperie de logique' (I evoke the mystics, mention St John of the Cross, Meister Eckhart, Ruysbroeck ... , ask him whether it ever comes upon him to reread them, whether he likes what emerges from their writings. – Yes ... I like ... I like their ... their illogicality ... their burning illogicality ... that flame ... that flame ... which burns away all that blasted logic) (Juliet 1986, 51).

With this statement – which forms the closing words of Juliet's study – Beckett makes clear his own alignment of the mystical experience with images of light and flame. In a notable full-length study of religious and ethical undercurrents in Beckett, Alice and Kenneth Hamilton explore how access to realms of light and spirituality are in some measure dependent in Beckett's work upon a commensurate downgrading of the darkness of materiality as perceived within the Manichean tradition: 'At least with respect to its view of creation, the Manichean myth is better adapted to Beckett's estimate of the human situation than the Christian one. Christianity asserts the goodness of the created order. Manicheanism holds this order to be a dark prison' (Hamiltons 1976, 52).

Beckett's interest in Manicheanism is indisputable and has been well-documented, particularly with reference to *Krapp's Last Tape*.[9] Laura Barge supplies a careful reading of the short story 'Assumption' in the light (or darkness) of Manicheanism. Hence, the protagonist's search for the ethereal, for some kind of mystical, non-material unity, is played out in the context of 'a divine Power that is man's enemy, the condemnation of the bodily or fleshly and exaltation of the spiritual, and a world order that is cosmically disordered' (Barge 1988, 80).

It must be stated at this point that, in this disordered Beckettian world, the term 'mystical' cannot be used to denote a disciplined and infinitely repeatable mode of progress towards a desired end, as might be taught by a master of contemplation. If mystical insight arises, it is by way of diversions and even evasions. As Shira Wolosky points out, in a study which assesses a writerly triumvirate (Eliot, Beckett, and Celan) in relation to language and mysticism: 'While Beckett certainly invokes the methods of negative theology, he should not be mistaken for a negative theologian. He does not necessarily use mystical practices to achieve mystical goals' (Wolosky 1995, 93).

Further, those 'mystical goals' are elastic ones, amenable both to finitude and to unforeseen directions, beyond the Christian tradition. For Paul Foster, in his book *Beckett and Zen*, Buddhism lends itself well to Beckettian dilemmas of subjectivity, since 'it is neither philosophy nor religion exclusively, nor psychology, yet it embraces them all; it is free from dogma since it does not have a code of divinely inspired rules to explain the circumstances of our existence' (Foster 1989, 31). Referring to a selection of both prose and drama, Foster uses Zen Buddhism in particular to try to show how Beckett's 'techniques towards a definition of self are similar to those found in Buddhist practice and that the dilemmas encountered in the quest for identity are those that the Buddha formulated and solved' (Foster 1989, 33). Nevertheless, that quest is not to be construed as an accomplished progress to a goal, for 'in truth, there is only one desire and that is the desire to know. However, the desire to know always leads Beckett into an impasse' (Foster 1989, 257).

The difficulty is that what is an 'impasse' for one may be a refuge for another. In an intriguing study, John Leeland Kundert-Gibbs brings Zen Buddhism and Chaos theory into dialogue with each other in an attempt to uncover new and dynamic patternings in Beckett's drama. If nothing else, this bi-directional analysis demonstrates that it is 'nearly impossible to characterize *the* interpretation of Beckett's work; indeed, there should never be such a consensus about work of this complexity and power' (Kundert-Gibbs 1999, 17).

As Paul Davies observes in a complementary insight: 'The Beckett character is close to the Buddhist just because he has not swallowed whole the apparent way of looking at things, but rather, he has seen there is a problem with the supposition that self and world are self-subsistent, real entities. Where Beckett takes the story up is on realizing that the supposition is unsustainable' (Davies 2000, 55). Davies's study takes the bold step of drawing together spirituality and the erotic. His observations, he warns, 'are not excursions into sexual biography so much as incursions into the potentially eroticised encounter between being and non-being' (Davies 2000, 7). If one wished to return full-circle to the Protestant focus with which this essay began, one might fruitfully turn to Michael Allen's 'A Note on Sex in Beckett,' in which he remarks that 'Beckett's work exploits vestigially a culturally Protestant way of calculating the significance of sex in God's absence' (Allen 1985, 46).

Despite this rumoured, resented absence, 'the question of God,' as Richard Harries concludes, 'is never quite closed' (Harries 1982, 11). Neither is it ever quite opened, for, as Lance St John Butler states: 'Religion is a raw place in Samuel Beckett's mind' (Butler 1992, 169). Does this then mean that, as K. M. Baxter laments, Beckett's writing has been shown to be 'without any real religious statement to make'? (Baxter 1964, 84). Certainly it does, if 'religious statement' be understood as dogma or categorical pronouncement. If, as André David observes, Beckett 'se tient dans l'expérience de la tragédie humaine. Il s'y tient et n'en sort pas' (remains within the experience of human tragedy. He remains there without leaving) (David 1992, 10), the impasse is precisely where Beckett has chosen to remain.

notes

1. Burial service, 1662 Prayer Book.
2. This series of notebooks, incidentally, also contains a very detailed 'doodle' by Beckett of a crucifixion scene, incorporating several elements of crucifixion narratives in the Gospels. It is reproduced and commented upon in my 'Figures of Golgotha: Beckett's Pinioned People' in John Pilling and Mary Bryden (eds), *The Ideal Core of the Onion: Reading Beckett Archives* (Reading: Beckett International Foundation, 1992), 45–62.
3. See Samuel Beckett, 'Peintres de l'empêchement,' in Samuel Beckett, *Disjecta: Miscellaneous Writings and a Dramatic Fragment*, ed. by Ruby Cohn (London: John Calder, 1983), 133–7 [135–6].
4. Here quoted in the King James (Authorized) version.
5. See Reading University Library MS 3000/1.
6. My own book, *Samuel Beckett and the Idea of God* (London: Macmillan – now Palgrave Macmillan, 1998) includes analyses of uses of the Bible within Beckett's writing. See particularly pp. 34–48 and pp. 102–12.
7. See Bryden 1998, Chapter 5.
8. This passage occurs in the Preface to *La Princesse Maleine*, *L'Intruse*, and *Les Aveugles*.
9. For an early exposition, see James Knowlson, *Light and Darkness in the Theatre of Samuel Beckett* (London: Turret Books, 1972).

works cited

Allen, Michael. 'A Note on Sex in Beckett,' in Gerald Dawe and Edna Longley (eds). *Across a Roaring Hill: the Protestant Imagination in Modern Ireland*. Belfast: Blackstaff Press, 1985, 39–47.

Anders, Günther. 'Being Without Time: On Beckett's Play *Waiting for Godot*,' in Martin Esslin (ed.), *Samuel Beckett: a Collection of Critical Essays*. Englewood Cliffs, NJ: Prentice-Hall, 1965, 140–51.

Baldwin, Hélène. *Samuel Beckett's Real Silence*. University Park: Pennsylvania State University Press, 1981.

Barge, Laura. *God, the Quest, the Hero: Thematic Structures in Beckett's Fiction*. Chapel Hill: University of North Carolina Press, 1988.

Barge, Laura. 'Beckett's Metaphysics and Christian Thought: a Comparison.' *Christian Scholar's Review*, 20, 1 (September 1990), 33–44.

Barjon, Louis. 'Le Dieu de Beckett.' *Etudes* (January 1965), 650–62.

Baxter, K. M. *Speak What We Feel: a Christian Looks at Contemporary Theatre*. London: SCM Press, 1964.

Beckett, Samuel. *Endgame*. London: Faber, 1964.

—— *Waiting for Godot*. London: Faber, 1965.

—— *Murphy*. London: Picador, 1973.

—— *Watt*. London: John Calder, 1976.

—— 'Peintres de l'empêchement,' in Beckett, Samuel, *Disjecta: Miscellaneous Writings and a Dramatic Fragment*, ed. Ruby Cohn. London: John Calder, 1983.

Bryden, Mary. *Samuel Beckett and the Idea of God*. London: Macmillan – now Palgrave Macmillan, 1998.

Butler, Lance St John. '"A Mythology with which I am perfectly familiar": Samuel Beckett and the Absence of God,' in Robert Welch (ed.), *Irish Writers and Religion*. Gerrards Cross: Colin Smythe, 1992, 169–84.

Cixous, Hélène. 'Une Passion: l'un peu moins que rien,' in Tom Bishop and Raymond Federman (eds), *Cahiers de l'Herne: Samuel Beckett*. Paris: Editions de L'Herne, 1976, 396–413.

Coe, Richard. 'God and Samuel Beckett.' *Meanjin Quarterly*, 24, 1 (1965), 66–85.

Cohn, Ruby. 'Endgame,' in Bell Gale, Chevigny. (ed.). *Twentieth Century Interpretations of* Endgame. Englewood Cliffs, NJ: Prentice-Hall, 1969, 40–52.

Cronin, Anthony. *Samuel Beckett: the Last Modernist*. London: HarperCollins, 1996.

David, André. 'Samuel Beckett: La Parole de Tragédie.' *Etudes*, 376, 2 (February 1992), 1–11.

Davies, Paul. *Beckett and Eros: Death of Humanism*. London: Macmillan – now Palgrave Macmillan, 2000.

Driver, Tom. Interview with Beckett, in Lawrence Graver and Raymond Federman (eds). *Samuel Beckett: the Critical Heritage*. London: Routledge and Kegan Paul, 1979, 217–23.

Duckworth, Colin. *Angels of Darkness: Dramatic Effect in Samuel Beckett with Special Reference to Eugène Ionesco*. New York: Barnes and Noble, 1972.

Durozoi, Gérard. *Beckett*. Paris: Bordas, 1972.

Foster, Paul. *Beckett and Zen: a Study of Dilemma in the Novels of Samuel Beckett*. London: Wisdom Publications, 1989.

Graver, Lawrence, and Federman, Raymond (eds). *Samuel Beckett: the Critical Heritage*. London: Routledge and Kegan Paul, 1979.

Hamilton, Alice and Kenneth. *Condemned to Life: the World of Samuel Beckett*. Grand Rapids: William B. Eerdmans Publishing Company, 1976.

Harries, Reverend Richard. 'Samuel Beckett and Christian Hope' (Drawbridge Memorial Lecture 1982). London: Christian Evidence Society, 1982.

Hokenson, Jan. 'A Stuttering *Logos*: Biblical Paradigms in Beckett's Trilogy.' *James Joyce Quarterly*, 8, 4 (1971), 293–310.

Hunt, W. H. *Pre-Raphaelitism and the Pre-Raphaelite Brotherhood*. London: Chapman and Hall, 1913 (2nd edn.), Vol. I.

Janvier, Ludovic. *Beckett*. Paris: Editions du Seuil, 1969.

Juliet, Charles. *Rencontre avec Samuel Beckett*. Saint-Clément-de-Rivière: Editions Fata Morgana, 1986.

Kenner, Hugh. *A Reader's Guide to Samuel Beckett*. London: Thames and Hudson, 1973.

Kiberd, Declan. 'Beckett and the Life to Come,' in S. E. Wilmer (ed.), *Beckett in Dublin*. Dublin: Lilliput Press, 1992, 75–84.

Knowlson, James. *Damned to Fame: the Life of Samuel Beckett*. London: Bloomsbury, 1996.

Kundert-Gibbs, John Leeland. *No-thing is Left to Tell: Zen/Chaos Theory in the Dramatic Art of Samuel Beckett*. Cranbury: Associated University Presses, 1999.

Mercier, Vivian. *Beckett/Beckett*. Oxford: Oxford University Press, 1977.

Morrison, Kristin. 'Neglected Biblical Allusions in Beckett's Plays: "Mother Pegg" Once More,' in Morris Beja, S. E. Gontarski, and Pierre Astier (eds). *Samuel Beckett: Humanistic Perspectives*. Columbus: Ohio State University Press, 1983, 91–98.

Onimus, Jean. *Beckett*. Paris: Desclée de Brouwer, 1968.

Pilling, John, and Bryden, Mary. *The Ideal Core of the Onion: Reading Beckett Archives*. Reading: Beckett International Foundation, 1992.

Ross, Ciaran. 'Homewards to the Centre of Nowhere: Difference and (Irish) Identity at Play in Samuel Beckett's Theatre.' *Cycnos*, 10, 2 (1993), 97–115.

Simon, Alfred. *Samuel Beckett*. Paris: Pierre Belfond, 1983.

Smith, Frederick. *Beckett's Eighteenth Century*. Basingstoke: Palgrave – now Palgrave Macmillan, 2002.

Wolosky, Shira. *Language Mysticism: the Negative Way of Language in Eliot, Beckett, and Celan*. Stanford: Stanford University Press, 1995.

10
beckett and psychoanalysis

angela moorjani

Deep into my dissertation on Beckett in the late 1960s, I found myself turning to psychoanalytic theory to buttress my attempts at understanding his elusive texts; the dissertation in hand, I called my first paper 'A Comic Oedipus' (1970). For me, Beckett's textual enfolding of unconscious effects and his allusions to psychoanalysis were not to be denied; at the same time the infusion of linguistic and semiotic insights into psychoanalytic theory provided a heady framework for new excursions in the field. Not everyone was of the same mind, I was soon to learn. Eventually, two major developments would moderate the unexpected resistance I experienced to anything smacking of a psychoanalytic reading: first, the light the biographies of Beckett shed on his impressive psychoanalytic culture; and second, the excitement generated by bold new incursions into the psyche: object-relations theory, other postKleinian analytical thought, and structuralist/poststructuralist psychoanalysis.[1]

Resistance to psychoanalytic criticism was based on a number of practices perceived as 'reductive,' or simplifying, such as diagnosing the symptoms of authors or their creatures or matching themes with psychoanalytic concepts. To counter the critique of 'applied analysis' as reductive, the object of psychoanalytic readings shifted from pathography and content to what may be broadly termed 'textual performativity.' In privileging the interplay of textual production and reception, such readings are akin to an analyst listening to an analysand for resonances between their conscious minds, unconscious minds, and the circuits joining these topologies (Anzieu 1992, 91–2; Schwab 1994, 15–16). As I introduce Beckett's psychoanalytic culture and a number of analytic methodologies and readings it will become apparent that the quasi-proscribed pleasures of 'applied analysis' are not easily denied.

beckett's psychoanalytic culture and intertexts

As we know from the biographies, while in mourning for his father who died in 1933, Beckett sought treatment at London's Tavistock clinic for increasingly debilitating symptoms. He remained in therapy for two years with Wilfred R. Bion, then a fledgling psychotherapist, whose later writings on psychoanalytic theory are considered among the most eminent and original in the field.[2] The intrauterine memories of entrapment that Beckett was to mention on several occasions surfaced while he was in Bion's care. It would be surprising then if Beckett did not echo to some extent his therapist in ascribing his terrifying symptoms to a 'negation of living' owing to arrogant feelings of superiority and his tendency to disengage and isolate himself.[3] Amply chronicled by Beckett's biographers are his troubled relation to his mother May; Beckett himself wrote to Tom MacGreevy in 1937 that 'her savage loving' made him what he was. In later years, Beckett was to conclude that the analysis with Bion most likely helped him to control the panic and come to a better understanding of his doings and feelings.[4]

The notebooks Beckett kept on his readings in psychology and psychoanalytic theory at the time of his treatment were discovered only after the author's death; the notes on his therapy are apparently lost (Knowlson 1996, 171–2, 652 n. 51). The relatively recent discovery, then, that Beckett read Otto Rank's *The Trauma of Birth* at the time of his treatment helps to shed light on Beckett's fictional and dramatic reenactments of intrauterine existence, expulsion from the womb, and fizzled-out births-into-death that readers have puzzled over for decades.[5] On reading *The Trauma of Birth* two or three years after writing *Dream of Fair to Middling Women*, Beckett may well have been startled by the convergence between his and Rank's conceptions of a prenatal and posthumous timelessness fused in the mind: 'the darkened mind gone wombtomb' and 'the umbra of grave and womb where it is fitting that the spirits of his dead and his unborn should come abroad' (Beckett 1992, 44–5). For Rank (1957), this phantasy in which a progression toward death is identical to a regression to the womb, or where the future after death is also conceived as a return to a past before birth, is an attempt at healing the trauma of separation at birth.[6]

The consonance between the young Beckett and the disciple of Freud that Rank still was when he wrote his book on birth trauma can be explained by the pervasive influence of Arthur Schopenhauer's concept of nirvana on writers, artists, and psychoanalytic thinkers in the first decades of the twentieth century. Taken from Hindu and Buddhist sources, Schopenhauer's nirvana posits a phantom inner self (part of the will) that is ultimately unknowable and whose timelessness is that of the unborn and the dead. This lost paradise of nonbeing (*Nichtseins*), the philosopher suggests, is the object of our unending nostalgia (Schopenhauer 1969, 2:§ 41). In connecting his own Nirvana/pleasure principle to the death drive's compulsion to return to zero, Freud is aware of his indebtedness to Schopenhauer.[7] Rank combines these influences in referring to nirvana as 'the pleasurable Nothing, the womb situation.' Beckett joined other writers and artists in identifying the 'dark' and 'will-less' endlessness in the mind, said to be so 'pleasant that pleasant was not the word,' with the space of artistic conception (Rank 1957, 119; Beckett 1957, 113). It is from this psychic location outside of space (and time) that the Beckettian text (after *Murphy*) repeatedly tries and fails to effect a birthing into death in a rapturous celebration of the always deferred return to nothing.

Freud's *Beyond the Pleasure Principle*, dating from 1920, is undoubtedly one of the most important of Beckett's Freudian intertexts. In this work, Freud associates both the Nirvana/pleasure principle and the repetition compulsion to the death drive and describes the *fort-da* game through which his grandson enacted repeatedly separation from mother and self (the latter by making himself appear and disappear in a mirror).[8] Beckett's fondness for this text is apparent from the direct and indirect references to the pleasure principle in *Murphy* and *Molloy* and from repeated textual performances of the *fort-da* game in his work.[9] Further, in associating stones and the metamorphosis into stone with pleasure and death, both Rank and Beckett echo the urge 'to return to the inanimate state' that Freud describes as inhering in organic life.[10] In his poetic transformations of the stone motif in *Molloy*, *Godot*, *Ohio Impromptu*, *Ill Seen Ill Said* (to mention only these), Beckett continued his homage to *Beyond the Pleasure Principle*, from which, unlike some other Freudian texts, he did not distance himself through ironic mockery.[11]

Increasingly in Beckett's work after the 1930s, one can detect the translation of inner stirrings of the unconscious mind into maternal and paternal metaphors that is matched by resistance to them and the undoing or debunking of oedipal figurations in the direction of unnamability, anonymity, or the indeterminate. (More on this later.) Among the reasons to value Rank (1957) as intertext are its many maternal metaphors, substitute objects, and forms of play that are echoed in Beckett's later fiction and theater.[12] Rank's views (1957) on aesthetics too are useful for understanding Beckett's at times poetic, at times playful, and at times parodic or ironic shaping of maternal metaphors, the substitutes for the ultimately unthought. In linking the repeated attempts at overcoming birth trauma and healing separation anxiety to a child's and the artist's playful productions of substitute objects and other reenactments of separation and reunion, Rank (1957) is harking back to *Beyond the Pleasure Principle* as well as anticipating later developments in object-relations theory, such as Donald W. Winnicott's (1971) transitional objects and theory of play.

Long known and frequently adduced by Beckettian critics is the importance Beckett attached to a statement made at a lecture by Carl G. Jung that he attended with Bion at the Tavistock Clinic. Jung's words, 'She had never been born entirely,' about a little girl whose archetypal dreams seemed to announce her early death, are echoed in the addenda to *Watt* and directly or indirectly in a number of later works (Jung 1968, 107). In conversations with Lawrence Harvey some twenty-five years later, Beckett applied Jung's words to himself, speaking of an 'existence by proxy' and the intuition of 'a presence, embryonic, undeveloped, of a self that might have been but never got born, an *être manqué*' (quoted in Harvey 1970, 247).

Two books completed shortly before the publication of the Knowlson biography (1996) concentrate on Beckett's psychoanalytic intertexts. James D. O'Hara (1997) argues that Beckett used Jungian and Freudian texts as scaffolding for many of his pre-1957 works. Although it is uncertain whether the specific essays O'Hara quotes are actual sources that Beckett had in mind or whether they are intertexts, which leave this question open, the intersecting Jungian, Freudian, Beckettian, and other philosophical and literary texts he assembles are skillfully and often wittily probed for analytic insights. In diagnosing *Molloy's* two self-narrators as patients in need of therapy, O'Hara (1997, 101–280), moreover, is aware of the 'applied' nature of this exercise (301): He portrays Molloy as a typical Jungian patient who fails to attain individuation, while the Freudian Moran suffers from a 'narcissistic psychoneurosis' (278).[13] In his conclusion, O'Hara admits that Beckett sided with Freud over Jung in the quarrel that pitted the founder of psychoanalysis against his disciple (292).[14] In the second intertextual study, Phil Baker (1997) contends that Beckett distances himself from his psychoanalytic intertexts by a strategy of 'quotation,' in effect transforming psychoanalysis into a 'mythology.' This claim is difficult to uphold throughout even within Baker's largely thematic approach. Still, his extensive matching of psychoanalytic narratives (mostly Freudian and Rankian) with Beckettian motifs, even as it recapitulates the work of previous critics, provides an intelligent compendium of psychoanalytic ideas in Beckett's works.

In addition to Freud, Jung, and Rank, the most renowned among the scions of psychoanalysis into whose thought Beckett delved at the time of his treatment are Alfred Adler, Ernest Jones, and Wilhelm Stekel. Further explorations of the psychoanalytic narratives interwoven in Beckett's works will from now on be facilitated by the publication of the Knowlson biography (1996) and the availability of Beckett's notebooks from the 1920s and 1930s along with his correspondence with Tom MacGreevy.[15]

beckett and bion and other postkleinians

After Beckett's psychotherapy with Bion became known, a number of analysts and critics began to draw parallels between the Beckettian forms of address and the analytic situation. For many, *Not I*'s disembodied Mouth spewing words at a silent, shadowy Auditor came to evoke an analytic session. For others, Beckett was transposing specific aspects of his analysis with Bion into his works. In the view of eminent French psychoanalyst Didier Anzieu (1989*b*, 1992), who authored a study of Freud's self-analysis among other influential books, Beckett pursued the interrupted psychotherapy with Bion in the shape of a fictionalized self-analysis in *Watt* through *How It Is*.[16] More specifically, Jean-Michel Rabaté (1984) tracks a number of allusions in *Murphy* to Beckett's therapy with Bion and his readings in psychology and psychoanalysis at the time. The practice that Beckett shares with many writers of devising fictional composites, with bits and pieces of friends, enemies, family, self, and figures from literature and myth blended together, and the fact that *Murphy* was a text in progress during Beckett's years in treatment lend credence to Rabaté's view that parts of Bion went into the making of Murphy's teacher Neary (Knowlson 1996, 200–04; Rabaté 1984, 138).

Another argument in favor of Rabaté's (1984) identification is Bion's interest in the reversible perspective celebrated by gestalt psychologists. Bion was to integrate such figure-and-ground reversals into all aspects of his clinical, theoretical, and fictional work (Bléandonu 1994, 180–2, 250). In having Neary declare to Murphy 'all life is figure and ground,' Beckett is referring to a form of visualization that he will favor as much as Bion (Beckett 1957, 4). Indeed, among Beckett's many textual reversals of perspective, the figure-and-ground oscillation bound up with the oedipal mother and father imagos in the two parts of *Molloy* is among the most spectacular (see Moorjani 1982, 110). In a stunning parallel, Bion (1963, 54–9) hypothesizes that in meeting the interpretations proposed to him with blankness, one of his analysands is reversing perspective to avoid the severe pain associated with the Oedipus myth. Who here is elucidating whom? Is this too a matter of figure and ground?

The extent to which Beckett and Bion continued to influence each other over the years is a topic of some contention. It is known that they had no more personal or professional contact after 1935; not known is how much they were aware of each others' subsequently published work (Simon 1988, 336). Anzieu (1989b) and Harvard analyst Bennett Simon (1988) both hypothesize that the 'imaginary twin' phantasy that Bion describes in a 1950 paper was based on Beckett's therapy with him (Bion 1967, 3–22). As Bion states in his 1967 commentary on 'The Imaginary Twin,' he distorted the past of the patient in question 'to prevent him or anyone who knew him from thinking it referred to him' (Bion 1967, 120). In mentioning only one patient, although there are three (A, B, and C) in the original paper, and in suspecting that an identification is inevitable, Bion is challenging his readers to identify a model for his composite patient whom he has put together with bits and pieces like a Beckettian figure. Simon (1988), Anzieu (1992, 220), and Rabaté (1996, 25) all agree that there is an unconscious 'connivance' or 'correspondence' between the former analyst and analysand. It does not appear far-fetched that akin to Beckett's own obsessive experimentation with form to accommodate psychic catastrophe, Bion would repeatedly, even compulsively, make use of his later analytic experience and theoretical sophistication to rethink and reframe unresolved issues dating back to his first years as an inexperienced therapist. Along the way, their transformations of a shared experience were bound to manifest an *air de famille*.

As Lois Oppenheim (2001) contends, such hypotheses remain conjectural. Indirect evidence, however, is available in the striking parallels between Bion's paper and Beckett's own obsessive reenactments of the drama of an unborn twin. Drawing on the theories of Melanie Klein, with whom he was in analysis from 1945 to 1953, Bion (1967, 8–9) concludes that the nonexistent twin, whom his patient kept from being born and who was keeping him from being born in turn, was a bad split-off part of his personality that he projected into his analyst in order to be rid of it. This patient was able to personify his splits successfully and, one might add, artfully, when one considers the theories of the origin of art in child's play. Bion (1967, 14) compares listening to the patient's personifications to 'watching a session of play therapy with a child.' Beckett, in the meanwhile, in words similar to those he used to Lawrence Harvey, told Charles Juliet (quoted in 1986, 14) of his feeling of not having been born and his identification with an inner being that was murdered before his birth whom he must bring back to life. This obligation corresponds in aesthetic terms to the only affirmation that Beckett finds available to the artist, namely the 'giving form to formlessness' (quoted in Juliet 1986, 28; my literal translation of Beckett's 'donn[er] forme à l'informe').

Beckett's third and fourth *Fizzles*, dating from the early 1970s, suggest that the speaking *I* is an unborn twin inside the one who 'wailed' (Beckett 1995, 232). It was he, my twin, not I, who was born, these speakers insist, a refrain taken up by Mouth in *Not I* that dates from the same time: 'who? ... no! ....she!' (Beckett 1984, 217–22). For the play, Jung's unborn little girl with whom Beckett identified and who has grown into an old fantasy comes to mind. Even more apropos is 'the injured girl' that Bion (1967, 14) describes as an object 'recovered from [the patient's] inside, which was to be subjected to the scrutiny of both his eyes.'[17] Continuing the much commented on confounding of bodily orifices (from *Watt* on) – eyes, mouth, vagina, anus – and their figurative compression into the birth passage, *Not I* offers to the scrutiny of the eyes and ears an uttering mouth suggesting another twin's botched birth or 'wailing.'[18] A parallel in Bion is not hard to find. In *The Dream*, a novel published in 1975, the first-person narrator imagines an 'amusing' view of his mouth from *inside* the body: By using his alimentary canal as a telescope, he could focus from the rear passage up at 'the mouth full of teeth and tonsils and tongue' (Bion 1991, 3). Bion's thought helps elucidate Beckett's play and Beckett's play in turn helps interpret Bion's novel.

A radio play predating *Not I* by about ten years already parodied the analytic situation as a failed birth. In 'Rough for Radio II,' the patient Fox tells of 'my brother inside me, my old twin' to a punishing analyst disguised as a grotesque (Kleinian) combined-parent (Beckett 1984, 119). Hilariously spoofed too are an analyst's attempts to make sense of the notes from a previous session. In Paul Lawley's brilliant reading of the rough for radio (1989), he finds instances of reversed perspective tying the play's male pregnancy and blocked self-birth to Beckett's preoccupation with 'imperfect being, utterance and the process of creation.' Beyond these specific dramatizations of the imaginary twin, Watt of the Sam–Watt couple, Molloy of the Molloy–Moran pair, the narrative voice of the other novels through *How It Is*, the speaking voices in *Company* and the late plays, such as *Ohio Impromptu, That Time, A Piece of Monologue*, as well as

Footfalls and *Rockaby* suggest an increasingly ghostly unborn twin, or a split-off part of the personality, either failing to utter himself or herself into birth or, in the later works, failing to enshadow the born twin's fading away into death.

Intriguingly, the Director–Assistant couple bringing/torturing the Protagonist to visibility in the 1982 *Catastrophe* recalls the earlier rough for radio's intersection of scenarios of catastrophic birth with the dynamics of aesthetic creation. Pointing out a psychoanalytic subtext in a play whose enactments of violence are linked to an overtly political situation permits me to focus briefly on the textual stacking-up, or the enfolded levels of interpretation, in a Beckettian text, with which the boundaries of a psychoanalytic reading necessarily overlap. The Beckettian twinning of birth and death, of love and destruction, is a psychic subtext bound up with the text's own fizzled coming into being in the manner of metafiction and metatheatre. The ghostly figures moving within an enwombed and entombed theater of the mind are doubled by their twinning apparitions in a theater of ritual repetition constrained by institutional demands, both of which in turn interconnect with the outer world of social/political interactions in a historical time and place. Or the perspective can be reversed. The intersections do not end there – as we know, nothing ever ends in Beckett – as these scenarios become analogies of the analytic situation, or connect anagogically with ontological and mystical concerns. And all of it is enfolded in the matrix of language, or the material textuality of performance and its far-reaching effects on unconscious, conscious, and social positionings. And that in turn is enshrouded in blankness and the unknown. Or the perspective can be reversed. And what about the playfulness and humor? Is it not they who frame it all?

At the end of Bion's paper on the twin, he connects in fascinating ways the role of vision in psychic development and thinking with the emergence of the oedipus situation for the patient in question (Bion 1967, 21). Based in part on 'an association' contributed by the patient about two 'eye men,' one of whom he referred to as an 'eye surgeon,' this theme relates to the patient's intent to subject his injured object to the scrutiny of his eyes and intellect (Bion 1967, 14). Murphy's 'surgical quality' comes to mind (Beckett 1957, 62, 80) along with the role of seeing as a structuring and positioning device in the tortured relationship between self and other (within and without the subject) in Beckett's writing. Rendering an injured object visible to the eyes is an intriguing approach to Beckett's ever renewed attempts at failing to find a visible form for the inner chaos. As we have seen, reversible perspective is one of his ways of questioning the stability of vision: figure and ground, inside and outside, contained and container, image and frame oscillate in and out of focus perhaps, as Bion suggests, as a way of dealing with psychic pain.[19]

To my mind, the overlap in Bion's early essays with Kleinian theory is another reason for the parallels between the analyst and his early patient. In developing the construct he called 'attacks on linking,' for example, Bion (1967, 93, 100–01) makes use not only of Klein's projective identification, but also of her description of early aggressive phantasies based on envy against the combined parent's body and the part-objects it contains. There is little doubt that Beckett was aware of Kleinian thought and play technique as early as *Murphy*, where the first zone of Murphy's mind contains 'the world of the body broken up into the pieces of a toy' (Beckett 1957, 112). Additionally, the use he made of the Kleinian combined-parent phantasm in 'Rough for Radio' is only one of many instances in his writing.[20]

The Bionian 'attacks on linking' are assaults on 'anything which is felt to have the function of linking one object with another' (Bion 1967, 93). Such destructiveness curtails psychic development and verbal thinking and the capacity to introject good objects. For Anzieu (1989b, 166) Beckett's *Watt* is the first of several novels to manifest Bionian attacks on linking in its lack of relations and destruction of verbal meaning. In a fortuitous connection, Oppenheim (2001, 775–6) maintains that Beckett's often-quoted 1937 letter to Axel Kaun, with its own programmatic 'assault against words,' recalls a Bionian attack on verbal thought. Yet, Beckett's linguistic volleys, or his 'unwording the world' through words, is a process precariously posed between a failure to destroy and a failure to create links (see Locatelli 1990). Or as Lawley (1997, 41) puts it in his essay on narrative and parental relations: 'Utterance has the impossible task of repairing what it has itself broken.'[21]

In the space available, I have been able to suggest only a small part of the richness of Bion's thought and its resonance with Beckett's writing and theater practice. For readers who are interested in pursuing the connections between the two (and the elucidation obviously works both ways), I recommend, in addition to the works by Bion and the exegetes cited earlier, the essays by Ciaran Ross who has read Beckett with Bion in profoundly responsive ways and who is reconceptualizing Beckett's space of writing and its relation to blankness in Bionian and Derridean terms.[22]

Although Anzieu (1992, 8) traces his obsession with Beckett to a 1953 performance of *Godot* while he was in analysis with Jacques Lacan, he draws almost exclusively on Freud, Bion, Winnicott, and his own theoretical elaborations to write about Beckett. Other Beckett critics have in turn made use of Anzieu's concept of the skin ego (Anzieu 1989a), a phantasmatic interface between the body ego and the outer world. For the skin ego, phantasies of protective envelopment that recall fusion with the mother in the womb or in a common skin defend against separation anxiety; phantasies of wounded skin reenact the tearing away from maternal envelopment (skin, voice, rhythm, color).[23]

Others besides Anzieu have drawn on the renowned theorist of play D. W. Winnicott and his 'potential space' and 'transitional phenomena' in order to explain Beckett's adoption of a foreign tongue and to examine his plays and fiction.[24] Winnicott postulates that the potential for play and its extensions into cultural productivity depend on an intermediate space between baby and caretaker and, in general, between what he termed 'me' and 'not-me.' This paradoxical space of play is neither a dreamlike inner space nor a socially shared outer space: It is both. The me's relation to the not-me is neither symbiotic nor separate, but both; and the me's illusory omnipotence and disillusionment follow the same paradoxical pattern (Winnicott 1971). Well-known British analyst Patrick Casement (1993, 229) locates Beckett's writing in French in such a 'potential space' that permits him 'to play out' what has remained unresolved in relation to his external, internal and fictional mothers; Beckett's self-translations into English, too, are a means of recovering his capacity to play (Casement 1993, 243). Similarly, for Anzieu (1983, 71–4, 82), Beckett's main topic is the transitional space of creativity. In melding Winnicott's transitional space to his own notion of the skin ego, Anzieu postulates that in switching to French Beckett was able to purge the maternal imprints that enclosed him like a poisonous tunic, while evoking paradoxically the return to an archaic envelopment in a common skin and shared rhythms.[25] Given the relatively few studies that draw on Winnicott's work, one hopes that scholars will be encouraged to build on the scintillating possibilities suggested, for instance, by Ross (1992) and Gabriele Schwab's reading of *The Unnamable* as a 'transitional text' (1994, 132–71).

beckett and poststructuralist performativity

One reason, no doubt, for the draw of poststructuralist psychoanalysis is the allure of intellectual fashion, but the exciting possibility of thinking anew about the psyche in terms imported from linguistics and anthropology, semiotics and phenomenology surely plays a part. Only a few introductory remarks are possible here about the ways Beckett criticism has been inflected by the linguistic and philosophical revision of Freudian psychoanalysis undertaken by Jacques Lacan.[26] Topping all other Lacanian reformulations in popularity is his transformation of primary narcissism into a 'mirror stage' between the age of sixteen to eighteen months (Lacan 1977, 1–7). Beckett's textual mirrors, doublings, and disintegrating forms echo the mirror stage's constitution of the *I* as other (self-estrangement) and the introjection and projection of virtual marionettes of bodily wholeness, on the one hand, and of bodily fragmentation and dissolution, on the other.[27]

The mirror stage has the subject looking in the mirror, whereas Winnicott (1971, 111–18) proposes a pre-mirror stage when the infant's self-image and emotions develop because of the way it is being looked at and held by its first caretakers. It is more often than not the mother's face and hands that function as the child's first mirror. Drawing on the phenomenology of Maurice Merleau-Ponty and others, Lacan, too, would thirty years after first theorizing the mirror stage in the mid-1930s, refocus from the subject looking to its constitution as the object of the gaze (Lacan 1981, 65–119). The ways in which a visual text situates spectators by its gaze became an issue widely explored in the arts and film theory. Lacan's take on this issue was to identify the gaze with an archaic maternal imago, or object *a* (see below). In a brilliant and polemical rejection of Lacanian (or other) gender and power identifications, experimental filmmaker and theorist Peter Gidal (1986) argues that Beckett's theatrical practice positions spectators in conflict with the ideological effects of language, gesture, and gaze. This positioning is effected largely by blocking stable identifications with the known, whether conscious or unconscious. One such instance involves *Not I*'s hysteria about gender identity based on an oedipal crisis. The dramatic maneuver of having this male hysteria uttered by a woman's mouth thwarts any fixed gender identification (Gidal 1986, 98–9). Gidal's along with Bion's, Winnicott's, and Lacan's elaborations of the gaze provide controversial views for further psychoanalytic explorations of the important function of vision in Beckett's texts.

A second area of Lacanian thought with consequences for readings of Beckett are his conceptualizations of what he termed 'objects *A/a*.' Object *a* came to stand for the first lost and desired other (*autre*) which Lacan relates to Freud's *das Ding* (the Thing). Experienced as an exteriority in the interiority of the ego, this first estranged other is forever lost and forever desired by the subject. Whereas Freud did not personify *das Ding*, and Lacan himself wonders whether it isn't best to conceive of it as an unknowable Kantian thing-in-itself, he came nevertheless to identify the Thing with the archaic mother imago (Lacan 1986, 64–85, 101, 127). On the other hand, we know that in making his object A (*Autre*) stand for the ego-ideal identified with the law of the (dead) father and with the internalized discourse of the cultural environment, or the 'discourse of the Other,' Lacan is outdoing Freud by limiting the symbolic mediation of language and culture at the oedipal phase exclusively to the 'symbolic father,' the 'phallic signifier' or the 'name-of-the-father.'[28]

In Beckett studies, the Lacanian division between object *A/a* has had particular important effects. One of these is related to abjection, which for Kristeva (1980b) consists in a prenarcissistic mourning for a maternal 'nonobject' (in the sense of the Lacanian object *a*) and a 'not I' that are constituted by the exile or expulsion of birth and the second birth into the language of the Other.[29] All that flows from the body in the form of waste is therefore particularly abject by repeating the first separation at birth (Kristeva 1980b, ch. 4, 127). Drawing on Melanie Klein's archaic maternal object and Jacques Lacan's paternally-coded symbolic, Kristeva (1980b) limits maternal authority to a precultural 'semiotic' body and its polluting excretions which are repressed with the advent of the paternal function encompassing the symbolic, the law, and naming. Writing, she submits, entails the resurfacing of the abject body in the body of the text; in cases where the abject is identified with lifelessness, writing permits embodiment and resurrection (Kristeva 1980b, ch. 1, 33–4, ch. 3, 87–90). Ceaselessly moving back and forth between ingestion and expulsion and 'maternal body and paternal name,' Beckett's writing in the Trilogy effects such an embodiment for Leslie Hill, but with a difference (1990, 100–20). In his intricate and subtle reading of the Trilogy, Hill (1990, 120) maintains that in functioning as a body, the Beckettian text succeeds in leaving a mark through the reenactment not of 'resurrection' but of its own expulsion or failed birth.[30] Agreeing entirely with Kristeva in describing a Beckettian esthetics of waste and bodily decomposition, Evelyne Grossman (1998, 41–74) suggests that Beckett attempts to counter his 'borderline' feelings of imperfect birth with embodiment in his writing. In his study of abject identity in Beckett and Jean Genet, David Houston Jones (2000), on the other hand, argues that abjection can fuel resistance against social oppression.

A number of critics have melded writing, and especially narrative in Beckett, to the paternal function, or more accurately, they have linked 'narratricide' (Abbott 1996, 1–22), or narrative dissolution, to the absence of the father.[31] Contesting such a paternal coding of writing are those commentators who have instead associated Beckett's writing with *écriture féminine*, or the feminization of male writing and creativity.[32] In an extended and intricately reasoned essay, Lawley (1997), on the other hand, examines episodes that Beckett recollects obsessively in which father and mother preside in turn over narration as parturition and separation. In demonstrating that in these episodes it is the mother who demands separation and the father who is identified with the procreating body, Lawley (1997) indirectly puts in question the orthodox readings derived from Lacan and Kristeva. In my own work I emphasize that Beckett's writing is bound up with archaic mother–father imagos and with both a paternal law *and* a maternal law from which it tries to break free (Moorjani 1982; 1992, 181–95). More than one reader of Beckett, then, maintains that in using reversible perspective, one finds everywhere in his work the double bind of maternal–paternal laws and a male–female engendering. Finally, though, most exegetes agree that ultimately the Beckettian text erases or destabilizes maternal–paternal inscription – however these are interpreted – so as to render them illegitimate, or illegible, or, alternatively by turning them into objects of play.

Thirdly, Lacan's rewriting of the Freudian unconscious as a linguistic-pragmatic topos influenced the examination of the status of the *I* in Beckett's texts (Lacan 1977, 30–113). In tracing the *I*'s dispersion, critics learned with Lacan to draw on the sign functions of Ferdinand de Saussure, the enunciation-enunciated distinction of Émile Benveniste, the *I*'s deictic or shifting status and metaphorical and metonymical mechanisms described by Roman Jakobson, and the structuring effects of culture analyzed by Claude Lévi-Strauss. As we have seen, the voice, no less than vision, is bound up with separation anxiety, repetition, twinning, failed birth, contested parental inscriptions, blankness, and the pleasure of play and its effects. In addition, it has its parallel to the mirror stage in the echoing and self-alienating effects of utterance. For a succinct and intelligent introduction to Lacan's thought on these and other topics, I recommend the slim and elegant study by David Watson (1991), in which he reframes in provocatively Lacanian terms the textual practices (in the fiction) that other critics of Beckett have been examining: the *fort-da*, narrative repetition, the *I* and the discourse of the Other, lack, desire, and the fictional body, vision, and ghosting.[33]

Some of Lacan's critics have come to realize that his linguistic unconscious is less Freudian than psychopragmatic. The influential

French analyst André Green argues that all of Lacan's theory on the linguistic-pragmatic structure of the unconscious can be found in the work of the American philosopher Charles Sanders Peirce. Indeed, the work of the language theorists on whom Lacan drew overlaps with his.[34] Other thinkers have drawn on the same pragmatic concepts as Lacan to investigate the unraveling of the subject in Beckett's work. One such attempt relates the splitting of the subject in discourse and its deictic dislocations to psychoanalytic theories of mourning and encrypting of self and (m)other.[35]

Finally, many commentators have bound Beckett's writing to figurations of mourning and melancholy, especially in Freud (14: 243–58), Klein (1975b), and Abraham and Torok (1986). For these psychoanalytic thinkers, phantasms of lost ones live on buried in the mind, pinioned in an enclave in the ego, banished to a place of exile within a subject divided from itself. This memorial space encloses a lost one both living and dead, hated and loved, as mourning is unremittingly deferred. Abraham and Torok (1986) call this site of unfinished mourning a crypt whose cryptonyms are fetish signs that hide the encrypted name and body and keep the subject exterior to itself. More than one reader has identified this enceinte in the ego with Beckett's wombtomb space of writing with which I began this chapter and with which I am now bringing it, on this elegiac note, to its end, or as Beckett would remind us, to its near-end.[36]

glossary

imago: 'The image of a real object that the subject absorbs by introjection into his or her ego and endows with the status of fantasy' (Roudinesco 1997, 109).

intertext: A previous text echoed directly or indirectly in a new one. It may be a source with which the sender is interacting respectfully or ironically, or it may be part of that vast network of utterances saturating all discourse of which the sender is not directly aware but the receiver is. See also **text**.

object-relations theory: A psychoanalytic theory that focuses on the interrelation between the subject and its environment, especially between the child and his or her first object, or caretaker, usually the mother. The object-relations school is largely associated with the British Psycho-Analytical Society.

poststructuralism: A contested term referring to the evolution of structuralism beginning in the 1960s. Whereas structuralism emphasizes that human subjects are constructed by impersonal systems, of which language is the model, poststructuralism privileges the undermining of such systems from within them.

pragmatics: The area of semiotics that is concerned with how much of what we understand depends on the unspoken context. The American philosopher Charles Sanders Peirce (1839–1914) is considered the founder of this field. See also **psychopragmatics, semiotics.**

projective identification: A form of identification described by Melanie Klein. It involves splitting off parts of the personality and projecting them into external objects of identification (Bion 1967, 93).

psychopragmatics: The area of pragmatics that focuses on psychic context or 'scripts,' consisting of the representations of drives and emotions and the unconscious language and culture acquired from our environment. See also **pragmatics.**

semiotic, semiotics: Pertaining to the study of all signifying activities, including the nonverbal and contextual dimensions ignored by linguistics.

semiotic chora/body: Kristeva's use of the term *semiotic* refers to a phantasized archaic container evolving from the infant's earliest sensory experiences with another body. Limiting the use of the term to a presymbolic 'body language' is unfortunate. Nonverbal interactions are culturally inflected from the beginning and extended into fully cultural systems of communication which are 'semiotic' (signifying activities) in a much broader sense. See **semiotic, semiotics.**

text: In semiotics, a *text* expands in meaning beyond oral and written discourse to include other structured cultural performances, such as a theatrical or musical performance, a painting, a film, or a recording.

notes

1. In the interest of space, I refer to the English versions of Beckett's works and most secondary sources. To supplement the present overview, readers are encouraged to consult collections that focus largely or entirely on Beckett and psychoanalysis: Ben-Zvi, 1990, Smith 1991b, Rabaté 1992, Houppermans 1996a, Engelberts *et al.* 2000. A glossary at the end defines technical terms not previously clarified in the body of the paper.
2. An excellent introduction to Bion (1897–1979) is Bléandonu 2000.
3. Quoted in Knowlson 1996, 173 from a letter to Beckett's friend Tom MacGreevy of 10 March 1935. Bion's later essays tie arrogance and feelings of superiority to neurotic or psychotic symptoms, such as 'denudation' or 'without-ness' (Bion 1962, 97–8).

4. The information found in this paragraph comes from Knowlson 1996, 167–73, 624 n. 113.

5. Otto Rank (1884–1939) was the youngest of Freud's early disciples. Largely ignored after his break with Freud over *The Trauma of Birth*, Rank attracted renewed interest in the 1980s as a precursor of object-relations theory. See Rudnytsky 1991, 2–69.

6. The spelling of *phantasy* by convention signals an unconscious fantasy.

7. On the Schopenhauerian source of Freud's Nirvana principle, see Laplanche and Pontalis 1973, 272–3, 324; on the Schopenhauerian intertext for Beckett's 'wombtomb,' see Moorjani 1996; Rabaté 1996.

8. Freud 1953–74, 18: 1–64. All subsequent parenthetical references to Freud in the text will be to the 1953–74 *Standard Edition*.

9. Beckett 1957, 2, 113; 1958, 99. On the Freudian pleasure principle bound up with narrative repetition and *mise en abyme*, a postKleinian transformation of the *fort-da*, and textual enwombing, see Moorjani 1982, 33–151; in his study of repetition in Beckett's writing, Steven Connor (1988, 1–14) connects Derridean and Deleuzian thought on the duality of repetition with Freud's *Beyond the Pleasure Principle*. For a wonderfully lucid Derridean reading of Beckett's 'mirror-writing' and doubling, see Begam 1996.

10. See Rank 1957, 112; Beckett quoted in Büttner 1984, 163 n. 200; Freud 18: 38.

11. Among the other Freudian essays that numerous critics have found echoed in Beckett's texts, the 1918 'From the History of an Infantile Neurosis' (The 'Wolf Man') and 'The Uncanny' of 1919 stand out (Freud 17: 1–122, 218–56).

12. On Rankian allusions in Beckett's work of the 1940s, see Baker 1997, 64–72. Although many of Rank's metaphors overlap with Carl Jung's 'Symbols of the Mother and Rebirth' of 1912 (Jung 1976, 207–73), Rank (1957, 27) criticizes Jung for his nonpsychoanalytic focus.

13. The text from which O'Hara took this diagnosis is of special interest: in 'Neurosis and Psychosis,' Freud (19: 147–53) traces 'narcissistic psychoneurosis' to a conflict between the ego and the superego. In the same short essay of 1924, Freud describes the role of the ego to 'humour all its masters at once,' that is, the id, superego, and the outside world. Knowlson (1996, 206) affirms that one page of Beckett's notebooks 'sets out and defines the "Id, Ego and Superego,"' although the source of this page is more likely *The Ego and the Id* to which O'Hara refers at length (Freud 19: 12–59).

14. O'Hara's psychoanalytic references are limited to Jung and Freud and to a single critic of Beckett's work: G. C. Barnard (1970) who diagnosed Moran as a schizophrenic (O'Hara 1997, 228). Scholars will have to make their own connections with the striking Jungian analysis of *Molloy* in Aldo Tagliaferri 1967, and the Freudian readings of the same novel in terms of ego, id, and superego in David Hayman 1970, or in terms of an ironic or erased Oedipus in Moorjani 1976, 1982 (with a nod in the direction of Deleuze and Guattari's antioedipal stand), to mention only these early studies that made use of Jungian and Freudian intertexts in reading *Molloy*.

15. For a list of Beckett's readings in psychology and psychoanalysis at the time of his therapy, see Knowlson 1996, 171–2, 652 nn. 48, 49. The correspondence with Tom MacGreevy and Beckett's notebooks on his readings of that period

are at Trinity College Dublin Library. The latter became available to scholars only in 2001.

16. For other extended versions of Beckettian self-analysis, or what Abbott (1996, ix) terms 'self-writing' (or is it self-unwriting?), see in addition to Abbott, for example, Moorjani 1982; Hill 1990; Begam 1996; Lawley 1997.

17. A number of other sources for Mouth are discussed in Knowlson 1996, 520–23.

18. See Lawley 1983 for a subtle analysis of Mouth's words as self-referential portrayals of its own doings on stage while suggesting simultaneously the functions associated with an eye and the body's other orifices.

19. See also the Bionian discussion of Beckett's 'visual thinking' and 'visual writing' in Oppenheim, 2001, 770–5.

20. See also Rabaté 1996, 26 for other Kleinian allusions in *Murphy* and Bair 1978, 519–20 for a discussion Beckett had in 1960 about Kleinian and Freudian analysis. See Klein (1975a) for her history of the play technique and interpretations of early phantasies she developed in the 1920s. Given the notoriety of Klein's theories in the early 1930s, it is unlikely that Bion would not have been aware of them at that time. For Kleinian readings of Beckett and others, see Moorjani 1982, 1992, 2000a.

21. For further analyses of Beckett's 'attacks on linking' see Simon 1988 and Souter 1999.

22. For a sampling, see Ross 1992, 1996, 1997, 2001.

23. On the Beckettian skin ego, see Anzieu 1992, 113, 169, 216; Grossman 1998, 38; 50–2; Moorjani 2000a, 93–9; 2000b.

24. One of the most influential object-relations analysts of the twentieth century, Winnicott (1896–1971) was both a pediatrician and a postKleinian child analyst. For an appreciation of his contributions, see Rudnytsky 1991, 96–114; on transitional texts, see Schwab 1994, 1–48.

25. Critical of Casement and Anzieu's 'reductive' use of Winnicott, Ross (1992) argues for a more complex assessment of the relation between play and writing, especially for *Godot*.

26. For an introduction to the controversial Parisian analyst and thinker (1901–1981) and the intellectual climate in which he developed his theories (overlapping with the context of Beckett's post-war work), see Roudinesco 1997.

27. For Lacan's many sources of the mirror stage, see Laplanche and Pontalis 1973, 250–2; Roudinesco 1997, 110–12. For extensive discussions of the mirror stage in relation to Beckett, see, for example, Roof 1987 and Hunkeler 1997, 179–92. Watson (1991, 127–45) in addition examines Beckett's *Film* in light of Lacan's later views on the gaze.

28. See Lacan 1977, 56–77, 192–9; Roudinesco 1997, 283–5.

29. Kristeva 1980b, ch. 1, 11–22. Unable to locate a copy of the English translation in time, I have added chapter numbers to the citations to the French edition.

30. For readings of anal expulsion in relation to writing and birth, see, in addition to Hill 1990, Lawley 1993, and Baker 1997, 64–72.

31. In addition to Abbott 1996, see particularly Kristeva 1980a; Hill 1990; Watson 1991; Cousineau 1996, 1999; Bernard 1996.

32. See the chapter on this topic.
33. Another book-length study that reconceptualizes the Beckettian subject in largely Lacanian terms is Bernard 1996.
34. On psychopragmatics and Green's and other thinkers' critique of Lacan's view of the unconscious, see Moorjani 2000a, 3–17, 139–40 n. 11. For a psychopragmatic reading of *Texts for Nothing*, see Moorjani 2000a, 29–37. Only lack of space prevents discussion of Green's work to which several Beckett critics refer, among whom Lois Oppenheim (2001).
35. See Moorjani 1990, rpt. in 1992, 175–81; on deixis and first-person utterance, see also Katz 1999, 19–24.
36. Unlike my focus on the encrypted mother imago (Moorjani 1990, 1992, 1996), Hill (1990) draws on Abraham and Torok to probe the failed incorporation of the father. On melancholy and mourning in Beckett, see also Smith 1991a, Baker 1997, 145–70; Grossman 1998; Houppermans 1996b and 2001. American analyst Joseph Smith (1991a, 198) holds that people read Beckett because '[a]ll development is catastrophically marked by deprivation, loss, separation, guilt, anxiety, and meaninglessness, more or less overcome.'

works cited

Abbott, H. Porter. *Beckett Writing Beckett: the Author in the Autograph*. Ithaca: Cornell University Press, 1996.

Abraham, Nicolas, and Torok, Maria. *The Wolf Man's Magic Word: a Cryptonymy*. Trans. Nicholas Rand. Minneapolis: University of Minnesota Press, 1986.

Anzieu, Didier. 'Un soi disjoint, une voix liante: l'écriture narrative de Samuel Beckett.' *Nouvelle Revue de Psychanalyse*, 28 (1983): 71–85.

—— *The Skin Ego*. Trans. Chris Turner. New Haven: Yale University Press, 1989a.

—— 'Beckett and Bion.' *International Revue of Psycho-Analysis*, 16 (1989b): 163–9.

—— *Beckett et le psychanalyste*. Paris: Editions Mentha, 1992.

Bair, Deirdre. *Samuel Beckett: a Biography*. New York: Harcourt Brace Jovanovich, 1978.

Baker, Phil. *Beckett and the Mythology of Psychoanalysis*. London: Macmillan – now Palgrave Macmillan; New York: St. Martin's Press – now Palgrave Macmillan, 1997.

Barnard, Guy Christian. *Samuel Beckett: a New Approach*. New York: Dodd, Mead, 1970.

Beckett, Samuel. *Murphy*. New York: Grove Press, 1957. First published 1938.

—— *Three Novels: Molloy, Malone Dies, The Unnamable*. New York: Grove Press, 1958

—— *Collected Shorter Plays*. New York: Grove Press, 1984.

—— *Dream of Fair to Middling Women*. Ed. Eoin O'Brien and Edith Fournier. New York: Arcade Publishing, 1992.

—— *Samuel Beckett: the Complete Short Prose, 1929–1989*. Ed. S. E. Gontarski. New York: Grove Press, 1995.

Begam, Richard. *Samuel Beckett and the End of Modernity*. Stanford: Stanford University Press, 1996.

Ben-Zvi, Linda (ed.). *Women in Beckett: Performance and Critical Perspectives*. Urbana: University of Illinois Press, 1990.

Bernard, Michel. *Samuel Beckett et son sujet: une apparition évanouissante*. Paris: L'Harmattan, 1996.

Bion, Wilfred R. *Learning from Experience*. New York: Basic Books, 1962.

—— *Elements of Psycho-Analysis*. New York: Basic Books, 1963.

—— *Second Thoughts: Selected Papers on Psycho-Analysis*. New York: Jason Aronson, 1967.

—— *A Memoir of the Future (The Dream, The Past Presented, The Dawn of Oblivion)*. London: Karnac Books, 1991.

Bléandonu, Gérard. *Wilfred Bion: His Life and Works 1897–1979*. Trans. Claire Pajaczkowska. New York: Other Press, 2000.

Büttner, Gottfried. *Samuel Beckett's Novel 'Watt.'* Philadelphia: University of Pennsylvania Press, 1984.

Casement, Patrick J. 'Samuel Beckett's Relationship to His Mother-Tongue.' In *Transitional Objects and Potential Spaces: Literary Uses of D. W. Winnicott*, ed. Peter L. Rudnytsky, 229–45. New York: Columbia University Press, 1993. First published in *International Review of Psycho-Analysis*, 9 (1982): 35–44.

Connor, Steven. *Samuel Beckett: Repetition, Theory and Text*. Oxford: Basil Blackwell, 1988.

Cousineau, Thomas J. 'The Lost Father in Beckett's Novels.' In *Beckett & la psychanalyse & Psychoanalysis*. Vol. 5 of *Samuel Beckett Today/Aujourd'hui*, ed. Sjef Houppermans, 73–83. Amsterdam and Atlanta: Rodopi, 1996.

—— *After the Final No: Samuel Beckett's Trilogy*. Cranbury, NJ and London: Associated University Presses, 1999.

Engelberts, Matthijs *et al.* (eds). *L'Affect dans l'œuvre beckettienne*. Vol. 10 of *Samuel Beckett Today/Aujourd'hui*. Amsterdam and Atlanta: Rodopi, 2000.

Freud, Sigmund. *The Standard Edition of the Complete Psychological Works*. Ed. and trans. James Strachey *et al.* 24 vols. London: Hogarth Press, 1953–74.

Gidal, Peter. *Understanding Beckett: a Study of Monologue and Gesture in the Works of Samuel Beckett*. London: Macmillan – now Palgrave Macmillan; New York: St. Martin's Press – now Palgrave Macmillan, 1986.

Grossman, Evelyne. *L'Esthétique de Beckett*. Paris: Editions SEDES, 1998.

Harvey, Lawrence E. *Samuel Beckett: Poet and Critic*. Princeton: Princeton University Press, 1970.

Hayman, David. '*Molloy* or the Quest for Meaninglessness: a Global Interpretation.' In *Samuel Beckett Now*, ed. Melvin J. Friedman, 129–56. Chicago: University of Chicago Press, 1970.

Hill, Leslie. *Beckett's Fiction: In Different Words*. Cambridge, UK: Cambridge University Press, 1990.

Houppermans, Sjef (ed.). *Beckett & la psychanalyse & Psychoanalysis*. Vol. 5 of *Samuel Beckett Today/Aujourd'hui*. Amsterdam and Atlanta: Rodopi, 1996a.

—— 'A cheval.' In *Beckett & la psychanalyse & Psychoanalysis*. Vol. 5 of *Samuel Beckett Today/Aujourd'hui*, 43–55. Amsterdam and Atlanta: Rodopi, 1996b.

—— 'Travail de deuil, travail d' il dans *Mal vu mal dit*.' In *Samuel Beckett: Endlessness in the Year 2000/Fin sans fin en l'an 2000*. Vol. 11 of *Samuel Beckett Today/Aujourdhui*, ed. Angela Moorjani and Carola Veit, 361–71. Amsterdam and New York: Rodopi, 2001.

Hunkeler, Thomas. *Echos de l'Ego dans l'oeuvre de Samuel Beckett*. Paris: Editions L'Harmattan, 1997.

Jones, David Houston. *The Body Abject: Self and Text in Jean Genet and Samuel Beckett.* Bern and Oxford: Peter Lang, 2000.

Juliet, Charles. *Rencontre avec Samuel Beckett.* Montpellier: Editions Fata Morgana, 1986.

Jung, Carl G. *Analytical Psychology: Its Theory and Practice: The Tavistock Lectures.* New York: Pantheon Books, 1968.

—— *Symbols of Transformation.* Trans. R. F. C. Hull. 2nd edn. Princeton: Princeton University Press, 1976.

Katz, Daniel. *Saying I No More: Subjectivity and Consciousness in the Prose of Samuel Beckett.* Evanston, IL: Northwestern University Press, 1999.

Klein, Melanie. 'The Psycho-Analytic Play Technique: Its History and Significance.' In *Envy and Gratitude and Other Works 1946–1963*, 122–40. New York: Delacorte Press, 1975a.

—— 'Mourning and Its Relation to Manic-Depressive States.' In *Love, Guilt and Reparation and Other Works 1921–1945*, 344–69. London: Hogarth Press, 1975b.

Knowlson, James. *Damned to Fame: the Life of Samuel Beckett.* New York: Simon and Schuster, 1996.

Kristeva, Julia. 'The Father, Love, and Banishment.' In *Desire in Language: a Semiotic Approach to Literature and Art*, trans. Thomas Gora, Alice Jardine, and Leon Roudiez, 148–58. New York: Columbia University Press, 1980a.

—— *Pouvoirs de l'horreur: essai sur l'abjection.* Paris: Editions du Seuil, 1980b. Trans. by Leon S. Roudiez under the title *Powers of Horror: An Essay on Abjection* (New York: Columbia University Press, 1982).

Lacan, Jacques. *Ecrits: a Selection.* Trans. Alan Sheridan. New York: W. W. Norton, 1977.

—— *The Four Fundamental Concepts of Psychoanalysis (Seminar XI).* Trans. Alan Sheridan. New York: W. W. Norton, 1981.

—— *L'Ethique de la psychanalyse (Le Séminaire VII).* Paris: Editions du Seuil, 1986.

Laplanche, Jean, and Pontalis, J.-B. *The Language of Psycho-Analysis.* New York: W. W. Norton, 1973.

Lawley, Paul. 'Counterpoint, Absence and the Medium in Beckett's *Not I*.' *Modern Drama*, 26 (1983): 407–14.

—— 'The Difficult Birth: An Image of Utterance in Beckett.' In *'Make Sense who May': Essays on Samuel Beckett's Later Works*, ed. Robin J. Davis and Lance St. J. Butler, 1–10. Totowa, NJ: Barnes and Noble, 1989.

—— 'First Love: Passage and Play.' *Beckett in the 1990s.* Vol. 2 of *Samuel Beckett Today/Aujourd'hui*, ed. Marius Buning and Lois Oppenheim, 189–95. Amsterdam and Atlanta: Rodopi, 1993.

—— 'Samuel Beckett's Relations.' *Journal of Beckett Studies*, 6.2 (1997): 1–61.

Locatelli, Carla. *Unwording the World: Samuel Beckett's Prose Works after the Nobel Prize.* Philadelphia: University of Pennsylvania Press, 1990.

Moorjani, Angela. 'A Mythic Reading of *Molloy*.' In *Samuel Beckett: the Art of Rhetoric*, ed. Edouard Morot-Sir, Howard Harper, and Dougald McMillan, 225–35. Chapel Hill: University of North Carolina Press, 1976.

—— *Abysmal Games in the Novels of Samuel Beckett.* Chapel Hill: University of North Carolina Press, 1982.

—— 'Beckett's Devious Deictics.' In *Rethinking Beckett: a Collection of Critical Essays*. Ed. Lance St. John Butler and Robin J. Davis, 20–30. London: Macmillan – now Palgrave Macmillan, 1990.

—— *The Aesthetics of Loss and Lessness*. London: Macmillan – now Palgrave Macmillan; New York: St. Martin's Press – now Palgrave Macmillan, 1992.

—— 'Mourning, Schopenhauer, and Beckett's Art of Shadows.' In *Beckett On and On . . .*, ed. Lois Oppenheim and Marius Buning, 83–101. Cranbury, NJ and London: Associated University Presses, 1996.

—— *Beyond Fetishism and Other Excursions in Psychopragmatics*. New York: St. Martin's Press – now Palgrave Macmillan, 2000a.

—— 'Beckett et le Moi-peau: au-del du fétichisme matriciel.' In *L'Affect dans l'oeuvre beckettienne*. Vol. 10 of *Samuel Beckett Today/Aujourd'hui*, ed. Matthijs Engelberts *et al.*, 63–70. Amsterdam and Atlanta: Rodopi, 2000b.

O'Hara, James D. *Samuel Beckett's Hidden Drives: Structural Uses of Depth Psychology*. Gainesville: University of Florida Press, 1997.

Oppenheim, Lois. 'A Preoccupation with Object-Representation: the Beckett–Bion Case Revisited.' *International Journal of Psychoanalysis*, 82 (2001): 767–84.

Rabaté, Jean-Michel. 'Quelques figures de la première (et dernière) anthropomorphie de Beckett.' In *Beckett avant Beckett: essais sur le jeune Beckett (1930–1945)*, ed. Jean-Michel Rabaté, 135–51. Paris: Presses de l'Ecole normale supérieure, 1984.

—— (ed.). *Samuel Beckett: intertextualités et psychanalyse*. Dijon: Université de Bourgogne, 1992.

—— 'Beckett's Ghosts and Fluxions.' In *Beckett & la psychanalyse & Psychoanalysis*. Vol. 5 of *Samuel Beckett Today/Aujourd'hui*, ed. Sjef Houppermans, 23–40. Amsterdam and Atlanta: Rodopi, 1996.

Rank, Otto. *The Trauma of Birth*. New York: Robert Brunner, 1957. First published 1924 (German), 1929 (English).

Roof, Judith A. 'A Blink in the Mirror: From Oedipus to Narcissus and Back in the Drama of Samuel Beckett.' In *Myth and Ritual in the Plays of Samuel Beckett*, ed. Katherine H. Burkman, 151–63. London and Toronto: Associated University Presses, 1987.

Ross, Ciaran. 'Aspects du jeu dans l'oeuvre de Beckett.' In *Samuel Beckett: Intertextualités et psychanalyse*, ed. Jean-Michel Rabaté, 79–90. Dijon: Université de Bourgogne, 1992.

—— 'La "pensée de la mére": fonction et structure d'un fantasme.' In *Beckett & la psychanalyse & psychoanalysis*. Vol. 5 of *Samuel Beckett Today/Aujourd'hui*, 9–20. Amsterdam and Atlanta: Rodopi, 1996.

—— '"Toute blanche dans la blancheur": la prédominance de la métaphore blanche dans l'écriture beckettienne.' In *Samuel Beckett: Crossroads and Borderlines / L'œuvre carrefour, l'œuvre limite*. Vol. 6 of *Samuel Beckett Today/Aujourd'hui*, ed. Marius Buning *et al.*, 267–77. Amsterdam and Atlanta: Rodopi, 1997.

—— 'Beckett's *Godot* in Berlin: New Coordinates of the Void.' In *Samuel Beckett: Endlessness in the Year 2000 / Fin sans fin en l'an 2000*. Vol. 11 of *Samuel Beckett Today/Aujourdhui*, ed. Angela Moorjani and Carola Veit, 64–73. Amsterdam and New York: Rodopi, 2001.

Roudinesco, Elisabeth. *Jacques Lacan*. Trans. Barbara Bray. New York: Columbia University Press, 1997.

Rudnytsky, Peter L. *The Psychoanalytic Vocation: Rank, Winnicott, and the Legacy of Freud*. New Haven: Yale University Press, 1991.

Schopenhauer, Arthur. *The World as Will and Representation*.Trans. E. F. J. Payne. 2 vols. New York: Dover, 1969. Originally published in 1819–44.

Schwab, Gabriele. *Subjects without Selves: Transitional Texts in Modern Fiction*. Cambridge, MA: Harvard University Press, 1994.

Simon, Bennett. 'The Imaginary Twins: the Case of Beckett and Bion.' *International Review of Psycho-Analysis*, 15 (1988): 331–52.

Smith, Joseph H. 'Notes on *Krapp*, *Endgame*, and "Applied" Psychoanalysis.' In *The World of Samuel Beckett*, 195–203. Baltimore: Johns Hopkins University Press, 1991*a*.

—— (ed.). *The World of Samuel Beckett*. Baltimore: Johns Hopkins University Press, 1991*b*.

Souter, Kay Torney. 'Attacks on Links in the Work of Samuel Beckett and Wilfred Bion.' *Psyche Matters*. March 1999. http://www.psychematters.com/papers/souter.htm (23 August 2002).

Tagliaferri, Aldo. *Beckett et l'iperdeterminazione letteraria*. Milan: Giangiacomo Feltrinelli, 1967. Translated by Nicole Fama under the title *Beckett et la surdétermination littéraire* (Paris: Payot, 1977).

Watson, David. *Paradox and Desire in Samuel Beckett's Fiction*. New York: St. Martin's Press – now Palgrave Macmillan, 1991.

Winnicott, Donald W. *Playing and Reality*. London: Tavistock Publications, 1971.

11
beckett and performance

s. e. gontarski

> 'Oh but the bay, Mr. Beckett, didn't you know, about your brow.'
> *Dream of Fair to Middling Women*

narrative and performance

The idea of performance preoccupied Samuel Beckett well before he began to explore its potential directly in the theater. Its roots are in the doubling of the self that is already implicit in the idea of representation and the quasi-Cartesian idea of the 'pseudocouple' that Beckett would hone into in his fiction and drama alike. A character named 'Mr. Beckett,' for instance, appears in *Dream of Fair to Middling Women* (written between 1931–2) as a belaurelled poet at the conclusion of the short chapter called 'Und': 'Oh but the bay, Mr Beckett, didn't you know, about your brow' (141). (In 1931 laurels for the young author were, of course, very much a fiction.) At that point the author no longer stood entirely outside his work, but inside and outside simultaneously, a part of and apart from the narrative. Such fictionalizing of the self, narrated and narrator overlapping, followed hard upon Beckett's one and only direct stage appearance; he was persuaded to appear as Don Diègue in three performances of Trinity College's 'Cornelian nightmare,' *Le Kid*, at Dublin's Peacock Theatre between 19–21 February 1931 (Knowlson 126). Later in the 1930s Beckett would write a 23-line poem in French, 'Arènes de Lutèce,' in which he explored more fully the fractured or doubled self, what Lawrence Harvey referred to as the experience of *dédoublement* (202–07). In his pseudonymous 1934 essay 'Recent Irish Poetry,' Beckett would refer to such doubling as the crisis of the subject. What we read as the narrative of *Watt*, moreover, has apparently already been performed (or at least rehearsed) for an audience, a character named 'Sam' then re-presenting the tale (with the inevitable modifications of any *metteur en scène*) to a second audience, the reader. The model for such fictionalizing and performance of the self may have been Beckett's beloved Dante, and perhaps Proust as well, whose 'Marcel' relates what becomes *Remembrances of Things Past*. The idea of the author as a fiction performing in his own work appeared most directly finally, if fleetingly, as a descriptor in *That Time* where voice 'B' (Beckett?) was referred to at one point as 'something out of Beckett.' Ruby Cohn prevailed upon Beckett to excise the self-reference before publication and performance (332; 404, n10), but such self-reflexion invites us to read Mr Beckett, Sam, or Samuel Beckett as, at least potentially, a series of voices in and for performance, in short as a text himself. For the most part, however, Beckett learned to heed the advice he gave himself about Dante in the *Whoroscope Notebook* (University of Reading Ms. # 3000) as he was writing *Murphy*, 'keep whole Dantesque analogy out of sight.' The advice would, on the whole, apply equally to one 'Mr. Beckett.'

With two stage works written amidst the three post-war, French novels, Beckett would explore the crisis of the subject, its doubling (at least), on stage and page. The second of the two plays, *En attendant Godot*, written between *Malone meurt* and *L'Innommable*, was the first (finally) to be staged, in January of 1953 by Roger Blin at the Théâtre de Babylone. Beckett had high hopes for its companion, *Eleutheria*, as well. On 8 March 1948 he wrote to confidant Thomas MacGreevy, 'Eleutheria is dithering, dithering and beginning to be spoken of a little. I think it will see the boards in time if only for a few nights. But never those of the Gate [Theatre in Dublin].' With the success of *Godot*, however, Beckett sequestered *Eleutheria* (published only in 1995 and never officially staged) to his trunk and turned his development of performance in another direction. Soon after writing his two longest plays, he would explore the performative in a personal, serio-comic, aesthetic commentary, 'Three Dialogues with Georges Duthuit,' which he published in the newly revived, post-war *Transition* magazine in 1949 as *Eleutheria* and *Godot* were circulating among producers and as he was wrestling with the last of his three French novels, *L'Innommable*. In the self-deprecating critical piece, Beckett exploited the performative and travestied both aesthetic debate and the philosophical dialogue favored by Plato.

The philosophical tradition through which Beckett was working included Denis Diderot (1713–84) and Bernard Le Bovier de Fontenelle (1657–1757), the latter a French polymath and skeptic who was associated with Diderot in the making of the *Encyclopédie* (1751–72). Beckett's rendering of Fontenelle's 'De mémoire de rose on n'a vu que lui [le même jardinier]' from *Entretiens sur la Pluralité des mondes* (1686) was cited in the *Dream Notebook* (reference no. 581 in Pilling's edition). SB's source appears to have been one of Diderot's three philosophical dialogues, *Le Rêve de d'Alembert* (1769, pub. in 1830), in which d'Alembert's dream is discussed by his *amie*, Mlle. de l'Espinasse, and Doctor Bordeu:

> *Mlle. de l'Espinasse*: Doctor, what is this sympathy of the eternal?
> *Bordeu*: That of a transient being who believes in the immortality of things.
> *Mlle. de l'Espinasse*: Fontenelle's rose, saying that within the memory of the rose no gardener has been known to die.
> *Bordeu*: Precisely; that is graceful and profound.

Beckett used the 'graceful and profound' image in 'Echo's Bones' (19), and punned on it in *Dream* where the aged gardener broods 'over the fragility of all life' (174). That fragility is most poignantly expressed at the conclusion of 'Draff,' the tenth and final story of *More Pricks Than Kicks*, as a conversation, with emphatic punctuation, among roses on time and immortality, 'No gardener has died, comma, within rosaceous memory' (191), the conceit there associated with his father's death as well. (The quotation remained on Beckett's mind as late as 14 September 1977 when he wrote it out for Anne Atik, a note she reproduced in facsimile in her memoir, calling it 'his own beautiful translation' [Atik, 87]). As interesting as theme and image is the dialogue format that both Diderot and d'Alembert favored for philosophical, literary, and aesthetic discourse, and Beckett admired Diderot's philosophical dialogue, *Le Neveu de Rameau* (written in 1760). Set in a Paris café with two interlocutors, 'Moi' and 'Lui,' it offered a model for 'Three Dialogues,' the 'Exit weeping' of the second perhaps playing on Diderot's final 'Rira bien qui rira le dernier.'

Beckett knew George Berkeley's (1685–1753) decidedly undramatic *Three Dialogues between Hylas and Philonous*, as well, echoes of which appear in his subsequent theater work, *Fin de partie (Endgame)* that he began writing, in fits and starts, shortly after the dialogues. Hamm's neo-Romantic dreams of fertility beyond the immediate sterility and decay, for instance, echo Hylas's admonition of Philonous's skepticism of the senses: 'Philonous – Look! Are not the fields covered with delightful verdure? Is there not something in the woods and groves, in the rivers and clear springs that sooths, that delights the soul?' Hamm understands that Philonous's profound skepticism leads to madness, like that of the 'painter – an engraver' whom Hamm apparently visited in the asylum and for whose Philonous Hamm played Hylas: 'Look! There! All that rising corn. And there! Look! The sails of the herring fleet' (44). Hamm's persistent hopes ('Let's go from here, the two of us! South!' and 'But beyond the hills? Eh? Perhaps it's still green. Eh? . . . Flora! Pomona! . . . Ceres!' [34, 39]) keep him, for better or worse, from the asylum that the painter apparently found. British publisher John Calder thought 'Three Dialogues with Georges Duthuit' dramatic enough to stage as part of 'an evening devoted to your work' (25 June 1965). Beckett's response, on 30 June, was polite but adamant, 'Whatever you like, but please not the Duthuit dialogues. We can always find something to replace them.'

Writing *Eleutheria* (which he began on 18 January 1947) and *Godot* (which he began to write on 9 October 1948), Beckett folded the idea of performance into both texts as meta-theater or plays within plays (an 'Audience member' and 'Stage-box Voice' interrupting the action in Act III of *Eleutheria* and Lucky's monologue and his performance of the tree in *Godot,* most obviously). Beckett then began to extend the idea of performance in his fiction to new levels, developing a form of dialogic monologue with a consciousness of audience that would eventually find its way to the stage with *Krapp's Last Tape* in 1958 and dominate the short, late theater thereafter. Thus we have Auditor's echo of the spectator, of an audience that makes him (her?) so critical to the performance of *Not I,* for example. Similarly, Listener mirrors the audience and so adds to the doubling effects of *Ohio Impromptu.* In *Mercier and Camier* (written in 1946, but only published in 1970 and in translation in 1974) the eponymous duo, whom Beckett called a 'pseudocouple' in his subsequent fiction (*The Unnamable* 297), feel the presence of another, or an other, an audience of some sort:

I sense vague shadowy shapes, said Camier, they come and go with muffled cries.
I too have the feeling, said Mercier, we have not gone unobserved since morning.
Are we by any chance alone now? said Camier.
I see no one, said Mercier. (19)

Strange impression, said Mercier, strange impression sometimes that we are not alone. You not?
I am not sure I understand.

Now quick now slow, that is Camier all over.
Like the presence of a third party, said Mercier.
Enveloping us. I have felt it from the start. And I am anything but psychic.
Does it bother you? said Camier.
At first no, said Mercier.
And now? Said Camier.
It begins to bother me a little, said Mercier. (100)

'Pseudocouple' would become the critical term of choice for Beckett's paired characters (like Vladimir and Estragon, Hamm and Clov, Nagg and Nell, Reader and Listener, among others) who often seem to be aspects of a single character, a doubled representation of a single being. In *The Unnamable* (published as *L'Innommable* in Paris by Les Editions de Minuit in 1952) Beckett imbedded the dialogic within a monologue and, more important, folded the sense of an audience into what was becoming a dramatic narrative:

Well I prefer that, I must say I prefer that, that what, oh you know, who you, oh I suppose the audience, well well, so there's an audience, it's a public show, you buy your seat and wait, perhaps it's free, a free show, you take your seat and you wait for it to begin, or perhaps it's compulsory, a compulsory show, you wait for the compulsory show to begin, it takes time, you hear a voice, perhaps it's a recitation, that's the show, someone reciting, selected passages, old favourites, a poetry matinée, or someone improvising, you can barely hear him, that's the show, you can't leave, you're afraid to leave, it might be worse elsewhere, you make the best of it, you try and be reasonable, you came too early, here we'd need Latin, it's only beginning, it hasn't begun, he's only preluding, clearing his throat, alone in his dressing-room, he'll appear any moment, he'll begin any moment, or it's the stage-manager, giving his instructions, his last recommendations, before the curtain rises, that's the show, waiting for the show [. . .] . (*Three Novels* 381–2)

That final comment, 'that's the show, waiting for the show,' is as much a nod to Dada and surrealist performance as it is a gloss on *En attendant Godot*. Subsequently, much of the late drama, like 'A Piece of Monologue,' became, almost inevitably, nearly indistinguishable from the late prose fiction. 'From an Abandoned Work,' for example, was initially

published as a theater piece by Faber and Faber after it was performed
on the BBC Third Programme by Patrick Magee (14 December 1957).
Although 'From an Abandoned Work' is anthologized with Beckett's short
fiction, Faber initially collected it among four theater works in *Breath
and Other Shorts* (1971), which grouping highlighted its debut as a piece
for performance. Beckett was so enthusiastic about it as a monologue
for performance that he wrote to director Alan Schneider on 29 January
1958, 'I think Magee's performance is very remarkable' (Harmon 33).
That performance set Beckett to work almost immediately (20 February
1958) on another monologue, this overtly for the stage and called, at
first, 'Magee Monologue' but, ultimately, *Krapp's Last Tape*. Beckett even
suggested to Schneider that 'From an Abandoned Work' might be used
to fill out the evening with the American premier of *Krapp's Last Tape*.
As we begin to see that narration itself became a mode of performance
for Beckett, we more readily understand not only the late drama but the
impulse of so many theatrical directors to stage, to perform the prose
fictions.[1] The 1980 novel *Company* alone has been staged by some six
major theater companies.[2] The key to the late texts, prose and theater,
where narrative dominates, what we might call 'non-dramatic theater' or
'narrative theater' is, then, Beckett's earliest fiction and poetry. In both,
identity is very much the spectacle.

performance as creation

As Beckett explored the implications of performance fully in the mid-
1950s, he began to understand its necessity to his theatrical creative
process. As he wrote to American friend Pamela Mitchell on 28 September
1956, 'The new play [*Fin de partie* but which at this point he thought
to call simply *Hamm*, 'a label – like the novels'] is now as finished as is
possible *before rehearsals*' (emphasis added). He was perplexed about the
work and didn't know what to think 'really until I start hearing it and
looking at it – not of course even then.' The full embrace of performance
would come shortly thereafter with the Royal Court Theatre production
of *Krapp's Last Tape*. Writing his American publisher, Barney Rosset, on 20
November 1958, Beckett was unrestrainedly enthusiastic about Magee's
performance (which he oversaw so closely that some have claimed that he
directed it, although the director of record was Donald McWhinnie):

> Unerringly directed by McWhinnie Magee gave a very fine performance,
> for me by far *the most satisfactory experience in the theatre up to date*. I

wish to goodness that Alan [Schneider] could have seen it. I can't see it being done any other way. *During rehearsals we found various pieces of business not indicated in the script and which now seem to me indispensable.* If you ever publish the work in book form I should like to incorporate them in the text. (Emphasis added)[3]

The following day Beckett sent an almost identical letter to Schneider:

> I am extremely pleased with the results [of the *Krapp's Last Tape* production] and find it hard to imagine a better performance than that given by Magee both in his recording and his stage performance [. . .]. In the course of rehearsals *we established a certain amount of business which is not indicated in the script and which now seems to me indispensable.* If Barney [Rosset] ever brings out the work in book form I shall enlarge the stage directions accordingly [. . .] . The most interesting discovery was the kind of personal relationship that developed between Krapp and the machine. This arose quite naturally and was extraordinarily effective and of great help in the early stages whenever the immobility of the listening attitude tended to be tedious [. . .]. At the end [. . .] we had a fade-out and the quite unexpected and marvelous effect of recorder's red light burning up as the dark gathered [. . .] . (Emphasis added, Harmon 50–1)

By the mid-1950s Beckett was already talking and working like a director, committed to the lexicon and processes of performance. In a letter to Rosset's editorial assistant, Judith Schmidt, 11 May 1959, Beckett referred to the *staging* of *Krapp's Last Tape* as its 'creation.' The Irish journalist Alec Reid reports a similar attitude towards performance when he noted that Beckett 'will speak of the first run-through with actors as the "realization" of the play, and when it has been performed publicly he will say that it has been "created"' (Reid 12).

Samuel Beckett's exploration of performance would culminate in a second career that spanned the last twenty years of his life. That career was almost forced upon him as the awareness grew that dramatic works needed to be created on stage. Such a revelation threw into high relief fundamental problems inherent in the idea of productions 'of' a text, that is, stagings 'of' pre-existing, ostensibly completed scripts. The revelation that scripts produced in the study, no matter how finely honed, remained incomplete until realized on the stage would drive Beckett reluctantly to the semi-public posture of theatrical director. Once Beckett began directing himself in 1967, staging became a full extension of his creative process – not only for new plays but for those already published and part of the theatrical repertory if not fully explored by him on the boards. Once he had grown deeply involved in performance he made it clear to his publishers that no final text could or should go to press before he worked on it directly in the theater with actors. Writing to Grove Press about *Happy Days* on 18 May 1961, for instance, Beckett said, 'I should prefer the text not to appear in any form before production and not in book form until I have seen some rehearsals in London. I can't be definitive without actual work done in the theatre.' Grove Press editor Richard Seaver acknowledged Beckett's request on 30 June 1961 simply repeating Beckett's instructions for clarification, 'You asked that the book [i.e., *Happy Days*] not go into production until you had a chance to work with the script in the theater.' On 24 November 1963 Beckett wrote to Rosset about his wife Susanne's disappointment with the world premier of *Play*, the German *Spiel*, reiterating his position on the relationship of performance to publication:

Suzanne went to Berlin for the opening of *Play*. She did not like the performance, but the director, Deryk Mendel, is very pleased. Well received.

I realize I can't establish definitive text of *Play* without a certain number of rehearsals. These should begin with [French director Jean-Marie] Serreau next month. Alan's text will certainly need correction. Not the lines but the stage directions. London rehearsals begin on March 9th [1964].

In fact, even after having read 'final' proofs for *Play*, Beckett halted its publication mid-production so that he could continue to hone the text in rehearsals, as he confirmed to Seaver on 29 November 1963: 'I have asked Faber, since correcting proofs, to hold up production of the book. I realize I can't establish text of *Play*, especially stage directions, till I have worked on rehearsals. I have written to Alan [Schneider] about the problems involved.' This would become the standard, if often frustrating, procedure between Beckett and at least his English language publishers. The texts that Beckett was working toward, those that reflected much of what he learned through his staging of his plays have, however, never been published in versions generally available to the public, even the *Krapp's Last Tape* he promised to revise for the Grove Press publication. To date, for example, the 'Purple nose' of the original script of *Krapp's Last*

Tape, a detail Beckett had deleted for the 1958 London production and which he systematically eliminated in private copies to anyone discussing the play with him, remains, almost half a century later, part of every text of the play, French and English, except that in the third volume of *The Theatrical Notebooks* where a fully revised performance text appears.[4]

As Beckett developed as his own director, and through that process created his own ideal reader or spectator, he staged not only new work, that is, work still obviously in progress, but he began to intervene into and alter texts already published. He intervened into his own established canon, into texts which not only already existed in print but which were often well-established in the critical discourse as well. Beckett's directing career has thus forced to the fore unique questions not only about individual texts in the Beckett canon and the stability of textuality in general, but about the relationship of theatrical performance to its published record and so about the nature, the quality, and the validity of theatrical art itself. That sense of 'creation' on stage, however, has received scant attention from critics and scholars often more comfortable with the apparent solidity of the published text (apparently *any* published text) than the vicissitudes of performance. Underestimating and so undervaluing Beckett's direct work in the theater, his commitment to performance, particularly from the inception of his full-fledged directing career in 1967 (see the list of Beckett's own productions appended to this essay), have often skewed critical assessments of his theatrical art, his growth as a theater artist, and the world-wide theatrical tradition he generated. Documentation of Beckett's work in the theater does, of course, exist, but it seldom finds its way into the critical discourse.[5]

The sheer complexity and fluidity of Beckett's creative vision, however, has puzzled some critics, forcing a few into retreat and critical denial. Beckett's textual revisions were admittedly often made in response to the exigencies of production, and therein lies much of the problem, at least according to critics like Colin Duckworth. Commenting on the video version of *Waiting for Godot*, part of the *Beckett Directs Beckett* series, Duckworth admits that with Beckett's revisions, '[W]e can now have a clear insight into his own view of his most famous play a third of a century after he wrote it' (175). But he finally recoils from exactly that insight, concluding 'It is difficult to explain this textual vandalism, perpetrated on some of the most magical moments of the play' (190). 'It makes one wonder,' he continues, 'whether authors should be let loose on their plays thirty-odd years later' (191). Duckworth's argument is based primarily on the fact that Beckett did not fully direct the San

Quentin Drama Workshop production, which is finally almost a mirror image of Beckett's 1975 Schiller Theater production. For the San Quentin Drama Workshop production much of the preliminary work was done in Chicago in December of 1983 by Beckett's assistant at the Schiller Theater production in 1975, Walter Asmus, who began rehearsals by reviewing Beckett's Schiller production. Duckworth seems puzzled that although the new cuts and changes were made by Beckett in 1975 they were never incorporated into the German or any other revised text, and so he takes these to be less than authoritative changes. He quotes the actor Rick Cluchey (hardly a textual authority) as saying, 'Beckett will not impose any of these cuts on the published editions of this play.' Cluchey goes on to quote Beckett's ambiguous phrase, 'The text is the text' (Duckworth 185). Since three very different English language texts of *Godot* were in print and available at the time of Beckett's comment (two separate British and one very different American edition), which text is 'the text' was very much an open question even then. Shortly thereafter Beckett authorized publication of a new text for *Godot* based on the revisions made in his two productions, and it has appeared as part of a series of acting texts, along with the theatrical notebooks (which Beckett preferred to the originals), but it has never been published separately as a commercial edition.

To suggest, as Duckworth does, that the San Quentin Drama Workshop production of *Godot* is far from a definitive production is not exactly news, and if this were his fundamental point one might agree with him.[6] No one who spoke to Beckett about his productions could come away from those conversations thinking that Beckett had a very high opinion of the acting abilities of the San Quentin Drama Workshop. Friendship for its founder, Rick Cluchey, kept Beckett working with the group. 'The possibility of a definitive production of the play,' continues Duckworth, 'analogous to the definitive version of a text that every scholarly editor wants to bring out, seems vitiated by two factors: first, the frame of mind of the writer-director during any given set of rehearsals [but of course, this is true of any production at any time, and so Duckworth's position is an attack on performance itself]; and secondly the fact that Beckett was having to work with and through the temperaments of actors whom he had not hand picked (as he had in the case of the Schiller Theater production)' (178). In an age of postmodern textuality and performance such neo-Romantic yearning for definitive productions or even a definitive texts seems at best anachronistic.

Critic Michael Worton has similarly argued that Beckett's direct work in the theater is contingent and so should be dismissed as irrelevant to any critical evaluation. Worton, too, is bent on devaluing performance by dismissing Beckett's work as a director, work Worton considers more impulsive than deliberative: '[W]e should focus on the text itself and not seek to make our interpretations fit with what the dramatist may have said at any particular moment.' The immediate question that arises is what is 'the text itself' or which of the texts available is 'the text.' Moreover, 'Any particular moment' presumably refers to Beckett's twenty-year directing career, which Worton would simply dismiss as irrelevant to textual production. Worton, finally, seems more than a little confused about what constitutes 'text' in general and in the theater in particular, and so he takes it to mean simply script, which, by implication, is static on publication. Worton does, however, isolate the crux of Beckett's theatrical work when he suggests that 'What Beckett says outside the text of his plays is undoubtedly worth considering, but when he comments on either texts or productions, he is just another critic, just as eligible for skeptical examination as any other interpreter' (Worton 68). Where Worton goes most wrong is in treating the published work as finished and so static and ignoring the fact that Beckett continued to 'create' his theater works on the stage.

Rarely does one find such overt critical resistance to performance as that displayed by Duckworth and Worton, where the critics seem to set themselves up as protectors of a sacred text, that sanctity defined by publication. Both critical positions seem, however, to contain fundamental contradictions about the nature of performance. Performance cannot be both the ultimate achievement of dramatic art and simultaneously critically irrelevant since it is subject to theatrical contingencies – that is, since it is *a* performance. Duckworth finally makes a reluctant concession in his ultimate sentence, that Beckett's revisions of his own work were 'an incomparable barometer of the evolution of the Beckettian world view over thirty years' (Duckworth 191). All that is missing is the admission that such evolution is the creative process in theater. As we continue to evaluate the relationship between the literary text and its performative realization, and the playwright's relationship to both, the case of Samuel Beckett's acting simultaneously as theater artist staging a play and author revising it, a unique instance of self-collaboration in the modern (and modernist) theater, may force us to re-evaluate the centrality of performance to the literary field of drama. For Beckett's drama, performance would stand as the principal text. The results of that direct theatrical process, his fastidious attention to the aesthetic details of the artwork, need to enter our critical and performative equations if we are not to underestimate and so distort Beckett's creative vision, and his own theoretical contributions to the modernist theater.

That's the theory. The praxis, the actual accommodation of performance (the whole show) into the critical discourse, is not easily achieved. As he began increasingly to work directly on stage, to use the stage as a theatrical laboratory, to trust his direct collaborations with actors and technicians, Beckett did not, unfortunately, always immediately record those insights or revise his texts accordingly, as Duckworth points out. For some productions Beckett simply never got around to making the full and complete revisions to his texts; he never committed his revisions to paper, revisions which were clearly part of his developing conception of the play, but let the production stand as the final text. The most obvious and stunning example is the movement piece (or mime) called *Quad* in English. Beckett's final version of the work, the production for German television, broadcast on 8 October 1981, is called *Quadrat I & II*, a title that suggests two acts – if not two plays. Near the end of the taping, Beckett created what amounted to an unplanned second act. When he saw a replay in the studio on a black and white monitor, he wanted that too; he decided instantly to sanction *Quad II*. Beckett's printed text (in any language) was, however, never amended to accommodate this remarkable revision. The Grove Press and Faber and Faber editions of *The Collected Shorter Plays of Samuel Beckett* and the Faber and Faber edition of *The Complete Dramatic Works* carry only the following footnote: 'This original scenario (*Quad I*) was followed in the Stuttgart production by a variation (*Quad II*)' (*CSP* 293, *CDW* 453). No details are provided about the nature of that variation at all. No printed version of the play bears even an accurate title of the production, no less an accurate text, one that includes Beckett's theatrical insights and revisions. Beckett's own videotaped German production, then, is his final word on that work; it remains the only accurate text for *Quad*. For *Quad*, as well as for all the works that Beckett staged himself, that's the show.

appendix a: samuel beckett as director

In Paris:
Va et vient (Come and Go) and Robert Pinget's *L'Hypothèse* at the Odéon Théâtre de France 28 February 1966 (uncredited for his own work).

La dernière band (Krapp's Last Tape) at the Théâtre Récamier 29 April 1970.

La dernière band (Krapp's Last Tape) with *Pas moi (Not I)* at the Théâtre d'Orsay (Petite Salle) in April 1975.

Pas (Footfalls) with *Pas moi (Not I)* at the Théâtre d'Orsay in April 1978.

In Berlin at the Schillertheater (Werkstatt except for *Godot*):

Endspiel (Endgame) 26 September 1967.

Das letzte Band (Krapp's Last Tape), 5 October 1969.

Glückliche Tage (Happy Days), 17 September 1971.

Warten auf Godot (Waiting for Godot), 8 March 1975.

Damals (That Time) and *Tritte (Footfalls)*, 1 October 1976.

Spiel (Play), 6 October 1978.

Krapp's Last Tape in English at the Akademie der Künste with the San Quentin Drama Workshop, Berlin rehearsals 10–27 September 1977.

In London:

Footfalls at the Royal Court Theatre in May 1976

Happy Days at the Royal Court Theatre in June 1979

Endgame with the San Quentin Drama Workshop at Riverside Studios in May 1980

Waiting for Godot with the San Quentin Drama Workshop; rehearsals began at the Goodman Theater in Chicago from early November 1983 to January 1984 under the direction of Walter Asmus. Beckett joined the group at the Riverside Studios, London on 2 February 1984 and rehearsed the actors for 10 days. Production premiered at the Adelaide Arts Festival in 13 March 1984.

Teleplays:

He, Joe (Eh, Joe), at Süddeutscher Rundfunk, Stuttgart, directed March 1966 (with Deryk Mendel and Nancy Illig), broadcast 13 April 1966. [First theatrical event to credit Beckett alone as director.]

Geistertrio (Ghost Trio), at Süddeutscher Rundfunk, Stuttgart, directed May–June 1977 (with Klaus Herm and Irmgard Foerst), broadcast 1 November 1977.

Nur noch Gewolk (. . . but the clouds . . .), at Süddeutscher Rundfunk, Stuttgart, May–June 1977 (with Klaus Herm and Kornelia Bose), broadcast 1 November 1977.

He, Joe (Eh, Joe), second version at Süddeutscher Rundfunk, Stuttgart, directed January 1979 (with Heinz Bennent and Irmgard Först), broadcast September 1979.

Quadrat I & II, at Süddeutscher Rundfunk, Stuttgart, directed June 1981 (with Helfrid Foron, Juerg Hummel, Claudia Knupfer, and Suzanne Rehe), broadcast 8 October 1981.

Nacht und Träume at Süddeutscher Rundfunk, Stuttgart, directed October 1982, broadcast 19 May 1983.

Was Wo (What Where) at Süddeutscher Rundfunk, Stuttgart, directed June 1985, broadcast 13 April 1986.

notes

1. For elaboration on this point see my 'From Unabandoned Works: Samuel Beckett's Short Prose,' *Samuel Beckett: the Complete Short Prose, 1928–1989*, edited and with an Introduction and Notes by S. E. Gontarski (New York: Grove Press, 1996), xi–xxxii.
2. *Company*'s interlocutory nature has encouraged several dramatic readings and theatrical adaptations, beginning with Patrick Magee's reading on BBC 2 in July 1980, and John Russell Brown's version for the National Theatre, London, in September that year, featuring Stephen Moore. Another London version was staged by Tim Piggot-Smith and produced by Katharine Worth, with Julian Curry (1987); it was seen at the Edinburgh Festival and in New York (1988). There had been two earlier American stagings. In 1983 Frederick Neumann directed the play for Mabou Mines, with Honora Ferguson; and in 1985 S. E. Gontarski's production at the Los Angeles Actors' Theater with Alan Mandell was the English premiere of Pierre Chabert's adaptation, which had opened 15 November 1984 at the Theatre du Rond-Point in Paris, a version with which Samuel Beckett had been closely associated.
3. Unless otherwise noted all letters to Barney Rosset and the Grove Press staff are in the Barney Rosset/Grove Press archives now at the George Arents Research Library at Syracuse University and the John J. Burns Library, Boston College; the latter holds the Schneider/Beckett correspondence as well. An edited edition of the Schneider/Beckett correspondence is available as *No Author Better Served: the Correspondence of Samuel Beckett and Alan Schneider*, ed. Maurice Harmon (Cambridge, MA: Harvard University Press, 1998). All material is used with the permission of the principals.
4. They are available, however, in the following four volumes published under the general editorship of James Knowlson by Faber and Faber in the UK and Grove Press in the US: Volume I, *Waiting for Godot*, ed. Dougald MacMillan and James Knowlson (1993); Volume II, *Endgame*, ed. S. E. Gontarski (1992); Volume III, *Krapp's Last Tape*, ed. James Knowlson (1992); and Volume IV, *The Shorter Plays*, ed. S. E. Gontarksi (1999). A prototype volume, *'Happy Days': Samuel Beckett's Production Notebooks*, ed. James Knowlson, was also published by Faber and Faber and Grove Press in 1985 in a different format.

5. His theatrical notebooks for his productions, for example, have been published under the general editorship of James Knowlson. In addition, the series of productions Beckett at least oversaw with the San Quentin Drama Workshop has been released on videotape by the Smithsonian Institution under the general, if not entirely accurate, title *Beckett Directs Beckett*. And Alan Schneider's remarkable thirty-year correspondence with Beckett (1955–84) has appeared from Harvard University Press (1998) as *'No Author Better Served': the Correspondence of Samuel Beckett and Alan Schneider*.

6. See my review, 'Beckett Directs Beckett: Endgame,' *Journal of Beckett Studies*, 2.2 (Spring 1992): 115–18.

works cited

Atik, Anne. *How it Was: a Memoir of Samuel Beckett*. London: Faber and Faber, 2001.

Beckett, Samuel. *Endgame*. New York: Grove Press, 1958.

—— *Three Novels*. New York: Grove Press, 1965.

—— *Mercier and Camier*. New York: Grove Press, 1974.

—— *The Collected Shorter Plays of Samuel Beckett*. New York: Grove Press, 1984; London: Faber and Faber, 1984.

—— *The Complete Dramatic Works*. London: Faber and Faber, 1986.

—— *Dream of Fair to Middling Women*. Dublin: Black Cat Books, 1992.

Cohn, Ruby. *A Beckett Canon*. Ann Arbor: University of Michigan Press, 2001.

Duckworth, Colin. 'Beckett's New *Godot*.' *Beckett's Later Fiction and Drama*, ed. James Acheson and Kateryna Arthur. London: Macmillan – now Palgrave Macmillan, 1987, 175–92.

Harmon, Maurice. *No Author Better Served: the Correspondence of Samuel Beckett and Alan Schneider*. Cambridge, MA: Harvard University Press, 1998.

Harvey, Lawrence. *Samuel Beckett, Poet and Critic*. Princeton, NJ: Princeton University Press, 1970.

Pilling, John (ed.). *Beckett's 'Dream' Notebook*. Reading, England: Beckett International Foundation, 1999.

Reid, Alec. 'Impact and Parable in Beckett: a First Encounter with *Not I*.' *Hermathena: a Trinity College Review*, ed. Terence Brown and Nicholas Grene. CXLI (Winter 1986): 12–21.

Worton, Michael. '*Waiting for Godot* and *Endgame*: Theater as Text.' *The Cambridge Companion to Beckett*, ed. John Pilling. London: Cambridge University Press, 1994, 67–87.

12

sources of attraction to beckett's theater

katharine worth

It is some time since a source of attraction to Beckett's theater was curiosity about something so new and totally astonishing. One pioneer director, Herbert Blau, in an interview with Lois Oppenheim in 1992, remarked how difficult it had become by then to reconstruct the reactions of the 1950s and convey 'just how startling these plays had seemed.' He recalled how two of the older actors he had cast in his first production of *Waiting for Godot* had withdrawn after the first read-through, deterred because they 'simply didn't know what was going on in the play.'[1]

Total incomprehension such as this would be unlikely now, at least in those parts of the world where Beckett has long been a cultural icon. But the plays retain their power to astonish and be new again; the sure sign of a classic. So what are the chief sources of attraction to Beckett's theater now and to what sorts of people? In the interview just quoted from, Blau suggested that by that time (1992) Beckett had been 'deified among Americans, particularly academics.' Deification aside, it is certainly true that Beckett's oeuvre has had a huge attraction for academics, world-wide; unsurprisingly, given its subtle and wide-ranging intellectual as well as imaginative powers. It offers exceptional opportunities for traditional scholarly activities: researching, editing, annotating, translating (Beckett set the pace here, himself translating his French texts to English and vice versa. The rest of the world has been following ever since, in many languages).

Writing about the life of Beckett can involve writing also about the cultural and theater history of half a century, as James Knowlson's remarkably comprehensive 1996 biography splendidly demonstrates. There is a sense of excitement about this and much of the academic enquiry associated with Beckett's work. Partly, that may relate to the illusion so potently conveyed in his fiction, of something unfinished. It might seem to be reinforced in the outside world from time to time by expectations of discoveries yet to be made; in the shortly to be published correspondence, for instance. Or discoveries of revisions or drafts turning up in unexpected places. Ruby Cohn points to these continuing possibilities with her careful use of the indefinite article in the title – A Beckett Canon – of her masterly record of the whole oeuvre, from the first publication in 1929 to the last, 'Comment dire' in 1989, the year of Beckett's death.

It can't but be a stimulus to academics working on the plays to know that their scholarly activity may result in live connections to the theater process, for instance when directors are considering what text to use for a production. Significant connections of that kind were made with the publication during the last decade of The Theatrical Notebooks of Samuel Beckett (general editor, James Knowlson). The Notebook relating to Waiting for Godot, edited by Dougald McMillan and James Knowlson, contained material which took the editors and will take readers into the heart of a particularly fascinating, still not so very distant theatrical event, Beckett's directing of his own play with a German company at the Schiller-Theater, West Berlin, in 1975. Anyone who saw that finely tuned, moving production, in Berlin or, as I did, when it came to the Royal Court Theatre, London, in 1976, will especially value the fine detail of Beckett's production notebook, though its value, of course, goes far beyond that. But it is the inclusion in the Theatrical Notebooks of revised texts that allow scholars an influential role in relation to the plays in performance. Directors remain free to stay with the standard texts or go to the revised ones which incorporate Beckett's second or third thoughts as he directed or advised on productions of his plays. As soon as the revised text of Waiting for Godot was available (well before its publication) for viewing at the University of Reading it was brought into use by Michael Rudman for his production at the National Theatre, London, in 1987. It was used again in Dublin at the Gate Theatre in 1991, unsurprisingly, as the director on the occasion was Walter Asmus who had worked with Beckett on the production of Warten auf Godot at the Schiller-Theater, in 1975. Asmus' production came to the Barbican Arts Centre, London, in 1999, in a Beckett program which mixed lectures, discussions, and productions and gave opportunities for meetings of theater people and academics, some of whom had collaborated on Beckett projects. Among these were the French director, Pierre Chabert, who had staged the novella, Compagnie, in Paris and Stan Gontarski, who had also directed a staging of the English version, *Company*, in Los Angeles. Gontarski was editor of two volumes in the *Theatrical Notebooks* that were by 1999 on the bookshop shelves at the Barbican, a timely reminder of how important collaborations of academics and theater practitioners could be, and how these possibilities must rank among the attractions of Beckett's theater for both groups.

A very different source of attraction has been its perceived susceptibility to theory-oriented critical approaches. Fiction had been first in this particular field. The slippery narrators of the novels – the Molloys and Malones who endlessly invent, deconstruct, and reconstruct themselves – soon attracted criticism geared to those mental processes, criticism inspired by Derrida and deconstruction in the 1970s and by postmodernism and various types of gender-theory now.

Performance theory has been a relative latecomer, maybe because discussion of plays demands more time for actual theater-going than some theorists may want to give. When they do, and are genuinely attracted to Beckett's theater, their theoretical arguments can profit, as do Steven Connor's, for instance, when he illustrates his ideas on replication and repetition from details to do with Beckett's creative adaptation for German television of the stage play *What Where*. Occasional allusions to Beckett in more general studies can have a similar effect: discussion of such concepts as 'decontextualisation' gains a further reach when illustrated from the 'strange' elements in Beckett's theater.[2] With gender, theories and discussions of interest to academics and theater people are possible over such matters as the ban on female casts performing the all-male *Waiting for Godot*. The sort of theory-oriented criticism which has really responded to the attraction of Beckett's theater can, as a rule, reach out beyond the professional academics and students who would be thought its natural readership. 'Queer' theory began, it has been said, as an 'elite' academic movement.[3] Yet, through its interest in such phenomena as 'drag' and 'cross dressing' it has links with a common culture, a broad, music-hall type of theatricality such as can also be found at times on Beckett's stage.

I now move to the theater world where Beckett's art attracts some of the most adventurous talents, in acting, directing, and designing. The play offers actors unusual opportunities to stretch their talents to the uttermost – and find unique rewards in the nature of their achievement. It is a kind of adventure, even for experienced actors, to undertake such roles as Krapp, or the Listener in *That Time*, Winnie, or Mouth in *Not I*. Billie Whitelaw has described the ordeal of playing Mouth, how she was totally cut off from others, high above the stage, clamped, swathed in a black hood, subject to panic attack; after the dress rehearsal she was for a time totally disorientated. Yet this stage experience came to seem her most meaningful one. She heard in Mouth's outpourings her own 'inner scream': 'I found so much of my self in *Not I*. Somewhere in there were my entrails under a microscope.'[4]

This terrifying physical experience is remote from that an academic has in approaching the play. Yet such is the power of Beckett's art that those who fully respond to it as critics have been able to convey (along lines of their own) similar intuitions to those the actress had. Enoch Brater does this in his perceptive interpretation of Mouth's terrible struggle; he sees the silent, intent Listener, compassionate but helpless, in Jungian terms as her 'shadow.'[5] This has been singled out as a particularly interesting response to the play by James Acheson who is also in tune with Whitelaw when he stresses the impression of a possible self-realization for Mouth even though she resists it so passionately.[6]

The directors who are attracted to Beckett's theater have to deal with a similar challenge to that facing the actors. In their case, it is to make the plays new for new audiences and yet keep within the austere limits laid down in Beckett's texts and meticulously precise directions. In 1991 Michael Colgan, Artistic Director of the Gate Theatre, Dublin, multiplied the hazards of this challenge by presenting with his company not one or two, but 19 of the stage plays; all of them, that is, except for the early *Eleutheria* which Beckett had not wanted staged in his lifetime and which was not published until 1995. The performances ran for three weeks in October, part of a Beckett Festival shared by the Gate Theatre and Trinity College Dublin. It was a wonderfully exhilarating event, not least because it extended to so many different kinds of people, of all nationalities. The relative smallness and the compactness of Dublin made it easy walking from the College to the theater: At times one had the impression that the entire Dublin public was taking a benevolent interest in the event. Some of the public came to performances (which took place in mornings and afternoons as well as evenings). They might have been regular patrons of the Gate or admirers of certain actors – Barry McGovern as Vladimir, Johnny Murphy as Estragon, Fionnula Flanagan as Winnie – or simply attracted by the novelty of it all. One such, I imagine, was the woman I heard on the way out from the performance of *Footfalls*, saying excitedly to a friend 'Oh, that was spooky!'

Beckett's theater could be felt reaching out to many kinds of people on this occasion, as probably happened when the program later went to Lincoln Center in New York, and certainly did so when, with some changes, it came to London (in 1999). A Dublin-like community feeling was generated there, against the odds set by the formidable spaces of the Barbican Arts Centre. I will return to this last event and its successor, the 'Beckett on Film' program which took place in the same venue. But first I want to glance at one or two other sources of attraction to Beckett's theater which relate to the main theme in what follows, the power of his art to stimulate artistic creativity in others.

One has to do with length. Colgan would not have been able to present all the plays in the course of a festival had they been even as long as *Waiting for Godot* and *Happy Days* (each in two shortish acts) or *Endgame* (in one longish act). 'Shorts' is the term that would cover most of the rest, including *Play* (which has proved equally fascinating as a film) and later works like those included in *Three Occasional Pieces* (Faber, London, 1982): *A Piece of Monologue*, *Rockaby*, and *Ohio Impromptu*. These plays can be a valuable gateway for they attract students or anyone seriously interested in Beckett's theatre to perform them, perhaps as an adjunct to studying the texts. I recall student performances of this kind at my own college, Royal Holloway, in the 1980s, almost as soon as the texts became available. Amateur or semi-professional groups would not usually have performance and technical facilities equal to the demands made by plays such as *Footfalls* and *Not I*. But the plays can still convey to audiences sitting in the same room with the actors something of their dramatic force.

The possibilities for presenting groups of 'shorts' in an open, simple space has been for professionals too a source of attraction to Beckett's theater. Katie Mitchell made the most of these opportunities when directing six of them, in two separate programs for the Royal Shakespeare Company in 1997 at The Other Place, Stratford-upon-Avon. The audience sat in the same space as the actors, moving from room to room as *Rockaby* succeeded *Footfalls*, to be followed by *Not I*. Juliet Stevenson's performance as May and then as Mouth would alone have ensured that this would be a moving and rewarding experience for an audience watching it at such unusually close quarters. I recalled the production, and how it had conveyed the distinctive ghostly quality of those plays, in an 'ordinary' space when seeing recently (in 2002) the same director's production of Chekhov's *Ivanov* at the Cottesloe Theatre of the Royal National Theatre, London.

Here again Mitchell kept the audience aware of our actual situation throughout, having divided us into two groups which faced each other across a platform stage. This was open to view, except when closed off by fine, Japanese-style screens which demanded attention as objects in a real world outside the action of the play as beautiful, yet entirely practical, items of stage furniture. The effect of this double emphasis, and of looking across the stage at others also looking at the characters in the space between us, was, curiously, to intensify the impression of being somehow, ourselves, part of the scene where Ivanov's drama was being played out. Other effects, such as the delicately long-held pauses and silences which deepened the emotional atmosphere, suggested that the characteristics of Beckett's art, to which Mitchell had responded in her RSC production, had continued to attract her – and to stimulate her creative re-animation of Chekhov's seldom-seen play.

Mitchell's staging of *Not I* in close proximity to an audience (kept standing throughout) in an ordinary room was a long way from Beckett's requirement for a Mouth situated 'upstage audience right, about 8' above stage level.' But it could be justified, were that necessary, simply as a practical means of bringing the play within reach of audiences who would seldom, if ever, have the chance to see a reproduction of the original, extremely difficult scenic effect. Other divergences from Beckett's directions have sometimes proved harder to justify. Much ink has been spilt in arguments for and against JoAnne Akalaitis' production in 1984 of an *Endgame* set in a derelict subway tunnel. Defending it in the theater program, Robert Brustein drew attention to a remarkably free treatment of the play in a Belgian production of the previous year, set in a warehouse flooded with water. Stranger approaches still have been taken in other parts of the world, as for instance those in Japan noted by Mariko Hori Tanaka.[7] Some of these may have been eccentric or out for publicity. But some, we may assume, will have been driven by the desire for creative artistic expression which is stimulated by Beckett's theater. The attempts of all-female companies to play the all-male *Waiting for Godot* might well be among that number.

From directing or acting in Beckett's plays it has been a short step for some practitioners to engage in adapting works of his not written for the stage. This is a huge subject, requiring a volume to itself. I touch on it here only briefly, in relation to my main theme, the many different sources of attraction there can be to Beckett's theater. One such source for theater people has always been its capacity to inspire their own creativity as performers/directors but also, in some cases, as makers of adaptations.

Beckett has sometimes collaborated with the adaptors, to the extent, at least, of approving or encouraging their plans and, occasionally, offering advice. He helped Jack MacGowran put together the program of extracts from the plays, fiction and poems which changed content and title as MacGowran took it around on highly successful tours. *Beginning to End* at the Lantern Theatre, Dublin in 1965 became *Jack MacGowran in the Works of Samuel Beckett* at Lincoln Center in New York in 1970. Jordan R. Young has commented on the surge of interest in Beckett among American audiences following this performance.[8]

It's not hard to see why MacGowran would be drawn to Beckett's theater and want to create his own theater fragment from it. He was a natural Beckett actor, in tune with the humour and oddity in the work and relishing the opportunities it allowed for comic rhetoric and disconcerting changes of key. It gave him scope to express his private personality as well as his acting and comedic skills. No one who saw it on stage or, as I did, on video will be able to read *Molloy* again without seeing in the mind's eye the elfish MacGowran taking us into his ritual of sucking in due order the stones in his pocket, whimsically inviting us to take it as seriously as he does. It's also easy to see why Beckett was pleased to support and encourage this so congenial actor when he turned adaptor. His performance in the anthology was probably one of MacGowran's best pieces of Beckett's acting. (When I saw some years ago the newly discovered video of his Krapp I thought it less satisfying than his performance in the scenes he had selected for himself.)

For another Irish actor, Barry McGovern, a different theater background and personality led into a different, more complex performance in a stage adaptation: that of the *Molloy* trilogy which took its title from the last line of the novel, 'I'll Go On.' Like MacGowran's production, this adaptation (by McGovern and Gerry Dukes) also travelled widely and was received with excitement; the closing sequence with a kind of awe. I recall from experience as an audience member in one or two European theaters (The Hague, Monaco) the absolute hush that fell on the house when the actor, cut off from his earlier insouciant wandering, stripped and immobilized, brought us, with an accelerating vocal rhythm to the end that promises to be no end:

Perhaps they have carried me to the threshold of my story, before the door that opens on my story, that would surprise me, it opens, it will be I, it will be the silence, where I am, I don't know, I'll never know, in the silence you don't know, you must go on, I can't go on, I'll go on.

A striking feature of adaptations of Beckett's fiction has been the involvement in them of actors and directors with a keen interest in

Beckett's writings as a whole. This was clearly so with Joseph Chaikin, founder of the off-Broadway Open Theatre, whose adaptation (with Steven Kent) of *Texts for Nothing* was performed by him to great acclaim in 1981 at the Public Theatre, New York, as it was in 1992 when he directed another actor, Bill Irwin, in the 'narrator's' role. The actor's feeling for work so far outside the well-known plays must have touched Beckett. He did indeed write to Chaikin that he was greatly moved by his effort to stage the 'bodilessness' of *Texts for Nothing*.[9] And he allowed him to use a page from *How It Is* to make a stronger ending to the adaptation of the 'play' that had emerged from the original piece of fiction.

The attraction of Beckett's plays takes such adaptors as Chaikin in and out of the plays proper. In September 2002 he would return to them by directing *Happy Days*. Similarly, in France, Pierre Chabert has directed influential productions of the plays (including the revised *What Where*) and also his own adaptation for the stage of the whimsical early novel, *Mercier et Camier*. Many others have moved between the straight plays and adaptations, either as directors or actors: David Warrilow has been prominent among the latter. All this is lively testimony to the power of Beckett's theater to extend itself and make those who feel its fascination yearn to have more of it by endowing the fiction with a stage voice and a scenic image.

Not all these adaptations have won Beckett's approval. JoAnne Akalaitis has said that he was not pleased when she adapted *Cascando*, a radio play, for stage performance. That was certainly a different matter from taking the fiction to the stage: I recall being astonished to hear of it, having myself been involved in a new production of *Cascando* which Beckett had given me permission to make in 1984. It had required all the technical skills of the director, David Clark, to create the exact and delicate balance required between the sound of the Voice (played by David Warrilow), the Opener (Sean Barrett), and Music, composed and conducted by Humphrey Searle.[10] It was stimulating, however, to try and imagine a work that had become so familiar in its radio form played live to audiences who would need to look as well as listen.

Whether or not we like a new adaptation or 'performance' of the fiction or other prose work, we can't help but be stimulated by new perspectives or the hope of them. For some people unfamiliar with Beckett's theater or with the art of reading a text, some new production, perhaps with a celebrated actor or much talked-of directorial treatment, could be a way in to a lifelong interest. This can happen even if a production is controversial or ill received by those who know the work. It might have happened, for all we know, for some who attended the latest Beckett adaptation seen in London, the performance at the Cottelsoe Theatre in 2002 of the prose poem, *Lessness*, performed by Olwen Foure and directed by Judy Hegarty-Lovett. It was certainly a theatrical event, opening with the performer arranged on a table, then moving into various positions – rather dangerously, given the flowing, pale bronze, classical gown she was wearing. It felt like a quite daring physical act when she slowly stood up or sat down with her back to us or left the table to make a slow exit across the stage. These movements were considered pointless or intrusive by friends and fellow-Beckettians as we discussed the production afterwards. They were of a piece, it was thought, with a lack of sensitivity to the rhythmic subtleties of the prose poem, its repetitions, doublings back and variations on key words and phrases: 'little body,' 'figment dawn dispeller of figments,' 'issueless.'

It was hard to disagree, yet I did also think that something had emerged from the performance which touched a vein. When I first heard *Lessness* in a BBC broadcast of the 1980s it had been spoken by a number of male voices, including that of Harold Pinter. It was no doubt more accomplished in regard to intonations and rhythm but, as I recall, it lacked tension, maybe because spoken by unseen actors reading from scripts. At the Cottesloe, in contrast, the voice was female and there was a sense of vulnerability about the arrangements of her body which she was required to make – in all her statuesque glamour. The woman was really 'performing' the words, without aid of script or company, raising some anxiety in the process. I thought this anxiety not altogether irrelevant to the brooding of the poem on the fate of the 'little body' – and that, in its odd way, the performance might have offered a way in to the work itself for at least some of the audience.

That will certainly have been true of the programs of extracts read over the years by actors such as Billie Whitelaw, Barry McGovern, and Ronald Pickup. It is the sense of the work crying out to be voiced, given body, that has attracted so many to Beckett's theater, as adaptors, directors, actors. There was just such a threefold pull when I met at a Beckett conference in Austin, Texas, Julian Curry, performing Krapp in a production directed by Tim Piggot-Smith. They were looking for opportunities to work on some short prose piece of Beckett's and I was drawn to the idea of 'voicing' *Company*. From this came the adaptation of *Company* for which Beckett gave me permission, and which we took to many different types of audience.[11]

In 2001 a vision was achieved which should allow many more people to share the experience of being attracted to Beckett's theater. This was the filming of all the plays (with the usual exception of *Eleutheria*). There were great gatherings in Dublin and London for the first public showings, accompanied by panels where some of those involved in the film-making spoke about the process itself, their reasons for taking a particular line, and so on. Some had come to appreciate certain plays for the first time through meeting the challenges involved in transferring them to the screen.

Michael Colgan was the driving force behind the filming, as he had been in 1991 when he set up the production of all 19 plays at the Beckett Festival in Dublin. He went on to create, with Alan Moloney, a production company, Blue Angel Films, working with co-producers, Tyrone Productions, and with the backing of Channel 4, RTE, and the Irish Film Board. Channel 4 was to transmit all the films, said their chief executive, Michael Jackson, during 2001 and the following year. The promise was being kept in the summer of 2001 when six were shown on Channel 4 television, including, of course, the play everybody had heard of though not all would have seen on stage: *Waiting for Godot*. The others were: *Play*, *Catastrophe*, *Rockaby*, *Not I*, and *Breath*. The first films were put out in prime time with some flourish. Later it became more difficult to catch the showings: They have been almost smuggled in under cover of unrevealing program titles like *4 Learning* (on Friday mornings). It was evidently thought risky to make a big public event of the achievement such as had happened in Ireland when all the films were put out over a three-week period, in Spring 2001. Video cassettes can be bought, though here again no great publicity is given to that possibility, at least in the UK. It seems that it is an easier matter in the US to obtain complete sets of films at a modest price. However, the films exist and for that we must be grateful to all the parties involved in what John Richmond, speaking for Channel 4, rightly called an 'extraordinary achievement.' It was, he said, 'An heroic undertaking to bring all 19 of Beckett's stage plays to the screen: not to pick and choose between them, but to do the lot. The films are already, so soon after completion, bringing Beckett to far larger audiences, all over the world, than have previously seen his plays.'[12]

A sense of lively engagement with the challenge of filming the plays was conveyed during the panel sessions after the screenings at the 'Barbican on Film' Festival in September 2001. A few themes kept recurring. One was to do with Beckett's humour which particular directors had enjoyed. The playwright, Conor Macpherson, spoke of his strong wish to convey to the audience that *Endgame* was a funny play and not the 'hard going' it was commonly taken for. Damien Hirst, entrusted with the shortest of all plays, *Breath*, felt the same; a pithy comment of his was quoted in the film program: 'I kept reading the text over and over and what really focused me was Beckett's direction "hold for about five seconds". That was when I realised that Beckett had this massive sense of humour.'

Another persistent theme was a kind of fellow feeling some directors felt they had with Beckett because of his concern with form and his interest in the relationship humans have with a mechanical world, their 'interaction with technology,' as Atom Egoyan expressed it. Enda Hughes, who directed *Act Without Words 2*, suggested in conversation with John Richmond suggested that Beckett would have been in sympathy with the idea of using the mechanics of film, perhaps by revealing them, to create appropriate effects when converting the plays into films. There was widespread feeling that inventive approaches of that kind would be in keeping with Beckett's own way of giving stage conventions and mechanisms a vital dramatic function, as he had done so memorably with the spotlight of *Play*. Theater and film-goers in these discussions often came together in their support for film makers who aimed, as Hughes had done, to make the medium itself an actor in the scene.

Similar comments were made by Karel Reisz, director of the other mime play, *Act Without Words 1*. (*Breath*, though also without words, is *sui generis*.) Reisz had directed in the 1990s the highly successful stage production of *Happy Days*, a play with many sharp in-jokes for theater goers, as when Winnie's umbrella goes up in flame and she consoles herself with the actor's practical thought that it will be there again the next day. Reisz brought to his film treatment of *Act Without Words 1* a particularly keen sense of Beckett's clever use of the artifice of theater and an intention similar to that of Enda Hughes, to find a filmic equivalent for it.

Perhaps rather unexpectedly, it emerged from the talks and answers to questions during these sessions that the rigour of Beckett's stage directions and precision of his demands on actors, directors and designers had been a source of attraction, not a deterrent, for many of the directors working on the screen adaptations. Michael Lindsay-Hogg, who directed the film of *Waiting for Godot*, drew attention to the attraction of this rigour, how it could serve as a creative challenge, not a frustrating curb.

To see the films and hear well-known film-makers like Anthony Minghella talk about the process of making them had evidently been a main source of attraction to many in the audience at these showings and discussions. Attraction to Beckett's theater in the shape of the plays themselves might well follow, if it was not already there. Such, at any rate, would be the hope of those who had set up this ambitious project: Only time will tell if it will happen so.

For those approaching the films from the other end, so to speak, as long-term lovers of the plays, the Barbican event, presumably like those in Dublin and elsewhere, gave opportunities to look at the plays through a different prism, enjoy the infusion of fresh ideas from young practitioners and students of film, and meet old friends, some celebrated for their theatrical engagement with Beckett's plays, who had moved into the filmic adventure. Chief among these was Walter Asmus, a modest, friendly presence, for all his fame as the director who had worked so closely with Beckett and had with loving care built up over the years a particularly fine production of *Waiting for Godot*, pure and austere in form but rich in humour and poignant human feeling. This production had been the star of the 19-play event in its various places of performance, Dublin, New York, and London. It had now been filmed, with its original actors though not its original director. Asmus was instead directing *Footfalls*, with an actress new to Beckett performance, Susan Fitzgerald as May.

These variations and moves around the plays were an intriguing feature of the film program. The casting was, of course, also carefully designed to attract those unfamiliar with Beckett's theater by way of the celebrated film and stage stars involved in the performances. The Barbican publicity brochure flourished a great list, from Neil Jordan to Juliet Stevenson, and the first six plays put out on Channel 4 television included some of the most famous names; notably (and poignantly as it was to turn out), John Gielgud directed by Harold Pinter; it was Gielgud's final performance before his death.

Will the films be a major source of attraction to Beckett's theater? And will they give a true impression of the plays? The answer to the first question must almost certainly be 'Yes.' The advance publicity just mentioned would be likely to whet curiosity in many who might otherwise be uninterested in Beckett's plays, along with many more who are interested but have few chances to see them on stage. Among the latter group will be students, scholars, and others seriously interested in drama who know that to see a performance is necessary for a full grasp of play texts, especially those of Beckett. It isn't easy, after all, even for a regular theater-goer or well-exercised imagination (and even with the aid of production photos) to conjure up for oneself the astonishing impact of Beckett's scenic images and such subtle low-key sounds as ritualistically recurring footsteps. As an adjunct to teaching too, the films can't help but stimulate interest. There is no surer way of provoking instant, lively discussion (trained on the plays rather than on ideas about them), than to show, say, the film of *Play* after people have had a chance to read the text. Ideally, this would be accompanied by accounts of stage performances and illustrations, such as Jocelyn Herbert's mesmeric designs for the faces in *Play*, 'so lost to age and aspect as to seem almost part of urns.'

Play is a good starting point for seeking answers to my second question: How true an impression of the plays do the films offer? None of the plays makes us more aware of the stage than this one, with its spotlight moving from face to face of the three heads in urns, letting one gasp out a sentence, then on to another, in irregular order, sometimes cutting them off in mid-sentence. Anthony Minghella succeeded brilliantly in finding an equivalent for that masterful piece of theater machinery in his bold use of the basic cinematic machine: the camera. Every director was using this, of course, as every theater director will on occasion use a spotlight. Minghella made the basic equipment into a threatening force by switching it with bullying speed from one face to another, forcing unusual speed of delivery from the actors. Juliet Stevenson, playing W1, told me that during rehearsals she had wondered whether the lines were being delivered too fast for viewers to take in their sense. This might have been so for some, but my American friend and theater critic, Alice Griffin, who was writing brief accounts of this and the other first-shown films for her website thought that the line 'came across more clearly and more easily understandable than sometimes in the theater.' This she attributed partly to Minghella's use of close-up, a recurring feature of the film versions, naturally enough.

What came over unequivocally in the film as in the stage version was the impression of three people, trapped in shared memories of a painful adultery, driven by some inexplicable force to return over and over to the experience. They were a long way from ordinary external reality, their faces invaded by blotches as if from the encroaching urns, their senses apparently unaware of the other two so near them. Close-up techniques made the most of this fantastic element while allowing for fleeting changes of facial expression which helped suggest a genuine movement, a real 'change' occurring in the nameless W1, W2, and M1, so grimly immobilized and parted from their bodies. Minghella added a sequence (repeated, like the narrative) which widened out from the isolated three to a vast landscape of urns from which inaudible mutterings emerged; a ghostly graveyard, it seemed, though quite how it was to be 'read' remained an open question. This was much turned over, along with doubts whether it should be there at all, in the animated discussions that went on throughout the Barbican meeting places.

The careful measure of freedom granted to directors by the Beckett Estate did often, as in this instance, allow those familiar with the plays in the theater to receive a fresh charge of interest within the firm lines of Beckett's dramatic structures. That could not quite be said for the changes made to *Catastrophe*, directed by David Mamet. When the director (D) made his peremptory demands for a light from his female assistant (A) he received it not for his cigar, as in the original, but in the form of torchlight for his script. This weakened the sense of gratuitous offensiveness hanging about the character (the cause was rumoured to be the actor's objection to smoking). D., played by Pinter, received rather too much camera attention and a patient John Gielgud rather too little, above all at the final heroic moment when he defied the tyranny that had 'arranged' him like an object by raising the head that had been humiliatingly bowed by A. and looked directly out to his audience.

Still, there was scope for critical argument there, worth pursuing because of the talents of those involved in the film. Something of the sort might be said too about the film of *Happy Days* where Winnie was played by an actress, Rosaleen Linehan, who had greatly impressed in the role when directed by Karel Reisz in his stage production. In the film her performance was somewhat undermined by visual emphasis on desert scenery (the company went to Tenerife for these effects) and perhaps by the director's attitude, if that can be judged from the printed Barbican program where she was quoted as saying that she wanted to direct this particular play 'because it's, well, so happy ... it all adds up to a must see movie.'

The most famous source of attraction to Beckett's theater, *Waiting for Godot*, posed the greatest test for the film makers. The director, Michael Lindsay-Hogg, chose to use Walter Asmus' much admired stage production, adapting it to film with few changes except those the medium more or less demanded. Close-ups were sensitively used to provide variety during the long conversation, occupying the larger part of the play, between Vladimir and Estragon. He did also extend the scenic background with a substantial mound in a derelict-looking quarry, with slate scattered about, but that was scarcely more than the mild scenic variations stage directors have occasionally tried. Some of those discussing the films at the Barbican (and others I have heard since) found the film lacking in dynamism, even tending to be inert. This had nothing to do with the performances. No actors could have given a more satisfying account of

Vladimir and Estragon than Barry McGovern and Johnny Murphy, with their Irish voices, attuned to Beckett's rhythms, and their capacity to move with ease from the droll into the poignant mood. So too the other pair: Stephen Brennan's rendering of Lucky's 'think' alone deserved a film recording – and will be much used by those seeking to convey the extraordinary nature of the theatrical solo turn.

The trouble was with the medium itself, its visual restlessness, the difficulty it has in holding attention for long stretches where no obvious change is occurring. Yet for all that, the film is a treasure house, rich in scenes that have the capacity to bring the play completely to life. That was Michael Colgan's hope in the beginning. As he said during the Barbican sessions, the plays were bound to be filmed some time and he wanted to see them captured on screen, made fully cinematic, without loss to them as plays. No one illustrating *Godot* for an audience from videos of this film would need to be concerned about losing the sense of the play.

Endgame might have been thought to pose similar problems for a film director, given the defiant physical immobility of its four characters – two stuck in dustbins, one in a wheelchair, one able only to hobble. In fact, of course, the play is full of movement, especially around the hobbling, as Conor Macpherson, directing, brought out with comic flair. In this case the film gave a truer impression of the play than those stage productions which take it at too slow a pace and make it too dour, altogether a long way from the 'bittersweet comedy' Macpherson discovered in it. Similarly, Atom Egoyan found a screen pace that was exactly right for *Krapp's Last Tape*, allowing John Hurt to give a performance of fine precision which was equally well suited to stage or screen. More questionable as a rendering of the original play, was the film of *Ohio Impromptu*. The director, Charles Sturridge, changed the impression an audience would receive of Beckett's Reader and Listener, those two white-haired look-alikes, by having both played by the same actor, Jeremy Irons. The 'oneness' was stressed by movements in space and changes of focus that only a cinematic technique could manage. In this way the play was recreated, though along a line hinted at in Beckett's stage directions – the two men should be as 'alike as possible,' he says; they seem to share the one black hat lying on the table between them, and so on. There was room for argument about this interpretation: It lessened the play's ambiguity by so clearly implying that Reader and Listener were elements in one personality. But the argument would be an interesting one that could not but lead back into the play.

The mime plays offered chances for silent film effects that were vivaciously taken up by their directors, Karel Reisz (*Act Without Words 1*) and Enda Hughes (*Act Without Words 2*). The latter ingeniously followed up tips from stage directions which seem to envisage cinematic possibilities. The narrow platform Beckett wanted for his two figures, A and B, became a film strip, brilliantly lit in accordance with Beckett's call for 'violent lighting.' Directors of the *Rough for Theatre* films responded with equal zest to the chance of handling these relatively unfamiliar plays. An extra layer of poignancy was added to *Rough for Theatre 1* by the director's idea of shooting it on location and filming it in black and white, with an affectionate title of his own fancy in mind: 'Street Corner – Day.' Laurel and Hardy were in the background here for Kieron J. Walsh, as he indicated in the Barbican program.

These particular films could serve as truthful accounts of the plays as well as being pleasing in themselves. A big issue looms up here, however. Given the difficulty many will always have in seeing the plays in the theater, are the films likely to become substitutes rather than interpretations? Whether or not we saw the stage *Not I* with Billie Whitelaw's terrifying, anguished Mouth, the red-lipsticked not-very-anguished Mouth of the 2001 film version offers viewers a far from riveting experience. But even more effective film treatments, such as that of *Play*, are at a distance from the stage original. It would be unfortunate if easy access to the video cassette of the 2001 films were to fix understanding of the plays.

The best way to avoid this would no doubt be to have more films, giving chances for comparisons of film treatments which would involve looking back to the plays, especially if the films were controversial or strikingly different from each other. Had a film been made of the Dublin Gate Theatre's 1999 stage production of *What Where* there would have been just such a chance of interesting comparisons with the 2001 film version, directed by Damien O'Donnell. The style of the stage play was stately, poetic. Tall figures in flowing robes, representing Bam, Bom, and the rest, stood in lighted niches, seeming not so much victims of a sadistic tyranny as participants in a mysterious process of searching for some truth. For O'Donnell, as quoted in the Barbican program, the play suggested a 'brooding, palpable evil.' He brought the scene closer to realism and created a dark, sinister atmosphere by homing in on the faces of the two actors playing the four interrogators/interrogated. As he said, 'Filming allows you to show a close-up of a terrified man, bringing a different edge to the work.'

This 'different edge' is what may be hoped for as new stage productions and new films appear, to show what a great range of possible responses there is to Beckett's plays. It is a theater that can astonish us by its inventiveness and wit, draw us into strange worlds with sympathetic humour, touch us by its human feeling and the spiritual dimension which is part of it. This was never more poignantly shown than when Barry McGovern's Vladimir, having sadly questioned the young Boy without hope of a real answer, sends him back to Godot with the only message he can give: '[T]ell him you saw me.' Stage and film both reminded us here what it is, at the heart of Beckett's theater, that so powerfully attracts us.

notes

1. Interview with Herbert Blau in Lois Oppenheim (ed.), *Directing Beckett* (Ann Arbor: University of Michigan Press, 1994), 52.
2. See, for instance, William W. Demastes, *Staging Consciousness* (Ann Arbor: University of Michigan Press, 2002.
3. See Arlene Stein and Ken Plummer, *Queer Theory/Sociology* (Oxford: Blackwell, 1996), 132–3.
4. Billie Whitelaw, *Billie Whitelaw ... Who He?* (London: Hodder & Stoughton, 1995), 124, 126.
5. See Enoch Brater, 'The I in Beckett's *Not I*', *Twentieth Century Literature*, 20 (1974), 189–200.
6. See James Acheson, *Samuel Beckett's Artistic Theory and Practise* (London: Macmillan, – now Palgrave Macmillan; New York: St Martin's Press – now Palgrave Macmillan, 1997), 172–81.
7. See Mariko Hori Tanaka, 'Special features of Beckett Performance in Japan', in Lois Oppenheim and M. Buning (eds), *Beckett On and On ...* (Madison & London: Associated University Presses, 1996), 226–39.
8. See Jordan R. Young, *The Beckett Actor* (Beverley Hills, CA: Moonstone Press, 1987).
9. Oppenheim, *Directing Beckett*, 125.
10. Katharine Worth, 'Words for Music Perhaps' in Mary Bryden (ed.), *Samuel Beckett and Music* (Oxford: Clarendon Press, 1998).
11. For an account of this adaptation see Katharine Worth, *Samuel Beckett's Theatre: Life Journeys* (Oxford: Clarendon Press, 1999, paperback edn. 2001).
12. Comments by the film directors shown as direct quotations are from the 'Beckett on Film' program available to audiences at the Barbican event in 2001. Other comments occurred during the sessions of talks and discussion.

works cited

Cohn, Ruby. *A Beckett Canon* (Ann Arbor: University of Michigan Press, 2001).
Connor, Steven. *Samuel Beckett: Repetition, Theory and Text* (Oxford: Blackwell, 1988), 200.
Knowlson, James. *Damned to Fame: the Life of Samuel Beckett* (London: Bloomsbury Publishing, 1996).
—— (gen. ed.), *The Theatrical Notebooks of Samuel Beckett* (London: Faber & Faber, 1992–9).

13
beckett and bibliography

david pattie

What is different about Beckett is not that he provokes a critical response
... but the protean, open-ended, 'undecidable' and inexhaustible quality
of the challenge he offers. In this, it seems to us, he is the poet of the
post-structuralist age. Not that he was *not* the poet of other ages too
for he was – Beckett as the quintessential *nouveau romancier*, Beckett
the Cartesian, Beckett the Existentialist, these have rubbed shoulders
with Beckett the nihilist, Beckett the mystic and Beckett the explorer
of the limitations of language.

(Butler and Davis 1988, ix)

i. beckett and the critics

This summary of the academic response to Beckett's work, first published
in 1987, still holds true; the steady flow of critical literature devoted to him
shows no sign of diminishing, and yet it is hard to see a fixed consensus
about his work emerging from the voluminous material already available.
On the contrary: Beckett's position in twentieth-century literature might
be secure, but the nature of his contribution is a matter of debate. He
is variously the last of the humanists, portraying the individual soul
surviving in the utmost extremity; the last of the modernists, in whose
work the experimental urges of the interwar years reach their endpoint;
one of the first post-modernists, pulling apart the underlying mechanisms
of the literary and dramatic text; a philosopher, in whose work the history
of Western thought can be discerned; an anti-rationalist, perhaps even
a mystic; and so on, and so on. Beckett's relation to academic criticism
has been both unstable and problematic and, at the same time, endlessly
fruitful. (One only has to look at the contents page of this collection

226

to gain a sense of the many critical uses to which his work has been put.) And yet there is no consensus. If we were to look to Beckett's own work for analogies, we might be irresistibly drawn to dismissals of the critical enterprise (Molloy farting into the *Times Literary Supplement*, or the despairing cry in *Catastrophe* – 'This craze for explicitation! Every i dotted to death!'); or to the warning at the beginning of 'Dante...Bruno. Vico..Joyce' ('The danger is in the neatness of identifications.') Perhaps, though, the best analogy comes from *Watt*, and from Watt's determined attempt to read meaning into the painting in Erskine's room. Try as hard as he may, Watt can never bring the elements of the image into a fixed relation with each other; he is left with an artwork whose features are simultaneously obvious and frustratingly vague. So the critic with Beckett. It has so far proved impossible to establish a fixed image of the work. The critical perspective on any artist will of course change over time, but the history of Beckett studies has contained more than the usual amount of academic re-evaluations. Even attempts to close off an area of debate (for example, the chapter on modernity and postmodernity in Lois Oppenheim's *The Painted Word: Samuel Beckett's Dialogue with Art [2000]*) are, it seems, answered almost immediately by analyses that continue the argument (see the essays collected in Richard Lane's *Beckett and Philosophy* [2002]).

This makes Beckett a uniquely frustrating figure, as far as academic exegesis is concerned; however, it also means that he is a very useful case study for anyone interested in the fate of literary and dramatic criticism over the past half century. His work straddles the great theoretical chasm that opened up in literary studies in the 1970s and 1980s, a chasm that, in simple terms, divided the world of the modernists from that of the postmodernists, but which in a more complex and perhaps a more truthful sense should be thought of as a divide between those who used literary texts to uncover the essential truth of human experience, and those who used texts to uncover the contingent nature of reality. As will be demonstrated below (and as is clear to those who acquaint themselves with the secondary literature his work has spawned), there is ample evidence in Beckett's work to support both cases. For the essentialists or, in another term as general, the humanists, his writing represents a heroically sustained and determined attempt to uncover the foundations of human experience. His central figures, stripped of all social restraints and encumbrances, are free to confront the human condition – the naked, uncomfortable truth of human existence in an indifferent universe. On the other hand, critics on the other side of the divide have drawn attention to the curiously self-generating nature of Beckett's texts. In the prose, the narrators seem to have only the most fragile control over the stories they tell, and in the plays, purposeful action has been replaced by activity that merely serves to fill the space and measure out the duration of the performance. From this, it has been concluded that Beckett's work demonstrates that all human communication is subject to *aporia* (a term, most closely associated with the work of the French poststructuralist Jacques Derrida, referring to the moment when the ostensible meaning of a text seems to collapse into undecidability). For these critics, Beckett's work is uniquely suited to a world in which definitive meanings can never be established; where there is no fixed, certain human condition for the writer to reflect.

It would be wrong, of course, to imagine the gap between theorists from these two traditions to be as wide as it is sometimes imagined. For one thing, the traditions themselves are multifaceted and complex; there is no such thing as a typical modernist critic or, for that matter, a typical postmodernist. For another thing, the history of literary criticism is not as linear as undergraduate primers in theory sometimes suggest. We have yet to pass through the moment where one style of criticism automatically yields to another. With the advent of postmodernity, previous generations of critics neither surrendered to the theoretically inevitable, nor did they retire defeated to private life. Rather, the two broad streams and their offshoots came into conflict and cross-fertilized. Once again, any time spent with critical commentary on Beckett's work will begin to acquaint the casual reader with a sense of the bewildering variety of critical hybrids currently available.

Perhaps what unites work undertaken on Beckett by both modernists (loosely defined) and postmodernists (again, loosely defined) is simply that his work seems to pose fundamental questions – about the nature of human experience, about our physical selves, about the role of rational discourse in an irrational world; or about the inherently fragmentary nature of the text, the impossibility of settled meaning, and the endless creation and re-creation of the self. What, perhaps, is ultimately most interesting about Beckett's relation to literary criticism is that, no matter what the particular approach taken by the individual theorist, his work is used as a lens through which to focus the critic's attention on perhaps the most basic theoretical enquiry: How do we make meaning in the world? It may very well be that, in essence, the debate between Beckett scholars of whatever persuasion comes down to the simple parsing of this question; for one broad tradition, how do we make meaning in a world that seems meaningless, and for the other, how do we as human beings make meaning happen in the world around us?

ii. making meaning in the world

The clown exploits impotence, to be sure, when he allows to bubble up into sustained mimetic coherence his own inability to walk a tightrope, missing his footing, misplacing but never dropping his bowler hat (which catches on a button behind his collar and, obeying immutable mechanical laws, is carried round out of reach as he turns to clutch at the space where it was) collapsing in an arc which carries his hands exactly to a graspable stanchion, retarding his pace to zero for long reflection, crowding six desperate acrobatics into a split second. He does not imitate the acrobat; it is plain that he could not; he offers us directly, his personal incapacity, an intricate artform. The man who imitates the acrobat himself (all ropewalkers are alike), adding to what we have already seen before in other circuses some new miniscule difficulty overcome, moving on felt-shod feet a little further along the dreary road of the possible. (Kenner 1961: pp. 33–4)

Hugh Kenner's *Samuel Beckett: a Critical Study* was published in 1961; the same year saw the first appearance of Martin Esslin's influential study, *The Theatre of the Absurd*. With them, the history of Beckett criticism in English decisively begins and the initial framework that will surround his work is (almost entirely) constructed. For Kenner and Esslin, Beckett was the poet of meaninglessness. The artist, in a world whose ultimate destruction could at worst be only hours away, was faced with a new, urgent task – to convey a sense of what it felt like to live in the knowledge that such universal danger rendered most human activity absurd. World War II (in which Beckett had played a small, yet heroic part) was a reminder of the worst that humans could do: An artist who confronted the horror at the heart of the human condition, and yet who at the same time refused to be cowed into silence by it, was an artist uniquely placed to understand the existential dilemmas to which modern man was prone. Esslin's introduction to a collection of essays in 1965 remains, perhaps, one of the strongest reflections of this critical position:

To be in communication with a mind of such uncompromising determination to face the stark reality of the human situation and to confront the worst without ever being in danger of yielding to any of the superficial consolations that have clouded man's self-awareness in the past; to be in contact with a human being so free of self-pity, utterly oblivious to the pitfalls of vanity and self-glorification, even that most venal complacency of all, the illusion of being able to lighten one's load by sharing it with others; to see a lone figure, without hope of comfort, facing the great emptiness of space and time without the possibility of miraculous rescue or salvation, in dignity, resolved to fulfil its obligation to express its own predicament – to partake of such courage and noble stoicism, however remotely, cannot but evoke a refilling of emotional excitement, exhilaration. (Esslin 1965, 14)

I have quoted from Kenner's and Esslin's work at length because between them they give a sense of much of the first responses to Beckett's work. Beckett is the writer of the age, not because he deals directly with the world in the wake of global conflict, but because he unerringly anatomizes the underlying existential state of our existence in a bleak and uncertain present. He tells us, clearly, unsentimentally, what it is like to live a life without hope, what it is like to live a life doomed to failure, what it is like to live – and to live heroically – in a world with no guarantees. The clown will never achieve anything; he is bound to one location, to one set of meaningless actions; his activities have been prolonged beyond laughter, and yet he still persists. It is in this sense of stubborn persistence that the first generation of critics identify the positive, redemptive, even cathartic nature of Beckett's art:

These fictions tell us simply but insistently the story of a fragile voice – a human voice – which refuses stubbornly to die, which flickers on, somehow resisting submersion and assimilation. (Fletcher 1964, 233)

It is no good trying to isolate Beckett from values: if he has been unable to establish them for others, or for himself, it is to their hypothetical postulation that he dedicates the full force of his work. He directs his laughter he says, against that which is not good, against that which is not true, against that which mocks suffering. That laughter is his testament – his legacy to that which is good, to that which is true, that which is compassionate. (Jacobson and Mueller 1964, 174)

The man who, like Beckett, continues to create [...] is, as Camus writes in *The Myth of Sisyphus*, 'the most absurd character'. The conflict between the world's irrationality and man's hopeless desire for unity is most acute in the artist who, having once believed in his near total omnipotence, is now forced to recognise his almost total impotence. Yet there remains [...] the right to fail. Creating, or not creating, changes nothing, and the words which are written will remain at best only a hesitant approximation of those finer words that, if they do exist, continue to elude his need. But if he persists in this endeavour which he knows to be futile he will have sustained his consciousness in the face of the universe and its absurdity. (Robinson 1969, 301)

If [Beckett] is a sounding board for suffering, it is not just his own suffering. He paints a picture, not recognised by all but responded to by most, of man in solitude imprisoned within the time and space of a silent and unresponsive universe. Only the very brash or complacent can fail to react to that. (Duckworth 1972, 104)

It is interesting to note that, in the above quotes, the figure of Beckett is subtly elided both with the figure of the Beckettian protagonist, and with the reader or spectator who follows Beckett's attempts to wrest art from chaos. The hell, or the infinite purgatory, experienced by Vladimir, Watt, Hamm, and Malone is Beckett's hell; by extension, because we live through the same experience of existential dread, it is also our hell. Beckett's main attribute (and his main claim to our attention) is the clarity and directness with which he states the underlying conditions of our lives. His victory – in Michael Robinson's terms, the sustaining of his consciousness in an absurd universe – is a victory won on our behalf.

This view of Beckett is, at base, an amalgamation of a number of critical approaches, explored in various ways (and with varying degrees of success) by critics in the 1960s and 1970s. Firstly, there is the notion of Beckett the Cartesian: His work demonstrates and expands on the idea, crucial to Descartes' thought, of a split between the mind and the body (Kenner's study in particular devotes a chapter – 'The Cartesian Centaur' – to the subject). In Descartes (and even more so in the work of his philosophical descendants, Geulincx and Malebranche, both of whom find a place in the Beckett canon), the link between the mental and the physical is merely a matter of relation, assured by the existence of a beneficent god. In Beckett god 'the bastard ... doesn't exist,' and therefore cannot ensure that mind and body can operate smoothly together. The Beckettian mind or spirit is, in Yeats' resonant phrase, 'tethered to a dying animal.' It is condemned to observe an inevitable process of decay, in which it is powerless to intervene. The Cartesian quest for meaning is for a fundamental order to existence;

the Beckettian quest will uncover the underlying absurdity of existence but will, heroically, persist in the attempt to make the irrational rational.

It will, in other words, become a purgatorial quest with no hope of redemption. But it remains a quest – a detail that, for many first generation Beckett scholars, provided an easy bridge between the avowed Cartesianism of his work and the then fashionable philosophy of existentialism. Indeed, the very concept of the absurd, under which much early Beckett criticism assembled itself, was an existentialist concept, expressed most memorably by Albert Camus in *The Myth of Sisyphus*:

> At certain moments of lucidity, the mechanical aspect of [human] gestures, their meaningless pantomime make silly everything that surrounds them. A man is talking behind a glass partition; you cannot hear him but you can see his incomprehensible dumb-show; you wonder why he is alive. This discomfort in the face of man's own humanity, this incalculable tumble before the image of what we are, this 'nausea' […] is […] the absurd. (Camus, *The Myth of Sisyphus*, Harmondsworth, Penguin 1955, 18–19)

Read in the light of the above quote, the Beckettian canon is full of absurd moments: The comings and goings of *Godot*, Hamm's tour of the world in *Endgame*; those moments in the post-war fiction when the protagonist finds himself lost in a senseless world ('Into what nightmare thingness am I fallen?' as the narrator of *The Calmative* puts it); the times when the unfolding tales and fables that provide an illusory sense of purpose and hope for those who write and those who speak, decay, and decline into meaninglessness – all betray the impossibility of arriving at a final, essential meaning in a world shorn of rational significance.

As indicated above, however, early critics were keen to emphasize that, for Beckett, the fact that human life was ultimately meaningless did not automatically translate into an art that simply mocked any human pretension to rational activity. Beckett's, in the first of the *Three Dialogues with George Duthuit* (a text first translated into English in 1965, and an endlessly fruitful source of inspiration for the Beckett critic), stated his preference for an art that acknowledged that the expressive urge was overpoweringly strong, but that true expression was impossible. The world was simply too chaotic, too unknowable, and any human attempt to come to terms with it was doomed to ultimate failure. The artist's duty, though, remained clear – to accommodate the mess, or to leave a stain upon the silence, while clearly recognizing that his work was not simply a reflection, but a direct expression of the tragicomedy of human existence. As Kierkegaard (a proto-existentialist whose work proved a fertile source of inspiration for early Beckett scholars) put it:

> Existence itself, the act of existing, is a striving and is both comic and pathetic in the same degree. It is pathetic because the striving is infinite: that is, it is directed toward the infinite, being an actualisation of infinitude, a transformation which involves the highest pathos. It is comic, because such a striving involves a self-contradiction. Viewed pathetically, a single second has infinite value; viewed comically, ten thousand years are but a trifle. (Kierkegaard, *Concluding Unscientific Postscript*, Princeton: Princeton University Press 1941, 84–5)

The above description seemed to encapsulate not simply the fate of the Beckett protagonist, doomed to record and ponder over the minutiae of his everyday surroundings, but the figure of Beckett the artist, struggling onwards to produce meaning in the full and certain knowledge that the world cannot be transformed into sense through human intervention – and that no other source of intervention is available to us.

If a framework can be built around the first fifteen or twenty years of Beckett criticism in English, it would largely be constructed from the raw materials provided by Descartes and the existentialists. Other names and figures loom large in Beckett criticism at this time: Schopenhauer (whose ideal mental state, that of will-less contemplation, seems a goal to which the Beckett protagonist frequently aspires); Democritus (whose aphorism 'Nothing is more real than nothing' looms large in discussions of the ultimate senselessness of the Beckettian universe); and, from literature (amongst a host of others), Kafka, Joyce, Proust, and, pre-eminently, Dante – whose *Divine Comedy* had, it was argued, provided Beckett with a taxonomy of suffering and endurance. However various the influences that operated in Beckett's work, however, the banners under which critics established their positions derived in part or in whole from the central image of the Beckett character as a suffering mind, trapped in a decaying body, struggling to assert meaning in a meaningless world.

This is not to say, though, that such a reading of Beckett was either universal or simplistic. In 1967, for example, the theorist Ihab Hassan published *The Literature of Silence: Henry Miller and Samuel Beckett*. This study is notable, largely because it is the work of an early theorist of what was, even then, coming to be known as postmodernity. For other critics, Beckett described a fundamentally meaningless world using words, because they were the best tools to hand. Hassan pointed out that, in Beckett's work, it could be argued that words themselves were (very nearly) meaningless. Language was an aporetic game and the game would end only when language's ability to express meaning had finally exhausted itself:

> In this rigorous fidelity to failure, he also reveals the secret tendency of literature to silence. Despite the monstrous skill of his words, Samuel Beckett may be considered the author who wants to seal the lips of the muse. Yet his silence, despite its grim, satiric note, has something in common with the silence of holy men who, after knowing pain and outrage, reach for a peace beyond human understanding. (Hassan 1967, 30–1)

This quote is interesting, for three reasons. Firstly, and most obviously, it invokes a key postmodern concept: the sheer untrustworthiness of language as a form of communication. Secondly, it demonstrates the persistence of a humanist reading of Beckett's work. The author is still there, grimly, satirically silent, ordering his fictional world even as he brings it to its silent ending. Thirdly, it invokes a spiritual reading of Beckett's work, a feature both of the humanist and many of the postmodern readings of the prose and drama. Hassan, writing in 1967 (the year when Jacques Derrida published three books – *Speech and Phenomena, Writing and Difference, Of Grammatology* – and decisively inaugurated poststructuralism), produced a work which catches the first stirrings of the postmodern within the mainstream modernism, not simply of Beckett criticism, but of literary criticism as a whole. Indeed, he marks the point at which criticism begins its long metamorphosis into theory.

Hassan cannot be called a Beckett scholar. His work knits Beckett into an evolving theoretical framework, but Hassan's engagement with the author did not form the main thread of his work. It is interesting, though, to find echoes of the ideas discussed by Hassan in the work of one of the pre-eminent Beckett scholars, indeed, in an author closely associated with Beckett studies from the first. Ruby Cohn's early work, *Samuel Beckett: The Comic Gamut*, discussed the work in relation to Bergson's analysis of the comic techniques of language. Her study (published in 1962 – early in the day for Beckett scholarship) invokes the figure of Beckett the hunger-artist ('All Beckett's fictions merge, finally, into the unique suffering artist-human'), but it also seems in retrospect to prefigure the debates of the 1980s and 1990s, in which Beckett's literary technique would, itself, move to the center of all discussions:

Beckett's motif [...] is that words are thoughts are emotions, that fiction is our only language, and all knowledge a fiction written in a foreign tongue. (Cohn 1962, 167)

Dramatic or fictional, Beckett's work paints an ironic portrait of man, Everyman, as artist-liar. He paints in words – in the words that his heroes revile and unravel, in the words he weaves into one of the masterly prose styles of our time [...].

Within each literary genre, Beckett undermines that very genre-fictional formulae in the fiction and dramatic conventions in the drama. By mocking the literary form within that form, Beckett questions the boundary between art and life, between fiction and fact. Such interrogation is part of the traditional stock in trade of the fool and Beckett plays it for all its farcical, metaphysical worth. He pommels existence with the questions of his characters, or with is frenzied affirmations immediately followed by more frenzied negation. These questions slap at life as well as art; for any interpretation of life as a construction, a game, a work of art. (Ibid: 298–9)

Read from the perspective of the early 2000s, Cohn's summary of Beckett appears prescient; it anticipates debate over the truthfulness of the Beckettian narrator, and with it the inherent truthfulness or otherwise of the narrative impulse. Significantly, her analysis invokes one of the key stances adopted by both artists and theorists whose work is generally classed as postmodern. Beckett's work demonstrates an inherent irony at the heart of human existence, because the very act of representing experience transforms that experience into fiction, into art. Cohn later retreated from the proto-postmodernity of her first book. In *Back to Beckett*, published in 1973, she wrote:

Beckett is not a metalinguist [...] he is a speleologist [a cave explorer – taken here to mean someone who digs deep below the surface of things] of human essence – call it being, self, identity. The essence defies verbalization, and Beckett defiantly tries to verbalize it. As human beings, most of us investigate ourselves and our worlds with words. As a writer, Beckett can dig only with words. (Cohn 1973, 6)

Subsequent books (*Just Play: Beckett's Theater*, and, in particular, *A Beckett Canon*) have been firmly within the humanist tradition of the above quote. Beckett's art is heroic because he delves into human experience working with words as the only tools to hand, no matter how inadequate they might be.

The philosophical and literary framework of this first phase of Beckett studies remained more or less fixed throughout the 1970s; however, the volume of critical attention that his work excited began to expand exponentially. It is fair to say that the study of Beckett turned into something of an industry; and, as it did so, attention moved from the underlying philosophy behind the work to an examination of the work in detail. Studies such as Lawrence Harvey's *Samuel Beckett: Poet and Critic* (written, unusually for the field, in partial collaboration with Beckett himself); Fletcher and Spurling's *Beckett: a Study of His Plays*; and H. Porter Abbott's *The Fiction of Samuel Beckett: Form and Effect* concentrated on individual genres, rather than on the oeuvre as a whole. David Hesla's *The Shape of Chaos* analysed the development of a coherent philosophical position in Beckett's work: James Knowlson and John Pilling's *Frescoes of the Skull* discussed both the earlier, as yet unpublished manuscripts, and the increasingly gnomic later fiction and drama. In other words, these and other studies began, necessarily, to bring a greater diversity to the critical options open to the Beckett scholar. For example, Hesla's version of Beckett's existential humanism was a great deal more nuanced than previous accounts; and studies such as John Pilling's *Samuel Beckett* provided not only a more comprehensive list of actual and potential influences on Beckett, but also a detailed discussion of the literary, cultural and intellectual currents that ran through Europe at the time when Beckett's art was developing.

As the field diversified, though, the question of Beckett's relation to artistic form began to come to the fore. For example, Pilling's study argued not that the Beckettian hero was existentially driven to expression, but that the existential state of Beckettian man and woman was that of a self constrained and confined by narrative:

> It is as if Beckett's own creativity has come under scrutiny; the necessary liberation to compose one's own narrative ... is ousted by the remorseless repetition of event – what the Proust book calls 'habit' – to which passing time commits us all. As the plays become more and more elemental there is less and less time for the narratives to tell themselves; but our fictions have their revenge by taking on independent life, and compelling us to go on telling them. (Pilling 1976, 109)

The essay collection *Beckett the Shape Changer* (edited by Katherine Worth) was concerned, not with Beckett the suffering artist, but with Beckett the formal innovator, whose work was at its most exciting when it operated on the boundaries of genre:

> It is as an artist of the protean kind that Beckett has appealed to the contributors to this volume. The transformation process is our subject; how Beckett renews and reshapes himself from one form, language, genre, medium to another; how the characters take us into the pains, terrors, and jokes of the reshaping, the Unnamable panting 'If I could be like Worm,' the voice in Cascando stretching itself to 'get' Woburn, say him, know him and change him; above all, how the illusion draws its strength from being exposed, handled, turned round for us to see how it is done, *until finally there is no distinguishing how it is done from how it is.* (Worth 1975, 193)

These studies are still couched in an existential framework (even though Pilling denies to Beckett's characters the freedom of choice inherent in most forms of the philosophy). What is interesting, though, is that they, and other studies of the period, already operate in territory more usually associated with poststructuralism, deconstruction, and postmodernity in general. All that is required is a shift in the theoretical paradigm, from a loosely described humanism to the multiple varieties of textual uncertainty uncovered by the postmodern theorist. The same points could be made about the underlying formal uncertainty of the Beckettian world, the curious link between existence and the fictional process, and the formal games and strategies that give a transitory structure to existence in the Beckettian universe.

iii. making the world mean

Repetition in Beckett's work does not just involve the mirroring or duplication of situation, incident, and character. From the beginning, repetition has been the dominating principle of his language; repetition of words, of sounds, of phrases, of syntactical and grammatical forms. And as the consciousness of language as a distorting or constricting force tightens its hold on Beckett [...] so repetition seems to become more and more necessary in his work [...]. [Where] repetition begins as a supplementary feature of language, secondary to and derived from the uniqueness of particular utterances, it comes to occupy the centre of his work. Repetition comes to be all there is, the only novelty being the variations in the forms of sameness. (Connor 1988, 15)

Steven Connor's *Samuel Beckett: Repetition, Theory and Text* (1988) is one of the most frequently cited examples of postmodern Beckett criticism. It invokes a staple feature of poststructuralist textual analysis: the law of the supplement – or the contention that repetition undermines the unique status of the original, by producing indistinguishable copies of it. Beckett's work, under this new dispensation, could not be a revelation of authentic human experience. There was, simply, no such thing as an easily accessible, authentic human experience for the individual artist to describe. The text does not reveal reality; the text is a game, a strategic interpretation of the greater text that is created through the process of living. (Thus, Connor argues, for example, that repetition is an important feature, not only of the Beckett text, but of the always unstable process through which we assign meaning to our actions.)

There is no one moment that marks the integration of postmodern discourse (itself a paradigmatically postmodern term) into literary criticism. As mentioned above, Derrida's work had been available in English since the late 1960s (and, indeed, had exercised an influence, certainly on American academics, before then). Of course, some contributions to Beckett studies in the 1960s and 1970s had been postmodern in all but name; and at least one (Hassan's *The Literature of Silence*) could be described as a postmodern text. It could be argued, though, that the full impact of the postmodern paradigm was not felt in literary studies as a whole, and in Beckett studies, in particular, until the 1980s. This new paradigm can be thought of as the reflection of a paradox at the heart of our need to shape the world that surrounds us. In shaping the world, we necessarily transform our experience into narrative. We then become the sum of the narratives that we have constructed, but these narratives are neither internally consistent, nor are they consistent with each other. The process that we employ to shape our lives, as individuals and as societies, will inevitably contain holes, gaps, unexplainable elements, and moments of undecidability. No matter how hard we try, our desire to uncover the truth of ourselves through narrative will always fail because we will never be able to construct a narrative that unambiguously describes the human experience insofar as the human experience is composed precisely of unfinished, ambiguous narratives. As Leslie Hill noted, in *Beckett's Fiction: In Different Words*, Beckett's fiction mirrored Derrida's model of a language and a narrative structure that were perennially caught at a moment of crisis:

[I]t is a theory committed to defending the autonomy of literary texts, and it defines fiction as an activity of language in which, paradoxically, the foundations of meaning are attacked by the uncontrollable, self-inverting character of meaning itself. (Hill 1990, 6)

This is both a counsel of despair, and of hope. It is despairing because we can no longer structure our world according to the 'grand narratives' (to borrow a term from Lyotard), those stories that seek to give an answer to the human condition; it is hopeful because the death of the grand narratives leaves us perhaps a little freer than before, free at least to construct our own narratives from the raw material of existence.

From the first, critics remarked on Beckett's fascination with the process of narrative. For the postmodern critic, however, narrative was no longer the tool that the heroic Beckettian storyteller used to beat their worlds into shape. Rather, our attention is turned to the process of narration, and the odd inversions and echoes that the Beckettian narrative contains. For example, Angela Moorjani in 1982 (*Abysmal Games in Samuel Beckett's Fiction*) took a staple of humanist Beckett criticism – the idea of the quest – and subjected it to postmodern analysis:

From an examination of Molloy's narrative [...] it appears that the components of the Oedipus myth are inscribed in duplicate. The Louisse episode condenses the entire drama into a dreamlike emblem in the middle of the narrative which, since it stages embedded inner journeys to the mother, traces Molloy's movements through regions that evoke the mother and the unconscious [...]. The quest, as we have seen, is both commanded and forbidden by multiple embodiments of a paradoxical law; maternal voices that order and forbid, paternal figures that obstruct and goad, sphinxes both male and female. The violence against the father, of which there are two versions, and the union with the mother figures, however, fail to lead anywhere. Indeed, rather than Oedipus, Molloy is an anti-Oedipus, for instead of solving the riddle of the sphinx and attaining sovereignty, Molloy in a regressive moment recedes from his mother's room via the sphinx to the killing of the stranger at the crossroads to the final crawling on all fours out of the forest and into the bowels of the earth. (Moorjani 1982, 106)

Molloy's narrative does not simply replay the Oedipus myth; it reverses it. The Beckettian hero is no longer engaged in a quest for ultimate meaning, one that can be comfortably described as heroic. Rather, he or she follows a trajectory that leads away from revelation into undecidability. In Moorjani's account, there is no sense that Molloy, in travelling away from his moment of Oedipal crisis, is returning to a state of primal innocence. His life cannot be made to yield meaning in such a simple, linear fashion. It is constructed out of a familiar pattern, but that pattern has been re-assembled, and its new meaning remains obscure.

Critics benefiting from increased access to Beckett's own manuscripts noted that, as Beckett's work moved through its various drafts, all attempts to relate the work to a specific set of locations were systematically removed. S. E. Gontarski's *The Intent of Undoing In Samuel Beckett's Dramatic Texts* subjected this process to a thorough examination:

> Often the early drafts of Beckett's work are more realistic, the action more traditionally motivated, the world more familiar and recognisable, the work as a whole more conventional than the final. Revision is often toward a patterned disconnection, as motifs are organised not by causality but by some form of recurrence and (near) symmetry. This process often entails the conscious destruction of logical relations, the abandonment of linear argument, and the substitution of more abstract patterns of numbers, music, and so forth, to shape a work. It is finally a consciously literary process, which results in what the Russian Formalists might call 'defamiliarisation' or what Brecht, in *A Short Organum for the Theatre*, termed estrangement. (Gontarski, 1985, 3–4)

This move away from the strictly linear forms associated with more conventional forms of prose and drama was, however, not simply a retreat from a world that made no sense. Curiously, the new theoretical readings of Beckett's work still contained something of the heroic tinge of earlier analyses. This appeared in two main forms: The very fact that Beckett's work resisted closure was in itself heroic for a generation of critics for whom the closed narrative, with every character fixed in place, was a fundamentally authoritarian device. Thus Anna McMullan, in *Theatre on Trial: Samuel Beckett's Later Drama* argued that:

> Beckett's theatre can therefore be seen as the site of a confrontation between the attempt to assume a position of control and judgement in relation to the visual and verbal representations of self and the laws

of representations of self and the laws of representation in general, and the opening up of spaces which challenge and disrupt the construction of the roles posited by representation, including those of the self and other, spectacle and spectator. Beckett's drama frames the operations of authority. But also stages the drama of a subjectivity which resists or exceeds the dominant codes of representation, questioning in the process the languages and limits of theatre itself. (McMullan 1993, 9)

If representation is a political act (an expression of the dominant power relations within a particular society), then the artist who attempts to rework or disrupt the process of representation is engaged in an act of rebellion against the way that things are. Beckett's work questioned the dominant structures of representation in Western culture. This allied it with a sceptical, politically progressive aspect of postmodernity, which sought to undermine the fixed relations of social and cultural power. Mary Bryden, writing about Beckett's relation to gender politics in *Women in Samuel Beckett's Prose and Drama*, borrowed the term 'deterritorialisation' from the French theorists Gilles Deleuze and Felix Guattari. In doing so, she argued that Beckett practiced a style of writing that existed beyond the familiar boundaries of gender and social organization:

Thus, as an illustration of the marked contrast between the women of Beckett's early fiction and those of Beckett's later writing (from his turn towards drama and thereafter), one may observe that the poles stasis/movement, sterility/fertility, absence/presence do not operate in like fashion throughout his work. Further pairs could be added, but these alone make the point that, while both male and female are insistently and indiscriminately associated with the values of stasis, sterility and absence in the later work, it is their opposites – movement, fertility, presence – which contribute towards the differentiation of women in the earlier fiction. (Bryden 1993, 89)

In other words, Beckett's art has broken free of the binary oppositions that fix women into a subordinate position within society. Although he might never espouse a directly feminist political perspective, his work can be read as feminist, precisely because his work rejects the narrative process through which male power is disseminated and maintained.

Beckett's work, then, undermined the process of meaning, and was therefore useful for those critics who wished to question that process as it operated in Western society. Other critics took the process even further, and discovered in Beckett an artist whose work destroyed the very foundations of Western thought. In this strand of Beckett criticism, postmodernity met psychoanalysis (especially in its Jungian incarnation). The potential influence on Beckett's work of Freud and his disciples had already been explored (perhaps the first determined attempt being G. C. Barnard's *Samuel Beckett: a New Approach* in 1970). Postmodern psychoanalytic readings of Beckett's work, however, revealed an underlying metaphysical framework that could be treated as an all out assault on the rational Western tradition. Mary Doll, for instance, wrote:

My critical approach to Beckett's work borrows from the implications of post-modern thinking, of which deconstruction theory is a part. Like the post-modernists, I see Beckett debunking the systems of Western thought that perpetuate a closed system. Like the deconstructionists, I see Beckett presenting contextual encounters in every text, communicating from within the shattered pieces. Consistent with this post-modern, deconstructed approach, I break with traditional Jungian criticism as it has been so often applied to literary texts, reifying characters into stereotypes of archetypes. Jung's depth psychology became, in the hands of modernist critics, just another system, like that of Kantian idealism, that owed little to the phenomena of images, patterns or sounds. My claim, on the other hand, is that Beckett's work lends itself wonderfully to a mythopoetic method precisely because it breaks form. It not only eschews the established systems of Western philosophy, it also rejects other systems such as Jungian criticism that impose themselves in grid like certainty [...]. Rather, Beckett's poetics of myth allows us to see patterns, and to hear patterns, and to read patterns afresh. (Doll 1988, 4–5)

Beckett, then, represents a decisive threat to the ways in which we ordinarily organize information; and, because our tendency is to organize that information in ways that shore up existing power structures and repressive modes of thought, his work has an unexpectedly positive effect. It calls the way in which we organize the world into question. As earlier, humanist critics of Beckett discovered something positive in the stoic resignation of the Beckettian character, so the new generations of Beckett critics found something useful in his denial of textual determinism. Beckett's work, the implicit argument would seem to be, is a site of resistance to domination, whether that domination is by an indifferent universe, or is exercised through the tyranny of apparently fixed and stable meanings.

Postmodern theorizing did not overwhelm all other approaches to Beckett's work during the 1980s and 1990s. It was a dominant trend, but there were other voices – some, like Brater (1987), guardedly affirming their commitment to humanism; others, like Kalb (1989) and Ricks (1993), using Beckett as a goad to attack the new developments in literary theory. For example, Kalb argued that Beckett's theatrical practice is unsettling, precisely because old divisions between the mainstream and the avant-garde still hold true:

Part of Beckett's importance as a cultural figure is that he blurs ordinary distinctions between mainstream and avant-garde. Because he was embraced so readily as a classic he was able, in effect, to smuggle certain progressive ideas across the border of mainstream culture, and that achievement is, rightfully, his most celebrated: he actually changed many people's expectations of what can happen, what is supposed to happen, when they enter the theatre. (Kalb 1989, 157)

After all, one can only blur ordinary distinctions if the ordinary distinctions are still there. Other critics ceded the existence of the postmodern, but argued that Beckett's work could not truly be given the title:

In Beckett's fiction what is stressed is the arbitrariness; here intertextuality is not allusive; it is centripetal rather than centrifugal. But if, in a new dispensation, sometimes called 'post-modernist,' writers as diverse as the noveaux romanciers in France, American fabulators like Pynchon, Barth and Gass, outsiders like Borges and Gombrowicz, have created fictions which, in various ways revel in the endless arbitrary profusion of representation, Beckett's name should not be too hastily allied to theirs. In his texts there is really no euphoric relinquishing of the bonds between the textual and the existential [...]. (Sherringham 1985, 82)

But even in the work of those who did not declare themselves postmodernist, it was sometimes possible to discern the trace of the new theoretical formations. Enoch Brater, in *The Drama in the Text* (1994), a study of the later fiction, wrote the following of the short prose work *Still*:

Set not in stone, but as prose on a page, Still makes us hear words interact: the process is a verbal kineticism whose protagonists are verbs, adverbs, adjectives and nouns. The drama is the spectacle and speculum of Beckett's language; the only hero in the play is the uncertain word. A nature morte 'impossible to follow let alone describe', Still, ironically, is not still at all. 'Trembling all over', the words of this piece quiver onto actuality. (Brater 1994, 70)

'The only hero in the play is the uncertain word': The locus of enquiry is no longer the Beckettian hero or heroine, struggling with the burden of existence; it is Beckett's language, burdened with the sheer insecurity of meaning.

iv. meaning and history

As argued above, there are odd echoes of humanism in posthumanist accounts of Beckett and moments of incipient postmodernity in earlier critical accounts of the work. The two streams, therefore, should not be thought of as distinct. They come from two separate – in fact, it could be argued, two diametrically opposed – sources, but they intermingle and flow into and around each other further down their respective courses. They share a common interest in the processes through which we assemble meaning in an unstable world; they share a common interest in the processes of language, whether imagined as emanating from an uncertain speaker, or as an inherently unstable force in its own right. They both contain a positive estimation of the impact of Beckett's writing, either as a document of eternal struggle or as an heroic attempt to escape the authority of fixed meanings.

They are also both ahistorical. It is true to say that, for the first three and a half decades of Beckett criticism, nearly all critics treated his work as something separate from the world in which it was produced. This is not to say that references to a wider cultural history were entirely absent from analyses of the work. They did appear – but when they did, they tended to be of the order established by Esslin in 1961. The Theatre of the Absurd was a response to the end of World War II, and the horrors of that conflict, but it was also and more properly an expression of the existential plight of humanity. A few critics did attempt to forge stronger links between Beckett and his time (Kenner [1973] and Gidal [1985], for example); but it was not until the mid-1990s that critics began to take an interest in Beckett as a representative cultural figure whose work could be discussed in relation to his time. This happened for a number of reasons: Firstly, the nature of theory itself was changing, as purely deconstructionist and postmodernist readings began to give way to rather more historically contextualized analysis. (For an account of this process, see the afterword in Norris, *Deconstruction*, 3rd edn. London: Routledge, 2002.) Secondly, Beckett's death in 1989, coming as it did at the end of (to borrow a phrase from the Marxist historian Eric Hobsbawm) the short twentieth century, served not only to fix him to a particular historical period. It also reminded critics that this apparently unworldly author had lived through – indeed, had participated in and been exposed to – some of the most tumultuous events and ideas of the period. (For more information on this, see Gordon [1996] and Knowlson [1996]). Thirdly, during the 1990s, Beckett studies received the fillip of two substantial biographies, one of which (Knowlson [1996]) was explicitly authorized by Beckett himself. Critics had far more access to historical material at a time in which literary theory in general was becoming more interested in the historical context surrounding texts.

From the mid-1990s, therefore, another strand of Beckett criticism began to establish itself. It is found, for example, in Baker's 1997 study, *Beckett and the Mythology of Psychoanalysis*:

> [The] mythic aspect of psychoanalysis has become something of a commonplace. The reified concepts within psychoanalysis – the ego, the id, the instincts and so on – can be said to constitute a mythology [...]. But there is a larger, more pervasively ambient sense in which the discourses of psychoanalysis have become mythological, which has to do not with its conclusions but with its legacy [...].

> There is a whole retrospective landscape of loss in mid-twentieth century culture, constituted by notions such as the paradise of the womb, pre-Oedipal plenitude, parental prohibition, oceanic regression, narcissism, and the narratives of mourning and melancholia. Taken together, these constitute a distinctive terrain, and I shall argue that much of Beckett's major work has deep investments in this landscape. (Baker 1997: xv)

In other words, it is not Beckett's relation to the theory of psychoanalysis that is interesting; it is his relation to psychoanalysis as a particular cultural formation. Oppenheim's (2000) analysis of Beckett's relation to visual art set out to 'rethink Beckett's place on the twentieth-century cultural horizon' (with regard, in particular, to the French philosopher Merleau-Ponty). She undertook this analysis in full awareness of the potential vacuousness of the modernist/postmodernist debate:

> For in the first place we have yet to come to terms with the notion of postmodernism as an extension versus rejection of the modernist

project, as something other than a crude estimation of periodization. And in the second it is the nature of Beckett's writing, and herein resides its singularity, to defy, despite the quality of engaging criticism to the contrary, such classification. In summary, then, the modernist/ postmodernist distinction simply cannot set Beckett's work as a moment in cultural time. (Oppenheim 2000, 27)

The critic, therefore, should not impose a periodization on Beckett's work; rather, he or she should examine Beckett's work in relation to its time – without expecting that a simple correlation between the writing and the time might emerge.

In the late 1990s, studies which probed Beckett's relation to other art forms and practitioners (Oppenheim [1999], Bryden [1998]) began to appear. The links between his most famous play and its time were explored by Bradby (2001) and Gordon (2002) and Beckett's relation to poststructuralism was given a historical context (Uhlmann [1999]). Even more theoretical explorations of the work sometimes gained a sense of historical and cultural perspective not always found in earlier studies (see, for example, Essif [2001]). It is too early to say whether this trend marks another, broad and loosely associated period in Beckett criticism (although the very fact that I have bracketed it off in a separate section suggests that, at least in my opinion, it might well be so). What is quite clear, though, is that it will not mark anything near the end of critical engagement with Beckett's work. Beckett is, as stated above, a writer whose work is taken to pose fundamental questions concerning our need to assemble meaning from the world. Arguably, the wording of these questions might change, but the need and desire to pose the questions in the first place is unlikely to fade. Given that, Beckett's work will continue to prove itself as a site in which critics struggle with the matter of meaning, for many years to come.

bibliography and guide to further reading

general studies

As one might expect, general studies of Beckett's work have become rather less prevalent since the 1980s; the proliferation of work on Beckett, and the increasing variety of critical approaches to it, have tended to militate against studies of the work as a whole. Important early studies of Beckett (particularly Kenner [1961] and Cohn [1962]) deal with both the prose and drama. Later books by these authors (Kenner [1973], Cohn [1973, 2001]) revisit the arguments posed in the earlier studies and partially revise them. Esslin (1965) collects some important early essays on Beckett's work, and contains the first English translation of *Three Dialogues*. Robinson (1970) is a strong assertion of the existential reading of Beckett's work; Mercier (1977) is an interesting, if idiosyncratic, reading of Beckett's work as a series of dialectical oppositions. Gontarski's edited volumes (1986, 1993) garner essays from a wide critical spectrum; Pilling (1994) provides a good overview of Beckett's work, with chapters from a number of prominent Beckett scholars. Accessible entry level studies of Beckett are provided by Ben-Zvi (1986), Kennedy (1989), and Pattie (2001).

prose

Fletcher (1964) is the first study devoted solely to Beckett's fiction; Federman (1965) is a useful early study of Beckett's development as an author up to the trilogy. Kennedy (1971) gives a detailed reading of *Murphy*; Finney (1972) is the first study dedicated to the later short fiction. Abbott (1973) is an interesting study of the relation between Beckett the author and his texts. This theme is expanded and developed in Abbott's later (1996) study. Useful theoretical approaches to the fiction are provided by Moorjani (1982), Hill (1990), Locatelli (1990), Murphy (1991), and Watson (1991). Brater (1994) provides an interesting discussion of the performative nature of the later prose. Pilling (1998) traces the development of Beckett the writer, traversing the same ground as Federman, but with the benefit of a greater access to biographical detail.

drama

Discussions of Beckett's place in twentieth-century theater begin (in more than one sense) with Esslin (1961). This work creates the theoretical framework for much of the discussion of Beckett's drama (and indeed his work in general). Dedicated early discussions of Beckett's theatre can be found in Fletcher and Spurling (1972), Duckworth (1972), Webb (1972), and Fletcher *et al.* (1978). Information and analysis of Beckett's attitude to the texts in performance can be found in Knowlson (1980, 1985, 1992) and Gontarski (1992, 1993). Discussions of the drama informed by recent theoretical developments can be found in Gontarski (1985), Ben-Zvi (1990), Bryden (1993), and McMullan (1993). Kalb (1989) deals with the problems and opportunities that Beckett's work poses for the performer; Oppenheim (1994) gathers a number of directorial responses to the drama.

poetry

To date, the only dedicated study of the poetry remains Harvey (1970).

tv/radio

Sections on the TV and radio plays can be found in many of the books on Beckett's drama. Zillacus (1976) remains the only study dedicated to the radio and early TV work. Homan (1992) gives an interesting perspective on directing the TV work.

special interest

Hesla (1971) is the first study of the philosophical underpinning to Beckett's work. Other notable works on the same theme are by Butler (1984), Davies (2000), and Lane (2002). Baker (1997) and Begam (1996) provide interesting studies of Beckett's response to the wider cultural movements that surrounded him; Oppenheim (1999, 2000) provides a detailed investigation of Beckett's relation to other art forms. Connor (1988) is a provocative poststructuralist reading of the work; Uhlmann (1999) is a more recent, more historically contextualized placing of Beckett's work in relation to poststructuralist thought. Fitch (1988) tackles the difficult area of Beckett the self-translator. Finally, Ricks (1993) is an idiosyncratic, astute, and frequently amusing study of Beckett's language.

biography

Of the five studies published, Bair (1978) is groundbreaking, but full of inconsistencies; Brater (1989) is a concise introduction; Cronin (1996) is especially strong on Beckett's Irish roots; and Knowlson (1996) is the most comprehensive work available as yet.

bibliography

Abbott, H. Porter. *The Fiction of Samuel Beckett: Form and Effect.* Berkeley, Los Angeles, and London: University of California Press, 1973.

—— *Beckett writing Beckett: the Author in the Autograph.* Ithaca: Cornell University Press, 1996.

Abel, Lionel. *Metatheater: a New View of Dramatic Form.* New York: Hill and Wang, 1963.

Acheson, James. *Samuel Beckett's Artistic Theory and Practice: Criticism, Drama and Early Fiction.* London: Macmillan – now Palgrave Macmillan, 1996.

—— and Arthur, Kateryna. (eds). *Beckett's Later Fiction and Drama: Texts for Company.* London: Macmillan – now Palgrave Macmillan, 1987.

Alvarez, A. *Samuel Beckett.* London: Fontana, 1973.

Amiran, Eyal. *Wandering and Home: Beckett's Metaphysical Narrative.* University Park, PA: Pennsylvania State University Press, 1993.

AMULA. No. 55: Samuel Beckett Special Issue, 1981.

Andonian, Cathleen Culotta. *Samuel Beckett: a Reference Guide.* Boston: G. K. Hall, 1988.

Art Press. No. 55. Samuel Beckett Special Issue, 1981.

Astro, Alan. *Understanding Samuel Beckett.* Colombia, SC: University of South Carolina Press, 1990.

Bair, Deidre. *Samuel Beckett: a Biography.* New York: Harcourt Brace Jovanovich, 1978.

Baker, Phil. *Samuel Beckett and The Mythology of Psychoanalysis.* London: Macmillan – now Palgrave Macmillan, 1997.

Baldwin, Helene L. *Samuel Beckett's Real Silence.* University Park, PA: Pennsylvania State University Press, 1981.

Barale, Michele A. and Rabinovitz, Rubin. *A KWIC Concordance to Samuel Beckett's Trilogy: 'Molloy,' 'Malone Dies,' 'The Unnamable.'* 2 vols. New York: Garland, 1988.

Barge, Laura. *God, The Quest, The Hero: Thematic Structures in Beckett's Fiction.* Chapel Hill: University of North Carolina Press, 1988.

Barnard, G. C. *Samuel Beckett: a New Approach.* London: Dent, 1970.

Beckett Circle, The. No.1 (1978)–present.

Begam, Richard. *Samuel Beckett and the End of Modernity.* Stanford: Stanford University Press, 1996.

Beja, Morris, Gontarski, S. E., and Astier, Pierre. *Samuel Beckett: Humanistic Perspectives.* Colombus: Ohio State University Press, 1983.

Ben-Zvi, Linda. *Samuel Beckett.* Boston: Twayne, 1986.

—— (ed.). *Women in Beckett: Performance and Critical Perspectives.* Urbana: University of Illinois Press, 1990.

Birkett, Jennifer. *'Waiting for Godot' by Samuel Beckett.* Macmillan Master Guides. London: Macmillan – now Palgrave Macmillan, 1987.

—— and Ince, Kate. (eds). *Samuel Beckett.* New York: Longman, 2000.

Blau, Herbert. *Sails of the Herring Fleet: Essays on Beckett.* Ann Arbor: University of Michigan Press, 2000.

Bloom, Harold (ed.). *Samuel Beckett.* Modern Critical Views. New York: Chelsea House, 1985.

—— (ed.). *Samuel Beckett's 'Waiting for Godot.'* Modern Critical Interpretations. New York: Chelsea House, 1987.

—— (ed.). *Samuel Beckett's 'Endgame.'* Modern Critical Interpretations. New York: Chelsea House, 1988.

Boulter, Jonathan. *Interpreting Narrative in the Novels of Samuel Beckett.* Gainesville: University of Florida Press, 2001.

Bradby, David. *Beckett: 'Waiting for Godot.' Plays in Production.* Cambridge: Cambridge University Press, 2001.

Brater, Enoch. *Beckett at 80/Beckett in Context.* New York: Oxford University Press, 1987a.

—— *Beyond Minimalism: Beckett's Late Style in the Theatre.* New York: Oxford University Press, 1987b.

—— *Why Beckett.* London: Thames and Hudson, 1989.

—— *The Drama in the Text: Beckett's Late Fiction.* New York: Oxford University Press, 1994.

Brienza, Susan. *Samuel Beckett's New Worlds: Style in Metafiction.* Norman: University of Oklahoma Press, 1987.

Bryden, Mary. *Women in Samuel Beckett's Fiction and Drama: Her Own Other.* London: Macmillan – now Palgrave Macmillan, 1993.

Buning, Marius and Oppenheim, Lois. (eds). *Beckett in the 1990s.* Amsterdam: Rodopi, 1993.

—— *Samuel Beckett and the Idea of God.* London: MacMillan – now Palgrave Macmillan, 1998.

—— (ed.). *Samuel Beckett and Music.* Oxford: Clarendon Press, 1998.

—— Garforth, Julian, and Mills, Peter. *Beckett at Reading: Catalogue of the Beckett Collection at the University of Reading.* Reading: Whiteknights Press & Beckett International Foundation, 1998.

Burkman, Katharine H. *The Arrival of Godot: Ritual Patterns in Beckett's Drama.* London: Associated University Presses, 1986.

—— *Myth and Ritual in the Plays of Samuel Beckett.* London: Associated University Presses, 1987.

Busi, Frederick. *The Transformations of Godot.* Lexington: University Press of Kentucky, 1980.

Butler, Lance St. John. *Samuel Beckett and the Meaning of Being: a Study of Ontological Parable.* New York: St. Martin's Press – now Palgrave Macmillan, 1984.

—— *Critical Essays on Samuel Beckett.* Critical Thought Series, 4. Aldershot: Scholar Press, 1993.

—— and Davis, Robin J. (eds). *Rethinking Beckett: a Collection of Critical Essays.* London: Macmillan – now Palgrave Macmillan, 1988.

Calder, John. *Beckett at Sixty: a Festschrift.* London: Calder and Boyars, 1967.

—— *As No Other Dare Fail: For Samuel Beckett on his 80th Birthday.* London: Calder, 1986.

Centerpoint, Vol. 4, No. 2. *Samuel Beckett* (part issue) 1981.

Chawla, Nishi. *Samuel Beckett: Reading the Body in His Writing.* New Delhi: Prestige, 1999.

Chevigny, Belle Gale. *Twentieth Century Interpretations of Endgame.* Englewood Cliffs, NJ: Prentice-Hall, 1969.

Cochoran, Robert. *Samuel Beckett: a Study of the Short Fiction.* New York: Twayne, 1990.

Coe, Richard N. *Samuel Beckett.* New York: Grove Press, 1964.

Cohn, Ruby. *Samuel Beckett: the Comic Gamut.* New Brunswick, NJ: Rutgers University Press, 1962.

—— (ed.). *A Casebook on 'Waiting for Godot.'* New York: Grove Press, 1967.

—— *Back to Beckett.* Princeton: Princeton University Press, 1973.

—— *Just Play: Beckett's Theater.* Princeton: Princeton University Press, 1980.

—— (ed.). *Beckett, 'Waiting for Godot': a Casebook.* London: Macmillan – now Palgrave Macmillan, 1987.

—— *A Beckett Canon.* Ann Arbor: University of Michigan Press, 2001.

Coots, Steve. *Samuel Beckett: a Beginner's Guide.* London: Hodder and Stoughton, 2001.

Cormier, Rebecca. *Waiting for Death: the Philosophical Significance of Samuel Beckett's 'En Attendant Godot.'* Tuscaloosa: University of Alabama Press, 1977.

Cousineau, Thomas. *'Waiting for Godot': Form in Movement.* Boston: Twayne, 1990.

—— *After the Final No: Samuel Beckett's Trilogy.* London: Associated University Presses (1999).

College Literature, Vol. 8, No. 3. Samuel Beckett Special Issue, 1981.

Connor, Steven. *Samuel Beckett: Repetition, Theory and Text.* Oxford: Blackwell, 1988.

—— (ed.). *'Waiting for Godot' and 'Endgame.'* New Casebooks. New York: St. Martin's Press – now Palgrave Macmillan, 1992.

Cooke, Virginia (ed.). *Beckett on File.* London: Methuen, 1985.

Copeland, Hannah Case. *Art and the Artist in the Works of Samuel Beckett.* Paris: Mouton, 1975.

Cronin, Anthony. *Samuel Beckett: the Last Modernist.* London: HarperCollins, 1996.

Davies, Paul. *The Ideal Real: Beckett's Fiction and Imagination.* London and Toronto: Associated University Presses, 1994.

—— *Beckett and Eros: The Death of Humanism.* London: Macmillan – now Palgrave Macmillan, 2000.

Davis, Robin J. *Samuel Beckett: Checklist and Index of His Published Works, 1967–76.* Stirling: The Library, University of Stirling, 1979.

—— and Butler, Lance St. John (eds). *Make Sense Who May: Essays on Samuel Beckett's Later Works.* Gerrards Cross: Colin Smythe, 1988.

Dearlove, J. E. *Accommodating the Chaos: Samuel Beckett's Non-Relational Art.* Durham: Duke University Press, 1982.

DiPierro, John C. *Structures in Beckett's 'Watt.'* York, SC: French Literature Publications, 1981.

Doherty, Francis. *Samuel Beckett.* London: Hutchinson, 1971.

Doll, Mary A. *Beckett and Myth: An Archetypal Approach.* Syracuse: Syracuse University Press, 1988.

Duckworth, Colin. *Angels Of Darkness: Dramatic Effect in Beckett with Special Reference to Eugene Ionesco.* New York: Barnes and Noble, 1972.

Eliopulous, James. *Samuel Beckett's Dramatic Language.* The Hague: Mouton, 1975.

Essif, Les. *Empty Figure on an Empty Stage: the Theatre of Samuel Beckett and His Generation.* Bloomington: Indiana University Press, 2001.

Esslin, Martin. *The Theatre of the Absurd.* Garden City, NY: Doubleday, 1961.

—— (ed.). *Samuel Beckett: a Collection of Critical Essays.* Englewood Cliffs, NJ: Prentice Hall, 1965.

Europe, No. 71: Samuel Beckett Special Number, June–July 1993.

Farrow, Anthony. *Early Beckett: Art and Allusion in 'More Pricks than Kicks' and 'Murphy.'* Troy, NY: Whitston, 1991.

Federman, Raymond. *Journey into Chaos: Samuel Beckett's Early Fiction.* Berkeley: University of California Press, 1965.

—— and Fletcher, John. *Samuel Beckett: His Works and His Critics.* Berkeley: University of California Press, 1970.

Finney, Brian. *Since 'How It Is': a Study of Samuel Beckett's Later Fiction.* London: Covent Garden Press, 1972.

Fitch, Brian. *Beckett and Babel: An Investigation into the Status of the Bilingual Work.* Toronto: University of Toronto Press, 1988.

Fletcher, Beryl, *et al. A Student's Guide to the Plays of Samuel Beckett.* London: Faber and Faber, 1978.

Fletcher, John. *The Novels of Samuel Beckett.* London: Chatto and Windus, 1964.

—— *Samuel Beckett's Art.* London: Chatto and Windus, 1967.

—— *Samuel Beckett: 'Waiting for Godot,' 'Krapp's Last Tape,' 'Endgame.'* London: Faber and Faber, 2000.

—— and Spurling, John. *Beckett: a Study of His Plays.* New York: Hill and Wang, 1972.

—— *Beckett the Playwright.* London: Methuen, 1985 [Revised edition of Fletcher and Spurling (1972)].

Foster, Alan. *Beckett and Zen: a Study of Dilemma in the Novels of Samuel Beckett.* Boston: Wisdom Publications, 1989.

Friedman, Alan. *Beckett in Black and Red: Samuel Beckett's Translations for Nancy Cunard's 'Negro.'* Lexington, KY: University of Kentucky Press, 1999.

—— *et al. Beckett Translating/Translating Beckett.* University Park, PA: Pennsylvania State University Press, 1987.

Friedman, Melvin J. (ed.). *Samuel Beckett Now: Critical Approaches to His Novels, Poetry and Plays.* Chicago and London: University of Chicago Press, 1970.

Gambit International Theatre Review. Vol. 7, No. 28: Samuel Beckett (part issue), 1976.

Gidal, Peter. *Understanding Beckett: a Study of Monologue and Gesture in the Work of Samuel Beckett.* London: Macmillan – now Palgrave Macmillan, 1985.

Gluck, Barbara R. *Beckett and Joyce: Friendship and Fiction.* Lewisburg PA: Bucknell University Press, 1979.

Gontarski, S. E. *Beckett's 'Happy Days': a Manuscript Study.* Colombus: Ohio State University Press, 1977.

—— *The Intent of 'Undoing' in Samuel Beckett's Dramatic Texts.* Bloomington: Indiana University Press, 1985.

—— (ed.). *On Beckett: Essays and Criticism.* New York: Grove Press, 1986.

—— (ed.). *The Theatrical Notebooks of Samuel Beckett, Vol 2: 'Endgame.'* London: Faber and Faber, 1992.

—— (ed.). *The Beckett Studies Reader.* Gainesville: University of Florida Press, 1993.

—— *The Theatrical Notebooks of Samuel Beckett, Vol. 4: The Shorter Plays.* London: Faber and Faber, 1999.

Gordon, Lois. *The World of Samuel Beckett 1906–1946.* New Haven: Yale University Press, 1996.

—— *Reading 'Godot.'* New Haven: Yale University Press, 2002.

Graver, Laurence. *Samuel Beckett: 'Waiting for Godot.'* Cambridge: Cambridge University Press, 1989.

—— and Federman, Raymond. *Samuel Beckett: the Critical Heritage.* London: Routledge and Kegan Paul, 1979.

Hale, Jane Alison. *The Broken Window: Beckett's Dramatic Perspective.* West Lafayette, IN: Purdue University Press, 1986.

Hamilton, Alice and Hamilton, Kenneth. *Condemned to Life: the World of Samuel Beckett.* Grand Rapids, MI: Eerdmans, 1976.

Harmon, Maurice (ed.). *No Author Better Served: the Correspondence of Samuel Beckett and Alan Schneider.* Cambridge, MA: Harvard University Press, 1998.

Harrington, John P. *The Irish Beckett.* Syracuse: Syracuse University Press, 1991.

Harrison, Robert. *Samuel Beckett's 'Murphy': a Critical Excursion.* Athens: University of Georgia Press, 1968.

Harvey, Lawrence E. *Samuel Beckett: Poet and Critic.* Princeton: Princeton University Press, 1970.

Hassan, Ihab. *The Literature of Silence: Henry Miller and Samuel Beckett.* New York: Alfred A. Knopf, 1967.

Hayman, Ronald. *Samuel Beckett.* London: Heinemann, 1968.

Henning, Sylvie Debevec. *Beckett's Critical Complicity: Carnival, Contestation and Tradition.* Lexington: University Press of Kentucky, 1988.

Hesla, David. *The Shape of Chaos: an Interpretation of the Art of Samuel Beckett.* Minneapolis: University of Minnesota Press, 1971.

Hessing, Kees. *Beckett on Tape: Productions of Samuel Beckett's Work on Film, Video and Audio.* Leiden: Academic Press, 1992.

Hill, Leslie. *Beckett's Fiction: In Different Words.* Cambridge: Cambridge University Press, 1990.

Homan, Sidney. *Beckett's Theaters: Interpretations for Performance.* Lewisburg PA: Bucknell University Press, 1984.

—— *Filming Beckett's Television Plays: a Director's Experience.* Lewisburg, PA: Bucknell University Press, 1992.

Jacobsen, Josephine and Mueller, William R. *The Testament of Samuel Beckett.* New York: Hill and Wang,1964.

Jeffers, Jennifer M. *Samuel Beckett: a Casebook.* New York: Garland, 1988.

—— *Uncharted Space: the End of Narrative.* New York: Peter Lang, 2001.

Junker, Mary. *Beckett: the Irish Dimension.* Niwot, CO: Irish American Book Company, 1997.

Journal of Beckett Studies, No. 1. (1976)–present.

Kaelin, Eugene. *The Unhappy Consciousness: the Poetic Plight of Samuel Beckett.* Dordrecht: Reidel, 1981.

Kalb, Jonathan. *Beckett in Performance.* Cambridge: Cambridge University Press, 1989.

Katz, Daniel. *Saying 'I' No More: Subjectivity and Consciousness in the Prose of Samuel Beckett.* Evanston IL: Northwestern University Press, 1999.

Kelley, Paul B. *'Stories for Nothing': Samuel Beckett's Narrative Poetics.* New York: Peter Lang, 2002.

Kennedy, Andrew. *Samuel Beckett: a Critical Study.* Cambridge: Cambridge University Press, 1989.

Kennedy, Sighle. *Murphy's Bed: a Study of Real Sources and Surreal Associations in Samuel Beckett's First Novel.* Lewisburg PA: Bucknell University Press, 1971.

Kenner, Hugh. *Samuel Beckett.* New York: Grove Press, 1961.

—— *A Reader's Guide to Samuel Beckett.* New York: Farar, Straus and Giroux, 1973.

Kim, Hua Soon. *The Counterpoint of Hope, Obsession and Desire for Death in Five Plays by Samuel Beckett.* New York: Peter Lang, 1996.

Knowlson, James. *Light and Darkness in the Plays of Samuel Beckett.* London: Turret Books, 1972.

—— *Happy Days / Oh Les Beaux Jours.* London: Faber and Faber, 1978.

—— *Krapp's Last Tape: a Theatre Workbook.* London: Berutus Books, 1980.

—— *Happy Days: the Production Notebook of Samuel Beckett.* London: Faber and Faber, 1985.

—— (ed.). *The Theatrical Notebooks of Samuel Beckett, Vol 3: Krapp's Last Tape.* London: Faber and Faber, 1992.

—— *Damned to Fame: the Life of Samuel Beckett.* London: Bloomsbury, 1996.

—— and Pilling, John. *Frescoes of the Skull: the Later Prose and Drama of Samuel Beckett.* London: John Calder, 1979.

Krance, Charles (ed.). *Samuel Beckett's 'Company'/'Compagnie' and 'A Piece of Monologue'/'Solo': a Bilingual Variorum Edition.* New York and London: Garland, 1993.

Kundert-Gibbs, John L. *No-Thing is Left to Tell: Chaos Theory in the Dramatic Art of Samuel Beckett.* Madison, NJ: Fairleigh Dickinson University Press, 1999.

Lane, Richard (ed.). *Beckett and Philosophy.* New York: Palgrave – now Palgrave Macmillan, 2002.

Levy, Eric P. *Beckett and the Voice of Species: a Study of the Prose Fiction.* New York: Barnes and Noble, 1980.

Levy, Shimon. *Samuel Beckett's Self-Referential Drama: the Three 'I's.* New York: St. Martin's Press – now Palgrave Macmillan, 1990.

—— *Samuel Beckett's Self-Referential Drama: the Sensitive Chaos.* Brighton: Sussex Academic Press, 2002 [revised edition of Levy (1990)].

Locatelli, Carla. *Unwording the World: Samuel Beckett's Prose Works after the Nobel Prize.* Philadelphia: University of Pennsylvania Press, 1990.

Lyons, Charles. *Samuel Beckett.* London: Macmillan – now Palgrave Macmillan, 1983.

McCarthy, Patrick (ed.). *Critical Essays on Samuel Beckett.* Boston: Hall, 1986.

McMillan, Dougald and Fesenfeld, Martha. *Beckett in the Theatre: the Author as Practical Playwright and Director: Volume 1: From 'Waiting for Godot' to 'Krapp's Last Tape.'* London: Calder, 1988.

McMullan, Anna. *Theatre on Trial: Samuel Beckett's Later Drama.* London: Routledge, 1993.

Marvel, Laura (ed.). *Readings on 'Waiting for Godot.'* Farmington Hills, MI: Greenhaven Press, 2001.

Megged, Matti. *Dialogue in the Void: Beckett and Giacometti.* New York: Lumen Press, 1985.

Mercier, Vivian. *Beckett/Beckett.* New York: Oxford University Press, 1977.

Miller, Lawrence. *Samuel Beckett: the Expressive Dilemma.* New York: St. Martin's Press – now Palgrave Macmillan, 1992.

Modern Drama, Vol. 9, No. 3: Samuel Beckett special issue (1966).
—— Vol. 19, No. 3: Samuel Beckett (part issue, 1976).
—— Vol. 25, No. 3: Samuel Beckett (part issue, 1982).
—— Vol. 28, No. 2: Samuel Beckett (part issue, 1985).
Modern Fiction Studies, Vol. 29, Part 1: Samuel Beckett (special issue, 1983).
Moorjani, Angela. *Abysmal Games in the Novels of Samuel Beckett*. Chapel Hill: University of North Carolina Press, 1982.
Morot-Sir, Edouard, Harper, Howard, and Dougald, McMillan. *Samuel Beckett: the Art of Rhetoric*. Chapel Hill: Department of Romance Languages, University of North Carolina, 1976.
Morrison, Kirstin. *Canters and Chronicles: the Use of Narrative in the Plays of Samuel Beckett and Harold Pinter*. Chicago: University of Chicago Press, 1983.
Murphy, P. J. *Reconstructing Beckett: Language for Being in Samuel Beckett's Fiction*. Toronto: University of Toronto Press, 1991.
——Huber, Werner, Breuer, Rolf, and Schoell, Konrad. (eds). *Critique of Beckett Criticism: a Guide to Research in English, French and German*. Colombia, SC: Camden House, 1994.
Murray, Patrick. *The Tragic Comedian: a Study of Samuel Beckett*. Cork: Mercier Press, 1970.
New Theatre Magazine, Vol. 2, No. 3: Samuel Beckett special issue.
O'Brien, Eoin. *The Beckett Country: Samuel Beckett's Ireland*. Dublin: Black Cat Press, 1986.
O'Hara, J. D. (ed.). *Twentieth Century Interpretations of 'Molloy,' 'Malone Dies' and 'The Unnamable.'* Englewood Cliffs, NJ: Prentice Hall, 1970.
—— *Samuel Beckett's Hidden Drives: Structural Uses of Depth Psychology*. Gainesville: University of Florida Press, 1997.
Oppenheim, Lois (ed.). *Directing Beckett*. Ann Arbor: University of Michigan Press, 1994.
—— (ed.). *Samuel Beckett and the Arts: Music, Visual Arts, and Non-Print Media*. New York: Garland, 1999.
—— *The Painted Word: Beckett's Dialogue With Art*. Ann Arbor: University of Michigan Press, 2000.
—— and Buning, Marius (eds). *Beckett On and On ...* London: Associated University Presses, 1996.
Pattie, David. *The Complete Critical Guide to Samuel Beckett*. London: Routledge, 2001.
Perspective. Vol. 11, No. 3: Samuel Beckett special issue (1959).
Pilling, John. *Samuel Beckett*. London: Routledge and Kegan Paul, 1976.
—— (ed.). *The Cambridge Companion to Beckett*. Cambridge: Cambridge University Press (1994)
—— *Beckett Before Godot: the Formative Years*. Cambridge: Cambridge University Press, 1998.
—— and Bryden, Mary. *'The Ideal Core of the Onion': Reading Beckett Archives*. Reading: International Foundation, 1992.
Pountney, Rosemary. *Theatre of Shadows: Samuel Beckett's Drama 1956–76: From 'All That Fall' to 'Footfalls' with Commentaries on the Latest Plays*. Gerrards Cross: Colin Smythe, 1988.

Pultar, Gonul. *Technique and Tradition in Beckett's Trilogy of Novels*. Lanham, MD: University Press of America, 1996.

Rabnovitz, Rubin. *The Development of Samuel Beckett's Fiction*. Urbana: University of Illinois Press, 1984.

—— *Innovation in Samuel Beckett's Fiction*. Urbana: University of Illinois Press, 1992.

Reid, Alex. *All I Can Manage, More Than I Could: An Approach to the Plays of Samuel Beckett*. Dublin: Dolmen Press, 1968.

Ricks, Christopher. *Beckett's Dying Words*. Oxford: Clarendon Press, 1993.

Robinson, Michael. *The Long Sonata of the Dead: a Study of Samuel Beckett*. London: Rupert Hart-Davis, 1969.

Rosen, Steven J. *Samuel Beckett and the Pessimistic Tradition*. New Brunswick, NJ: Rutgers University Press, 1976.

Samuel Beckett Today/Aujourd'hui, Vol. 1 (1992)–present.

Schlueter, June and Brater, Enoch (eds). *Approaches to Teaching Beckett's 'Waiting for Godot.'* New York: MLA, 1991.

Scott, Nathan A. *Samuel Beckett*. London: Bowes and Bowes, 1965.

Sherringham, Michael. *Beckett: 'Molloy.'* London: Giant and Cutler, 1985.

Smith, Joseph H. (ed.). *The World of Samuel Beckett*. Psychiatry and the Humanities 12. Baltimore and London: Johns Hopkins University Press, 1991.

Smith, Frederick N. *Beckett's Eighteenth Century*. London: Palgrave – now Palgrave Macmillan, 2002.

Solomon, Philip H. *The Life After Birth: Imagery in Samuel Beckett's Trilogy*. University of Mississippi: Romance Monographs, 1975.

Spurling, John and Foster, Paul. *Beckett and Zen: a Study of Dilemma in the Novels of Samuel Beckett*. Boston: Wisdom Publications, 1989.

States, Bert O. *The Shape of Paradox: An Essay on 'Waiting for Godot.'* Berkeley: University of California Press, 1978.

Stevens, Richard. *The Insanity of Beckett's Art*. Parker, CO: Parker Distributing, 1997.

Sussman, Henry, and Devenney, Christopher. (eds). *Engagement and Indifference: Beckett and the Political*. Albany: State University of New York Press, 2000.

Tindall, William York. *Samuel Beckett*. New York: Colombia University Press, 1964.

Topsfield, Valerie. *The Humour of Samuel Beckett*, London: Macmillan – now Palgrave Macmillan, 1988.

Toyama, Jean Yamasaki. *Beckett's Game: Language and Self-Referentiality in the Trilogy*. New York: Peter Lang, 1991.

Trezsie, Thomas. *Into the Breach: Samuel Beckett and the Ends of Literature*. Princeton: Princeton University Press, 1990.

Uhlmann, Anthony. *Beckett and Poststructuralism*. Cambridge: Cambridge University Press, 1999.

Via, Dan O. *Samuel Beckett's 'Waiting for Godot.'* New York: Seabury Press, 1968.

Watson, David. *Paradox and Desire in Samuel Beckett's Fiction*. London: Macmillan – now Palgrave Macmillan, 1991.

Webb, Eugene. *Samuel Beckett: a Study of His Novels*. Seattle and London: University of Washington Press, 1970.

—— *The Plays of Samuel Beckett*. Seattle: University of Washington Press, 1972.

Wesberg, David. *Chronicles of Disorder: Samuel Beckett and the Cultural Politics of the Modern Novel*. Albany: State University of New York Press, 2000.

Wilmer, S. E. (ed.). *Beckett in Dublin*. Dublin: Lilliput Press, 1992.

Worth, Katherine (ed.). *Beckett the Shape Changer*. London: Routledge and Keegan Paul, 1975.

—— *'Waiting for Godot' and 'Happy Days': Text and Performance*. London: Macmillan – now Palgrave Macmillan, 1990.

—— *Samuel Beckett's Theatre: Life Journeys*. Oxford: Oxford University Press, 2001.

Zillacus, Clas. *Beckett and Broadcasting: a Study of the Works of Samuel Beckett for and in Radio and Television*. Abo: Abo Akademi, 1976.

Zurbrugg, Nicholas. *Beckett and Proust*. Gerrards Cross: Colin Smythe, 1988.

The Samuel Beckett Society
http://beckett.english.ucsb.edu/sbs/society.html

The Beckett International Foundation at the University of Reading
http://www.library.rdg.ac.uk/colls/bif/index.html

The Dutch Beckett Foundation (in English)
www.samuelbeckett.nl

Samuel Beckett Endpage
http://beckett/english/ucsb/edu

The Journal of Beckett Studies
http:/www.english.fsu.edu/jobs

Samuel Beckett Today/Aujourd'hui
See 'Series and Journals' under Rodopi
www.rodopi.nl

Apmonia
http://www.themodernworld.com/beckett/images/beckett_spash_left.gif

Samuel Beckett On-Line Resources and Links
Pageshttp://home.sprintmail.com/~lifeform/Beck_Links.html

Roussillon Association
http://www.luberon-news.com/samuel-beckett

index